PRACTICAL CLINICAL PSYCHIATRY

Practical
Clinical Psychiatry

JACK R. EWALT, M.D.
Clinical Professor of Psychiatry, Harvard Medical School; Commissioner,
Department of Mental Health, Commonwealth of Massachusetts

EDWARD A. STRECKER, M.D. Sc.D., LL.D.
Formerly Professor of Psychiatry, University of Pennsylvania Medical
School and Graduate Medical School

FRANKLIN G. EBAUGH, M.D.
Clinical Professor of Psychiatry, University of Colorado School of Medicine; formerly Director, Colorado Psychopathic Hospital

EIGHTH EDITION

The Blakiston Division

McGraw-Hill Book Company, Inc.
New York Toronto London 1957

THE MAPLE PRESS COMPANY, YORK, PA.

Foreword

It is with much pleasure and satisfaction that I greet the eighth edition of this text. First published in 1925, it has lived through more than three decades of American psychiatry. This is an expression of confidence—from physicians in all areas of medicine, from psychiatrists, from psychologists, and from workers in the ancillary disciplines—of which we are deeply aware and appreciative. I think it means that our text has kept abreast of psychiatric progress in diagnosis, research, and therapy. Occasionally we have been prophetic. As the years go on, my debt of gratitude to my coauthors and colleagues, Franklin Ebaugh and Jack Ewalt, grows larger. This eighth edition represents the careful thought and labor of Jack Ewalt. In my opinion he has produced a splendid and practical text.

Edward A. Strecker

Preface

This book is written for the medical student, the physician beginning training in psychiatry, and the physician in practice who wishes to learn something of psychiatry for the better handling of his patients. With improvement in medical education and greater emphasis on psychodynamics in the premedical and medical school curricula, it becomes necessary to increase the technical nature of the psychologic material in each succeeding edition of the book to keep pace with the sophistication of our readers.

In earlier editions we devoted much space to the presentation of case histories. In times past this was essential, as many teaching centers lacked adequate clinical facilities for the demonstration of live case material. With the further spread of clinic and hospital services and the uniform availability of suitable teaching material, the presentation of long case histories seems unnecessary and undesirable. We have, accordingly, devoted correspondingly more space to theoretical discussion to increase the student's understanding of the cases he will have an opportunity to examine. To this goal we have also added new information on psychoanalytic psychology. Succeeding generations of students and patients convinced us of the fundamental value to all psychiatry of the knowledge promulgated by the psychoanalytic school of psychology. New knowledge in the social sciences made it desirable to present the beginnings of information on the social aspects of mental illness. Future editions of the book will probably show larger amounts of space devoted to the rapidly growing information in this field. In this edition it seemed worthwhile to include a chapter on the prevalence of mental illness. We hope that future editions will contain a chapter that can be honestly labeled The Epidemiology of Mental Illness.

In further attempts to make this book useful as a textbook and for reference in studying available material in the clinic and in the hospital, we have organized it into three general sections.

The first section deals with the more purely theoretical material and medical psychology, or if you prefer, psychobiology.

The second section is devoted to the symptomatic description of the various illnesses and to additional material concerning their causes. The sparse knowledge in some disorders we hope will stimulate students to research in these areas. For convenience in translating information from the patient's symptoms to the record room classification, we have followed the official classification of the American Psychiatric Association. Here and there we have remarked on its inadequacies in some areas.

The third section is devoted to the various types of treatment in common use in mental disorders. The student is advised to use the sections on drug therapy as reference points and to go from there to the literature, because at this writing many new drugs are in experimental use.

The chapter on child psychiatry has changed authorship. Dr. Leo Kanner, who was our coauthor for this chapter in the last three editions, was unable to contribute to this one owing to other professional and writing commitments. We feel our readers will be pleased with the contribution of Dr. Warren Vaughan. We have also added a chapter on the mentally subnormal child, by Dr. Malcolm Farrell, because new interest in this area merits the opinion of an expert.

Deep appreciation is expressed to the secretarial staff who worked long and energetically on the preparation of this manuscript. Special gratitude goes to Ann White, Marie Brown, and Helen Trainor for their efforts in checking spelling, punctuation, and accuracy of references and correcting English structure. Ann White also prepared the index and aided in reading proof.

In closing we take this opportunity to thank our many loyal readers whose support through the years encouraged us to bring forth an eighth edition. The change in line-up of the coauthors of this book is due to the shifting of major responsibilities for the writing and for the content.

Jack R. Ewalt
Edward A. Strecker
Franklin G. Ebaugh

Credits

Specific acknowledgment is made to the following publishers and authors for permission to quote excerpts from their works. The excerpts are quoted in this book on the pages shown in brackets at the end of each listing.

AMERICAN ACADEMY OF ARTS AND SCIENCE, Cambridge, Mass.
BRIDGMAN, P. W.: The Task before Us. *Proc. Am. Acad. Arts & Sc.,* **83**:95–122, April, 1954. [Pages 37 and 38]

AMERICAN BOOK COMPANY, New York.
GOLDSTEIN, KURT: "The Organism." 1939. [Pages 45 and 47]

ASSOCIATION FOR RESEARCH IN NERVOUS AND MENTAL DISEASE, New York.
ANASTASI, ANNE: The Inherited and Acquired Components of Behavior. In "Genetics and the Inheritance of Integrated Neurological and Psychiatric Patterns." Vol. 33. Edited by D. Hooker and C. C. Hare. 1954. [Page 72]
BLEULER, E.: "The Theory of Schizophrenic Negativism." Monograph No. 11. 1912. [Page 195]
KALLMANN, F. J.: The Genetics of Psychotic Behavior Patterns. In "Genetics and the Inheritance of Integrated Neurological and Psychiatric Patterns." Vol. 33. Edited by D. Hooker and C. C. Hare. 1954. [Pages 73 and 200]
WHITE, WILLIAM A.: "Outlines of Psychiatry." Ed. 10. 1924. [Page 180]

BASIC BOOKS, INC., New York.
ARIETI, SILVANO: "Interpretation of Schizophrenia." 1955. [Page 203]
FEDERN, PAUL: "Ego Psychology and the Psychoses." Edited by Edoardo Weiss. Basic Classics in Psychiatry. 1953. [Pages 191 and 210]

FENICHEL, OTTO: "The Psychoanalytic Theory of Neurosis." Ed. 2. 1945. Also in "The Collected Papers of Otto Fenichel." Edited by Hanna Fenichel and David Rapaport. 1953. [Pages 25, 183, 203, 225, 236, and 262]

SEELEY, JOHN: Social Values, The Mental Health Movement, and Mental Health. In "Mental Health and Mental Disorder." Edited by Arnold M. Rose. 1955. [Page 53]

PHILOSOPHICAL LIBRARY, INC., New York.

EINSTEIN, ALBERT: "Out of My Later Years." 1950. [Page 19]

THE PSYCHIATRIC QUARTERLY AND PSYCHIATRIC QUARTERLY SUPPLEMENT, Utica State Hospital, Utica, N. Y.

POLLOCK, HORATIO M., MALZBERG, BENJAMIN, and FULLER, RAYMOND G.: Hereditary and Environmental Factors in the Causation of Manic-Depressive Psychoses and Dementia Praecox. 1939. [Pages 179 and 200]

THE RONALD PRESS COMPANY, New York.

ALEXANDER, FRANZ, and FRENCH, THOMAS MORTON: "Psychoanalytic Therapy." 1946. [Page 63]

CHARLES SCRIBNER'S SONS, New York.

SAROYAN, WILLIAM: "Bicycle Rider in Beverly Hills." 1952. [Page 20]

THE TECHNOLOGY PRESS, Massachusetts Institute of Technology, Cambridge, Mass., and JOHN WILEY & SONS, INC., New York.

WIENER, NORBERT: "Cybernetics." 1948. [Page 44]

UNIVERSITY OF OKLAHOMA PRESS, Norman, Okla.

WILLIAMS, ROGER J.: "Nutrition and Alcoholism." 1951. [Page 266]

JOHN WILEY & SONS, INC., New York.

"Cerebral Mechanisms in Behavior: Hixon Symposium." Edited by Lloyd A. Jeffress. 1951. [Pages 48 and 73]

THE WILLIAMS & WILKINS COMPANY, Baltimore.

COBB, STANLEY: "Foundations of Neuropsychiatry." Ed. 5. 1952. [Pages 39 and 46]

FULTON, JOHN F.: The Frontal Lobes. *Proc. A. Res. Nerv. Ment. Dis.* Vol. 27. Dec. 12 and 13, 1947. [Page 46]

KENNEDY, F., FRANTZ, A., and HARE, C. S.: "The Inter-relationship of Mind and Body." 1939. [Page 4]

YALE UNIVERSITY PRESS, New Haven, Conn.

BARCROFT, JOSEPH: "The Brain and Its Environment." 1938. [Page 39]

Contents

PRACTICAL CLINICAL PSYCHIATRY

SECTION I

Basic Concepts

This section reviews current theories and knowledge of personality development. We present basic mental mechanisms that explain some elements of behavior and psychopathology.

The current status of knowledge in the fields of physiology, chemistry, epidemiology, and genetics, as they relate to behavior, is discussed.

CHAPTER 1

The Development of Normal Personality

Human behavior can be understood if we have sufficient information about a person's development—his biologic, psychologic, and sociologic history. Our methods of observation and study remain crude, but the behavioral sciences have progressed and we can now see some pattern in human behavior and make some useful predictions. Our knowledge in the field of psychology, biology, and sociology grows each year. A quotation from Tracy Putnam made several years ago to the effect that there is still an enormous gap between the facts of neurophysiology and those of psychology is still appropriate, and one could paraphrase this remark to include the fields of sociology and genetics.

Before we consider man as an individual biologic unit we remind the student that man exists in a world filled with other humans, other animals, and myriad natural phenomena, all of which influence his life. This has been discussed from factual, theoretical, and interpretive points of view by many anthropologists, sociologists, and other scientific groups. From this group of facts, interpretations, and theory, we conclude that man is composed of a group of atoms which in proper combination form molecules. The molecules make substances, and these form cells. The cells in proper combinations form tissues, which in predetermined ways form organs, each contributing its own peculiar part to the effective function of the living man.

In our own culture human beings in combinations form small groups, usually referred to as families, who in turn form larger groups known in some areas as tribes and in others as neighborhoods, towns, or social sets. These groups of persons form larger groups known as nations.

At present we believe that the world is part of a solar system, which is only an insignificant part of a group of larger constellations known as

3

a universe. All these elements are part of an integrated or organized system, each portion of which has some influence over the others.

If a few cells in a man's liver decide to "overthrow" the rules by which they grow, to multiply and to pursue their own selfish desires as to direction and type of growth, in so far as their basic abilities allow, we find the liver and then the organism show poor function. We say that the man has a malignancy. Whether the cells were incited to nonconformist behavior by physiologically or chemically "unhappy" or "underprivileged" atoms or molecules, we do not yet know, but we do know that in their own self-seeking at the expense of their environment, they bring about the disintegration of the system in which they live, and the price they pay for victory over their environment is death for themselves because they accompany their environment into disintegration.

In another perspective, this occurrence produces a break in the integrity of the family, with greater or less effect upon the community, depending on the position of the family unit in the community's economy. By becoming "malignant," persons within a family may also bring about a similar series of events. In the recent past the world has experienced the agonies of radical surgery involved in removing "malignant" nations which interfered with and threatened integration. Kennedy has stated, "Who knows but that we humans may be the blood corpuscles of the world or of God, Himself."

The importance of socioeconomic integration upon man's function and upon his health is great, and the student is advised to review the facts as well as the theories and interpretations of workers in these fields.

The subtle interweaving of one's biologic functions and cultural influences starts even before birth. To take a rather simple example as an illustration of the infinite possibilities for differences in people and their behavior, let us recall that many children born of mothers who have German measles during pregnancy will develop congenital cataracts. Let us tease this situation to see what varieties of interaction may enter into the development of a blind child. In the first place, some people apparently have a high degree of immunity to German measles which carries throughout life. Had the blind child's mother been immune, the situation would not develop. But most people are not immune to German measles, and this hypothetical mother was not. However, had she been exposed to German measles during her own childhood and developed the disease at that time, the disease would not have resulted in a blind child. Thus, the time of exposure interacting with the biologic factor of immunity to German measles, or lack of it, results in a blind or sighted child. The element of time was obviously important. Had the mother become pregnant a month or more after developing German measles, her child would not be blind. In this case, however, we can understand why this particular child had congenital cataracts, if we understand the particular patterning of cultural forces, life experiences, and the biologic heredity and experience of the mother. All factors neatly dovetailed at that particular instant in time, when this woman, pregnant and susceptible to German measles, was exposed to the disease, contracted it, and later gave birth to a child with congenital cataracts. Varying any one of several facts in this constellation would have resulted in a different pattern in the child. This leaves unexplained the children who do not develop congenital cataracts whose mothers had German measles during their gestation. This may be due to some influence of the father, to some different substrain of German measles, as yet unappreciated, or to any one of many factors not presently understood. We do not completely understand either why German measles (a rather minor illness) in the mother should have such disastrous results on the embryo, or why it should select the lens for its attack.

If the cause of such a relatively simple thing as congenital cataracts involves such a variety of factors, more difficulty will be encountered when one attempts to explain complicated situations, such as why one man holds up banks, another becomes a banker, and a third becomes a schizophrenic. Many people have commented on the variety of events and circumstances that explain human behavior.

Attempts to make generalizations based on observation of the effects of cultural forces on individual development have led to interesting new facts, which are often of use in the over-all management of ill people and in the promotion of good habits of mental health. These will be discussed later, but studies in cultural anthropology tend to show that much of the behavior of man and many of his beliefs about the proper way to satisfy biologic needs depend upon the time and the particular tribe into which he is born.

Hollingshead and Redlich show that with a nation such as the United States, one's social position depends to some extent on the occupational skills of the head of the family. This position seems to influence the kind of diagnosis and type of treatment offered in cases of mental illness. They have also shown that the geographic location within the country will have important effects on one's beliefs and one's choice of acting out.

The psychoanalytic school has contributed much to the understanding of an individual's behavior, and has produced many explanations of his attempts to act out within the cultural situation in which he finds himself.

The combination of the social sciences and psychoanalytic theories has made important contributions to understanding human behavior. One may call this fascinating complexity "the will of God," "the rules of nature," or "the master plan of time," depending upon one's religious and philosophic leanings. Life as we know it is a dynamic or energy-consuming and -producing process, an energy-exchange system.

As we presently understand it, the fundamental unit of structure is the atom, which is composed of electrical entities. These electrical units combine to form atoms, which have mass, and these atoms combine to make up molecules by a balance of attraction and repulsion. The whole particle is a very stable but extremely kinetic organization. Man's tinkering with this fundamental unit of structure has resulted in widespread sociologic and cultural forces, which even influence our death rate and tax rate in a way that the fundamental scientists first inquiring into the nature of things never dreamed of.

Certain molecules combining in certain ways make up tissues, as mentioned before. One thing common to all living matter is the continuous energetic process. From the simplest unicellular organism to the complex organization known as man, living tissue is in a continual process of utilizing combinations of chemical elements, which are only arrangements of atoms, to build tissues. This results in a continual state of flux and balance between the processes of building and destruction and consumption of energy. When the constructive process exceeds the destructive, we say that we have growth, but if the destructive force exceeds the constructive, we have deterioration, or if it becomes extensive, death. It is interesting to note, however, that if the growth exceeds normal bounds, death may also result, as illustrated by cancer.

In the simplest form of animal, the ameba, we find that the individual ameba repeatedly perishes but achieves a kind of immortality by his manner of death. He divides himself, and, while he ceases to exist as an individual, he now is two. By this manner of procreation we say that the species is being continued.

In higher forms cells take on a more specialized function and do not reproduce themselves in this manner, but, as individual cells die, they are replaced by new ones in ways not wholly understood.

It is quite a jump in biology and time from a single-cell protozoan to man, but the tissues of man involve energy exchange, growth, and destruction. The building up and consumption or destruction of tissues goes on throughout life. Thus, this basic push to create and destroy is found in all forms of life. The individual cells of human beings must, as long as they live, show a neat balance between the forces of creation and destruction.

Psychonanalysis shows that the essentials of human behavior, that is, of man's behavior in relation to other men, may also be best understood if studied as a balance between the forces of creation and destruction, usually dubbed by the analyst as "libidinous strivings" and the "death instincts," or "aggressive strivings."

Even these basic urges of man have a certain natural history as they develop. At the moment of birth we are, in effect, the summary of the biologic inheritance of mankind as represented by our particular racial and family strains. For each it is slightly different. This heritage is a fact that cannot be altered in its fundamental, even though the vicissitudes of life may grossly alter the way in which these fundamentals can be used. As mentioned earlier, this effect of environmental influences on the tissue potentials starts with the status of maternal health, the condition of the uterine mucosa, where the ovum lands in the uterus, and many other factors that occur during the period of gestation. These environmental influences continue to operate throughout life, and, in fact, will operate after death until our final resolution into the anonymity of the surrounding earth. Thus, any consideration of man must include the items of heredity and constitution, as well as the environmental influences and their effect upon him.

In spite of the hazards and vicissitudes possible during the stage of gestation, the fact remains that this is perhaps our greatest period of security. Here we are in an insulated, temperature-controlled environment, which is safe and dependable as long as our supporting mechanism, the mother, does not break down. We are oxygenated without breathing and fed without eating. Even our excretions are handled by the maternal organism. There is perhaps a philosophic lesson to be learned here, in that man seems to strive continually to achieve again security akin to this, but these strivings are not successful in any form of government, pension system, or combination of social and engineering processes. Those who strive for such security should perhaps consider the regressive features present in such behavior, and the fact that the great security of intrauterine existence was paid for by shortcomings in terms of environmental choice, mobility, and available recreation. In the adult world perhaps the nearest to such security in our present-day life is provided for the patient in a well-run mental hospital or for the inmate in a well-run prison.

In the act of being born, or beginning an independent existence, man makes one of the greatest adjustments he will ever be called upon to make. He enters the world in a most undignified and uncomfortable fashion by being forcibly ejected from the uterus through a passageway uncomfortably tight, and the trip is often hurried by hands or by tools of steel. He is then severed from his physiologic link to the mother, and, if he is to survive, he must breathe. This inhalation is usually accompanied by a cry, and we find that inhalation fulfills a basic need.

Satisfaction of basic needs, or relief of physiologic tension and threatening disaster, is later interpreted as gratification or as giving comfort or pleasure. Whatever our original sensations may have been, the act of inspiration and expiration must be repeated at reasonably frequent intervals from that moment forward, until what we call "death" is announced by the permanent cessation of this act. Thus, our first responsibility becomes our most pressing one, and one which is forced upon us as the price of our first step toward an independent existence. Claude Bernard states, "The fixity of the internal environment is the condition of the free life," but we find that this environment must have material to work upon.

Soon sensation appears, to be later interpreted as hunger, which is relieved by the breast or by satisfactory substitute. Other sensations find relief in evacuation of bowel and bladder. These sensations of internal need recur periodically and become uncomfortable and unpleasant if long ignored, because they arouse an impending state of physiologic imbalance that impairs existence if allowed to persist. The fact that their satisfaction gives pleasure is manifested by the almost universal enjoyment of eating, drinking, smoking, or chewing, and the frankly erotic sensations induced by kissing a suitable person under the proper circumstances. The more introspective student may even admit of some pleasure in evacuation of bowel or bladder when the physiologic tension has become great.

Almost at once the environment begins to establish rules under which the needs may be satisfied. These rules vary with the age of the infant, the time in which he lives, the cultural group in which he finds himself, and even the financial and social status of his family at any particular moment under discussion. One fact remains: whatever the obstacles or hardships imposed by the environment, the basic needs of the tissues must be met, and the infant must work out some sort of compromise which will enable him to satisfy these drives and at the same time adapt himself to the demands of his environment.

In most cases the needs of the infant are supplied by the same person or persons. He now seems to find added pleasure in the attention and affection which these persons bestow upon him, and soon he behaves in a manner which we interpret as showing a desire for love and a desire to give love to these persons. These first manifestations which we interpret as "love" are closely related to the care and comfort incident to feeding, excreting, and being provided with shelter. This blending of feelings in relation to the various biologic functions and the emotion known as love is never completely lost.

Those phenomena in infants which we interpret as love, anger, hate, and fear must also be modified and adapted to the rules and demands of the environment. The infant finds feeding comes at regular intervals, and soon the hunger sensations appear about the time the feeding is due. He discovers that his cries may hasten the preparation of food, bring dry clothes, cover when cold, or comfort when in pain. This association between certain acts on his part and certain environmental responses leads to conditioning in the neurophysiologic sense. By a similar process the child may learn that unscheduled crying may bring him added attention or isolation in the nursery, depending upon the parents' attitude toward such behavior.

The foundation for patterns of adjustment to life situations is started in this manner. One child loudly demands attention, and another gets it by smiles and adaptive behavior. Some children find it hard to establish a pattern of behavior or adaptive conditioning because their families act in an inconsistent manner, responding to outbursts in various ways and thus making it difficult for the children to know what to expect. This results in much tension, confusion, and unrest in the whole situation.

As the child develops he is required to adapt his needs to the rules of his particular family. These seem to vary somewhat in our culture with the current fad on advice on child rearing.

At a certain age the breast or bottle is withdrawn and semisolid and, finally, solid food substituted. The sensations previously associated with the sucking phenomena are not obtained by biting and chewing, and as adults we interpret the child's actions as giving pleasure or satisfaction. At least it gets him fed! It is perhaps the manifestation of the wisdom of nature that the acts which aid his graduation to a more easily obtained type of food and to the cutting of teeth are also a source of pleasure which he prolongs—gnawing puppy fashion on his toes, shoes, toys, or the furniture.

In our particular culture the child soon discovers he is not allowed to pass his excretions when and where he wishes. In fact, he finds he is supposed to exercise these functions at a given time and in certain specified places. In our bathroom-conscious culture, the place is usually a bead-festooned toidy seat. Passing excretions in response to physiologic need is obviously essential to continued existence. It is also true that the child's use of the particular sanitary device at the time and place desired by his mother or nursemaid brings him added attention which also seems to give pleasure and may help prove to him the value of this particular product of his physiologic processes. Thus he can experience a relief of physiologic tensions with its associated pleasure, and at the same time win rewards in terms of praise and loving attention from his attendants. After some time, usually at about 2 or 3 years of age, the child begins to withhold the stool and finds that this may bring rewards in terms of added attentions and bribes, or at least create an emotional upheaval in the nursery. The child may withhold until the rewards become satisfactorily great. The child apparently gets satisfaction from the retention itself and from having brought forth this doubly prized object. He may use the product for fingerpainting himself or the nursery. If the mother, as is often true, puts prohibitions on this, he substitutes by decorating the home or himself with crayons, lipsticks, or other reasonably satisfactory substitutes for the feces.

There are many variations in the demands of the child's environment, especially those of his parents and attendants, and the rewards and punishments forthcoming as a result of his adaptation to these demands undoubtedly influence his future behavior.

We believe that much of a child's future development may be dependent upon the degree to which the mother accepts and loves him. Studies of children, in this country and in England, raised without the care and affection of a mother, show that separation from the mother of the infant, with the lack of a satisfactory substitute, can make profound differences in his development, particularly in the emotional and intellectual spheres. It is obvious, of course, that in more primitive cultures the child's life itself may be dependent on the mother or a wet nurse being present to breast feed him. Regardless of where he lives at this stage, however, the child is completely dependent on factors in the external world for his continued existence. This dependency is thought to induce certain anxieties within the child, particularly if the necessary elements of care and affection are not forthcoming on need. This system of unobjectified anxiety becomes a danger signal and an important factor in the child's organization and adaptation to life from that moment on.

As mentioned earlier, the culture or portion of the world or the social stratum of the family all make differences in the attitude of the child and his family toward these early basic processes.

Our type of life and attitude toward cleanliness, sanitation, and human excrement, and our emphasis on early toilet training in this culture are by no means universal. The tendency to regard any product of one's own activities as of particular importance is probably exaggerated beyond nature's intention. Our use of toilet seats and our attempts to housebreak the child in order to cut down on the diaper changes necessary and the soiling of expensive rugs and polished floors are known to introduce later many desirable and undesirable psychologic traits. Some are considered attractive features of people in our cultures. In America the general respect for wealth, the great awe for the person who can organize, accumulate, and properly distribute wealth, and the honor in which the so-called executive is held are parts of our culture that certainly owe some of their origins to our earlier experiences with toilet training.

At about 1 year of age a child seems to notice certain oral sounds that are associated with feeding, excreting, lovemaking, anger, and play. His attempts to reproduce these sounds, when successful, make it easier for him to make his desires known to those about him. Certain persons are associated with other sounds, and these sounds come to stand for, or symbolize, certain objects, acts, and desires. Once he masters a few of these simple symbols, he is said to be talking.

In the beginning he uses the symbols in a general way. The entire hunger-feeding activity is often symbolized by one word such as "eat," "cookie," "milk," or some similar word. In this manner, the name of his dog, Jip, becomes a symbol for all similar hairy four-legged animals, and all men are "Daddy."

At 3 to 4 years of age, we find the child forming more specific associations to these word symbols, and the symbols become very rigid. Thus, "cracker," may come to mean a square, salty biscuit, and anyone using the term to describe a native of Georgia or a nut-breaking device will be incomprehensible to the child. With further experience the child finds that many words have several meanings, and his concept of words broadens to symbolize more than one thing. He finds that the meaning of a word intended by the speaker varies in terms of the situation in which it is used. The final step in the management of word symbols is a confusing and difficult one for children and is not fully achieved until the eighth to tenth year. Some persons unfortunately never fully grasp or understand that the speaker or writer uses a word in terms of his own experience with the word and with knowledge of the situation as understood by himself. The person who hears or reads the material interprets in terms of his own experience with the words and his own concept of the situation in which it is used. This often results in complete or partial misunderstanding. The child's first efforts at speech are made with what seem to be little or no appreciation of the fact that his meaning may not be clear to his audience. He understands and seems to assume that they also understand. This phase is sometimes referred to as *egocentric speech* and is probably our best example of the verbalization of thought. As the child develops he recognizes the necessity for making his meaning clear to his audience or socializing his speech, but at play will continue to indulge in speech for himself alone until 8 to 12 years, when it gradually becomes subvocal and he uses only the adult form of thinking.

The emotional manifestations of a child also go through a period of change and adaptation to the environment. In infancy we see all-out reactions usually expressed in terms of physiologic needs and with no obvious attempt to regulate the degree of the outburst to the urgency of the situation. When the same situation is repeated, the child will show bebehavior which we interpret as apprehension and anxiety even though pain has not yet occurred. The avoidance of the radiator after a painful experience with it, even though the heat is turned off, is a common example in our culture. In a similar manner the child learns that cooing, smiling, and certain tricks bring forth prizes of various sorts. He may learn that nocturnal yelling or crying brings no reward, and he gives this up because the effort and trouble he goes to bring no dividends. If his lonesome cry brings a reward in terms of attention, it will be repeated, and many parents take unwanted nocturnal walks to the nursery because they have failed to learn that infants are not above getting as much as they can from the environment in terms of pleasure or other rewards.

Just what constitutes too much or too little attention for infants is a matter about which there is no general agreement. The "wise ones" in the field go through fluctuations; at this writing they are in the "shower-them-with-love" phase. Since more persons tend to follow their own natural inclinations and desires in these matters anyway, I doubt that the confusion produced in mothers' minds or the damage that may or may not be done to a child is as great as is sometimes claimed.

As the child grows, he begins to manifest curiosity about his genital organs. Digital explorations and prolonged stimulation on the hobby horse or stair bannisters seem pleasurable and are repeated. Performed openly at first, these acts become surreptitious and a source of mixed pleasure and shame only after parents or grandmother have expressed disapproval or horror at the act. Threats of bodily mutilation may impress the child, and questions concerning loss of various external organs are common at this age. The curiosity concerning their own bodies leads to comparison with the structure of siblings or playmates. Finding that girls lack a penis is supposed to cause considerable anxiety at this time because the child fears either that the organ has been or his own will be mutilated. These anxieties are dubbed "castration anxieties" by the psychoanalyst.

About the same time the child may show a difference in his display of affection for his parents and siblings. He demands increased affection from the parent of the opposite sex and may be observed competing with the other parent and siblings for it. Displays of affection between parents are met with demands for attention or openly aggressive acts against the rival. This change in emotion, experiencing mixed feelings toward the members of the family, has been interpreted as the child's sexual strivings for the parent of the opposite sex. At the same time the parent of the same sex is regarded as a rival and, as such, is looked upon with mixed hatred and fear and yet still loved to some extent. This situation is referred to in psychoanalytic literature as the *Oedipus situation* or *Oedipus complex*.

This directing of affection and attention from one's own body to the surrounding world is soon followed by an expansion of interest. Children become interested in playing in groups and attending school, parties, and other forms of children's social life. The emphasis in our culture is toward association with members of the same sex, but this is no longer true to the extent it was 10 to 15 years ago. The period in life when this is most evident has been called the *latency period* because most children display little activity that could be interpreted as heterosexual in nature, although one might make homosexual interpretations of certain phases of juvenile activity in these years.

With puberty we see the child displaying frank adult sexual interest. Sex tension mounts and in our culture is offered no relief except masturbation, nocturnal emissions, and auto-seat skirmishing. Even these acts are surrounded with so much social disapproval, superstition, and misinformation that they become more worry- and tension-inducing than tension-relieving in the life of the adolescent.

To this point we have carried the child along as a unit. One would like to stress the fact that he continues to live as a physiologic unit in the culture in which he finds himself. For purposes of organization, however, it is now necessary to divide our discussions into the further details and development of the psychologic functions; what is known of the physiologic aspects of behavior; and the cultural or social influences on these functions and aspects. The student should recall, however, that all these things fuse into the behavior known as life. It will also be obvious that there are gaps in our knowledge and that the simple addition of what is known of psychology, physiology, and sociology by no means explains all the phenomena we observe in our fellow man.

The student is familiar with anger, fear, sadness, and happiness as subjective phenomena in his own experience. These phenomena are termed *emotions.* But in spite of this personal familiarity these expressions are difficult to define. Like the odor of the goat, once experienced, they are easily recognized on repetition, yet they defy adequate description in words. In one sense emotion may be said to represent an attitude or thought. It may be said to be a subjective or inner experience concerning some external object which we invest with feeling or energy. This feeling is accompanied by physiologic alterations due to the concomitant activity of the autonomic nervous system and certain autonomic chemical regulating systems within the body. The physiologic phenomena will be discussed in a separate section.

In infancy the emotional phenomena are usually shown by a child in terms of external situations or internal needs. As his experience becomes more extensive, we see emotional phenomena being reproduced by environmental events which suggest renewed contacts with familiar situations; for example, the child who, having been inoculated on one trip to the physician's office, begins to cry when he sees the physician on subsequent visits without first determining whether painful procedures are planned. This is closely akin to the conditioning seen in animal experiments originating with Pavlov. As the child grows older, further broadening of experience will enable him to show external behavior appropriate to the planned procedures, but he will probably never completely overcome a certain degree of apprehension and uncertainty when approaching his physician's office and a feeling of relief when dismissed.

In all instances our subjective feelings about things, or our emotions, are invested with energy or drive. Many workers believe that emotions are produced by situations which either facilitate or oppose the instinctual urges. At any rate, the energy or drive created is either expended upon the primary object of the drive or some suitable substitute in an appropriate manner, or it is denied or "frustrated."

In the latter event, the energy expresses itself in physiologic tension which may accumulate to the explosion point or may sputter out along the network of the autonomics. More details will be discussed later, but a simple example would be the soldier who develops hatred for a domineering company commander. He may hit the officer, but probably not. His tension may accumulate until he goes AWOL and gets drunk, or it may be expressed in heroic acts against the enemy, or it may be expressed with diarrhea and disgust with the entire Army.

In psychiatry we also speak of *affect* or *feeling tone* in relation to the emotions. Affect is a quantitative term and is used to express the person's emotional capacity and the degree of his reaction to given situations. For example, one person may react to the death of a loved one with silent grief and a "carry-on" attitude. His brother may be affected differently and weep, become retarded, and perhaps develop a reactive depression. The schizophrenic sister, on the other hand, may show a disassociated affect and apparently regard the death as a good joke on the victim.

The term *mood* is also used in psychiatry and is closely related to emotion, the difference here being that mood is a subjective term and is generally used to describe a more prolonged state of feeling in which the person is not aware of the object toward which the energy of the mood is directed. For example, you may get angry at your roommate, but this anger expresses itself in some manner and emotion subsides. Throughout the same day you may have a general feeling of well-being without being entirely aware of what causes your moods to be euphoric. The mood is probably determined by some event or thought of the past to which you have become conditioned, and something in the day's activity determines your mood through this conditioning process. A simple example is the nostalgic or amorous mood which certain odors or music may engender if they have been a pleasant part of your early life.

In understanding these phenomena one must recall the early comments on thinking. The adult's concept of a total situation is the important factor in determining his emotional reaction. One thinks of the Virginian's advice, "Smile when you say that," to those persons making disparaging remarks about his ancestors!

Human beings are aware of their environment by means of the sensory receptors of the body. This awareness is commonly referred to as "consciousness." During infancy and in childhood there seems to be some difficulty in separating the concepts of self from surroundings, and we observe children referring to themselves in the second and third person. The term "conscious," or "consciousness," causes some confusion in the total medical literature because, as used, it may mean "awareness"; or receipt of a stimulus from one of the sensory receptors and reflex action to it; or complicated psychologic processes following the receipt of a stimulus, involving perception and identification of the stimulus and realization of its significance at that particular moment. The ability to form concepts of stimuli appropriate to the nature and the time and place they occur depends on the development of language and thought functions not fully matured until about 8 years of age. As a child reaches the age of 3 or 4, the memory and language functions achieve a level which enables him to distinguish clearly between that which is himself and that which is of the environment.

This awareness of self is commonly called *ego reference*. As an example, a person may speak of "my toothache" with ego reference, or "the toothache" without making a personal connection. This consciousness of self is an ever-changing, fleeting thing which Allport likened to "a pencil point of light flicking over life experiences." The ideas, concepts, emotions, and attitudes of any person at any particular moment are influenced by past experiences. Some of these past events are available on call, and we become conscious of them when and if we choose, and we say, "I remember." Other material is not so easily recalled and only with effort or prompting does the skeleton outline appear. Perhaps because of the confusion of concept formation prior to the third and fourth year, rarely do persons clearly and accurately recall the events prior to that age. At times the recollections after the third- to fourth-year level are factual; at others, they are as we wish they were. Nietzche (rather freely translated) stated, "'That is what I have done,' says my memory. 'I could not have done *that!*' says my pride, and gradually my memory gives in."

The almost-forgotten material that can be recalled only by a process of association and the promptings association brings has been referred to as the *unconscious*. Psychoanalytic research has revealed that much of this material is forced out of the mind or repressed because it conflicts with the person's sense of fitness of things and threatens his efficient functioning as a person. This material from the past has important influences on our total behavior. For example, your preferences for blonds over brunets, and for a particular blond over all others, is determined by factors in experience that have accumulated in that repository we refer to as the unconscious. The more important the event, and the more closely it is bound up with the instinctual strivings, the more important it will be so far as future behavior is concerned.

In certain pathologic states we find a disturbance of consciousness, which will be discussed in later sections. We see one interesting type of partial disturbance of consciousness of self in persons who identify themselves with a parent or friend or some highly esteemed person. Women's attempts to emulate the latest Paris or Hollywood dictate in terms of hairdo and bust-and-bottom profile are ever-present examples of this identification in our American culture.

Memory is a function closely related to consciousness and to the functions of thinking and speech. The memory process consists of several steps: Stimuli from the environment are received, and we become aware of them. Then, by association, a concept of the stimuli is formed, and this concept is retained. Later the concept is reproduced; usually the associations of the concept facilitate the reproduction. Human beings seldom recall events occurring prior to the third year, probably because the language function is not sufficiently developed to permit the formation of adequate concepts or association with the stimulus. Since the concepts are confused, reproduction is difficult and in most persons impossible.

Memory is dependent upon a healthy, functioning brain, and cortical defects and injuries impair the memory function. The intensity of the original stimulus is also important in facilitating memory. If the intensity is great and the associations many, or the emotional significance great, reproduction is facilitated. On the other hand, events that are too painful or too heavily charged with emotion may be pushed out of memory or repressed. In memory the time factor is important and must be evaluated. The events highly charged with emotion may be clearly recalled after a long period of time, while trivial events are forgotten in a short time. In every instance memories are dependent upon concepts or the individual's interpretation and understanding of the original phenomena. This may vary slightly from person to person.

A good example of this is the spread of rumor or gossip. A person who hears a statement interprets the facts in terms of his own understanding and experience. This will vary in terms of his previous experiences, beliefs, prejudices, and use of language. This person later, in repeating his interpretation of the original statement, explains it in his own way and in his own words to make this concept clear to the listener. The third person in turn forms still a third concept of what person number two means, because the third person is also influenced by experiences, beliefs, and his concept of the meaning of words. After the original material makes a few such transitions, it is often barely recognizable as the original version.

We wish to emphasize that all mental activity results from the integration of a person's psychologic and somatic functioning, as influenced by the world in which he lives.

The succeeding three chapters will contain what have been useful concepts for us in understanding the behavior of human beings when observed in the context of present knowledge of psychology, physiology, chemical processes, and cultural forces.

CHAPTER 2

Psychoanalytic Concepts of Behavior

In understanding the function of human beings it is necessary to begin with fundamentals. The phenomenon known as life is characterized by a production and consumption of energy. It is essential for this energy production that oxygen, water, and food be assimilated and that worn out or injured tissues be replaced; a person at any one time is, therefore, an integrated mass of chemical processes. The urge to provide the body with these basic needs for its maintenance is referred to as a *basic drive*, a *primitive drive*, or an *instinct*. It is also necessary for the organism to reproduce itself, and this drive or urge or impulse to reproduce is also called a basic drive or instinct.

These drives have their origin in the tissues (as we shall discuss later) and assure the body of the fundamentals needed for life and for procreation. In some form they are seen in all living matter. As adult man became civilized, the genital strivings and the strivings for shelter and food began to take on secondary elaborations which now become important to the individual and have almost the force of the basic urges.

The discussion of instinct psychology has undergone many trends in the past hundred years, but at present the majority of practicing psychiatrists base most of their psychologic interpretations on Freudian concepts. Within the Freudian school there have been differences of opinion on fundamentals. Certain non-Freudian and anti-Freudian groups propose different explanations of behavior. With each succeeding edition of this book the authors become more thoroughly convinced of the vast importance of Freudian teaching in understanding human behavior. This section will be devoted to current "orthodox" Freudian psychology. We choose to discuss Freud's contribution in this edition because we feel that the orthodox Freudian viewpoint is most useful in explaining human

18

psychologic processes and that it is a viewpoint that will be less confusing for the student. If given an orthodox orientation, he may then use this as a framework of reference for wider reading in the field. He is encouraged to do this.

The term *psychoanalysis* is used in the literature in two ways to designate:

1. A body of knowledge based on the researches of Sigmund Freud and his followers.

2. A therapeutic method based on the facts and theories of Freudian psychology.

In this section we will be using the term to designate the body of knowledge and theories based on the work of Freud and his followers. Our present concepts of psychoanalytic psychology are based on:

1. A series of observations made by Freud, his pupils, and other adherents to the psychoanalytic movement. From these observations of adults in psychoanalytic treatment, and on children observed in treatment and in day-nursery experiences, a set of postulates or theories was drawn which proposed to explain the behavior of the adults and children.

2. Further experience with the treatment of patients and candidates for training in the psychoanalytic method, plus a large number of psychologic and sociologic experiments which test these postulates.

3. A reasonably ordered arrangement of proved postulates which most of us regard as facts. Some original concepts or postulates were proved to be false and have since been discarded or modified, and there are still theories which are workable but which have not been fully proved.

Difficulties in establishing a science of psychology of human behavior are inherent in the fact that in studying his own mental process man must use his intelligence and emotion in studying those very elements in himself and his fellow man. Einstein expressed it, "What does a fish know about the water in which he swims all his life?"

Freud's factual observations were not unique nor original, but Freud was the first to develop workable theories that explained these observations, and he was the first to develop definitive proof of the truth of some of these theories. The fact that there are dissension and disagreement over details should not deter the student. One can only point out that in recent articles Max Born emphasizes the fact that physicists are still not agreed on whether the fundamental particle of the universe has mass.

In the fields of astronomy, mathematics, politics, economics, and religion there are divergent points of view. The fact that there are also different points of view in explaining human behavior is evidence for accepting the postulates and theories as an integral part of science rather than of dogma. In spite of these differences and divergent points of view, psychoanalytic psychology is a workable science of the operation of the human mind.

Freud postulated and later proved that the mental activities of a person go through definite stages of development, and that man functions as the result of the experiences he has lived, both those he recalls and those he has forgotten.

Understanding the importance of both conscious and unconscious material in explaining human behavior has been reported periodically by great writers throughout recorded history. Most recently William Saroyan states, "First, it is not easy to live purposefully; that is, consciously. Second, it is not easy to remember, certainly not easy to remember accurately, for the unforgettable events of a man's life are not necessarily more important than the insignificant events which do not seem to be remembered at all. A man has his memories, but he is also the things he forgot."

Freud postulated, and it has been frequently proved, that certain significant desires and memories are actively "forgotten" or pushed out of the realm of consciousness by a process called *repression*. This repressed material continues to generate energy, and the organism seeks to discharge or use up the energy without permitting the original thoughts to become conscious. These events which influence behavior without the person's conscious knowledge Freud called the *dynamic unconscious*.

He observed that patients resist attempts to bring this unconscious material into the field of consciousness because it would again produce anguish. Freud observed patients who used a variety of mental tricks as defenses to prevent the return to consciousness of repressed ideas, thought, or acts. This activity he called *resistance*.

The matter of resistance has been a subject of much inquiry in the development of psychoanalytic technique and its comprehension, and detecting its manifestations is essential to any understanding of human behavior. Edward Glover and many others have written extensively on this subject. Resistances are encountered in all phases of mental activity. Glover states:

First of all the ego uses the customary defense resistances against id excitations . . . keep unconscious presentations from consciousness in analysis. These are repressions or defense resistances. Secondly, we have the transference resistances which endeavor to avoid memory work by keeping alive a new enactment of old situations in the transference period. The third is the resistance due to the gain through illness which is connected with the ego's manipulation of symptoms. All these are ego resistances. The fourth is the type we have described where guilt feelings and self-punishment tendencies indicate a conflict between

the super-ego and the ego. This is a characteristic of super-ego resistance, sometimes called the negative therapeutic reaction, when the need for punishment
continues to exploit symptom formation and is the sole remaining barrier to their
resolution. The fifth is the resistance of the id which is indicated in the process
of working through.

In working with patients Freud noticed that some individuals expressed
emotions, thoughts, and sentiments toward the physician which had originally been felt for one of the significant people in their lives. This phenomenon he called *transference*. Later developments of techniques have
shown that the detailed analysis of these transference phenomena gives
much understanding of the development of the personality of the patient
and contributes much to the unraveling and reformation of his character
structure. Based on this understanding and reformation, healthy ways of
handling emotional problems may be developed.

In his attempts to explain these phenomena described as repression,
resistance, transference, and the dynamic unconscious, Freud postulated
a structure of the mind. Students should bear in mind that this structure
is not correlated with any particular anatomic structure but is only a concept used to explain mental phenomena resulting from the total functioning
of the organism.

The Id

The term *id* was invented by Freud to designate those mental phenomena called the basic or primitive drives, sometimes referred to as the
instincts.   These drives are found in all human beings and in modified
forms in all other animal life.   The energies associated with these drives
result from metabolism in the tissues. Chemistry and physiology teach us
that metabolism is a continuing process of building up, or creating, and
tearing down, or dying, of tissues throughout the life of the organism. This
process uses a combination of essential chemicals for the body called food,
plus oxygen and water which are necessary for life.

This derivation of energies from metabolism in the tissues is said to be
the *source* of the instinct. The *aim* of the instinct is to derive from the environment those elements necessary for carrying on these basic processes.
Where the nurture of the organism is concerned, this is the acquisition of
food, oxygen, and water. For procreation in man and the higher animals,
the aim is to find a suitable object of the opposite sex. The *object* of the
instinct is the source in the environment from which the instinct may
achieve its satisfaction or the elements necessary for satisfying its drives;
for man, a woman.

Freud was able to show that in the organization of the cells, tissues, and organs which we call man, the processes of creating and dying in the tissues have their counterparts in the total behavior of the individual. These also can be classified and studied. In a historical sense we know that civilizations also rise and fall.

We know that the drives, when expressed in the behavior of man, reflect this basic balance between creation and destruction found in the fundamental elements of the cell and, so far as we know, in the total pattern of the universe. To describe these forces Freud used *eros* for the creative or growth functions and *thanatos* for the destructuve and death functions as expressed in the total behavior of the person. He postulated that psychologic growth and development depended on the balance of these two factors being somewhat in favor of the creative mechanism, just as growth and development of the organism are dependent on the creative and growth processes exceeding the destructive ones. Thus, reduced to its bare fundamentals, the basic instincts or drives in the id have as their function the carrying on of life by a system of replacement of cells and substances, by the creation of new ones during the death of the old ones, and, periodically in the higher organisms, by death of the total organism following its replacement by new ones which we call children. Thus, life of the individual and life of the species are assured. Services to the cell or to the race in terms of food, water, oxygen, shelter, and procreation ensure the safe carrying on of these primitive functions. The fact that man develops elaborate means of acquiring these necessities, which can be classified and studied, does not alter the fact that these secondary elaborations are less essential than the fundamental necessity of carrying on the life of the species.

In our complex society some of these secondary elaborations have become so much a part of our culture that they too produce changes and alterations in behavior, but must in the long view be thought of as complicated elaborations of primitive and fundamentally simple functions. Evolutionary changes may be constructively viewed as adaptations serving these same functions.

These basic forces as they operate in man Freud termed the *libido*. He postulated that these basic energizing forces have a natural history of development. This has been repeatedly verified in the analysis of adults and by the observation of children who are going through these stages of development. Analytic psychology has demonstrated that these drives or instincts are implacable in seeking an outlet or expression for their energy and demanding their satisfaction. We know that external situations may stimulate or accentuate the force of these drives in some circumstances, and, in others, attenuate them, but in no instance can they be created or completely obliterated by external circumstances except killing of the organism.

Certain portions of this drive directed toward the person's own character development and stimulated by the needs of the person as determined by the world in which he lives are called the *ego libido* or sometimes the *narcissistic libido*. Those portions of the basic drives or instincts directed toward objects outside the individual, that is, to things or persons in the environment, are called *object libido*. In his earlier years Freud believed that the drives concerned with love, the sexual urges, and the creative and aggressive strivings were all manifestations of the libido. He felt that destructive, aggressive tendencies and hate and death wishes were manifestations of the basic balance in nature between creation and destruction, or life and death if one wishes to express it so.

In his later years he became more occupied with a study of the destructive elements, which he termed the *death instinct* and to which he ascribed the aggressive and hostile strivings of a person when these drives were directed outward. Originally analytic psychology called the libido the *basic force*, and it was understood to consist of both creative and destructive trends. This more clear-cut separation of the destructive elements into the death instinct adds to the concepts of analytic psychology.

Freud has conclusively demonstrated that the psychologic development of the individual contains the elements of creation and destruction, as the atom, the cell, society, and the universe seem to do. He was also able to show that the libidinous strivings go through certain definite natural cycles in time and development which in our culture are predictable. He was able to show that our culture and social custom place restrictions on the gratification of these drives and a person's mental health or ill health and much of his character formation and adaptability to his society will depend upon how successfully he directs these drives in constructive activities. The degree to which he finds solution and satisfaction for these drives in our society will have much to do with his mental health. The details of this evolution will be discussed later.

Researches to date have not shown similar evolutions of the death instinct as distinct from those of the libidinous strivings. Workers report clinical evidence of the death instinct, and Karl A. Menninger in *Love against Hate* and in *Man against Himself* discusses some of these manifestations as they are observed by physicians.

The Ego

Ego was the term Freud used to describe those functions of man that deal with the external world and form his concepts of himself in this world. It is the ego which finds ways of satisfying his primitive needs in the world while at the same time adapting him to the rules and conditions of the culture at the time and in the place in which he finds himself. The equation of the term ego with self has become a part of our common language. Much of this functioning of the mental processes is on a conscious level, but there are important unconscious elements influencing all phases of ego function. Freud recognized that there were certain ego needs, though less basic than those of the id, which in themselves create a type of secondary energy around which the desire to do good and similar strivings must find constructive outlet. This phase of the ego, its needs and the energies it develops, has not been studied in the same detail as the development and the vicissitudes of the libido.

In modern times, as the result of more study, some minor alterations in basic analytic concepts of the ego and some disaffections from the core groups have occurred. Many studies of the ego and its functions deal with its capacity for adapting the demands of the libidinous forces to the rules and circumstances of the environment and doing it in a way that will keep the organism comfortable and avoid anxiety, pain, and guilt. These functions of the ego have been described and studied in detail and are called the mechanism of defense. Sigmund Freud, and later Anna Freud, divided these defenses into several groups. The fact that the usefulness of these groups depends upon the opportunities of the environment and that the study of the environment is of value hardly seems to require setting up a whole new theoretical structure as some propose. This point will be discussed later in the section on cultural forces.

These ego defenses are of two general types:

1. Defense which succeeds in disposing of drives which are unacceptable, by finding substitute satisfactions for them or by abolishing the need for satisfaction at that particular moment

2. Defenses which are less successful and lead to repeated recurrences of the drive and the need of defense

These latter defenses usually result in pathology of some sort and may result in one of the functional neuroses or psychoses depending upon the prior history of the particular organism, the type of stressful situation, and the mechanism of defense selected by the ego.

SUBLIMATION

Sublimation is the term applied to successful defenses. Sublimation involves changing the object of the instinctual striving to one that is acceptable to the superego and ego, and in some instances both the aim of the instinct and the object are changed. It is said to be *desexualized*. In this successful adaptation the basic striving is satisfied with a substitution of one object which is acceptable to the person for one which is unacceptable. Sublimation is possible if the phases of the pregenital development (narcissistic phases) have been successfully negotiated so that each phase contributes elements of stability and satisfaction which can be used constructively in later phases of development. All the pregenital adjustments enter into the development of adult heterosexuality.

Various forms of sublimation are common to the experience of the student. The discharge of excessive hostile competitive urges in sports such as football, hunting, and activities of that type is part of American culture. The identification of the boy with his father and the semideification of the concept of Mother in our culture are other examples of the sublimation of urges not entirely acceptable to the individual but which are handled in a socially acceptable and culturally constructive way by the process of sublimation. In all these situations the aim of the instinct is altered; the sexual components being removed, the substitute object provides a satisfactory outlet for the instinctual striving. Fenichel expresses it:

Conflicts between instinctual demands and fear or guilt feelings are not necessarily pathological. The way . . . the conflicts are handled determines whether the further course is a normal or pathological one. As long as normal instinctual demands have their place within the total personality and can achieve periodic satisfaction, the remaining conflicts have a relatively minor intensity and can be solved without pathological results. The ability to discharge instinctual tensions by periodic gratification is the best guarantee for mental health and also a prerequisite for undisturbed sublimation.

Those portions of the instinct which are in conflict with the customs and the demands of the environment must be handled by other methods of defense. These drives produce feelings of shame, disgust, or guilt in the child, and as a result they are not satisfied directly or by sublimation but are repressed. To keep this material out of consciousness and thus avoid the painful recognition of it, certain other defenses become necessary. Because the energy from the repressed drive remains in the unconscious, the drive is continually seeking satisfaction and will associate itself with another impulse, thus increasing the intensity of the other impulse and at times actually changing the emotional coloring of it. The utilization of these mechanisms of defense explains some neurotic symptoms, many of the psychoses, and much other human behavior that may seem illogical or strange.

Denial. Denial is perhaps the simplest form of ego defense. Denying the presence of painful sensations or anticipated unpleasant experiences is one of the common ways of reducing anxiety. The child in the doctor's office who repeatedly reassures himself that the needle prick will not hurt, although past experience tells him otherwise, is an example of the beginning of this type of mechanism. The grownup who fancies that a marriage or divorce or changing jobs will solve all his problems is using a more adult version of the same type of reaction.

Projection. This is another commonly used form of adaptation to the environment. The buck passing and alibiing so commonly seen after personal failures in love, business, or sports activity is a normal manifestation of projection. The unfair umpire, the bad lie on the golf course, the "general condition" causing business failure are all examples of persons projecting their own failures and inadequacies onto persons or objects in the environment, thus alleviating a great deal of anxiety, guilt feeling, and sense of failure. Projections may progress in severity until we have a complete distortion of the external environment with delusions of persecution and hallucinatory experiences of a fearsome type seen in certain paranoid and paranoid schizophrenic patients.

Introjection. Introjection is another commonly used mechanism of defense. It is closely related to the earlier pleasurable sensations associated with taking food and the incorporation of other things into the body. Because this incorporation not only affords the body pleasure, but at the same time destroys the identity of the external object, the person may later rid himself of hostile impulses or symbolically eliminate a feared person by incorporating certain qualities of the feared person into the personality. This identification with other persons is commonly seen and undoubtedly plays a role in the child's attempt to imitate the father during and after the period of the oedipal conflict and castration anxiety. The old political adage, "If you can't lick 'em, join 'em," is an example of one form of introjection.

Repression. Repression is the type of ego defense most familiar to the student. Unacceptable or painful impulses may be pushed out of consciousness, or, if you like, "forgotten." This material may seek an outlet in certain body systems as in hysteria or may exist as voids in the memory pattern. It is not uncommon in psychotherapy to find that patients have periods of 1 or 2 years during their childhood for which they have little or no memory. Other patients have no recollection of one of their parents prior to 8 or 9 years of age. This repressed material may become manifest through feelings or ideas that the patient adheres to very rigidly.

Reaction Formation. Reaction formation is closely related to repression and is a method of handling or discharging the repressed material. The completeness and the success of this maneuver will vary considerably from one patient to another. For example, the person who has many hostile or aggressive wishes toward people around him or unacceptable urges in the sexual sphere may become a very rigid, rabid religious fanatic, denying and inveighing against all manifestations of pleasure because all of them represent threats to him. The compulsive person who is meticulous about his clothes and surroundings and about his physical effects becomes quite anxious and upset at the slightest disarrangement of his preconceived order of things. This person may be reacting against strong anal impulses to smear and spread filth around him. The mother who did not wish her child, tried to have an abortion, and has a great deal of hostility toward him may react to the situation with so much anxiety and guilt that as a result she becomes an oversolicitous, hovering mother who continually fears that something harmful will happen to her child. Secondarily, of course, by this projection she also "grinds him down" and shows a sweet form of hostility which is frequently openly accepted and embraced by her women friends. The Don Juan, or particularly aggressive he-man type of male, may actually be using this type of supermasculine activity to ward off homosexual impulses.

Undoing. Undoing is a form of defense closely related to reaction formation. A good example is a medical student who had many compulsions. Among them was a necessity of leaving out part of examinations, but he felt forced to undo this by offering a quick prayer in which he promised God that he would answer all the questions completely. This undoing of the original ideas results in attenuation which is temporary, and must be repeated to be effective.

Isolation. Isolation is a type of defense most commonly seen in compulsive neuroses. The patient retains in consciousness the memory of the psychogenic trauma, but he has isolated it from its original significance and from all or most of the emotional feeling that went with it. It is extremely difficult to get these patients to tie their emotions into the original situations. Patients will tell you of the situations in a calm manner during their therapy but discharge their emotions on apparently isolated objects. For example, we treated a young woman who spent all her time in her bathroom in washing rituals. She would wash her hands and clothes and then wash the bowl in which she had washed her hands and clothing. Then, having contaminated her hands because she washed the bowl, she had to wash her hands again, but in this act contaminated the bowl, etc. In therapy it developed that the thing she actually feared was paper, and her hands had touched paper which set off the washing mechanism. She feared paper because letters, newspapers, and magazines were brought by the postman. He, in turn, in getting to her house, walked by the public library where there were books. The patient feared library books because she had been told once that she could contract scarlet fever from library books that had been handled by patients with the disease. It developed that she feared contracting scarlet fever because a small boy of her acquaintance had had scarlet fever. It also developed that the patient had a great deal of sexual play with this boy who subsequently developed scarlet fever, and the patient had guilt feelings and anxiety about this. She was able to discuss the play with the boy and his part in her past without much display of emotion but became panicky with anxiety and fear if anything connected with paper came near her. In this rather extreme example of isolating, we see how obsessive symptoms may develop. That patient, having taken the original fear and guilt concerning her play with the boy out of the incident, felt responsible for his scarlet fever. This idea produced too much discomfort and had then been transferred step by step to irrelevant and partially avoidable objects.

Regression. This is the return to an earlier type of adjustment, and patients resort to it in trying to adapt to a difficult or impossible situation. Regression in the social sphere is quite common. Persons who are promoted to new positions of responsibility will sometimes find they cannot handle them and ask to have their old jobs back. Country boys going to the city may find it necessary to return home in order to get along. In a psychologic sense, persons who fail to adjust on an adult level may develop various types or varieties of childish dependency. Going home to Mama for support, either financial or emotional, is regression. They may regress in even more infantile forms of behavior. An attempt to return to the breast or bottle may result in prolonged alcoholism, pregenital sexuality, and other types of infantile behavior. The degree to which regression takes place plays an important role in determining the type and severity of the neurotic or psychotic reaction the person summons to his aid when external situations become too severe to handle in a constructive manner.

Blocking. Blocking is the handling of emotional changes the patient feels inadequate to cope with by repressing or denying. Classic examples of this type of defense are frigidity in the sexual sense and the extreme passivity of the individual who is actually very hostile. There are facts which are blocked and are often postponed and discharged later on a substitute object. Thus a patient of ours was prone to weep when he heard certain types of music or when he attended children's plays. Investigation in this case revealed that the patient had been instructed or compelled to repress his emotions as a child and was not permitted to react to punishment or disappointment with weeping or anger. The affect had become blocked and was later discharged in a seemingly irrelevant situation.

Displacement. This is closely related to blocking. The above patient is an example of blocking, postponement, and displacement of affect from rage and grief toward parental action to some child's play or a bit of sad music. This displacement frequently operates in obsessive patients.

Superego

Freud coined the term *superego* to describe those mental activities dealing with our personal moral code or sense of ethics. When we stop to think about it, most of us are conscious of our moral and ethical beliefs, but the original experiences and the training which lead to the formation of these beliefs are made up of some things we remember and many that are forgotten.

The function of the superego was studied in some detail in the early phases of the development of psychoanalytic psychology, but the major emphasis was on the vicissitudes of the id functions. In recent years psychoanalytic research, especially by psychologists, has studied the superego function extensively. Some writers suggest the possibility that the superego is as basic in tissue origins as the libidinous strivings. Psychoanalytic psychology, like other fields of science, is continually developing, and one therefore cannot positively say that this is not so, but the evidence presented to date is not convincing.

The superego is the result of the religious and moral teaching of the child by his parents and other significant persons during his formative years. The form of the superego will vary with the social, educational, and disciplinary actions of the parents experienced by the child. These teachings are further modified by the ethics he experiences at the hands of his schoolmates, scout masters, teachers, and other persons with whom he comes in contact.

In effect, the superego establishes rules and determines methods by which the ego can find satisfactions for the id impulses in terms of the superego's sense of the fitness of things. If the ego violates or anticipates violating the individual's moral code as expressed by the superego, anxiety results, and if the behavior takes place in spite of this anxiety, guilt feelings will develop. The situations which produce feelings of guilt vary among individuals because of the different ethical teachings, the demands of their culture, and the differences in experience as they are trained. The extent to which the superego controls the ego in its functions depends upon the strength or the energy which a superego can summon to this controlling function.

The strength of the superego is the result of the circumstances under which it develops. In infants in the pregenital phase, the superego is present as a potential or rudimentary function. It begins to take definitive form at 4 or 5 years of age. At this stage in the evolution of his libido the child develops hostilities directed outward, as well as positive feelings directed outward to persons in the environment, usually the parents. If the feelings of hostility, as a result of castration anxiety and the oedipus complex, are directed toward a parent whom the child loves, he will have a strong sense of guilt and some fear of punishment. If, in spite of this hostility, the parent remains loving, the hostile impulses are repressed and sublimated, and we say we have a healthy handling of the so-called oedipus complex. If the hostility is too great or the parent is restrictive, withholding love, or is absent at this time, sublimation may be impossible, calling for continual efforts at repression and development of other defenses. Frigidity and rigidity may result.

If, on the other hand, while in this phase of development, the child is handled by a parent he does not love or who, because the parent is cruel, deserts him or does not love the child, the guilt feelings toward this person in the face of hostility are minimal, the repression of the hostility is incomplete, and the basic foundations of a strong superego are not formed. The child's subsequent experience in terms of contact with teachers and other persons in the community and the degree to which he can obtain emotional support from persons outside his immediate family will determine whether he develops a strong superego of a healthy sort, one that is overly strict and inhibiting, or one that leaves him at the mercy of his own basic impulses as he tries to adapt himself to living in a world full of other people.

A superego that is too strict results in a rigid, frigid, unhappy person who usually produces unhappiness for other people about him as well as for himself. A superego that is not in control of the situation gives little anxiety and few guilt feelings when the ego uses hostile or antisocial methods for gratification. This leaves the person at the mercy of his basic impulses and results in various types of antisocial behavior, some of which may be criminal in nature.

Mechanisms of Defense

Other mechanisms of defense not described in the analytic literature should now be discussed.

Hallucinations. Hallucinations are sensations perceived in the spheres of the special senses without external stimulation. Hallucinations commonly occur in the schizophrenic reactions, the affective disorders, some of the organic states, and, most commonly, in the toxic reactions. No adequate explanation of hallucinations has been made, although the best discussion is Schilder's. It seems most productive to consider hallucinations, as we do all other symptoms, as attempts of the organism to solve situations in which it finds itself. A psychosis represents the individual's attempt to find satisfactions for his basic strivings in an environment where they are not available. The individual regresses and begins to distort the environment into forms that are more satisfactory to him. He resorts first to fantasy, then later to hallucination. It seems logical to assume that the ego, confronted with situations which are tremendously confused either because of anxiety and threats to it from the id or the environment, or from toxic processes threatening it by interference with cortical functions, attempts to organize the external world into a less confusing place to protect itself. Inasmuch as the major portion of our awareness of the world around us is through the organs of the special senses, it seems only logical to assume that the sick person would likewise use these senses to distort the environment around him to make it more satisfying to him. As a result he probably begins to objectify things in the environment and, due to old conditioning responses, interprets these sensations as actual sensory perceptions, where in actuality none exists.

Delusions. The same material discussed for hallucinations would apply to delusion formation. The projecting outward of one's need in order that one may make the environment more satisfactory and the interpretation of environmental events in terms of one's own needs at the moment are commonly called delusions. It would seem that the principal difference between hallucinations and delusions, which are frequently associated, would be that in the former the projection organizes the world into sensations of objects which are perceived by the special senses, and in the latter it is done in the sphere of concepts, thoughts, and ideas.

Illusion. In this concept of hallucinations and delusions an illusion becomes little different from hallucination. The outstanding difference is that in illusion the individual actually chooses some stimulus and interprets it in a manner which aids him in solving his problems, while in hallucination the environmental object is projected in its entirety. It seems likely that illusions may represent less serious psychopathology in that the individual needs some object to misinterpret, while in hallucination he can create the object and interpret it in any way he sees fit.

Origin of Instincts or Drives

The basic drives or instincts have their origins within the tissues and guarantee satisfaction of needs that the organism must meet if it is to survive. The things or persons in the environment which satisfy a particular need are known as the *object* of the drive. The desire to avail oneself of the particular object is referred to as the *aim* of the instinct; that is, the instinct seeks to find satisfaction by working toward or availing itself of the above-mentioned object. The *source* of the instinct is thought to be within the chemistry of the tissues and represents the basic need which must be satisfied if the organism is to survive.

The Development of the Libido

Freud discovered the infantile phases of sexual development in the course of analysis of adults and verified them by observations in children. These observations in both adults and children have been repeated countless times by other analysts. These early steps in the development of the libido were described by Freud as going through certain rigid phases. Analysts still believe that the libido develops through certain specific stages but with perhaps more overlapping and less rigidity than originally believed.

In the early portions of the introductory chapter we described the behavior of children as they go through the phase in which most of their emotional satisfactions are received at an oral level. In the primary sucking or passive phases, the child receives pleasures as well as nourishment through the oral passages. This is known as the *oral* or *primary phase* of libido development. The pleasure is prolonged by sucking thumbs, toes, or toys and, as mentioned earlier, will carry over into adult life in the satisfactions gained from smoking cigars, excessive eating, and kissing suitable persons.

The second oral phase is known as the *oral aggressive*, or, if you prefer, the *biting phase*. This is closely akin to the first phase but is a more active stage in which the primary pleasure is not in the passive reception of objects into the mouth but is in the drive to incorporate aggressively external objects through biting, chewing, and swallowing. This aggressive phase carries over into many areas of early childhood even after other phases of libidinous development have achieved ascendancy. A child's game of "eating people up," the love of bubble gum, and other commonly observed phenomena are residuals of this oral aggressive phase.

The second large phase in libidinous development, the so-called anal phase, was also discussed in Chapter 1. In this phase the child finds much emotional satisfaction and develops great interest in his excretory function. In the anal phase we have retentive and expulsive or aggressive phases.

These oral and anal phases are sometimes called the *narcissistic* or *pregenital phases* of libidinous development because in these early stages the pleasures and drives which originate within the body are also satisfied with the infant's own body. Hunger and feeding, sucking, chewing, a full bowel, an evacuation, caresses, and fondling are all examples. These several stages of satisfaction of the body with the body in which the ego libido is predominant comprise the narcissistic phase. Later, as the child becomes more fully aware of things and people as distinct from himself and finds that others offer satisfactions for his basic urges, the object libido or energies directed toward other persons become a more important factor. In all well-adjusted persons, however, both object and narcissistic or ego libido are present and show a nice balance in utilizing basic drives.

The next step in the development following the anal phase is the first of the genital phases and is of great importance in psychopathology because for the first time the infant's emotional drives are directed outward and require other persons for their satisfactions. He begins to look to the persons in his environment for satisfaction of his instinctual urges, particularly those with affectionate and sexual coloring. In this phase of one's emotional development, referred to as the *first genital phase*, guilt feelings over hostile wishes toward the parent of the same sex and guilt feelings over sexual strivings of an infantile sort directed toward the parent of the opposite sex first appear. Accompanying the guilt is fear of retaliation from the parent, which results in objectified anxiety. This anxiety is called *castration anxiety* because many of the child's fears at this time are colored by thoughts of genital mutilation by the parent as a form of retaliation. This whole complicated stage of emotional development is called the Oedipus complex because a situation of this sort has been immortalized in the Oedipus myth by Sophocles.

In the male child this anxiety is handled by repressing the sexual components of the strivings toward the mother, and sublimation is achieved by a semideification of his feelings toward the mother. It is further sublimated by developing identification with the father and incorporating into his own behavior many of the father's attitudes and imitating his behavior. At this phase, which occurs at about 5 years of age, we have the beginning development of the secondary sexual traits as the child emulates the father. If the father proves to be weak or unworthy or rejecting of the child, great confusion in this identification takes place, laying groundwork for later serious psychopathology, especially in the areas of sexual identification and development.

Even in the most successfully sublimated children, however, the strong bond of affection and, at times semiseductive behavior on the part of both mother and child will be seen by the astute observer. Also lingering antagonism between father and son is a matter of common observation in our culture. Another manifestation of this carryover of early impulses is seen in a boy's choice of a wife. Very often the wife will have some traits which are closely related to character traits of the mother. One also sees jealousies between the mother and the daughter-in-law which have been immortalized in our culture by the mother-in-law jokes.

The female child has a somewhat different course of development in this stage because of sexual anatomic differences. Both children suffer castration anxiety, but the female child, lacking a penis, may feel that she has actually been cheated or mutilated. The child, in her attempts to identify with the father, is also anxious to share or possess his phallus. This aggressive desire to possess a penis is doomed to frustration, and the guilt feelings and subsequent identification with the mother require a slight regression to a more passive feminine phase. The desire to conceive a child originates at this time as the desire to receive a child from the father and identify with the mother in her relations with him. Little girls almost uniformly play at being mothers and have identifications in the possession of dolls. Some girls never entirely achieve a successful resolution of the Oedipus situation, and they are attracted to older men and are often somewhat aggressive, rather than typical, passive, feminine persons. This aggression may show itself in distinguished careers or it may reveal itself through pursuit of men in the desire to take from them the envied penis.

These anxieties and their resolution produce a phase in the development known as the *period of latency*, in which a child runs away from his heterosexual strivings. The male child in particular joins a boys' club, imitates his father, plays cowboy, and engages in other types of socially acceptable activity with persons of his own sex.

Little girls also have a latent period but carry into this situation the identification with the mother and the desire to possess a child from the father. This is manifest by the great preoccupation with playing house, playing with dolls, or playing doctor.

The latent period in libidinal development is sometimes referred to as the *homosexual phase*. This is an unfortunate term because actually the child is running away from sexuality and seeking solace and safety in the friendship of persons who either directly or indirectly symbolize the object of his fear. It is as if he were trying to ingratiate himself with the enemy as a self-protective device.

With the biologic changes that come with puberty, there is a revival of the genital strivings and, if the Oedipal situation has been satisfactorily negotiated, the individual enters into adult sexuality as we understand it. Masturbatory experiences started during the first genital phase may have been suppressed along with the castration anxiety or may have continued through the latency period. With the sexual tensions that develop with the puberty changes, masturbation is almost universally practiced, and with it many culturally induced conflicts and difficulties arise. Masturbation is only a symptom of the first stage of adult sexual strivings. It usually persists or is replaced by nocturnal emissions until marriage or other types of heterosexual activities are established.

Vicissitudes in accomplishing the transition of the libido from one of the earlier phases to another, or fixation at one of these phases due to unusual frustrations, or excessive satisfactions at any phase, may produce what is known as a fixation at the oral, anal, or primary genital level. Later in life, situations with which the ego cannot cope may result in a return to one of these earlier forms of satisfaction as a way of finding expression for one's emotional needs and as a safety measure to preserve the ego. This going back is dubbed *regression* in analytic terminology.

In closing this section, the student is again reminded that these psychologic phenomena occur, so far as we know, only in the living body. This ongoing chemical factory which is a semisolid state or phase in the transition of organic material from the vegetable garden to the sewer system is known as man because it exists as a discreet movable object said to be endowed with a soul and thought to be endowed with a mind. This thing known as man also exists in a world full of rules, natural forces, and effects from which he cannot escape.

These observations on libido development are not new with Freud. He was the first to organize the observations, describe them, and make them clinically useful. Sophocles in the Oedipus myth was perhaps the first to describe them. However, prior to this Confucius described man's basic needs as being food, drink, and women. Many modern authors have also described all or part of these things. As an example, in *Rock Wagram*, William Saroyan states:

Every man is an animal; he is the animal all men are, but after that he is also his own kind of animal. He is a small and lovely thing, not unlike all of his breed, all alive at the same time.

He is his own poor friend, his own proud stranger, his own cunning enemy, watching with sharp eyes his mother's own son, and he knows more than he is ever able to tell. Whatever the acts of his life, his own cunning friend and his own forgiving enemy watches and marks and comforts him, and a man lives out his time in secret, leaving behind no word of what he was or did or knew. Or leaving half a word mixed with laughter or half an act of dancing mixed with love, in the warm light, along the bright floor of his own mother's kitchen, when he was five and she was his girl baking bread for him.

Before leaving the psychologic phenomena and going to the more physical, it should be pointed out that the existence of man as an entity is dependent on those around him. The work of Spitz and Bowlby shows that isolating infants or removing them from their loved ones results in a lower level of intelligence, and they believe it may produce emotional disorder.

CHAPTER 3

Organic Components of Behavior (Chemistry and Physiology)

The development of the highly integrated culture in which we live is apparently dependent upon man's possession of a better developed nervous system. This nervous system enables us to develop certain facilities not possessed by the so-called lower animals. Cicero (as translated by Gordon Allport) said:

Nature then has generated and fashioned man's body in such a way that some parts of it were perfect at birth. Others were formed as age increased without much use of external and adventitious aids. Now in other respects she made the mind as perfect as the body, endowing it with sense capable of perceiving things so that little or no assistance of any sort was needed to supplement them, but that faculty which is highest and most excellent in man she left lacking. She furnished the rudiments, nothing more.

Lin Yutang expresses it in a more popular way:

Our mind was originally an organ for sensing danger and preserving life. That this mind eventually came to appreciate logic and correct mathematical equation I consider a mere accident. Certainly it was not created for that purpose. It was created for sniffing food, and if, after sniffing food, it can also sniff an abstract mathematical formula, that is all to the good.

As previously stated, these higher functions must have their basis in physiology, but the how of this process is not completely understood at this time. With each succeeding edition of this book, more information is available. Since the last edition there has been a delightful expansion of interest in this field, and many mathematicians and physicists as well as neurophysiologists, psychologists, and sociologists have interested them-

36

selves in the problem. Perusal of this material is refreshing, particularly after one attends a session in which our colleagues berate and argue over psychologic interpretations and minutiae. Arguments that systems are incomplete, or that "there is no proof," for example, of psychoanalytic psychology or the role of oxygen in the central nervous system must be viewed in their proper light. One recognizes that there has been difficulty in proving the facts and logic of arithmetic when viewed by modern mathematics.

One of the best self-orienting documents, which is recommended to all serious students, is *The Task Before Us* by P. W. Bridgman. In an essay read at the American Academy of Arts and Sciences in Boston, he quotes Gödell and his theorem, stating Gödell proved that

. . . it is not possible to prove that a logical system does not contain concealed self-contradictions or inconsistencies by the use of any theorem which can itself be derived from the basic postulates of the theorem in question. In other words no system can ever prove itself free from contradiction. If you want to prove freedom from contradiction you have to go outside the system to do it, which implies using a theorem for which there is no proof in its original context.

He points out that the efforts of mathematicians who sought to "prove by the principles of arithmetic that arithmetic contains no concealed contradictions which may some day be discovered and bring down the whole intellectual edifice in ruins" are not only futile but impossible. One can perhaps prove that arithmetic contains no self-contradiction, but to do it one has to use methods other than arithmetical. These other methods used to prove that arithmetic has no contradiction cannot be proved not to have contradictions in their own systems, and one must now go outside this extra arithmetical system ad infinitum. "The regress has no end, but actually there is an end, for in any epic the system containing all men and their activities is an upper limit which may not be exceeded. Logical certainty is unattainable, and in hoping for it we are deceived by a mirage of our own creation."

As stated earlier, it is difficult in observing one's own behavior and the behavior of one's own kind, particularly in the intellectual sphere, to avoid contradictions and difficulties. In recent times the psychologists, sociologists, neurophysiologists, and physicists who have been dealing with the technical problems of communication and communication theory have become interested in the basic problem of what sort of thing the brain is. The Macy Foundation has repeatedly brought together groups of scholars to consider various facets of mental functioning. The Hixon Symposium pursued this topic at great length with many interesting suggestions and discussions but raised far more questions than it answered.

Norbert Wiener has written at length on control and communication in animal and in machines. He dubs this theory *cybernetics*.

Bridgman commented on the difficulty in studying what sort of thing the brain is:

This I think can only result in a better understanding of the whole situation. One of the results which is beginning to emerge is the realization of the extent to which our conscious activities have to be selected from the overwhelming number of potentialities. Ever since Freud people have known that large parts of the activity of the brain never get into consciousness. It is only recently, however, that calculations have been made of the numerical possibilities of our conscious awareness. The figures that one gets are no less than stunning. It is known that the neurones in the brain serve in some way as basic elements in brain processes, and it is known that the brain contains something of the order of ten billion neurones. Let us suppose for the argument that different states of consciousness correspond to different ways of connecting the neurones together. Furthermore, suppose that recognizably different states of consciousness cannot follow each other more rapidly than one hundred per second, much too generous an estimate. Then it may be calculated that in a lifetime of one hundred years a man will be able to have about three hundred billion different conscious experiences! But the total number of conscious experiences, with which his mental machinery is capable of providing him, is so great that the number of lifetimes of one hundred years required to experience them all, is a billion times the total numbers of electrons in the entire universe! It follows that the pictures which our perceptions are capable of giving us must be inconceivably abridged and conventionalized. Yet with such an instrument we have set ourselves the goal of knowing ourselves and our neighbors and the incomparably more complex external world which we have clothed with the concept of reality, independent of the brain that conceives it. I cannot help feeling that it will have a pretty sobering effect when the significance of this simple calculation gets under our skins. I think a certain decent humility is inevitable. The problem for us becomes not to find the absolute truth, but to find how to do the best we can with what we have.

The rest of this section will follow Bridgman's dictum to "Do the best we can with what we have."

As the student will readily perceive, the best we have is none too good. The possession of an intact healthy brain is essential for optimum mental functioning. The effects of disease, injury, drugs, and deficient blood supply on the structure are well known in so far as structure is concerned, and the effects that these structural and chemical changes have upon mental processes have been studied. In spite of this, much of man's activity and thinking cannot be correlated with specific alteration in the brain or other body structures or processes. New information on this subject increases, and it is still our belief that function is dependent upon structure. Sigmund Freud expressed it, "Because of the essential unity of the two things that we divide into somatic and psychic, one may prophesy that the day will come when the avenue from biology and chemistry to the phenomena of neurosis will be open for our understanding, and we hope also for therapy."

Stanley Cobb along the same lines states, "In spite of the fact that handedness is inherited and therefore dependent upon the structure of the genes, no difference can be seen between the right and left hemispheres of the brain. Grossly and microscopically nothing significant has ever been found to distinguish the dominant from the secondary hemisphere." Cobb further states, "If the reader insists on classification as of 1943, the difficulty is probably chemical rather than histological. To say that the trouble is 'functional' is just as stupid in this connection as in others. There can be no function without a structure behind it, and function is not inheritable."

Sherrington states, "Inside the animal form sits the brain, its work broadly to increase the animal's grip on the world about it, and hardly less the grip of the external world upon the animal. . . . But the dominant partner in the driving of the brain is the outside world in commerce with the animal."

All these quotations serve to emphasize the oneness of living function and of the interdependence of structure and environment in determining the individual's reaction to any situation.

With these facts firmly in mind and with the philosophy of Bridgman casting its shadow over them, we will present some phenomena observed in the laboratory on interrelation between physiology, chemistry, and behavior. The importance of regulation of the chemical environment of the body, as well as the brain, has been studied, and new evidence is available in this edition.

In earlier editions we quoted Barcroft:

We have therefore arrived at the point where we can say not only that the form of life, man, which has developed an intellectual power far beyond any other, is that in which the constitution of the fluids that bathe his cells is almost exactly regulated, but also the most immediate effect of interference with the chemical or physical properties of the brain is impairment of the higher qualities of the brain.

The brain, one of the great users of oxygen in our body, utilizes more than 4,000 ml per gm of brain per hour. To ensure this supply, the blood flow averages 1,400 ml of blood in a minute or 100 ml per 100 gm of brain per minute. The brain receives, at rest, about one-third of the output of the left ventricle, although the brain represents only 2 per cent of the body weight. Interference with the blood supply of the brain, either through heart failure or sclerosis of the vessels with decreased flow, will produce confusion and impaired intellectual function. Acute arrest of cerebral circulation produces unconsciousness in a few seconds. The blackout experienced by combat pilots is due to the sudden interference of cerebral blood flow caused by pullouts at high speed.

Further examples are the observations on the decreased mental efficiency in any field of intellectual activity when the oxygen concentration of the environment drops below certain critical levels or below certain pressures. These phenomena have increasing importance in our age of high-altitude flying, but have long been observed in hospital patients with pneumonia, or other respiratory illness, who develop confusion, intellectual dysfunction, and delirium if the oxygen supply to the brain is long impaired. Prolonged interference with an adequate oxygen supply causes permanent changes in the brain. Doust found by spectroscopic methods that the "constitutional schizophrenic" patients showed a significant degree of chronic anoxemia, that other kinds of schizophrenic patients showed lesser degrees of anoxemia, and that neurotic patients showed anoxemia in the same degrees as the patients with physical illness. Other workers noted that oxygen therapy after head injury hastened recovery, and they reported that injury produces variable changes in oxygen use by the brain.

It was long thought that the brain could utilize only glucose as food. This has been shown to be untrue by Gerard. He noted in cat brains that the organism could be kept alive with perfusion fluids completely free of glucose. It has also been shown that in vitro brain slices can utilize glutamate. There is also new information available by Gerard and his group on the metabolism of the phosphates in the brain. Other workers have shown changes in general body metabolism associated with various emotions and forms of behavior. Schottstaedt, Grace, and Wolff report:

Persons responding to situations calling for fight or flight or aggressive behavior or feelings of excitement, intensive anger, and apprehension showed sodium and water loss and that this behavior reduced activity; produced slower, decreased speech; feelings of despair, hopelessness, and depression and were associated with retention of fluid and electrolyte. These elements were retained in terrorizing situations and reaction to severe, noxious stimulation and pain. When faced with situations eliciting restless behavior, increased alertness, or readiness for action or mixed feelings of confidence, uneasiness or tension; excretion of water and sodium were decreased and body weight increased. With the end of the threat, water loss and salt loss occurred.

They point out that this is the same as for the body's response to threat from bacterial invasion. For example, during consolidation in pneumonia, there is retention, and as consolidation resolves, diuresis. This seems to be a general response to threats of all sorts.

Roy Grinker and his associates in extensive studies on stress situation, particularly in pilots, have shown profound chemical changes, secondary to psychologic response.

Hyden and Hartelius found that large nerve cells contain considerable amounts of ribose, nucleic acids, and other protein substances. They found that a stimulation of the nerve cell produced extensive changes of a catabolic nature which were followed by recovery and return to the previous state. They believe that this metabolic change is governed by a specific protein-forming system in the nerve cell and that the nucleoprotein is associated with the motor and sensory functions of man. They conclude, "Malononitrile stimulates the nerve cells to an increased production of nucleo-protein. This effect is shown to be restricted to cells of the nervous system." They use malononitrile to treat certain patients with schizophrenia and depression and report that the patients showed some improvement. They believe that the whole procedure was one of stimulation of psychic function, and from this conclude that psychic functions appear to be correlated to the nucleoprotein metabolism of the nerve cells.

Recent researches have confirmed lay observations from ancient times that the ingestion of certain chemicals can produce temporary hallucinations and artificial psychotic states. Rinkel, Hyde, and Solomon in one journal and Levine and his coworkers in another report that the ingestion of lysergic acid produces an artificial psychosis with specific and measurable changes in various phases of psychologic functioning. Because the effects of lysergic acid are transitory and clinically somewhat similar to those of schizophrenia, it has proved a valuable vehicle for artificially inducing psychoticlike behavior in normals. The ultimate significance of this drug and its ability to produce psychosis is not clearly understood. It makes an excellent tool, and the admirable work, particularly of these two groups, does much to improve our knowledge of the interdependence of brain physiology and the mental process.

New leads as to the role of chemical processes in psychologic functions have developed from experimentation with certain of the hallucinogens, particularly LSD (d-lysergic acid diethylamide). Woolley and Shaw discuss the similarities in chemical structure of the compounds producing hallucinations in humans, and they point out the chemical similarities to the neurohormone serotonin (5-hydroxytryptamine) which occurs in the brain but which was first observed in smooth muscle. They suggest that the hallucinogenic substances prevented the action of serotonin in the brain and that the abnormal psychologic functioning, at least hallucinations, is due to the blocking of the action of serotonin by the hallucinogenic substances combining with those receptors ordinarily used by serotonin. This would imply that in abnormal mental states some other substance was present which prevented the action of the serotonin.

Himwich says that reserpine resembles serotonin in chemical structures and causes the liberation of serotonin. He further demonstrates that reserpine causes an early temporary increase in serotonin but with continued use produces a late and enduring diminution in serotonin:

If these results yield a clue to the action of reserpine on the brain, and this is yet to be proved, then I would like to offer a tentative explanation for the therapeutic effects of reserpine, namely, that the abnormal activity of disturbed psychotic patients is associated with an excess of serotonin and that under continued dosage of reserpine its concentration of serotonin in the brain is reduced.

He also points out that this concept could explain the lag in effect of reserpine when first administered to a patient and the fact that the beneficial effects persist for some time after the drug is discontinued.

In contrast to these statements, Sjoerdsma, Kornetsky, and Evarts at the National Institute of Mental Health studied two patients with elevated blood serotonin levels resulting from malignant carcinoid. They found that "the psychological changes produced by LSD in these patients are of the order which have been observed in normal subjects receiving LSD. It is concluded that elevation of blood serotonin levels does not alter the central effects of LSD." They point out, however, that the brain levels of serotonin in carcinoid patients are not known, and these studies do not entirely refute the hypothesis that psychologic effects of LSD are due to blockage of some central action of serotonin. They do point out, however, that other serotonin antagonists such as chlorpromazine and ergotamine do not cause hallucinations.

Funkenstein and his coworkers have in a series of articles detected chemical differences in populations of people. They feel there is a distinct group of people, which may be designated as Group A, in which the drop in blood pressure following Mecholyl infection is sustained, and the preinjection level of the blood pressure is not reached within a substantial period. In Group B, the drop in blood pressure following the injection is not sustained, and the preinjection level is reached within the observation period. They believe that these are distinct groups of people. In their opinion a person secretes either epinephrine or norepinephrine, or perhaps a mixture is secreted, and the greatest quantity of the excreted substance determines into which group a person falls. They also feel that this has definite meaning for determination of the results of treatment of various disorders.

There has been much study of the effect of ACTH and cortisone on the behavior of man: its influence in the production of psychoses, in the treatment of psychoses, and on the instinctual drives. Some outstanding work in this field was done by Henry M. Fox, Sanford Gifford, and their associates in the psychiatric and medical services at the Peter Bent Brigham Hospital in Boston. They conclude that corticotropin and cortisone increase instinctual tensions. Basically they show that the nature of psychologic response depends on the possibility of gratifying psychologic needs in terms of the realities of the patient's total life situation and his present ego structure. These studies were done on a variety of patients facing stress, including persons presenting themselves for cardiac surgery, patients in analysis, and the Harvard crew before, during, and after the Yale contest.

Hoffer, Osmond, and Smythies produced artificial psychosis with deteriorated or "pink" Adrenalin. They also noted hallucinations and other severe psychologic disturbances which they thought were due to the adrenochrome in the deteriorated Adrenalin. They suggested, since Adrenalin is a naturally occurring product and adrenochrome is one of the steps in its destruction, that this might be a causative agent in some psychoses. This work has not been confirmed at this writing but is an interesting subject for speculation.

A group of Minnesota workers studies 90 chronic psychotic patients by EEG with intracerebral electrodes. In 15 of these patients without convulsive history they recorded short periods of high, slow voltage discharge. These paroxysmal bursts of 2- to 5-per-second waves were found in depth recordings. They report a close relationship between the acute psychotic behavior and the elicited exacerbation of the electrical activity. They offer no conclusion.

Ewalt and Bruce and, later, Himwich found that the administration of glutamic acid to certain types of schizophrenic patients, particularly of the retarded catatonic or simple variety, produced transitory improvement in their symptoms.

Kitzinger and her coworkers found that glutamic acid in 23 schizophrenic patients produced different effects on different types of patients and individuals, and that in general it produced definite changes in behavior.

Kaadabirger and his coworkers found that stimulation of the amygdaloid nucleus in unanesthetized cats produced searching responses of the eyes and head which they interpreted as being due to auditory or visual hallucinations.

Hans Selye showed that artificial inflamation and granulation due to chemical stimuli in rats could be inhibited by injection of cortisone at an appropriate time which he called the "critical period." He also reports that tying the animal and subjecting it to psychogenic stress at these same critical periods will also suppress the inflammation. He concluded that the effect of systemic stress in suppressing inflammation is not dependent upon the introduction into the body of any toxic foreign substance or upon the production of any direct physical injury to the tissue.

J. W. Lovett Doust found that capillary pressures are higher in neurotic patients than in healthy patients and that they showed an increasing curve of abnormality to the highest level in the so-called "process" or "constitutional schizophrenic." In other words, the capillary-pressure determinations form a spectrum along which psychiatric patients may be placed in accordance with the severity of their mental disorders. He believes that this partially explains the relative anoxemia seen in some of these patients. This work has not been confirmed but is an interesting finding and deserves further exploration.

These scattered findings, of which the diligent student can find hundreds of examples and contradictions in the literature on chemistry, physiology, and pathology, lead us back to the consideration of the problem of the organization and integration of the body.

Norbert Wiener has written on the problems of organization, and he uses for analogy the breakdown in telephone systems when one part is either overloaded or defective, and how it results in throwing out the functioning of the entire system. He states:

This suggests three ways in which the broken-down organization and homeostasis observed in mental and psychiatric disorders may be attacked. The simplest is to use the psychiatrist and his judgment as a homeostat, attacking each symptom of departure from the norm as it occurs. The next, more complicated, is to put the patient in an environmental situation, which is itself more or less automatically homeostatic and will tend to counter serious departures from equilibrium. The third, which is at once the most difficult and, in my opinion, the most hopeful, is to try and locate the particular links in the homeostatic chain which had become ineffective, and either to find a way of bolstering them up or replacing them by automatic links, perhaps learned by training, which will in the long run have much the same effect.

We hope that researches in chemistry, physiology, sociology, and psychology will some day detect these "links" and provide means of replacing them or for using alternates.

There can be no doubt that over-all deterioration of the brain produces profound changes in behavior and in symptoms. This will be discussed in more detail under Organic Psychoses. In spite of this, the effect of focal lesion on intellectual functioning has not received much attention from experimenters in the laboratory and clinic. It is known that disease, trauma, or atrophy of the brain produces changes in the intellectual process. Attempts to localize certain functions in certain areas of the brain have for the most part been unsuccessful. Putnam stated, "There is unquestionably some degree of special representation of certain behavior patterns in the brain. On the other hand, the brain unquestionably acts as a unit in the sense that it consists of a network of neurones, so that every part of it has some connection with and presumably some dependence upon every other part."

Goldstein states:

If we mean by the mosaic theory that every part of the cortex contributes something different to the performances which in themselves are related to the functioning of the whole cortex, even the whole organism, then it is correct. . . . There are no isolated performances which are merely expressions of the function of single parts of the organism, especially not of a separate part of the brain cortex.

The work of Halstead and others shows that there are no "silent" areas of the brain. Conclusive evidence that silent areas exist only as deficiencies in the method of examination, and not in human function, has been furnished. Lashley demonstrates the importance of the total mass of the brain for functions.

Emotional reactions are undoubtedly total organism reactions with participation of all body systems in their expression. They are generally assumed to be under the control of the central nervous system. Gellhorn expresses it, "These observations (on electrical stimulation of the hypothalamus) obviously indicate that these somatic and autonomic responses which are the overt signs of emotional display are integrated in the hypothalamus."

Alpers stated, "In this sense then the hypothalamus may be regarded as a group of nuclei concerned with the expression of emotional reaction. These are ordinarily controlled by the cerebral cortex which exercises an inhibitory influence over such reactions." Recent work with the new drugs, particularly reserpine and chlorpromazine, which act on the midbrain and grossly influence behavior and emotional response to the symptoms of psychoses, seem to offer further clinical evidence of the correctness of these statements.

The cerebral cortex is the governing or controlling link between emotional experience with the environment and the autonomic system. Fulton expressed it:

These considerations make it evident that the cerebral cortex governs not only the somatic system, but all the systems involved in emotional expression, psychological tension, fears and phobias, etc. This means that the cerebral cortex may drive the heart, the gut, and other visceral organs. Thus, there is a sound physiologic basis for the long-time recognized association between mental activity and visceral processes.

Miller compared the cortical function to a rheostat which determines and regulates the proper shade and degree of emotional expression to be manifest in terms of a given situation.

Interesting animal work was done by Otto Weininger. He demonstrated that gentled rats show significantly greater weight gain, display more activity and less fearful behavior in an open field situation, and as adults sustain less physiologic damage to the endocrine, cardivascular, and gastrointestinal system under prolonged emotional stress than does a comparable group of controls. In other words, gentling the animal early in life produces a type of protection to stress in later years.

Ruegamer, Bernstein, and Benjamin report that albino rats, gentled and given extra handling during the developmental period, gain more rapidly and grow more rapidly on the same amount of food than littermates not handled in the same manner but otherwise subject to the same environment. These interesting studies confirm the interrelation of the psychologic and physiologic activity. The role of the central nervous system and the total reaction of the organism to events is to increase the number of associations possible. In the rats we are not certain what the associations were, but apparently they were constructive.

This increase in the number of associations made possible by use of a better-developed cortex has been called "long circuiting" by Fulton. Cobb described this function as

. . . the mechanism that allows for an enormous increase in associations, it gives higher integration, and leads to delayed action. This process of spread is essential for coordination. Its acme is found in the cerebral cortex where stimuli arriving at one receiving station (example of visual center) spread in innumerable directions to many other cortical areas, awakening associations, habitual responses, memories, etc. . . . The longest way round would seem to be just what is needed to cause a delay in response, probably a most necessary and useful mental process, for, while delay persists, the spreading impulses are making more and more contacts. They are rousing more and more associations. This allows the past experience of the individual to affect his behavior, and if there is any distinction between man and lower mammals it would seem to be this. Adult man usually looks ahead and acts in the light of past experience.

The attempts to understand in physiologic terms the phenomena of human or animal behavior in various situations have led to many ingenious experiments and interpretations. Goldstein made many conclusions from observations of humans with neurologic lesions and from animal experiments. He repeatedly stressed the total function of the organism. He believes symptoms are answers given by the modified organism to definite demands: "A defective organism achieves orderly behavior only by a shrinkage of its enviroment in proportion to the defect." He further comments on behavior sources:

From whence comes the direction of the activity in the organism. . . ? One, the direction is effected through a specific environment in which the organism lives; two, it is effected through a certain determination and force issuing from the organism itself. . . . This tendency in nature to actualize itself is the basic drive, the only drive by which the life of the organism is determined.

Masserman, basing his interpretations upon experience and training in the field of psychobiology and psychoanalysis, conducted many experiments on hypothalamic function and upon experimental neuroses in animals. He has written extensively on the subject to the effect that humans behaving rather complexly secure consummation of their needs and avoid unpleasant psychobiologic tensions in the same manner that a dog in a simpler situation reacts to conditioning experiments when given food, attention, or some other reason to be motivated to take an interest in the procedure.

Lidell, Scott, and others have worked extensively along similar lines to explain human behavior in terms of lessons learned in the laboratory. The difficulties in interpreting human behavior and making analogies to animal behavior have been well demonstrated by Masserman and his group. A recent symposium on group processes further highlights this difficulty. Only through the continuation of research and the interdisciplinary discussion of results will we finally reduce behavior to an exact science. At least we can hope! (The student is advised to reread the quotations from Bridgman in the early parts of this chapter.)

Pavlov culminated his study on conditioned reflexes by attempting to interpret certain types of abnormal human behavior in terms of conditioned reflexes. These researches brought valuable information but no workable or conclusive theories.

Andersen and Lidell stated, "It seems to us that the essential feature of the technique of establishing a conditioned reflex is that it suppresses spontaneous activity through habituation." They noted that animals in a maze test may solve their problem by extra locomotion. This has an interesting analogy in human behavior where people may achieve their biologic needs through extra effort to overcome their own deficient capacities or unusual demands of the environment. When the extra effort results in successful achievement of the goal, the individual is satisfied, but if he fails, the reaction is often more severe because of the extra effort that went into the attempt.

We have previously mentioned Wiener's work in cybernetics in which he attempts to describe the functioning of the brain in terms of a feedback communication system. In the Hixon Symposium, John Von Neuman read a paper on the general and logical theory of automata. By use of mathematics he offered a possible explanation of the functioning of the nervous system. He also pointed out the tremendous efficiency and small energy use of the nervous system as compared to present electronic calculators. He did not pretend to explain how the nervous system works, but the fact that it is possible to design a machine that will perform some of the functions of the human brain in an efficient manner is encouraging. To quote Brosin:

> In summing up the Hixon Symposium, Dr. Von Neuman's brilliant exposition of man's essentially intuitive relation to the machine provides us with some consolation since this is the familiar position of the clinician. We can profit by his example in not regarding the problem as insurmountable.

Brosin in commenting on this brilliant seminar also stated:

> In spite of the encouraging progress exemplified in these papers, there are some notable gaps. We still do not have much material about those operations labeled motivation. For example, why do people do things? What does the organism do in order to maintain harmony between the internal world and the external world? For the student of medicine, the future opportunity for constructive contributions and development in this are unlimited.

If this short excursion into the attempts to explain human behavior on a physiologic and chemical basis has served to stimulate the student to further thinking and researches, the time and space devoted to it in this book will be amply justified.

To summarize, the laboratory data in this field, as now understood, show that much of animal behavior including man's is motivated by the wish and the need to satisfy certain physiologic demands. Interference with these satisfactions produces tensions with common changes in the

autonomic hormonal system. Many details as to how this is done remain
to be filled in. These changes are regulated by the cortex and the hypothalamic nuclei. Human beings are animals and show the same types of
behavior as other animals, modified by the better-developed nervous system in man.

The motivations received from a particular environmental demand will
vary somewhat with individuals in terms of their previous experience and
tissue needs of the moment. Whether a person will adjust to a situation
will depend upon his ability to satisfy his needs either directly or symbolically in terms of the opportunities and handicaps offered by the environment. The necessity of making unsatisfactory compromises in too
many situations will result in a maladjustment or a neurosis or a psychosis. Thus, maladjustment or neurotic symptoms come as a result of
the individual's attempting to satisfy these basic needs in the face of
shortcomings in his own capacity or experience, or from excessive demands made by the environment. The individual's capacity to achieve
satisfaction from his environment may be altered by structural damage
to some part of the body, by toxic influences due to poisons or disease, or
by accumulated faulty habits of reaction. In this instance the person cannot adjust to ordinary environmental conditions, and he will need a specially prepared and protective environment pending his recovery. Other
persons are confronted by environmental situations that offer very little
opportunity for satisfactory living. In these cases the environment must
be manipulated, or the person must make unusual efforts to meet his
needs in the face of the difficult situation.

From these preliminary observations concerning the developmental
structure of the human personality, it is a long step to the personality
as it appears to the student of psychiatry. At least one may state that
any given cross section of any person is the result of the constant previous interplay and interaction between the individual and his environment. Somewhat dramatically, but still authentically, the student might
think of human personality as a given cross section of an individual life,
as a composite—but exact—record of everything that has happened in
the life of a person.

However, human personality is more than this because the foundation
layer of its structure is derived from inheritance. Very rapidly during
childhood and then, as the span of life lengthens, more slowly, there are
innumerable additions, some of which eventuate as physical characteristics, intelligence, emotional traits, bias, prejudices, and intolerance. It
is obvious of course that sex and its larger implications and connotations
occupy a significant place in the personality.

In this chapter we have attempted to discuss some of the known organic factors of behavior and indicate areas in which the student may improve his knowledge in terms of understanding behavior in neurophysiology and neurochemistry. The following chapter will present in more detail the growing knowledge of the influence of environmental or cultural situations on the organism.

CHAPTER **4**

Social Concepts of Behavior

The past two chapters have been devoted to studying variations within the individual human. In Chapter 1 we stressed the fact that man himself is only one small unit in a large and complex universe. Since we may only view ourselves with the equipment with which nature endows us, we consider man as the basic unit of our society. The interrelations of man to man, of groups of men to other groups, and of man to the other living and nonliving natural phenomena of the world have occupied man's attention throughout history.

In the early phases of history it was a struggle for existence. As man has succeeded in subduing more of the natural forces of the world, or, perhaps more accurately, learned to utilize them for his own survival and comfort, he has turned more attention to understanding each individual's behavior, and to understanding the individual's reactions to groups, and the interaction of larger groups with each other. These studies have been rather loosely categorized as psychology, sociology, anthropology, politics, and statesmanship with contributions from history, art, and literature, to say nothing of geology and archeology. The details of this history will be left to other works and authors more competent on the subject.

In this chapter we shall review briefly some of our current knowledge of the influence that social and cultural forces have on the behavior of man. Certain simple ones are easily illustrated, and others are more complex. For example, we know that if the food supply of the environment is not sufficient for the organism to acquire an adequate supply with the effort and skills he possesses, he will starve. We know that certain natural phenomena in the environment may or may not be adequately met with the equipment at hand. An example would be two aircraft decompression accidents reported in the press within a few weeks of each other. In one, the observation dome on a high-altitude aircraft blew out, and the navigator was extruded into the air at about 25,000 feet over the North Atlantic. Not having a parachute and not being equipped by nature for soaring, he undoubtedly perished because he was suddenly confronted with an environmental situation for which he was not equipped by inheritance or experience. Shortly after this, another aircraft flying at high altitude had a cabin window blow out. By coincidence in this case one of the stewardesses was standing near the cabin window at the moment of decompression, and certain substantial segments of her anatomy were extruded into the space. Fortunately, her natural equipment, intended by nature for other purposes, proved sufficient to stop the hole and saved not only herself (she was injured but recovered) but the other passengers in the aircraft from an extremely hazardous situation.

Wartime experience, as well as civilian experience, shows that human beings placed under unusually stressful situations may break but if removed to more ordinary or average life situations, adjust adequately. That these maladjustments under stress are related to individual experience has been shown by several studies, among them those of Menninger, Grinker and his coworkers, and Bond and his associates.

In recent years, more complex studies have been undertaken by sociologists and anthropologists. Sociologists, many of whom are analytically oriented and trained, have attempted to explain in analytic terms, or in other terms, the dynamics of the interrelation of people within groups and of groups to each other. Some studies have attempted to explain the effect of sociologic forces on man's behavior and on the incidence, course, treatment, and prognosis of mental disorder. Other groups through observations of primitive tribes, of civilizations other than ours, and of our own civilization have attempted to work out a sociologic theory of personality and behavior. A new subspecialty known as *social psychiatry* is emerging and is fortunately attracting competent sociologists, anthropologists, and psychiatrists, each with respect for and knowledge of ways of interacting with others in this multiprofessional group.

It has been found productive to being sociologists and anthropologists into our hospital and clinic settings to make observations on the group interactions. From these observations we have learned many things about the administration of hospitals and factors influencing patient and personnel morale, behavior, and response to therapy. A serious student is referred to the abundant literature on this subject. The field has been rather well summarized in *Mental Health and Disorder*, and the literature on psychiatry, anthropology, sociology, and psychology contains many studies. The following material is excerpted from the literature that has proved of particular value to us. No pretense is made that this is a complete review of the subject.

Orientation as to the view of the social scientist is stated by John Seeley:

What the social scientist is contending is that no matter what light may be shed on man's nature by any analysis (not merely present analysis) that is couched in terms of physics or biology, these sciences furnish explanations only of necessary conditions for the behavior of human beings as human beings, and not explanations of sufficient conditions. There are physical, chemical, physiological, and anatomical conditions without which a man cannot exist or continue as a man; but no compilation of such statements of conditions will account for that in him which is distinctively human. We may account in physical, chemical and physiological terms for the fact that men grow periodically hungry, but this they share with the animals. But to account for the fact that they—or some of them—will go into a restaurant, read a menu, smile seductively at the waitress, have a moment of guilt or elation about that, and then proceed to order lobster newburg because it is a prestige-laden food (as against, say, shepherd pie) we have to turn to an order of explanation that is not physical, chemical, physiological; for these are distinctly human acts.

To the charge of triviality (that the social scientist is saying what everybody already knows; namely, that social behavior is a part or aspect of human behavior) the answer is that this is not what the social scientist means either. He means that (given the necessary physical and biological conditions) all that is distinctively human about man must be wholly and solely accounted for in terms of his social nature. He means that man is made human by humans and in society. He means that it is in social life and only in social life that the welter of mere potentialities with which man is born is organized and given form and operability and access via communication to a share in the common human life, and via that to a human life of his own.

Recent work on isolation at the National Institutes of Health, by John Lilly and colleagues, has shown that individuals isolated from all sensory stimuli occasioned by contacts with other humans develop definite mental symptoms and that in time the situation becomes unbearable. As a child living in the west, the senior author heard many stories and fables of Indian braves who periodically isolated themselves in a hut or lodge, and after a period in these lodges received visions which guided their activity in future hunts, warfare, and movements of the tribe. Similar fables and lore concerned young Indian girls who, after a prolonged period of isolation, would see a vision of their lover or future mate. It was assumed by the people that these prolonged vigils resulted in hallucinations due to visitation by spirits, and later, with the advent of the

scientific age, that these visions were induced by starvation and suggestion. These recent studies suggest that the phenomenon of isolation also
played a part. This offers interesting sidelights on the origin of mirages
among old prospectors and persons becoming lost and isolated in desert
and mountainous areas. The work of Bowlby, Spitz, and others on dis-
placed children in England, and studies done on institutionalized children in this country, show that intellectual development is impaired by
isolation from love objects. In an earlier section we reported influences
on growth in albino rats and the influence on tolerance to stress, induced
by contacts with persons who engendered affection and, presumably, feelings of security.

From all these studies one should not make unwarranted conclusions.
It seems valid, however, to conclude that man in his present state of development is dependent on some type of contact with other human beings
in order to exist in a healthy or normal fashion. Social scientists now occupy themselves with an attempt at better understanding the details of
the mechanisms and how they may be manipulated or guided for the bet-
terment of the race and the individuals within it.

Cultural anthropologists and sociologists have studied the psychoanalytic theories and have made substantial changes in their concepts of the
origins and functioning of human culture. Both the medical and social-
science professions have been immeasurably enriched by their mutually
sponsored agreements and differences, and by researches projected into
the fields of their mutual interests.

Freud made several basic observations relevant to the field of understanding man's relations with man:

The love that instituted the family still retains its power; in its original form it
does not stop short of direct sexual satisfaction and in its modified form as aim-
inhibited friendliness, it influences our civilization. In both these forms it carries
on its task of binding men and women to one another, and it does this with greater
intensity than can be achieved through their interest or work in common. . . .
We have seen that culture obeys the law of psychological economic necessity
in making the restriction, for it obtains a great part of the mental energy it needs
by subtracting it from sexuality. Culture behaves toward sexuality in this respect
like a tribe or section of the population which has gained the upper hand and is
exploiting the rest to its own advantage. . . . The bit of truth behind all this—
once so eagerly denied—is that men are *not* gentle, friendly creatures wishing for
love who simply defend themselves if they are attacked, but that a powerful
measure of desire for aggression has to be reckoned as part of their instinctual
endowment. The result is that their neighbor is to them not only a possible helper
or sexual object, but also a temptation to them to gratify their aggressiveness on
him, to exploit his capacity for work without recompense, to use him sexually

without his consent, to seize his possessions, to humiliate him, to cause him pain, to torture, and to kill him. . . . I am convinced that very many processes will admit a much simpler and clearer explanation if we restrict the findings of psychoanalysis in respect of the origin of the sense of guilt to the aggressive instincts. . . . I would not say that such an attempt to apply psychoanalysis to civilized society would be fanciful or doomed to fruitlessness, but it behooves us to be very careful not to forget that after all we are dealing only with analogies, and that it is dangerous not only with men but also with concepts to drag them out of the region where they originated and have matured.

Kardiner, Linton, DuBois, and West made cultural anthropologic studies of the habits of American Indian tribes, of certain island groups, and of a contemporary United States town. Each of these studies has been subjected to analytic study and interpretation to determine the effect of the culture on the biologic drives and behavior. Not all authors agree with the interpretations in these studies, but the studies represent the type of interdisciplinary action that can contribute much to the fundamental knowledge of man's behavior toward man.

In *The Science of Man in the World Crisis* (edited by Ralph Linton) was an attempt to bring to the lay person a knowledge of his own time. This was made by psychology and anthropology (explaining the behavior of men) with the hope that this improved understanding would result in more rational behavior by men toward one another. Now, years later, the statement in the preface seems prophetic:

At the same time some of these findings are of the utmost importance both for the intelligent planning of the new world order which now appears inevitable and for the implementation of any plans which may be made. The builders of such an order are foredoomed to failure unless they understand the potentialities and limitations of their human material. . . . Scarcely less important, is the knowledge of those trends which operate over long periods of time, and of the problems which specialists can foresee before they arise, or can recognize before they become acute enough to call for drastic action. Lastly, even plans which take all these factors into account cannot succeed without the use of adequate techniques. At all these points the science of man can provide some aid.

For a sequel to these statements, the student is referred to the daily newspapers.

The social sciences have had and will continue to play an important role in psychiatry. At the dedication of a psychiatric hospital, Charles S. Johnson refers to the contributions of Freud in understanding the social sciences and to the contribution of Harry Stack Sullivan in adding the interpersonal factor dimension to analytic psychology. Johnson comments that these workers influenced social psychology to shift its center

of gravity "from concern with specific items of behavior and attitude to
dynamic situational concepts also involving interpersonal relationships."
He also refers to work by the Group for Advancement of Psychiatry in
this field, and quotes Helen McLean:

Over fifty years of investigation have made it clear that the total personality
of any human being is a socio-psycho-biological complex. The complexity of
interrelationships between forces in personality and forces in the environment
is so great as to be almost beyond comprehension. The number of variables is
staggering. The scientists' task is made more difficult by the added effect of one
group on another. For full understanding there must be cooperative investigation by men in the psychobiological sciences and men in the social sciences, particularly sociology and anthropology.

More specifically in the psychiatric field social scientists and psychiatrists collaborated in studies which are yielding new information and may
prove to have wide-sweeping significance.

Hollingshead and Redlich have made a study of 5 per cent of the community of New Haven, Conn., as a control of the census of patients receiving psychiatric care. These patients are studied as to psychiatric diagnosis, type of treatment, and their relation to the class structure of the
community. Patients classed as schizophrenic and paranoid, under treatment on Dec. 1, 1950, made up 44.2 per cent of all patients hospitalized
in that area and 58.7 per cent of psychotic patients in the psychiatric
center. Of these patients, 97.6 per cent had been hospitalized sometime,
and 94 per cent were in the hospital at the time of the census. Hollingshead and Redlich found a marked association between social class and
prevalence of schizophrenia in the community. Instead of an equal distribution of patients by class, the indexes were:

Social class	Expected no. persons in class by population distribution, %
I	23
II	33
III	48
IV	84
V	246

Their hypotheses to explain these differences are that either schizophrenic patients are downwardly mobile toward class V, the lowest stratum, or that class differences reflect differences in treatment and rehabilitation. Their data point to the latter hypothesis. They found that the
schizophrenic patient of the upper and middle class is more likely to be
treated by psychotherapy and that the lower-class patient by organic
treatment or by no treatment at all. The lower-class schizophrenic pa-

ticnt is also less likely to leave the hospital permanently and rarely has more than one chance in the community. They assume that the community and the family are of enormous importance in determining who stays in the hospital and who becomes reintegrated with the family. Patients in the upper class seem to come earlier. Thus, the combination of late case finding, inadequate treatment, and poor rehabilitation in families already poorly organized may account for the increase of chronic patients in the lower-class level.

The same authors in collaboration with J. K. Myers, after a study of 1,963 patients under psychiatric care in a New Haven area (the same group referred to in the other paper), reported that 67 per cent of these patients were cared for in state hospitals, 19 per cent by private practitioners, and 14 per cent in clinics or Veterans Administration hospitals. In this study they again reported that patients in the higher social levels —classes I, II, and part of III—tend to receive psychotherapy predominantly, and those in the lower levels tend to receive organic therapy or no treatment. As an example: in class I 54 per cent of the patients received psychotherapy, as compared to 20 per cent in class II, and 9 per cent in class III. Ninety per cent of the patients receiving psychoanalysis were in the first group.

These studies tend to show that treatment depends not on psychologic and medical determinations alone but on the social status of the patient. These studies, if shown to be true for other communities and other populations, have tremendous significance in future management of psychiatric care.

Alfred H. Stanton and Morris Schwartz, and Milton Greenblatt, Richard York, and Esther L. Brown have made extensive studies of the influence of the social environment of the hospital on the care of the patient and the morale of the patient and employee. These studies are of tremendous significance because they show the importance of proper administration in the hospital environment. Employees with high morale, an understanding of what they are doing, a sense of important status, and a feeling of empathy for the patient invariably find themselves in pleasanter working conditions and with fewer disturbed patients than is true of the reverse situation. The effect of extra attention on ward morale and the general level of custodial patients' behavior has been capably shown by Paul Barraby.

Such studies have led me to believe that the whole concept of the mental hospital needs to be carefully restudied.

Studying disease and its social contexts makes relevant the attitudes toward psychiatry of the rest of the medical profession and of the public.

Opinion surveys in this field disclose interesting information. Some of the best have been done by Myers. In brief, his studies reveal that the public seems ready for guidance and education for the basic knowledge in the field of mental health and that the New Jersey population seems prepared to cooperate and finance a well-organized program for combating mental illness.

Robert Myers' study on *The Influence of Age on Physician's Views Concerning Mental Health Matters* shows that younger physicians tend to have a better concept of a mental-health program and a better knowledge of the potentialities for treatment in this field. These studies are significant because of the recurring myth that both the public and the medical profession are afraid of mental illness and not interested in it. These studies suggest that perhaps the fears exist more in the mind of the mental-health workers and that what is needed is more active participation in a mental-health education program, both at the medical and public level.

Before proceeding to a study of the individual reaction types, a few words are necessary. We have discussed factors which enter into individual development and the interrelationships of men with one another. These pages contain some explanations of the things which make up human beings. The reason one person adjusts well to the vicissitudes of life and others do not can be understood in individual cases. In all cases it becomes necessary to evaluate the individual and all things that make him what he is. In doing this we must evaluate the so-called "constitutional" and "hereditary" factors. These factors, acted upon and modified by the environment both internal and external, as the individual grows, will determine his total capacity to react or adjust to life. Thus a person with great potentials can handle almost anything that may come up. His contemporaries, possessing fewer resources, will have difficulty in adjusting to anything beyond minor vicissitudes. The degree to which a person can adapt himself to difficulties in life, his resilience of character, and his accomplishments will depend on his over-all reaction and the general environmental configuration in which he finds himself. It should be remembered, however, that incidents which happen to a person, and his education, friends, economic and social position, religion, or politics— all go to make up the final reactive capacity of the individual.

In order to predict how a person will adjust to life's experiences, it is necessary to evaluate *all* the factors mentioned above in addition to the person's total personality resources. These are in terms of the person's constitution and inheritance, his total life experiences and his reaction to them, the success with which he adapts to them, the influence these will have on his subsequent experiences, and, finally, his total self, as we see him at the moment.

Students are sometimes concerned because psychiatrists spend so much time worrying about the child's reaction to life and the various stages of infantile development. In some instances whole new schools of psychiatry have been formed on the issue of the relative importance of the past versus the present social milieu. In practice both things must be considered. It should be remembered that events which happened yesterday will influence your life pattern and modify your adaptation to life from this day forward. Today those events of yesterday have been influencing your reaction and way of thinking for only 1 day, but 30 years from now they will play a more basic and integral part in your reaction because they will have been influencing your behavior for 30 years.

So it is with events that happen in infancy and early childhood. At age 20, incidents which occurred at age 5 have been playing an integral part in your reaction for 15 years. Thus they play a larger role, other things being equal, than similar events which happened on the day before. It is thus common to say that in childhood one's basic patterns of reaction are set. This is true for the simple reason that patterns of reaction formed at this time continue to modify behavior throughout the rest of one's life. It is equally true, however, that other events happening at other periods of time also modify one's behavior. However, they modify one's behavior for a shorter period and thus less fundamentally. The student would be negligent if he did not consider all significant events that happen to a person throughout his life, giving to each its proper weight and evaluation. The severity of the reaction and the importance of it will depend on its general emotional significance to the individual at the particular time. Thus in evaluating the effects of any event, its emotional significance, as well as the time of occurrence, must be determined in order to estimate accurately its total importance to the individual's personality pattern.

CHAPTER 5

The Prevalence of Mental Illness

We hope that subsequent editions of this book contain a chapter on the epidemiology of mental illness. To head such a chapter with this term would be presumptuous at this time. The origins of many forms of mental illness are unknown, and those which are understood have multiple causes. The term "mental illness" is a general one which has never been satisfactorily defined.

In the broad spectrum of human behavior it is easy to decide that the acute or chronic schizophrenic person is suffering from a mental illness. Not even judges deny that a suicidal depression is mental illness. At the other extreme, few people would believe that the active, productive, happy, well-adjusted adult person was mentally ill in spite of the stresses, ambitions, and worries that may beset him in the normal routine of life.

In between these two extremes, however, exist the improvident ones and the successful men who risk their personal happiness and their business or professional careers to pursue a small and not-too-desirable secretary for a few fast laps around an office. There is also the person in an executive position of good income who becomes involved with bookies to the point that it is necessary from his point of view to steal from his company in order to pay off his illegal debts which could otherwise be collected only by physical violence.

What and who then comprise mental illness? In 1951 one of us wrote an essay describing difficulties in this definition and, unfortunately, to date the same information may be used without appearing old. Is it the bed-wetting child? Is it the hallucinating woman? Does it include stomach ulcers, the interracial tension in certain sections of our cities, the international tension manifested at the United Nations councils? Is it

60

the drunken driver? The speed-mad driver, skillful though he may be? Perhaps as a starting point we could all agree that it goes beyond the Shakespearean definition of "madness is but to be mad."

Freud describes neuroses and psychoses as follows: "Neurosis is the result of a conflict between the ego and its id, whereas psychosis is the analogous outcome of a similar disturbance in the relation between the ego and its environment (outer world)."

The symptoms of a neurosis, if defined as conflict between the ego and the id, would then include in them many types of people using reasonably acceptable modes of adjustment. Would the person who abides by the biblical directive, "Blessed are the meek, for they shall inherit the earth," be looked upon as a victim of a neurosis because of this manifestation of passivity compensated for by hopes of a reward guaranteed by faith alone? Are persons epitomized by Edna St. Vincent Millay's little couplet to be considered as suffering from a neurosis?

> My candle burns at both its ends. It will not last
>   the night,
> But ah, my foes, and oh, my friends, it makes a
>   lovely light.

Goldstein speaks of "catastrophic behavior" in a situation in which the patient is confronted with a sense of failure on a level which is unacceptable to him, in contrast to the ordered behavior of a person in situations with which he can cope.

The general context of all these proposals would suggest that a person may be said to be mentally ill when situations with which he is confronted so far exceed his adaptive capacities that he must resort to distortion of body function, to distortion of the facts of the real world about him, or perhaps in a broader sense when he resorts to behavior that is detrimental to persons in his environment; this protective behavior being necessary if he is to escape flooding his consciousness with anxiety or repressed material unacceptable to him.

Thus we would come to understand mental illness as being a type of adjustment that an individual makes to certain demands made upon him. The adjustment, unsatisfactory though it may be, is the best possible one under the circumstances.

We call it mental illness because the resultant total behavior pattern does not conform to the standards of the time and the situation. For example, a patient in a clinic in dungarees and sans shave would be accepted, but if the author gave a lecture so dressed, you would think he was psychotic. If he came to a picnic in full dress, you would think that odd. If he chaired a panel discussion while drunk, you would say, "An alcoholic!" but if he delivered a temperance lecture you would think that even more peculiar!

Thus we are labeled ill, a genius, brilliant, or a fool, depending upon how well our ego can adapt our means of satisfying the basic drives to the demands of our particular culture and time.

If we are to understand mental illness, we must therefore understand what goes to make up the person. That is, we must understand his basic needs and his capacities to satisfy these needs in the environment in which he finds himself. We must study carefully the interaction between the patient and the environment if we are to have a complete understanding of his illness. A study of the basic needs of man, sometimes dubbed the "instincts," has been the preoccupation of philosophers, religious leaders, scientists, and psychiatrists for many generations.

Confucius wrote that the basic needs of man were for food, drink, and women. Goldstein states that the basic drive in all humans is for "actualization." By this he apparently means the need to find oneself in a satisfactory relationship with the other persons in the environment and the ability to live in a satisfactory manner in this situation. The basis of modern psychology and its understanding of human function rests in the works of Sigmund Freud. These are presented in Chapter 2.

It would be superfluous to repeat here the emphasis in Freud's ultimate teachings of the basic urges of the sexual and death or aggressive instincts. As stated in Chapter 4, the understanding of a patient's distortion of behavior in the present is not to be fully realized by the investigations of the vicissitudes of his ego development as though they existed in some Erlenmeyer flask in the sterile room of a tissue-culture laboratory. The investigation of these earlier developmental phases is essential if one is to understand what goes to make the individual who is reacting to the situation as of now. On the other hand, it would be equally serious to ignore the actual situation in which he is at present reacting. It should always be remembered that the earlier material is essential because one cannot understand the individual or his reactions to the present situation that hurts unless you have an understanding of his earlier development.

The importance of considering the present demands of reality has been emphasized by practically all profound writers on the subject, but is often neglected or overlooked by the neophyte. Mark Twain once said, "Circumstances make man; not man, circumstances." Freud himself stated it as clearly as any.

Or to express it yet another way, neurosis does not deny the existence of reality; it merely tries to ignore it. Psychosis denies it and tries to substitute something else for it. A reaction which combines features of both of these is the one which we call normal or healthy; it denies reality as little as neurosis but then, like a psychosis, it is concerned with effecting a change in it. This expedient, normal attitude leads naturally to some active achievement in the outer world and is not content like a psychosis with establishing the alteration within itself; it is no longer autoplastic, but alloplastic.

Fundamental in comprehending the interaction of these two activities is an understanding of what Franz Alexander has called "the power of regressive forces." He points out that human beings in general have a tendency to refuse to accept changes, especially those which require a greater independence and expenditure of energy. They have an inclination to revert to earlier behavior patterns whenever a new situation requires a new adjustment. He emphasizes that regression does not mean an exact repetition of older methods of behavior or older attitudes but merely a coloring of present behavior by earlier attitudes. Thus the examples he uses are, "Drinking alcohol is not identical with suckling; cigar smoking or chewing is not the same as thumbsucking; and the street phobia is not precisely the old fear and insecurity of the child when he is first called upon to do an errand by himself." He goes on to state, however, that they are attempts to revive earlier situations which will enable the person to avoid in some manner the unpleasant demands of the present.

Balanced against these regressive trends with their tendency to economize on nature are the basic urges and drives of man to create. This is manifest in the sexual sphere, in the growth and development of children, in man's desire to acquire new mastery over his environment, and in new spheres of knowledge. Irrational competition between people probably does not fall within this particular sphere of activity. A broad concept of sociologic factors is necessary in order to understand fully the interreaction between these two forces. It is also indicative of the degree to which technologic factors have expanded beyond the concept of sociologic factors in the interrelationships of people.

The reasons for the neglect of religion and philosophy and the concentration on television and jet motors are matters for study by our colleagues in the allied disciplines. Psychologically speaking, it must be a manifestation of the regressive tendency in man.

Another regressive trend is the desire to lead an increasingly parasitic existence where a man works and sweats and, if he avoids dying of coronary disease, can retire into a thermostatically and automatically controlled old age, where the only efforts necessary to live are to digest his own food and to pass his own excretions. All these factors present individually and as a group in our culture may have an important bearing on the development of mental illness and its diagnosis and treatment.

Thus mental illness may stem from any one of several causes. The simplest situation would be one in which the environment was so difficult that no amount of adaptive capacity would make a person get along entirely well.

A different category but closely akin to this is the plight of a person precipitated into this difficult world who has been by nature under-equipped in terms of cortical tissue to understand at least some of the implications of the things that go on about him.

Various combinations of difficult situations and varieties of basic capacities go into explaining many other types of illness. If persons in their emotional growth fail to develop sufficient ego strength to enable them to cope with an ordinary environment, they inevitably succumb to some type of mental illness unless the environment about them is extraordinary in terms of protective and ego-supporting potentials.

We have other persons who, in the process of growth, build a strong ego or a great capacity for integrating their needs with the demands of the environment, but meet with an extraordinary situation. These patients, faced with failure, retreat to earlier and more successful types of adjustment, usually referred to as "symptoms," or, if you prefer, "regressive phenomena."

We also have the person who, during the phases of his ego development, gets along quite well and is able to cope with the ordinary environment, but who, due to sclerosis, the aging process, syphilis, tumor, trauma, or other cortical-depleting processes, begins to lose some of the adaptive functions which he has developed and then begins to have difficulty in conforming to the demands of his environment as he attempts to satisfy his basic needs.

Patients in this latter category are referred to as *organic*. Those in the former category are referred to as *functional*. Actually there is little difference except that in the case of patients with functional illness their ego, which lacks the ability to respond to the demands of the environment, takes cognizance of the needs of the organism and works out a solution that is unsatisfactory to their society.

In the so-called organic case there is actual loss of cortical functions, which reduces the patient's capacity to function. Abilities formerly present and relied upon in establishing behavior patterns are gone. To survive, the patient must change his behavior to conform to the new top limit of his capacities.

In the so-called functional cases this process is a little more complicated, but the end results are essentially the same. In these categories the person, by reason of experiences in the process of taking from his environment those things necessary for his continued existence, comes upon situations which threaten him because of old conditioning or which exceed his capacities by reason of previous imperfections in development.

In either instance the patient is now in a situation which is no longer tenable so far as he is concerned, and it is necessary for him to begin to simplify the environment. In some instances the situation is sufficiently superficial or sufficiently controllable so far as environmental manipulation is concerned so that relatively simple procedures result in successful mastering of the situation.

For example, a person in a job with which he is incompatible or which makes him very apprehensive may quit and take a job making fewer demands upon him. In this case we may say that he has worked out a type of solution which is in general satisfactory to him, and no further activities are required on his part.

In the case of the organic patient, if he has reached a certain specified chronologic age, perhaps he can retire and thus reduce the demands upon him, and in this manner simplify his environment and solve his problems.

Other patients find that such solutions are either unacceptable to them or in some instances impossible. This is particularly true where the difficulty involves personal attitudes of the patient and the environment as such does not lend itself readily to manipulation or significant change. In these instances the patient will resort to what we call nervous or mental symptoms. In effect, he is still attempting to simplify his environment but is using a different method which results in the formation of symptoms such as faints, pains, amnesia, and periods of anxiety.

The selection of symptoms will depend upon the individual, his physical make-up, and the situation in which he finds himself. In some, the development of such symptoms solves the problem, and they go through life as chronic neurotics. Others, more fortunate, receive therapy and, if successful, grow in ego strength so they can cope with the aforementioned difficulty. In still others, time takes care of the environment and precipitates the patient into situations more nearly satisfactory; and with some reluctance the patient may give up his illness.

Some patients find that so-called "neurotic symptoms" will not provide a satisfactory solution. They are still threatened, and the situation continues to stir up anxieties and insecurities until what Goldstein called a "catastrophic situation" looms—a state which the analysts call "flooding the consciousness with anxiety."

Whichever term you prefer, the patient is sorely threatened and, if he is to exist, must bring about more drastic changes by distortion and misinterpretation of the environment, bending it into shapes more acceptable to him. We commonly call such a patient psychotic. We say that the patient has regressed and ignores the demands of reality. Actually the patient has regressed, but to state that he ignores the demands of reality is taking a very superficial view. Actually, he is so much aware of the demands of reality and what they mean to him consciously and unconsciously that he finds it necessary to distort them into a form more satisfactory to him, or at least into a form he is able to cope with, using the particular resources and abilities available to him at the given time.

The importance of considering what we mean by mental illness is by now obvious. First, the attempt to define mental illness highlights the areas in which we have little or no information. Therefore, we have a more accurate guide in future investigation. Second, the attempt to define mental illness and its causes enables us to plan therapeutic programs more intelligently and make a more efficient use of the knowledge of our colleagues in the allied disciplines. Third, when we understand what happens to a patient when he develops mental illness, it supplies many clues for our activities in the preventive field. It enables us to give more intelligent guidance to our colleagues and coworkers who must play the major role in the actual mechanics of the prevention of possible mental illness.

Thus our understanding that general paresis is due to a patient's failure to adapt himself to an environment because of the spirochetes' damage to the cortex makes treatment, intelligently planned, go along the lines of:

1. Combating the actual infection.

2. Decreasing the patient's responsibilities and otherwise simplifying his environment so he can cope with the disease in terms of the resources he has left.

3. Enabling the patient, through psychotherapy, to accept more readily and understand what has gone on in order that he may more nearly adapt himself to his new position in life.

Understanding the infectious origin of this illness also makes it possible by early treatment and cooperation with the social hygienist and other anti–venereal-disease workers to cut down the over-all incidence of infection.

Understanding the meaning of functional disorders, both neurotic and psychotic, makes our cooperation and work with the parents and teachers who deal with youngsters during the formative years an important part of our activities. Certainly time spent in indoctrinating pediatricians and the general practitioners who first advise mothers on the care of the children and working with schoolteachers is time constructively spent in health promotion.

This dissertation should pinpoint the difficulties involved in our present concept of mental illness and should highlight for students the desirability of more work in epidemiology in these disorders.

In the remainder of this chapter, the figures presented will be based on patients who have been diagnosed as suffering from a mental illness in some form, using as the criterion the fact that the person has been diagnosed by a physician as suffering from some type of nervous or mental disorder. The projections onto the general population from specific samples are based on these same criteria. It is not possible to correct for differences in concepts among the physicians or for differences in criteria of diagnosis between civilian physicians and physicians examining soldiers for recruitment into military service. A student must therefore accept these cases as representing those counted by competent professional people who have made no attempt to correct the figures for possible differences in criteria dictated by circumstance and moral and cultural pressures at the time and place of the examination.

Most estimates of the incidence of psychiatric cases in the general population are based on projections of three population studies, but the criteria for inclusion varied among the three groups. On the basis of selective-service examinations, patients rejected for service and discharged for mental illness, which includes adult personality disorders, adult delinquencies, epilepsy, and mental deficiency, projected onto the general population, would give an estimated figure of 8,500,000 cases suffering from some type of mental disorder in the total population of the United States. These estimates were arrived at in 1948, amplifying a study made in 1945.

Lemkau, Tietze, and Cooper made an estimate on a population survey in the Baltimore area. This sample was based on 50,000 persons in one of the health districts of Baltimore, and they reported an incidence of mental illness of 60.5 per thousand. This, projected onto the total population of the United States, would also give a figure of approximately 8,500,000.

Roth and Luton made a survey of individuals in a Tennessee county and found a prevalence of mental illness of 69.30 per thousand individuals. Projecting their figures onto the general population of the United States, the number would be approximately 9,000,000.

In 1951, Warren T. Vaughan, Jr., used the Luton statistics to project the expected number of mentally ill in the population of Massachusetts. He pointed out the differences in the population of rural Tennessee and of Massachusetts and noted that the Luton statistics were based on information as of Sept. 1, 1938, while the Massachusetts estimate was made in November, 1951. With this limitation in mind one can expect the "psychiatric disorders" in Massachusetts on Nov. 30, 1951, to number approximately 325,000 persons. As a result of a survey on Nov. 30, 1951, Vaughan was able to count the actual number of patients known to be mentally ill in Massachusetts. On this day, Nov. 30, 1951, there were 24,055 patients in state hospitals for the mentally ill; 5,000 in veterans' hospitals and private sanatoriums for the mentally ill; and 5,100 attending community psychiatric outpatient clinics, private and public. There were approximately 2,500 seen by private psychiatrists and 6,300 were being cared for in family and child agencies by caseworkers. A total of only 42,955 persons out of the 325,000 estimated to have psychiatric disorders were receiving services. To this figure could logically be added the 5,000 children in state schools for the retarded, approximately 5,000 other children known to be in public school classes for retarded children, and about 1,200 persons in prison. This would still bring the known total "psychiatric population" on that day to approximately 54,200 persons.

This count took place on one day, and a legitimate complaint could be that mental illness is a prolonged disorder, and that other patients not actually ill on that day would later come to the attention of the medical authorities sometime during that year. For example, we know that the clinics, while having 5,000 cases under their care on that particular day, during the course of a year give care to approximately 35,000 different persons. Schools for the retarded in a year care for approximately 6,000 different persons, and, if we assume that the rate of turnover for private practitioners is the same as for private and public outpatient departments in Massachusetts, they would annually care for about 5,000 different persons. This still totals far less than 325,000 patients, and we don't know where the others are! In fact we cannot be sure that they exist, although an objective look at general human behavior in this or any other community suggests that they are undoubtedly there uncounted.

Reports of the health agencies indicate that there are more than 700,000 cases in mental hospitals of the country, most of these in government-operated hospitals, principally state operated, and that these hospitals admit approximately 120,000 new cases per year.

The National Health Education Committee Inc. published statistics showing that 1 out of every 12 persons will spend some part of his life in a mental hospital. These statistics are based on publications by Malzberg. Figures show that 1 per cent of the persons admitted to mental hospitals are under 15 years of age; about 16 per cent are between 15 and 29 years of age; about 45 per cent are between 30 and 39; and 38 per cent are 60 and older. Each year the older age group increases in proportion. It is estimated that over 13,000,000 people now living in the United States will some time during their life be hospitalized for mental illness.

About 21 per cent of the admissions to mental hospitals are for schizophrenia alone. Approximately 30 per cent are for mental illnesses accompanying old age. Manic-depressive psychoses make up about 6 per cent of admissions to hospitals. Alcoholic psychoses and simple alcoholism combine to make up about 11 per cent.

The biggest drop in recent years has been the admission rate from syphilis of the nervous system, due to the use of penicillin. Previously psychiatric hospitals reported from 10 to 12 per cent of their admissions due to various types of syphilis of the nervous system. At present most hospitals report almost none, and 4 per cent is considered a high admission rate.

While not directly associated with epidemiology, students should recognize that approximately half the hospital beds in America on any day are occupied by mental patients. It should be pointed out, however, that less than 2 per cent of the admissions to the hospitals are for mental illness because of the long stay of most mental patients and the short stay of general hospital patients for acute surgery, obstetrics, and short-term illness.

The fact that mental hospitals grow larger each year and admission rates go up at a more rapid rate than the increase in population leads to speculation that the world is becoming mentally ill. These theories are without foundation in fact. Goldhamer and Marshall, as a result of the study of the Rand Corporation, found that there has been no increase in psychoses over the past hundred years in patients under the age of 50. Their figures are based on New York State figures and show that at the age of 25, a person has 1 chance in 74 of becoming mentally ill; 1 chance in 25 at age 45; 1 chance in 13 at age 65; and 1 chance in 9 at age 75. One concludes that the increased use of mental hospitals is due to better education of the public, better recognition of the problem, and the offer of facilities and hope for effective therapy. This better utilization and increase in available facilities is common in other health fields.

The complexity of studies of this sort and the need for accuracy in observation and reporting are well illustrated by a report of Paul Lemkau in which he describes a visit during a survey of mental hygiene facilities in Yugoslavia. In most of the nursery schools, run by the government, which care for children of working mothers or for orphans, the schools were run well and the children were active and appeared normal. In one school, however, the children were stultified. Had this survey of government-operated schools in Yugoslavia concentrated on only the last school, the result would be an unfavorable report. Concentrating on one of the former schools, however, would result in an excellent report on the influence of government schools on the mental health of children.

Similar difficulties are highlighted by Kingsley Davis who, in commenting on marriages, notes that the divorce rate is an indication of disturbed family relations, but is not an index of what goes on in the community. He points out that the divorce rate does not include separations or parents living apart within the same household.

The attitude of a community toward aberrant behavior, in tolerating it and supplying community resources to cope with it, undoubtedly influence the reported rate of mental illness. The whole future of the epidemiology of mental illness depends on an agreed, even though artificial, concept of who shall be included as "mentally ill" and on some well-financed method for sampling these in a sufficiently varied population, in order to arrive at a reasonable rate of incidence and of prevalence of these disorders in our population. An important counterpart to this study would be research on the community's attitude toward these cases. There are several studies of ethnic and religious influence on mental illness. Barrabee and Von Mering found a definite difference in Jewish, Irish, and Italian families in their attitude toward stress within the family and the pressures placed upon members in the family.

I emphasize the importance of such study to persons working with family groups either on a professional or counseling plane.

Rose and Stubb compiled a long table on the incidence of the various types of disorder for age, marital status, location in urban or rural populations, socioeconomic status, and nativity. Their statistics based on publications particularly of Massachusetts, New York, and the Federal agencies indicate correlations in these factors, but the significance or reasons for these remain to be discovered.

More definitive studies in this field are imperative for a full understanding of the significance of epidemiology of mental illness and in order to work out more productive health promotion and true preventive activities.

This dissertation should emphasize the complexity in defining mental illness and the need for arriving at some workable definition acceptable to most people in the field by which the criteria for mental illness can be used comparably between various groups surveying the incidence of the prevalence of these disorders in the population.

Our problems are not eased by the present confusion in medical epidemiology owing to a shifting from single to multiple causes of disease. This is so even in diseases thought to be due to specific bacteria. For example, it is no longer thought that tuberculosis is caused solely by the presence of the tubercle bacillus, but rather is caused by the tubercle bacillus plus certain social, genetic, physiologic, and psychologic forces bearing on the prospective victim. Psychiatrists have long been aware of the multiple forces bearing on their clients but have yet to come upon the equivalent of the tubercle bacillus as a common factor in all persons with certain types of mental disorder.

Rose and Stubb also compiled in an extensive table a survey of relevant English literature dealing with mental disorders as related to various social variables for which they found significant data. The data deal with the incidence of the various diagnostic categories for various age periods, marital statuses, distributions among urban and rural populations, social-economic statuses, nativities, races, and incidences among members of religious groups. More studies of this type need to be done, and perhaps some of them can be made by the Joint Commission on Mental Illness and Health.

CHAPTER 6

Genetics

The genetic aspects of mental illness have been studied with greater frequency in recent years, but our knowledge is still fragmentary. Certain components of behavior such as handedness are thought to be inherited. A recent symposium on genetics and the inheritance of integrated neurologic and psychiatric patterns was devoted to this topic, and Anne Anastasi epitomized the problem:

The more precisely heredity and environment are defined, and the more fully their operation is investigated, the more evident it becomes that they are inextricably intertwined. The very distinction between them no longer appears as sharp as it once did, and the study of behavior, the difference between organic and experimental etiology, seems to have more promise from both a practical and heuristic point of view. Since heredity must necessarily operate through the medium of structural organic factors, it follows that the applicability of the concept of heredity to behavior phenomena is indirect and remote. . . . It should also be borne in mind that heredity and environment are themselves abstractions. Each covers a multiplicity of factors which interact with each other. It is not enough to imply that "environment" causes a particular behavior deviation. We must know what specific factors in the environment brought it about. Similarly, when we attribute a behavior characteristic to "heredity," we have not solved a problem; we have only formulated a problem. We must find out what is inherited. What is the hereditary condition which ultimately and indirectly leads to this behavior deviation, and how does it operate in bringing about the behavior under consideration?

Arnold Gesell, in the same symposium states, "The human infant comes by his behavior as he comes by his body, through the organizing processes of growth. As behavior grows, it assumes lawful forms, characteristic of the species, and of the individual." The gist of Gesell's re-

72

port is that human development goes through certain definite sequences of behavior that seem to be innate in the tissues. He believes:

Improved methods for the periodic developmental diagnosis and analysis of infant behavior, therefore, should provide one approach to the problem with which this symposium is concerned—the inheritance of integrated neuropsychiatric patterns. With full recognition of the reciprocal interdependence of heredity and environment, this paper has stressed inherent factors which established the basic trends and sequences of behavior patterning. Environmental factors support, inflict, and modify, but they do not generate the progressions of development.

From an entirely different point of view the work of the psychoanalytic school shows that the development of the personality, particularly the libidinous strivings, goes through definite time and sequentially predetermined phases, modified somewhat by the environment and the culture.

It was one time assumed that intelligence was inherited, but now many people feel that the genetic development of intelligence is not clearly understood. There seems to be little doubt that some elements of intelligence or the more basic ability *to be intelligent* is inherited, but work has shown that environmental stimulae or their lack can have a tremendous effect on this basic intellectual capacity. This is confirmed in both animal and human studies. W. R. Thompson discusses these factors in great detail.

In discussing Thompson, K. S. Lashley states, "We do not know the functional significance of such individual variations (between brains), but it is inconceivable to me that two brains differing in cell density of the temporal lobe by thirty per cent, could function the same way. The one monkey in which we found huge stellate ganglion in the auditory cortex may well have been a potential Bach among monkeys."

Among the mentally retarded certain states are known to be inherited, most notably the phenylpyruvic oligophrenias.

Lennox and Jolly show a definite genetic factor in convulsive disorders. The detailed genetics are not understood, but there is a correlation and a high concordance of seizures and similar brain wave patterns in monozygotic twins.

Kallman has studied the genetics of psychoses. He believes that the incidence of psychoses follows selected patterns of distribution. He has made studies on twins and studies by use of the proband and sibship methods to indicate that the prevalence of schizophrenia is significantly higher in the proband family than in the normal population. He states:

The corresponding rate for relatives of schizophrenics varies from 7.1 percent for half sibs through about 14 percent for full sibs and two-egg co-twins to 86.2 percent for one-egg twin partners. Children of one schizophrenic parent have an expectancy of 16.4 percent, while the incident rate from the parent of schizophrenic index cases is 9.3 percent. Next to one-egg co-twins, the children of two schizophrenic parents have been found by all investigators to have the highest expectancy of the disease. [Genetically it has to be demonstrated] that the tendency to develop a severe psychosis is specific in nature, that it follows a statistically predictable pattern of distribution, and that it increases in proportion to the degree of blood relationship to a family member affected by the given type of psychosis.

He concludes, "It may be said, that in order to understand certain basic principles in the formation of psychotic behavior patterns, it is necessary to delve into the substratum of gene action as well as into the subconscious." While Kallman's work has not received universal acceptance among psychiatrists, it certainly must be given the careful consideration accorded to any carefully and conscientiously done scientific study. Only the consideration of all factors will ever explain the great complexity of mental illness.

The manic-depressive reactions are thought to have a familial tendency, but no true Mendelian pattern of inheritance has been demonstrated.

Huntington's chorea with mental deterioration is one form of mental illness that seems to be definitely of genetic origin.

Much more careful work is required in this field. It seems too much to expect the many complexities of behavior patterns, events, and time required for development of schizophrenia to be genetically determined. Rather one would expect some genetic factor, as yet unknown, which makes a person potentially schizophrenic if hit by the proper combination of environmental events and time.

CHAPTER 7

Methods of Psychiatric Examination

It is essential for the successful approach to psychiatric problems that: (1) the examiner have a clear idea of the data necessary for the understanding of the case; (2) he have a sense of continuity and purpose in the examination; (3) he approach the patient in a genuine spirit of sympathetic understanding and helpfulness; and (4) he be willing to spend whatever time and energy are necessary to achieve the establishment of that mutual rapport which will work toward a solution of the problem. It will be apparent that in general these are the considerations which apply in any medical approach.

Therefore, the same methods used in general medicine are employed for psychiatric investigation, namely: (1) the indirect examination of historical data concerning the chronologic evolution of the difficulty as focused in the complaints concerning the past performance and the family tendencies; (2) the direct examination of the mental status and the physical status, which gives a cross section of the present behavior; (3) the contributory information from special examinations and the patient's course under observation and treatment.

Too often the examination of the psychiatric patient is described in a way to make it appear to be a difficult and formidable task. Actually, if the examination is made in an easy and natural manner with some background of experience, it is not at all difficult and is extremely interesting. The objective of a psychiatric examination is *not* to discover the condition of the patient's mind, but to come to an opinion concerning the patient as a person, body and mind together. They are inseparable.

History

An obvious starting place for the examination is the history. It naturally separates itself into four major divisions:

1. Complaint
2. Present illness
3. Past history
4. Family history

Complaint. An easy way to start is to say to the patient, "What seems to be troubling you? Tell me about it."

Not infrequently such an opening may loosen the patient's tongue and there will emerge an account which is worth a dozen formalized histories. Above all else, let the patient *tell his story in his own way*. Gaps may be filled in and details supplied later on.

The patient's chief complaint may be vague—he is "tense," "blue"—or it may be concrete, and the patient may at once and in no uncertain language damn his "persecutors." The patient may recite a list of psychosomatic symptoms: headache, backache, nausea, vomiting, etc. At this early cross section the examiner has no magic way of knowing whether these symptoms may be indicative of organic pathology, liver cirrhosis or even brain tumor, of an emotional marital tangle, or of a remote, deeply buried emotional conflict, dated in childhood. The patient may not have any particular complaint. For instance, he may be quite content with his fantasy life. The complaint may come from his parents or his children, wife or husband, or employer; those who are deeply concerned about his behavior.

Present Illness. Again if the patient is cooperative, let him tell his story in his own way. Fill in the chronologic order and sequences later on. The nature and incidental setting at the onset are always important. Generally, the more acute and dramatic the onset is, the more favorable it is prognostically, as compared to a gradual, sometimes almost imperceptible withdrawal from the realities of life. Likewise, it is relatively favorable if the onset coincides with a severe environmental insult, as in one of our patients who "blacked out" and had an amnesia for the incident of her 15-year-old daughter's confessing to her that she was illegitimately pregnant. All in all, the history of the present illness gives the examiner a clear idea of the illness, from its beginnings, and traces its development and progress.

Past History. The past history is the record of everything that has happened to the patient, from the environment and from inside himself, and his reactions thereto.

As the past history unfolds, there is revealed the sum total of the patient's reactions to the psychosomatic onslaughts and liabilities of his life—and also to its assets. Every effort should be made to lift the curtain separating childhood from adult life. The core of psychopathology is very likely to be laid down in the early relationships of life, first with the mother, then with both parents, and finally as a unit in the family constellation.

Something very important emerges from the interreaction between man and his environment—*the human personality*. It is too vast and dynamic to be confined in the cage of a definition. It is the determinant of behavior at any given cross section of life, the condensed record of everything that has happened to the individual. Yet it is ever-changing from cradle to grave. The nucleus of personality is derived from the ancestry, but from birth on, at first rapidly and later in life slowly, it is molded and fashioned this way and that.

We can give only the barest minimum of the personality's vast content—physical build and characteristics, intelligence, directions of thinking, affectivity and emotional traits, enthusiasms, ideals, bias, prejudice, hostilities, and sometimes shameful and bloody intolerances, habits, interests, hobbies, drives, tendencies, energy output, aggression and submission, selection of vocations and avocations, social adaptability, the potentiality for success or failure, for happiness or misery, and many other ingredients. The measure of the stature of the personality is the degree of emotional maturity.

Birth and Development. These are reviewed with special reference to childhood maladjustments: nail biting and thumb sucking; fears of the dark, of storms, or of animals; finickiness with food; social adaptation, noting outgoing or seclusive tendencies in the home, school, or play; and the more asocial traits of lying, stealing, truancy, or cruelty to other children or to animals, etc.

Health Record. This is made with a careful survey of previous diseases of all kinds. There should be included the patient's attitude toward his health: his disregard, neglect, overconcern, or other reactions.

School Record. This should include dates of beginning and ending of schooling, number of grades taken, grades repeated, isolated failures, and degree of scholarship. Special school interests should be noted as well as liabilities, including speech and writing disabilities. With children who are brought to the physician because of school difficulties, a copy of the official school record and the teacher's estimate of the child are useful sources of information.

Work Record. This should contain the kind of work done, specific jobs with chronologic sequence, degree of skill in the craft or profession, salaries, reasons for leaving jobs, attitude toward work responsibility, satisfaction in the work, and economic status—debts, responsibilities, habits of saving.

Interests and Habits. This category comprises the patient's assets in collateral interests, as in religion, art, theater, literature, sports, clubs, various cultural movements, etc. It also should contain an inquiry into habits, specifically eating, sleeping, play, alcohol, tobacco, drugs, coffee, tea, etc.

These considerations are important in view of the breakdown in patients of the appreciation and utilization of native or acquired assets through neglect, lack of opportunity, or unwholesome rut formations. Often therapeutic hints are derived from a careful check of interests and habits.

Previous Attacks. Information about previous attacks of like or unlike character is valuable with specific data as to time, duration, symptoms, course, outcome, and where hospitalized.

Sex Development. The past history of sex development should delineate a clear picture of the first awareness of sex; how, when, and with what preparedness and attitude this took place; evolution of the sex interest, and specific data on the sex pace, as noted in overt sex activity (physiologic and psychologic data of erections, emissions, menstruation), as well as the more mental factors of sex fancies and dreams and their effects; autoerotic, homosexual, and heterosexual features; attitude to family formation.

Marital Data. This includes the date of marriage; marital adjustment with degree of satisfaction, special gratifications, disappointments, and difficulties; pregnancies and their results; attitude to the specific sex factors and satisfactions therefrom; contraceptive methods, reasons for the methods used, safety coefficient, and fear of pregnancy; conflicts aroused by sexual practice.

Family History. Families tend to overemphasize the influence of the ancestral record. It is one way of escaping feelings of personal culpability and guilt. Of course, the family account of the direct and collateral ancestry is important. The examiner will note carefully the familial record of psychoses, psychoneuroses, suicide, mental defect, epilepsy, alcoholism, drug addiction, and many other conditions. Occasionally, direct inheritance is highly significant, as in juvenile paresis with a history of parental syphilis and in certain types of epilepsy, feeblemindedness, and manic-depressive reactions. More often the family life is important because of its environmental liabilities. Children readily imitate psychotic and psychoneurotic displays in other members of the family. The family history should include the data of family life—the interfamilial relationships, with special allegiances, dislikes, frictions, etc.

The history has now been taken not only from the patient but also from all other available sources. It can never be considered a closed book and should be kept open for supplementary data which will be obtained from time to time. A reasonably complete, well-taken history serves a double purpose. It is a two-beamed searchlight. It illuminates the motivations and drives which shaped the psychiatric illness and its symptoms. It in turn is illuminated by the patient's particular psychotic or psychoneurotic reactions.

Physical Examination

From time to time, we will present various good reasons why it is imperative to make a thorough physical examination of each patient. At this place, it suffices to say that no conscientious physician would think of treating any patient for any serious condition unless he was familiar with the state of the systems and organs of the body. Sometimes the physical survey may yield conclusive information. Complaints and symptoms of patients do not carry distinguishing labels. Sometimes symptoms which at first view seem to be due to unconscious mental conflicts are finally shown to be the result of organic diseases, arteriosclerosis, syphilis, intoxications, or metabolic disorders.

Sometimes it is good judgment to make a preliminary physical examination at the first session with the patients. Many people are reassured at seeing the familiar instruments of the doctor—the clinical thermometer, the stethoscope, the sphygmomanometer, the reflex hammer.

Physical Status. The physical examination must be complete. Experience shows that special attention should be paid to body build (pyknic, athletic, asthenic, dysplastic types); evidence of endocrine dyscrasia; focal infections; the gastrointestinal functions; the genital development and workings; the neurologic status, including the autonomic participations in emotional reactions; and the serologic and blood chemistry studies.

The physical findings may appear purely incidental in the behavior pattern, or more closely integrated into that picture, or may be as yet largely a matter of research interest. Reference will be made later to the more common somatic findings in certain behavior patterns.

Neurologic Examination. Every psychiatric patient should have a careful neurologic examination. The student should follow one of the standard examination outlines until he has familiarized himself with a systematic examination procedure. In patients with evidence of neurologic abnormality special procedures such as vestibular tests, pneumocncephalogram or ventriculogram, arteriograms, and electroencephalograms must be performed as indicated by the findings in each case. Special attention to the endocrine and autonomic nervous systems is indicated in many psychiatric cases.

Direct Mental Examination

The examination should be an easy, natural procedure, never formalized or a bristling questionnaire: "What is the date? Are you sad? Suspicious? How much is 9 × 14?"

Put the patient at ease; try to establish a friendly relationship; encourage the patient to talk freely and then let him talk. Sometimes we say to a patient, "Let's forget what your family said; just tell me in your own way how you feel about it." The examiner should never be stern, rebuking, or judicial, but rather interested, helpful, kindly.

The mental examination should cover certain areas, but there should not be insistence upon sequence. Gaps in the patient's story can be filled in later by a few judicious questions.

In his examination the examiner covers the following areas:
1. General appearance and behavior
2. Stream of talk and activity
3. Content and special preoccupations
4. Mood
5. Sensorium and intellectual resources
6. Insight

General Appearance and Behavior. For years we have been trying to teach our students to use their powers of observation to the full extent. Scientific advantages have accrued from the many available instruments of precision, yet we have paid a penalty. There is some danger that our powers of observation may atrophy from disuse as has our sense of smell.

Careful observation reveals a wealth of information. Here are a few things that may be seen:

General appearance of the patient—well-groomed and neat, or untidy? Physical bearing—tense and stiff, or nonchalant? Speech—much, or little? Movements and gestures—purposeful and in touch with the surroundings, or aimless?

Is there negativism? Formerly in its restricted sense, negativism applied to automatic-like muscular resistance to any attempt by the examiner to move a muscle or part, like the downward pull of the eyelid by the patient if pulled upward. Now, the clinical meaning of negativism is much broader—for instance, the retention of urine and feces, and, indeed, a pathologic resistance against any demand the environment may place on the individual.

Catalepsy may be observed. In catalepsy the limbs may be placed in awkward, strained positions which may be retained beyond the period of physiologic tolerance. Cerea flexibilitas is an extreme degree of catalepsy, in which the limbs seem to the manipulating hands of the examiner as though they can be molded, like wax. Mannerisms are bizarre, and there are exaggerated ways of doing ordinary things, for instance, hopping every third step.

Echopraxia is the reproduction by the patient of physical motions, such as gestures made by those in his vicinity, as echolalia is the imitation of speech. These and other catatonic-like symptoms, such as automatic obedience (in which the patient is unable to resist protruding the tongue to have it stuck with a sharp needle), whatever be their deeper significance, have in them a strong element of suggestibility reminiscent of posthypnotic behavior suggested during hypnosis.

Catatonic stupors may be witnessed. In many of these stupors, even exhaustive examinations fail to uncover satisfactory evidence of somatic pathology. Often the stupor is so profound that there is no observable reaction to painful stimuli, and there seems to be an abeyance of emotion and motion. For some patients, the stupor is symbolic of death, and the emerging from it, of rebirth.

In stuporous conditions the following observations should be carefully made: (1) the degree of alertness to environmental distractions, such as the eyes following the examiner, even when gross bodily movements are absent; (2) the degree to which the patient responds to spoken commands, or exhibits negativism (active, by doing the opposite of what is requested; or passive, by a more stubborn resistance to casual attempts—change of posture, etc.); (3) the presence of sustained queer postures, as holding the head off the pillow; (4) the presence of drooling; (5) the reaction to painful cutaneous and deep sensory stimulation; (6) spontaneous changes in the motility (especially during sleep), the speech, etc.; (7) whether spoon feeding or tube feeding is necessary; (8) evidence of spontaneous or reactive emotional display with smiling, laughing, tears, playfulness, anxiety, etc.; (9) catalepsy, or the holding of postures imposed on the patient, in marked cases the so-called "waxy flexibility" being present.

We have indicated merely a small segment of the vast amount of clinical evidence which may be discovered by observation. Some years ago, one of us made a purely observational study (without benefit of history, without asking any questions, and confined to one examination of 100 consecutive admissions) and the diagnostic impression was almost 80 per cent correct.

Stream of Talk and Activity. Awake or asleep, the stream of thought flows on unceasingly. Speech expresses thought, but semantics has emphasized the fact that, as often as not, speech is used to conceal rather than reveal thought. At first survey, the examiner views the stream of speech in general terms, amount, speed, pressure, just as the internist at first determines the volume, speed, and pressure of the blood stream. This is a good time to remember that, both in normal and abnormal mental life, the emotions control thought and speech, accelerating or breaking it, according to happy or depressed moods. Indeed, emotion is the dynamo of psychic life, and normal mental processes and mental symptoms (delusions, hallucinations, and obsessions) alike derive their strength and driving force from the emotions. Finally, it is well to remember that there is no symptom of psychosis or psychoneurosis which may not be found in miniature in so-called "normal" mental life. The difference is not in kind but in degree. But degree is important.

For instance, in *distractibility*, frequently seen in the manic phase of manic-depressive psychoses, thinking and its speech expression are tossed about this way and that at the behest of external distracting sensory stimuli (what is seen and heard) and by internal thought associations.

In the extreme of distractibility, *flight of ideas*, these reactions are so marked that the patient never completes the goal of his thought and his productions sound delirious.

The opposite, slowing or *retardation* of thought and speech, sometimes drying up into mutism, commonly occurs in the depressed phase of manic-depressive psychosis.

Many other disorders of thought and speech occur—the *dissociated thinking* of schizophrenia, in which the parts of a single sentence seem on the surface to have no relationship to each other; *neologisms* or words coined by the patient and having significance only in his mental life (one of our patients spoke of the "dartleroid," a thought-collecting machine); garrulous and repetitive speech; obsessive or "must" thinking, seemingly in spite of the determination of the patient to inhibit it; confused, incoherent, inarticulate speech, as seen in severe toxic reactions and in deterioration (dementia); and many other thought and verbal symptoms.

In examining the stream of talk and activity, the examiner looks specifically for: (1) underactivity, with general slowing of motility, speech, and thinking; (2) overactivity, with restlessness, agitation, or more purposeful expansive or playful motility, ease of thinking, and association, with distractibility, and pressure of talk with play or words, rhyming, flight of ideas; (3) incongruous, distorted, bizarre activity, with queer mannerisms, grimacing, stereotyped movements or mutism, catalepsy, scattered and incoherent talk, "word salad," queer condensations of words or parts of words, or new word formations; or (4) blocking of thought processes, poverty of thought, or feelings of a multitude of random thoughts crowding in.

Accompanying thought disturbance are motor acts seen as slowing of physical motion, restlessness, agitation, mannerisms, grimacing, stereotyped movements, mutism, catalepsy, etc., and they have already been noted in viewing the general appearance and behavior. But now, in the setting of speech, their meaning becomes clearer and their interpretation often is made possible.

Content and Special Preoccupations. The psychiatric examiner should look carefully into the *content* of the stream of thought for pathology, as revealed in the *special preoccupations* of the patient.

He may find *illusions*—sensory misinterpretations, not dissipated, as are the illusions of everyday experience, by logical proof of the sensory deceptions.

There may be *hallucinations*, often vivid experiences, described as things seen, heard, smelled, tasted, touched. It is assumed that hallucinatory experiences do not have any stimulus or starting point in actual sensory perceptions.

The examiner may find *delusions*, or gross false beliefs of all kinds—grandiosity, belittlement and inferiority, depression and self-blame, persecution, nihilism, and many other types.

There may be *ideas of reference* in which erroneous and pathologic significance is attached to causal happenings in the environment (an accidental cough, for instance), which are interpreted by the patient as referring to him, usually with deliberate insulting or direful intent.

Then there may be *obsessions*, dominations of the personality by certain trends of thought, *compulsive behavior*, that is, behavior which cannot be inhibited even though the patient may try strenuously to control his conduct, and phobias or fears of all kinds. Obsessions, compulsions, and phobias are nice examples of cover-up or camouflaging symptoms, psychologically designed to protect the ego and representing an unconscious choice of the lesser of two perils—the greater one being the danger of the appearance in consciousness of repressed material, which the ego cannot face. Obsessions, compulsions, and phobias often determine amazingly elaborate rituals, which are utilized slavishly as "protective" devices.

So too, particularly in the psychoneuroses, the examiner may uncover tension, anxieties, unconscious hostilities buffered by guilt feelings, sexual conflicts of all kinds, death wishes, etc. We have mentioned only a fractional part of the rich pathology of thought content and preoccupations.

There has been much discussion about the difference between delusions and merely false opinions, which are so common in everyday life and considered to be within the range of "normal" mental thinking. True enough, both are founded in early acquired strong emotional impressions, biases, prejudices, and, perhaps, intolerances, emotionally isolated from and insulated against the intrusion of logical proof to the contrary. But a delusion is a very strong and invulnerable false belief in ego-belittling and shaming material, such as a strong latent homosexuality, which the patient would rather accept than face in consciousness. If this intruded itself into consciousness, it would be repugnant to the remainder of the personality and to society or the herd. Incidentally and in a general way, the psychologic necessity for the personality to disown certain of its ego-shaming and herd-disapproved segments is the chief undercover motif of mental and psychoneurotic symptoms.

We wish to repeat that every psychotic and psychoneurotic symptom has its miniature "normal" mental life representation—blueness of spirits, instead of pathologic grief and melancholia; innumerable superstitions, beliefs, and practices, instead of compulsive behavior and phobias; slight inferiority reactions, instead of psychotic and psychoneurotic self-accusation; mild worry, instead of intense anxiety, etc.

We reiterate, too, that prevailing mood and emotion determine the strength and direction of psychotic and psychoneurotic symptoms, just as they control the thinking in "normal" psychic life. A thought without emotional support would be pallid and ineffectual.

Finally, it must be remembered that in themselves, psychotic and psychoneurotic symptoms at the mere descriptive level mean little or nothing. For instance, merely to note hallucinations of hearing or psychosomatic displays is scarcely modern psychiatry. It would be much like memorizing the sound of a heart murmur as heard through the stethoscope, without understanding the genesis and mechanics of its production. If we understand that the "voices" which accuse the patient of sex perversions are derived from a marked latent homosexuality or that psychosomatic genitourinary symptoms represent an unconscious escape from the sexual component of marital life, perhaps because the wife does not represent the mother figure to which the husband is still tied, then we are beginning to uncover hidden psychopathology.

In concluding our discussion of content and special preoccupations, we present a few sample questions. We do not recommend that the examiner use these particular questions. If questioning becomes necessary, it is better for the examiner to frame his own questions. Otherwise there is danger of the examination becoming too stilted.

This portion of the examination is very difficult since it is directly concerned with material about which the patient may be sensitive, at least sensitive to sharing in discussion. The completeness of this portion of the examination is in some cases a good measure of the degree of rapport between the patient and the examiner.

As will be noted, the mood may be intimately linked with topical (content) considerations, such as worry, anxiety, ecstasy, etc. The transition to this portion of the examination is made immediately by inquiring as to *why* the patient is worried, or anxious, or ecstatic, etc. One might naturally expect some relation between the content in such a case and the precipitating factors as determined in the history of the present illness. The greatest divergencies may be seen and should occasion no surprise. For example, a man who apparently becomes depressed by the loss of his savings in a bank failure may speak of worry over masturbation as the principal complaint.

In addition to the type of content associated with mood, the following are important and must be inquired into:

Obsessions and Compulsions. These are thoughts (also fears and doubts) which course through the mind and cannot be erased—they are usually recognized as absurd or relatively meaningless, or at least as parasitic on the personality, yet a part of the personality—and acts performed through some inner need, the omission of which produces feelings of tension.

Do you have any thoughts which you can't get rid of?

Do you find yourself thinking of things and can't stop, or are you ever aware of thoughts, or words, or phrases, or tunes going round and round in your mind, and do you find yourself unable to control them?

Are you afraid of storms, heights, crowds, traffic, etc.?

Do you have difficulty in making decisions, finding yourself wavering constantly?

Do you feel compelled to do certain acts, or rituals? And, if so, do you feel tense until they are done, even though you know they are foolish or unimportant (e.g., hand washing over and over again, locking and relocking the door, certain rituals for dressing and undressing, feeling of need for the curtains to hang just so, or all on a level, etc.)?

Are you able to stop these actions at will?

The variations with causes are to be inquired for.

Familiarity (Déjà Vu Experiences) and Unfamiliarity Feelings (Depersonalization and Unreality, Benumbing). Have you ever been in a strange place or situation of any sort and suddenly had the feeling that you had been there before, or had experienced it all before?

Describe the experience.

Have you felt strange or lost in your own room or other familiar place?
Do friends ever appear strange or changed in appearance or action?
Do things in general seem strange, queer, or unreal?
Do strangers often look familiar to you?

The inverse situation and experience are also inquired into:

Do these experiences occur in any special setting?
How long do they last?
Do things seem natural (real) to you? How different?
Are you aware of any change in yourself?
How does it affect you?

Ideas of Reference, Paranoid Ideas. These are projections to the environment of internal insecurity or sensitiveness, or dominant motives with feelings of being the object of environmental attention, especially of being the target of persecution or unfair dealing of some sort.

Do you feel at ease?
How do people (the world) treat you?
Have you had a square deal from life?
Are you bothered by crowds?
Do people look at you on the street?
Have you ever felt singled out for special attention?
Do people like you?
Does anyone "have it in" for you? Has anyone a grudge against you?
Under what circumstances, or why and how does it affect you?

Passivity Feelings. These are feelings of being under the control of an external force.

Do you ever feel that your thoughts or actions are under any outside force (influence) or control?
Do you ever feel hypnotized?
Do you ever feel made to do or think things against your will?
Are your thoughts ever suddenly taken away from you?
Can people read your mind?
Does the radio have any special influence over you?

Inquire into the reverse phenomena—the feeling of being able to influence others, to read minds, etc.

Delusions (False Beliefs) and Hallucinations (Imaginary Sensory Elaborations without External Stimuli). The former may appear in the detailed present illness or in the mental status as ideas of reference and paranoid ideas. Grandiose ideas may be elicited. Both delusions and hallucinations are inquired into as follows:

Have you had any unusual experiences lately (since you have been sick)?

Has anything out of the way happened to you?

Any peculiar experiences?

Any imaginations?

Any daydreams?

More pointed questions with reference to hallucinations may be:

Have you seen (heard, smelled, tasted, felt) anything unusual?

Do you ever hear your name called when no one is about?

Do you hear people talk about you (or when you are alone in your room)?

Do you ever get messages from heaven?

Have you been bothered by any unpleasant odors?

Have you felt the need for bathing frequently? (Hallucinations of body odor.)

Any affirmative answer is to be taken as a lead for the further description of exactly how the phenomena occur, what the exact content is, how they affect the patient, and the means of their control.

Dreams. Ask concerning the dreams, especially for troublesome, anxious dreams or frequently recurring dreams, and the patient's interpretations.

Hypochondriacal Ideas. Ask for the presence of aches or pains or unusual physical sensations. Questioning may reveal unusual physical concern, excessive physical complaining, or bizarre, distorted somatic delusions.

Mood. The significance of the emotions has been emphasized. They are the life-giving essence of the personality. In psychiatry, much turns upon the emotions. For instance, in a general way, the prognosis depends upon the viability of emotions and their appropriateness to the content of thought.

The way *not* to reach a satisfactory opinion concerning the emotional life of a patient, as we have said before, is to throw at him, at once, a barrage of questions: "Are you sad? Elated? Irritable? Suspicious?" etc. We are quite adept in judging the moods of our friends without endless cross-examination. Unconsciously we note the facial expression, physical posture, and gestures, the eyes, the intonation and cadence of the voice. These and similar indications are more valid criteria than mere verbal responses.

The examiner trained to observe closely has available many more criteria—pallor, flushing, dilation of the pupils, throbbing of the neck vessels, clenched fists, rapid, shallow breathing, etc. He may supplement his observation by such clinical examinations as blood-pressure readings.

Before emotional reactions can be considered pathologic, they must have endured for some time. In the life of almost every human being, there are transient episodes of emotional disturbance, perhaps murderous rage, jealousy, "blue" spells, elation, etc.

Questions, if needed, should be used sparingly and must be framed to elicit an unprejudiced answer concerning the mood or affect, how it makes the patient feel, its variations and causes, and its controls. The mood may be rather diffuse, such as blueness, sadness, melancholy, depression, or lonesomeness, or elation, euphoria, expansiveness. The mood may be more topically conditioned, such as worry, anxiety, fear, or ecstasy. Again the variations and their cause and controls are important.

Begin with the most casual, naive questions and proceed to more pointed ones only when they clearly will not prejudice the answers. The following have been found useful:

How are you?

How do you feel?

How are your spirits?

How is your mood?

Any initiative? Optimism?

Then

How does this mood affect you?

What do you mean by "blue" or "anxious"?

How do things (the world, life) look to you?

Any ups and downs? Are these under any special conditions, or at any time?

Do you feel better in the morning or evening?

How is this mood different from your usual feeling?

Does it ever drive you to despair?

Does life seem worth living?

Sensorium and Intellectual Resources. The accommodations of consciousness and the placing or orientation of ourselves in relation to space, time, and person are so usual that we are apt to forget how frequently the binding threads of consciousness are parted—in sleep, anesthesia, hypnotism, fever, infection and intoxication, mental deterioration, etc. Even fatigue loosens the connections. In *disorientation*, which may be complete or partial, the patient is no longer able to interpret correctly the incoming sensory messages.

Not always is it true, as has been said, that we rarely forget that which makes a deep impression. In *amnesia*, ego-painful and belittling material has been "forgotten," repressed. Memory may be impaired by organic brain disease. For instance, in many senile deteriorations, *recent memory* may be annihilated. Later *intermediate* and *remote* memories are affected. There are many interesting memory disorders; for instance, in Korsakoff's syndrome, there may be *falsification of memory*, in which events that probably did occur sometime in the past are woven into the present. One of us was demonstrating a Korsakoff patient, weak, unable to stand, indeed, he had been bedridden for months. In reply to the question, "Where were you last night?" he said, "You know, in that night club. Don't you remember the girls? You liked the little fat blondie!"

In this division of sensorium and intellectual resources belong the testing of counting and calculation, of writing spontaneously, from dictation and from copy, of attention, of school and general knowledge, and of familiarity with current events. All the needed tests should be made without mystery or formality; otherwise patients may become frightened or suspicious. In making intellectual tests, the examiner must bear in mind the intellectual equipment and educational background of each patient and keep well within its limits.

A simple testing outline is reproduced. This portion of the examination is liable to provoke annoyance in being put to the test. It is useful in introducing the subject to preface with the question, "Have you had any difficulty in thinking, concentration, or memory?" This gives many patients a welcome opportunity to excuse errors in advance, at the same time orienting the examiner toward special difficulty. The data are taken in the following order:

Orientation to Time, Place, Person.
Have you kept track of the time?
What day (month, year, time of day) is it?
You know where you are, don't you?
What sort of place is this?
What is this building?
What is your full name?
You know who I am, don't you?
What is my job? What do I do?

Memory. Is this recent, intermediate, or remote? It is best checked by the dates of the history with reference to the facts and to consistency in the story. Recent memory may be checked with events of the past 24 hours, which of course must be corroborated from authentic outside sources.

Retention and Recall. The patient is given three objects to remember and is told that he is going to be asked to reproduce them within a specified time (3 to 5 minutes). The examination proceeds as usual and then the patient is asked for the three objects. This is a test of active retention. Also the patient may be led to mention three things in a casual conversation, and later asked to reproduce them. This tests the passive retention.

The retention of digits: For this purpose one may make up his own list, or use the numbers from the Stanford revision of the Binet-Simon test as follows:

Repeat forward	*Repeat backward*
3 1 7 5 9 (year 7)	6 5 2 8 (year 9)
5 2 1 7 4 6 (year 10)	3 1 8 7 9 (year 12)
9 7 2 8 4 7 5 (year 14)	4 7 1 5 9 2 (year 16)
7 2 5 3 4 8 9 6 (year 18)	

It is always advisable to begin with an easy task so as to avoid the sensitiveness a failure might produce. Progress then to the next higher number. The digits are to be pronounced at about the rate of one per second, and care must be taken to avoid repetition of digits or their arrangement, or emphasis or punctuations, which would aid in the reproduction.

The patient then is given a simple story to read and asked to reproduce immediately the substance of the story. The "Cowboy Story" is useful:

A cowboy from Arizona went to San Francisco with his dog, which he left at a dealer's while he purchased a suit of new clothes. Dressed finely, he went to the dog, whistled to him, called him by name and patted him. But the dog would have nothing to do with him in his new hat and coat but gave a mournful howl. Coaxing was of no effect, so the cowboy went away and donned his old garments, whereupon the dog immediately showed his wild joy on seeing his master dressed as he thought he ought to be.

Calculation. Calculations should be without pencil and paper, unless the patient has too great difficulty. In this case the fact should be noted.

Use simple calculations, or at least calculations within the range of the patient's educational advantages and life opportunities as determined by the history—addition, subtraction, division, and multiplication of increasing complexity.

Serial subtraction—100 minus 7s—is a most useful test. It requires keeping in mind the goal, retention of the last figure, and brings out slowing, late errors (fatigue), blocking, carelessness, or lack of appreciation of errors, tension, anxiety under load, etc. Ask the patient then to divide 100 by 7, and note if he gets the same fraction left over as in serial subtraction, and if he notes any inconsistency.

General Information. These are events of the day—newspaper items, politics, economics, art, etc. Facts of geography and history (local, national, and international) within the probable range of the patient's opportunities and interests are also included. We do not test to see how much the patient knows, but if he knows as much as he reasonably should. The list of questions will be adapted to the patients, and of course the answers must be known beforehand to the examiner.

Judgment. Judgment is formally tested by discriminations as: "What is the difference between a mistake and a lie (dwarf and child, tree and bush, etc.)?" It is also tested by reference to the absurdities in the Binet-Simon fables for years 10 and 14, etc.

Questions concerning the patient's plans for the future elicit a more spontaneous performance.

In many adults and in all children, more exact knowledge concerning the intellectual level is desirable. Recourse may be had to any one of several "intelligence tests" which have been standardized as to method of administration and scoring of the results. For ordinary psychiatric work, the Stanford revision of the Binet-Simon test or the Wechsler-Bellevue test will be found very useful and practicable. For the best results with these tests, considerable skill in obtaining cooperation of the patient and in interpreting the behavior during the test is necessary. A quantitative estimation of the intelligence is to be considered as adequate only when given under the optimal conditions. Poor rapport, physical distress, fear, and environmental distractions are common vitiating factors and should always be noted in the body of the test.

In children, the intelligence scoring may be compared with the scholastic record. Special difficulties in reading, writing, or calculation are frequently discovered in applying the tests.

Insight. Under this heading we get the verbatim statement of the patient's summing up or formulation to himself of his present situation. There are many instances when the physician's use of the word "sick" or "ill" will meet with an uncooperative attitude. The questioning had best proceed then from the most casual beginning:

What do you think about all this you have told me?

How do you explain your present situation?

Is anything wrong with you? What?

What do you think is the matter with you?

What would you say was the nature of your trouble?

When things do not go right with us, we naturally look about for explanations.

Have you come to any conclusions concerning yourself (this situation you find yourself in)?

Do you consider yourself as any different now from what you have always been?

How do you explain the interest (concern) of your family (friends) in wanting this examination made? (When the patient has denied anything being amiss.)

Are you sick?

SUMMARY OF THE DIRECT EXAMINATION

At this point summarize briefly the facts which seem to be of significance in the direct examination for their natural hanging together or for their inconsistency or incongruity. Compare these findings with the points of interest in the history for their similarities and incongruities and the understanding gained in view of their developmental story in an experimental formulation of the material. Note what gaps are present and keep them in mind for future investigation through additions to the history or the mental status of the patient.

The Laboratory Examination

It is important that the physical examination be reinforced by laboratory studies. The types and number of laboratory procedures indicated will vary according to the total health picture presented by the patient. It seems advisable to do routine blood and urine studies and chest x-ray on all patients. Spinal-fluid studies should be made in all patients with major psychotic symptoms. In general the principles to be recommended are those of good scientific medicine, making any and all laboratory examinations indicated but avoiding unnecessary procedures motivated by a desire to make an impressive chart full of normal reports.

CONTRIBUTORY EXAMINATIONS AND SPECIAL TESTS

This category leads directly into highly technical fields, for the most part still problems in research, but often special tests have great practicability. Our colleagues in psychology have developed a variety of helpful tests. The test results plus the psychologist's diagnostic formulation should be part of the clinical examination of the patient.

Pentothal Sodium or Amytal interviews have proved of particular value. The technique for Amytal interviews is too well known to warrant detailed discussion at this time. In brief, the technique consists of the slow administration of Sodium Amytal or some similar preparation by vein to a point of lethargy and "grogginess" in the patient. During the period of induction a patter of conversation along neutral lines of interest should be maintained. When the speech becomes thick and the patient develops slips of the tongue and momentary lapses, probings into the conflict material and amnesic or willfully withheld material may be started. During this phase much can be accomplished by the use of direct and positive suggestion, by reliving conflict situations with formulation of better ways of adaptation to these situations. Caution is necessary to avoid overdosage with a resultant sleep and inability to respond to questions.

The Rorschach test is one of the most valuable contributory examinations. It gives information concerning the patient's basic personality configuration, his capacity for control, and offers a quick yet surprisingly accurate means of determining what the patient has to react with in terms of instinctual drives, affective control, type and quality of intellect, intellectual capacity, manner of approach to problems, and nature and quality of conflict material. In skilled hands the test enables one to predict with some certainty what the individual's behavior would be in a given situation. In clinical practice it is of definite value in the differential diagnosis of difficult cases, although this is the least valuable of its many uses. The technique of administration is simple but the interpretation rather complex. Those interested are referred to the excellent works of Rorschach, Klopfer, Beck, and the members of the Society for Projective Techniques. Special training in the use of this method may be obtained in certain teaching centers in this country. Such training is necessary for successful utilization of the test.

Funkenstein has devised a test based on the patient's reaction to epinephrine and mecholyl. He believes it differentiates populations and is of aid in prognosis for certain types of mental illness (see Chapter 3). Other tests using Amytal and Pentothal Sodium for prognostic study have also been devised. The tests seem reliable in the hands of persons experienced in their use, but they are still tools for the specialist in their present stage of development.

Summary

There should be a complete summary made of the indirect, direct, and contributory examinations. These summaries constitute an abstract along with detailed progress notes describing the course in the hospital. This complete abstract should close with a formulation.

Muncie's outline of the formulation is as follows:

1. The essential descriptive character of the leading and incidental lines of behavior as reactions to life situations

2. Degree of involvement (and the degree of preservation of normal functioning)

3. Etiologic factors: those more and those less directly concerned; those more and less obvious to patient and physician

4. Immediate therapeutic need and the opportunities for management

5. Gaps in the understanding; treatment possibilities which must await further information

The purpose of the formulation is to summarize and stress the genetic-dynamic factors in the particular patient under consideration. In each case the gradual evolution of the problem must be understood by both patient and physician.

GRAPHIC SUMMARIES

Some students find it helpful to organize the case material graphically. Two types of graphic summary are presented as examples.

Life Chart. The longitudinal approach devised by Adolf Meyer is self-explanatory. The formula in Fig. 1 represents a schizophrenic reaction showing the development of the schizophrenic process from the earliest stages when treatment should have been instituted. It can readily be seen that in the study of a psychosis through the genetic-dynamic approach the patient's present difficulties or symptoms are not the only or even the main objectives for study but are only one part of the large series of things which later must be studied from the earliest beginnings and dealt with as a whole.

I + S Chart. The second graphic method of study of mental disorder has been developed in the clinic of one of the authors, and is termed by the student the I plus S equation, which represents a cross section of behavior taken at any significant period of an individual's life. The first graphic presentation deals with behavior primarily in its genetic aspects and relationships and evolution of reaction patterns. The second deals primarily with the dynamic aspects of behavior, showing it as a reaction to specific situations. We feel that these methods are of fundamental importance to the physician and the student in the understanding of mental disorders, and that they offer in a compact, understandable form a fairly accurate presentation of the case history in all its aspects. Records of this type are invaluable from the standpoint of teaching psychiatry, and they are essential to demonstrate effectively the rationale of each therapeutic measure undertaken and the results obtained from it. The value to the physician of such a formulation of the case graphically lies in the fact that his attention is immediately directed toward the factors of the individual's make-up or the situations which may be modifiable or correctable. The etiology of a psychiatric case is often as definite and clear-cut as the etiology of other forms of illness. A great degree of in-

CASE NUMBER: 3291. M. L. White, Female, Age 42. Single, File Clerk. Schizophrenic Reaction Type.
HEREDITY: Father and mother rather reticent and high strung. Patient fifth of eight children, all living and well, with no significant history.

YEAR:			BIRTHDAY: November 6th
1886		Gestation and birth uneventful.	Denver, Colorado. *Age*
1887		Early development normal.	1
1889		Fear reactions. *Afraid of the dark.*	3
1892		*Afraid of thunderstorms and high places.*	Started school. 6
1894	Chickenpox.	*Blue spells.*	8
1896		*Tense, anxious, insecure.*	10
1897	Measles.	*Had to have bed just so or she could not sleep.*	11
1898		Sex curiosity. *Beginning of rituals.*	12
1899		*Overtidy.*	13
1900	Measles (?)	*Always looked under bed at night.*	Graduated from 8th grade. 14
1901		Stayed out of school to help mother, in poor health.	15
1902	Onset of menses.	Went out with boy once.	Started high school. 16
1903		Thought that people talked about her.	17
1904	Dysmenorrhea.	Stepped to avoid cracks in sidewalk.	18
1905		*Anxiety, fears, rituals, prudishness.*	High school graduation. 19
1906		Hated shady jokes. *Definitely psychasthenic.*	Post graduate review. 20
1907		Got teacher's certificate. Taught 3 months.	Teaching. 21
1908		*Taught 8 months. Lacked confidence.*	22
1909		Went east with sister. Liked it.	Pittsburgh, Pa. 23
1910		Thought family needed her, came home. *Saleswoman, failed. Began withdrawal to world of phantasy.*	Denver. Taught 3 mos. Cashier in grocery store. 24
1911		*Went out a few times with a man. He quit. Patient very disappointed.*	Changed employment. Worked as file clerk. 25
1912		*Prudish and feelings easily hurt.*	Bookkeeper at dry goods store. 26
1913		*Ill at ease with other girls in the office.*	File clerk for merchant. 27
1914		*Took up Christian Science. Mystical interest.*	Father died. 28
1918		Head of department. Thought self unworthy. Quit.	32
1919		Christian Science treatment for throat and nerves.	33
1921		*Autistic love affairs.* "*Felt crazy about men.*" *Tried to flirt with them.*	Many employment changes, 3 jobs in 6 months. 35
1922		*Feared dirt. Thought people were talking about her and watching her.* Delusions of being watched.	36
1923		*Thought people watched her by television. Receiving messages.*	37
1924		Thought something terrible was going to happen.	Visited in California. 38
1925		*Outbursts of anger at times. Thought self worked on sexually. Fear reactions and rituals.*	39
1926		*Washed hands frequently. Nightmares.*	40
1927		*Thought food was poisoned and ate little. Very worried and anxious.*	41
1928		*Washed hands constantly. Thought people watched her by television and scolded her by telepathy.*	42
1929		Refused to bathe because she was watched. Burned clothes. Improved after 5 weeks hospital treatment.	Admitted to Colo. Psychopathic Hospital. 43

SEX-LIFE
THYROID
THYMUS
KIDNEYS
DIGESTION AND LIVER
HEART
RESPIRATION
REFLEX LEVEL
CEREBRUM

FIG. 1. Life Chart.

Case 10091

Main Facts

Pt. a 28-year-old, married white female admitted 60 days postpartum with the complaint that the desire to kill her children constantly recurs. She is frightened by these ideas, but cannot rid herself of them. Considering suicide as an escape and as a means of preventing herself from injuring her children.

Individual Make-up	Plus	Situation	Equals	Reaction

Reaction Type

Psychoneuroses, obsessive type.

Reaction

A. *Reaction Type:*
Psychoneuroses, obsessive type.

Brief Symptomatic Description of Illness:

Friendly, dominant, aggressive individual, who developed obsessive thinking in a setting of conflicts over marital responsibility and business ambitions with disappointment over the sex of her second child.

Results:

Marked improvement. Patient keeping house, allowing husband to manage the business. Still desires male child. Still aggressive.

A. *Physical:*
1. Body habitus: Pyknic.
2. Physical defects: None.
3. General health: Good.

B. *Intellect:*
1. Level of performance:
 (a) School: High school, good.
 (b) Work: Good, runs dairy.
2. I.Q. Binet—105.

C. *Instincts:*
1. Self-preservation: Strong.
2. Sex drive: Good, well directed.
3. Herd: Strong desire to dominate.

D. *Emotions:*
1. General emotional tone: Cheerful, happy.
2. Stability: Poor, tends to periods of irritability and sadness.

E. *Personality Pattern:*
1. Degree of organization: Good.
2. Type of response to environmental stress: Aggressive.
3. Special interests and ambitions: Interested in expanding business.
4. Amount and efficiency of drive toward goals: Unusually good.
5. Personal habits: Neat, clean, energetic.
6. Social habits: Friendly, outgoing, a leader.
7. Religious habits: Very little interest.

F. *Heredity:*
Good. Irish-German stock.

A. *Toxic Factors:*
Illness developed in setting of pregnancy and delivery, but there were no toxic symptoms.

B. *Organic Factors:*
None.

C. *Psychogenic Factors:*
1. Much humoring in childhood.
2. Fear and anxiety about father, with over-dependence on mother.
3. Failure to emancipate.
4. Seduction by brothers ages 10–11.
5. Resultant protest and aggression toward men.
6. Conflict between business ambitions and marital responsibilities.
7. Birth of second female child when boy was wanted.

Recommendations:
1. Treatment of physical factors: None indicated.
2. Psychotherapy: Distributive analysis with careful direction and synthesis.
3. Modification of Environment:
 (a) Emancipation from mother.
 (b) Lessened responsibility in the business.
 (c) Cultivation of interest in children.
4. Follow-up therapy through general practitioner and community clinic: Frequent interviews aid patient to adjustment in new routine.

Fig. 2. I + S Chart.

dividual variation in the forms of human behavior renders it imperative that the etiology be worked out individually in each separate case.

Personality Study. A different type of study which is of invaluable aid to the understanding of an intelligent patient is the autobiography or the planned personality study. The student is urged to learn to study his own personality as a preparation for the study of patients. We feel that a personality study is indispensable for good teaching. It is not within the scope of this book to reproduce the complete plan of a personality study but a practical guide for the study as devised by Adolf Meyer is presented in Billings' *Handbook of Psychobiology and Psychiatry* and in Muncie's *Psychobiology and Psychiatry*.

Classification of Diagnosis. In earlier editions we have discussed classification from many points of view and for presentation used the seven diagnostic groups of Adolf Meyer.

Experience demonstrates that this confuses the student who must translate from the textbook classification to the one used in the standard nomenclature of the hospital medical record library. This edition discusses the reaction types under the headings of the Standard Nomenclature of the American Psychiatric Association, using their headings and classification numbers.

In viewing his patient, the student will be aware that no case exactly fits the classification summaries, but the use of subcategories according to the American Psychiatric Association will enable one to classify the patient with reasonable accuracy.

Medical-Legal Consideration. In the practice of psychiatry, at times it becomes necessary to have patients confined against their will. Therefore the psychiatrist will need to familiarize himself with the local laws in any state in which he practices. Some states have provision for patients entering hospitals as voluntary cases. It is also necessary to have some type of emergency commitment. Some states, such as Massachusetts, make it possible for any police officer or other official person, a member of the patient's family, or his family physician to take him to a hospital and apply for his observation. Preliminary examination by the superintendent or admitting officer determines whether he shows sufficient symptoms to warrant his detention for 10 days. States should also have provision for prolonged periods of observation on medical certification when such observation is warranted, and they should have provisions for prolonged or more or less permanent commitment of patients who will need continued confinement.

In this latter category various state laws differ. In Texas, for example, it is necessary to have a trial before a 6-man jury. In Massachusetts and

New York, it is possible to have indefinite commitment on certification by 2 physicians. In Massachusetts, it is necessary to notify the patient and the family that he is to be committed, and, if the patient so indicates, he may have a hearing before the committing court. These hearings are held in private and a small proportion of cases avail themselves of this privilege. Most states also provide some appeal by the patient from the commitment, either at the time of the commitment or subsequently. Of course all cases should have this right to have their commitment reviewed by a court, and the court should avail itself of the best psychiatric testimony as to the patient's medical condition. The suspicion that judges have of psychiatry and mental hospitals in general still exists, but decreases steadily in most areas of the country. Psychiatrists should work with the courts to educate them and should encourage them to spend time familiarizing themselves with the various types of symptoms shown by mental patients. The student going into a new community who plans to handle mental patients, either in his capacity as a psychiatrist or family physician, should familiarize himself with the local laws. The local judge of probate or the court handling such matters can usually inform the physician of the rules and regulations. The clerk of the court will almost always have appropriate blanks and be glad to instruct the physician on the proper method of procedure. In most states, the State Commissioner of Mental Health will have procedure books or blanks available for the physician's instructions. The variations among the states are so great that to outline examples of laws here would be impractical.

SECTION II

The Clinical Syndromes

This section will contain the symptoms, what is known of the pathology, and recommendations for treatment for the more important clinical syndromes. We will follow the classification manual of the American Psychiatric Association. This classification manual makes it easy for the student to transpose from it to the standard and international nomenclature manual, as it has a transposition chart in the back. Most psychiatric hospitals use the American Psychiatric Association nomenclature manual which is identical with the standard nomenclature except for the numerical system.

The special treatments will be discussed in a separate section because many treatments are used in more than one disorder.

PART ONE

Disorders Caused by or Associated with Impairment of Brain-tissue Function

CHAPTER **8**

Acute Brain Disorders

Any disease, injury, or condition of physiologic decompensation which produces pathology of the nervous system may result in organic defects which, if severe enough, will produce mental symptoms classified as *the organic psychoses*. The principal differentiation between toxic or reversible organic reactions and more permanent or irreversible organic reactions is that in the former, the pathologic state is temporary and the brain recovers. In the latter, the changes are usually permanent and the brain function remains impaired. These changes may be focal or diffuse. In all these reactions stemming from impairment of the function of the brain tissue, there are certain symptoms due to the structural change in the nerve cells, and others due to the patient's earlier experience and his habitual pattern of reaction to the world. Symptoms due to impairment of brain-tissue function may be found in any age in life, beginning with birth injuries and terminating with the changes of senility.

Acute brain disorders are called *toxic* or *delirious reactions*, or *reversible organic reactions*. The psychotic episode is largely caused by various toxic states in the body and characterized by periods of confusion, fluctuating levels of awareness, and, in the more severe cases, episodes of hallucinatory and illusory experience. Acute organic reactions of this type make up only about 10 per cent of the admissions to psychiatric clinics and hospitals, but they are among the more common mental disorders treated by the general practitioner and the specialist who has a general hospital practice. Every practitioner of medicine should be familiar with these toxic states because they frequently accompany all types of severe infections and metabolic diseases.

Psychopathology and Symptomatology

The earliest and one of the outstanding symptoms in any toxic reaction is a fluctuating impairment of consciousness, the degree varying from mild confusion and disorientation to complete stupor. The patient may be acutely confused during part of the day and be relatively clear at a later time. These fluctuations may cause the student to doubt his own powers of observation, but actually they are often the first clues to the true nature of the patient's mental symptoms. Closely allied with these changes are defects in memory. Patients forget earlier instructions of the physician; they forget the physician's explanation of the treatment routine and may at times accuse the physician of neglect because the patient has forgotten his visits on the same day. These changes in memory, which are principally disturbances of retention and grasp of current situations, fluctuate in severity to a remarkable degree during the day. In spite of these variations, careful examination will usually elicit some impairment in the level of awareness and some impairment in retention and recent memory function at all times and in all patients suffering from toxic or delirious states. These early changes in the level of consciousness and in the memory functions are the first and outstanding symptoms in a delirious state.

As the condition progresses, the more spectacular content disturbances appear. These are for the most part hallucinations. These hallucinations occur in all spheres of sensation but are more commonly of an auditory type. Visual hallucinations and tactile hallucinations occur with some frequency in the delirious state, particularly when patients suffer from the various drug intoxications. These hallucinations in most instances are frightening to the patient or colored with anxiety and are often bizarre. In almost all instances the patient interprets them as being a threat or warning of some impending danger.

Delusions occur in many of these toxic reactions, and the delusions are usually of a fear-producing type with persecutory or paranoid overtones. The delusions often include members of the patient's immediate family, and in some cases the delusional system becomes fairly well organized and resembles that seen in some of the other psychotic states, particularly schizophrenia.

In some patients one finds an unusual combination of somatic hallucinatory and somatic delusional experiences. These are the patients who feel some type of tactile hallucinations, and upon this experience build a delusion of bugs or worms crawling under the skin. Classic descriptions of such cases occur in cocaine poisoning, but similar ideas are encountered in other types of toxic reactions. The hallucinatory and delusional experiences also come and go during the day. At times the patient is free of these experiences and will discuss the ones he has had in a good-natured manner. Later, during the same conversation or in other interviews, the patient will insist that these experiences are true. Some patients admit that certain productions of their imagination have been hallucinations but will pick out one or two ideas which they insist are true experiences. These are apt to be the paranoid projections, but in some instances the most absurd ideas are accepted. In the majority of cases the content of hallucinations and delusions changes considerably from time to time. If the toxic states become chronic, as they do in some of the alcoholic reactions, the delusions tend to become a little more fixed as to content.

Other types of experience disturbance frequently encountered in the toxic state are called *illusions*. These are closely allied to the above-described hallucinations and delusions. In this instance, however, the patient actually has an environmental stimulus but he misinterprets or misunderstands it. Patients, hearing nurses talking in the nurses' office, frequently interpret this as threats or plots to poison them. Patients sometimes misidentify the thermometer or enema tube as weapons with which the nurse or attendant intends to injure them. Noises around the hospital are often interpreted as gunshots fired at them.

In almost all instances the content of the illusion is of a fear-producing or anxiety type. The mood is one of apprehension and fear, usually in response to the hallucinatory or delusional experiences. When a patient is clear, the mood may change to euphoria. Patients in a toxic state weep easily and show irritability at the minor restrictions of the ward, but the mood is easily influenced by explanation and persuasion on the part of skilled nurses or physicians. Unfortunately the mood is labile, and, while patients may have their fears and apprehensions allayed, it will be necessary to repeat this reassurance as the apprehension and fears return with the hallucinatory experiences.

The stream of talk varies with the degree and severity of the delirium. Patients in a mild delirium respond to questions coherently, and spontaneous remarks are clearly expressed but usually colored by past experiences. In the more severe reactions speech becomes incoherent and in some instances consists of unintelligible muttering. Even in these cases, rousing the patient and fixing his attention on simple questions will usually result in coherent and often logical answers to the questions. Long or involved questions usually confuse the patient, and in the midst of a sentence he may wander into irrelevant or incoherent speech.

Behavior in these patients also varies considerably depending upon the degree and severity of the delirious reactions. Mildly delirious patients often react rather actively to their hallucinatory experiences. In some instances they attempt to run away from their imagined persecutors and may injure themselves by falling out windows or down stairs. Other patients believing that they are being threatened may assault nurses or attendants or fellow patients. These outbursts are usually controlled by explanation and reassurance, but the behavior is apt to recur frequently, and the patients require almost constant attention and nursing care. If the delirium becomes more severe, the patient becomes stuporous and will lie in bed muttering to himself, thrashing around, or picking at the sheets. Patients with tactile hallucinations will often spend hours picking bugs from themselves or pulling wires out of their fingers. Their behavior may seem bizarre and irrelevant upon first glance, but an understanding of the delusional content will make it seem more logical in terms of the patient's belief that he is covered with vermin or has wires running out of his fingers. The fact that the patient is a potential danger to himself and to his environment should always be borne in mind in planning the nursing routine.

The physical findings in toxic reactions are of importance. Details of the physical examination will vary somewhat with the particular etiologic agents. In all instances, however, the patient looks ill. At times the vasomotor instability is evidenced in terms of flushing, sweating, rapid but fluctuating pulse rate, and a widely fluctuating respiratory rhythm. There is usually a tremor of the fingers, hands, and lips. Patients frequently have a low-grade temperature and in some instances a high temperature, depending upon the etiologic agent and the individual somatic resistance. During the lucid intervals patients usually complain of headaches and feelings of general weakness and debility. Details of the physical findings vary in severity depending upon the etiologic agents; and, as might be expected, in the endogenous reaction the physical findings are more important and often specific for the individual diseases.

Blood pressure likewise tends to fluctuate, being high during periods of apprehension and excitement, and dropping to normal or below during periods of stupor. Persistent hypertension should make one suspicious that the cardiorenal system is beginning to decompensate, and this dysfunction may be the cause of the toxic picture.

Laboratory findings may be decisive and reflect a particular type of disorder from which the patient is suffering. In most instances, there is a moderate leukocytosis. All patients suffering from toxic reaction should have a complete physical and laboratory investigation even in those cases where the type of toxic reaction is thought to be obvious. In some cases the primary toxic agent is thought to be a kind of exogenous poison such as drugs or alcohol, but detailed investigation will show the patient to be suffering from some serious metabolic disorder and that a combination of the physiologic decompensation plus the exogenous toxin has produced mental disturbance.

Etiology. Any toxic or poisonous substance which adversely affects the metabolism in the body may produce a toxic reaction in the psychiatric sense. For convenience these toxic sources are usually divided into two types, endogenous and exogenous, or poisonous substances coming from within and from without.

Among the more common exogenous poisons are alcohol, sedative drugs, industrial poisons, opium derivatives, marihuana, and similar preparations.

In the endogenous group anything that interferes with the general metabolic efficiency of the body may produce toxic states. Modern research on vitamin therapy shows that toxic states are at least in part due to deficiencies in certain essential vitamins. There is also some evidence to show that a deficiency of certain proteins within the body has a tendency to produce delirium.

It is generally believed that the toxic states all produce reversible pathologic changes in the brain—primarily swelling of the nerve cells as well as of the supporting tissues. There is evidence which suggests that circulatory efficiency of the nervous system is an important factor in maintaining the normal liquid distribution between tissues and the vascular system. Ewalt and Ruskin showed electroencephalographic abnormalities with heart failure which would tend to support such a view. Engle and Romano found electroencephalographic abnormalities in patients suffering from minor degrees of confusion. In these series, clearing up the circulatory deficiency in one series and the delirious episodes in the other resulted in a restitution of a normal electric pattern in the cortex.

The utilization of oxygen by the brain is also an important factor in preserving a clear sensorium. The deficiency states play a role in the poor use of oxygen in the tissues, and this is probably a fundamental defect in the toxic and delirious states. Work by the Air Force on the impaired intellectual functioning in low-oxygen concentration and low-oxygen tension tends to support such a view.

Occasionally patients expire during the toxic episode. The postmortem findings are rather uniform irrespective of the etiologic agents. They are principally those of brain edema or "wet brain," which is generalized. Microscopic examination reveals the accumulation of fluids in the interstitial spaces and swelling of the neurons themselves. The changes are all of a reversible kind, and it is usually assumed that the toxic symptoms roughly parallel the degree of brain edema.

Acute Brain Syndrome Associated with Intracranial Infection 009–100

This type of reaction is not very common. Most cases are due to epidemic encephalitis or encephalitis secondary to measles or mumps. Meningitis of various types and vascular syphilis sometimes produce delirium. The psychiatric symptoms tend to be mild and usually appear after the patient is known to be quite ill, and after the correct diagnosis has been made. Among the first symptoms to appear are irritability and restlessness, accompanied by deepening lethargy and coma. The restlessness may be manifest by picking at the covers, tossing in the bed, or by marked motor agitation. At times these patients show hallucinatory reactions, and some have illusions. Paranoid delusions may also appear, but usually in those patients with paranoid personality predispositions prior to the illness. The symptoms either clear up or progress into deepening stupor and coma. Even in the stupor many of these patients show restlessness and motor agitation.

Pathology. Many of these patients recover. Those dying during the acute phase usually show involvement of the nerve cells, principally with edema and swelling. More permanent findings are usually confined to the midbrain, but some patients show chronic cortical pathology. Syndromes, particularly in children, known as postencephalitic behavior disorders, are assumed to be due to organic damage of the nervous system, residual from these acute infections. This is by no means clearly proved except by frequency of association.

Treatment. There is no specific treatment for this disorder. In general, the principles of management of any delirious reaction should be followed. Treatment should be directed toward the basic disorder if it is known and if it is treatable. In general, the treatment will be supportive. Sedatives should be prescribed with great caution in these patients because of their tendency to lapse into stupor, and should be used only if the patient becomes very excited and unmanageable.

Prognosis. Most of these patients recover. Some show residual symptoms, such as parkinsonism and anomalies of behavior, but the mental disturbance usually clears up. If not, what is left is usually chronic irritability and paranoid-like symptoms, similar to those seen in older patients or posttraumatic cases that will be described in a subsequent section. In the acute phases, practically all these patients should be handled in a general hospital.

Acute Brain Syndrome Associated with Systemic Infection 000–100

In any acute infectious disease accompanied by fever and toxic symptoms, the patient may become confused and delirious. Typical symptoms are a fluctuating level of awareness, confusion, disorientation that varies, and a general clouding of consciousness. As they become more ill, these patients begin to have illusions and hallucinations. At times they may become stuporous and have convulsions. These syndromes in varying degrees of severity may appear in pneumonia, influenza, acute rheumatic fever, malaria, and in the rare cases of typhoid. The patients may become depressed, overactive, or suspicious, depending upon their previous personality pattern.

Pathology. The general pathology in patients who die at this stage is that of a "wet brain." The psychopathology is colored by the sensorium disturbances produced by the brain pathology and by the patient's previous personality set.

Treatment. The treatment is directed toward combating the underlying infection. Concentrated plasma and whole blood are thought to be of value in treating the cerebral edema. At one time glucose and sucrose injections given intravenously in hypertonic solutions were recommended, but it is now believed by some that these are of only temporary benefit and that the final reaction to them is a more severe brain edema. With our increased skill in treating acute infections such arguments are usually academic because the infection can as a rule be promptly handled, and the patient's condition clears up rapidly. The general measures to be discussed under the management of delirium in the treatment section are particularly applicable to this group of patients.

Prognosis for recovery from the mental disorder is good, providing the patient recovers from the systemic infection. The improvement in the mental picture may lag behind improvement in the physical picture, particularly if the patient shows a good many depressive or paranoid tendencies. The sensorium improvement, however, should more or less directly accompany the improvement in the infectious state.

Acute Brain Syndrome, Drug or Poison Intoxication 000-3

The opium alkaloids may on rare occasions produce pipe dreams if taken as the Orientals do. These are transitory periods of well-being with pseudohallucinations and, in extreme cases, true hallucinations. Rarely does one see a psychosis precipitated by narcotics. Occasionally one sees a patient in a panic reaction because of the unavailability or abrupt withdrawal of the drug. Bromides and barbitals may produce prolonged delirious episodes of the Korsakoff-like type. Cocaine may produce somatic hallucinations and occasional acute paranoid delusions. These usually clear up promptly with detoxification. The problem in these cases is the addiction (see under Addiction) to the drug and not the acute delirious episode.

Certain chemicals used in the manufacturing industry may produce deliria. Carbon tetrachloride used in cleaning processes, for the fumigation of wheat in ships' holds, and in other industrial processes may induce deliria. These symptoms are usually transitory and not serious, but should alert the physician to test the patient for the more serious signs of liver damage sometimes induced by these drugs. Any volatile drug inhaled over a period of time may induce intoxication. In some areas of the country, in lower socioeconomic groups, certain persons voluntarily inhale the fumes from gasoline or from ether in a process known as "sniffing." This provides the same type of state seen in others using marihuana, barbitals, or heroin. It is not popular, and I have encountered it only among laborers in the Southwest, but it undoubtedly occurs periodically in other areas.

Acute Brain Syndrome, Alcohol Intoxication 000–3312

Alcoholism is a major sociopsychiatric problem of our time. Under the addictions we shall discuss the general problem of chronic alcoholism. In this section we shall deal with only those patients showing symptoms that are due to the acute recoverable brain syndrome characterized by delirium and other symptoms typical of any toxic reaction. These acute syndromes may occur in patients who are discussed under the general category of Chronic Alcoholism or Alcohol Addiction, or they may occur in persons who have been on a single isolated prolonged alcoholic bout.

Not all individuals develop a psychosis as a result of their drinking. We believe that the nutritional and physical status is important in producing the psychiatric reaction, and that the psychiatric reaction will be colored by the general personality pattern of the alcoholic patient. The alcoholic psychoses are usually subclassified according to their symptomatology, and this will be discussed under each common subclassification.

Pathologic Intoxication. This is an acute mental disturbance due to varying amounts of alcohol, usually small, manifesting over a short period of time excitement or furor with confusion and hallucination followed by amnesia. Persons showing this type of reaction usually are basically quite unstable and make a borderline adjustment when sober.

Delirium Tremens. This reaction often begins acutely and is characterized by motor restlessless, distractability, hallucinations (particularly auditory and visual), illusions, great apprehension, tremor, and ataxia. In effect it is a severe delirium with marked tremors. As the disease progresses, the motor and mental activity becomes greatly increased. Tremors of the tongue and fingers are severe. The patient is sleepless and has fever, rapid pulse, low blood pressure, and loss of weight. There is albumin in the urine. In favorable cases the delirium terminates abruptly in a few days. Delirium tremens is often inadequately treated. If resort to elimination and hydrotherapy were stressed and reliance on narcotic drugs abandoned, the recovery rate would be much higher. Vitamin therapy (with emphasis on vitamin B) and the use of insulin with glucose drip usually result in the prompt remission of symptoms.

Korsakoff's Psychosis. This is a chronic prolonged form of psychosis which is actually more organic than toxic because many cases show permanent changes in the central nervous system. They are characterized by loss of memory and plausible confabulations which bridge gaps in the memory, but the confabulation changes from moment to moment. Patients are reasonably well-oriented as to person and are easy to orient as to time and place, but they do not remain in contact with their environment. In initial phases the patient may have hallucinatory and delusional experiences similar to those seen in delirium tremens, but if the condition becomes chronic, the hallucinatory episodes will probably subside. The striking thing about the Korsakoff reaction is the marked confabulation and severe loss of memory. Peripheral or polyneuritis usually accompanies this diagnosis although strictly speaking, the Korsakoff reaction may occur without neuritis. Korsakoff's reaction is usually due to prolonged and excessive drinking. Polyneuritis produces muscular aches and pains, and patients often incorporate these sensations into their delusional systems, imagining them to be bugs or wires. Research indicates that the polyneuritic changes are due to a deficiency in the vitamin-B complex, and it is probable that many of the central nervous system changes are on the same basis.

Acute Hallucinosis. This form of alcoholic psychosis is characterized by hallucinations of hearing, with marked apprehension and fear, and fairly well-organized delusions of persecution. In contrast to the other forms of alcoholic psychosis, the sensorium is relatively clear in acute hallucinosis. The absence of confusion, disorientation, and retention defects is the principal difference from other forms of delirious reaction.

Chronic Hallucinosis. This is usually a prolongation of acute hallucinosis. As the state becomes chronic, the apprehension and fear in reaction to the hallucinations tend to subside. Some of the cases seem to be the first manifestation of a schizophrenic psychosis, and some authors consider chronic hallucinosis actually to be initial stages of a schizophrenic reaction precipitated by the alcoholic psychosis and not due to the alcohol per se. This reaction is also characterized by hallucinations and delusions, the former principally of the auditory type.

Acute Paranoid Type. The patients in this group are suspicious, have systematized persecutory delusions, and frequently misinterpret environmental events as having special application to themselves. These patients are distinguished from those who have hallucinosis by the absence of hallucinatory experience. The sensorium in these reactions is also clear.

Chronic Paranoid Type. This group includes those cases under the acute paranoid type which do not clear up within a few months. Many become chronic custodial patients, and future examinations usually reveal them to be suffering from a schizophrenic disorder. Because of the absence of confusion and hallucinations, and because the principal symptom is projection content, it is likely that these two forms do not properly belong to the toxic reactions but are to be considered as deeply seated personality disorders in persons who have been borderline psychotics but who first begin to form delusions when there is an additional burden of supporting a toxic reaction.

Treatment. All these disorders are treated by withdrawal of alcohol, as will be described under the treatment section, and by therapy to relieve the cause of the alcoholism.

Acute Brain Syndrome Associated with Trauma 000–4

Under this heading will be included those reactions which develop immediately after an injury to the head produced by some external force or following neurosurgery. The traumatic reactions include:

1. Acute delirious cases following trauma to the brain
2. Amnesic episodes, usually with limited retrograde and anterograde amnesia
3. Posttraumatic constitution or prolonged changes produced by head trauma
4. Defect conditions such as aphasia, asymbolia, or deterioration, with or without seizures as a late result of trauma
5. Terminal deterioration due to progressive alterations of the injured parts of the brain, with or without arteriosclerosis

In this section one would properly classify only the so-called traumatic deliria in the first group. Most of these cases follow head injuries from falls, auto accidents, or blows on the head. The delirium may appear as the patient awakens from a period of unconsciousness. Other patients may not be unconscious but only confused after the accident and the symptoms develop progressively. The symptoms are manifest by confusion, disorientation, and at times hallucinations and delusions. A typical case is that of a boy, age 17, who was injured in a motorcycle accident. He was taken to a general hospital after preliminary treatment in a physician's office. Two days after the injury, as he regained consciousness, he began to show confusion and delirium. He became so difficult to handle that he was finally brought to a psychiatric hospital. There he was uncooperative, hallucinating, and so restless it was necessary to use restraint to keep him in bed. He was extremely profane and cried often. At times he would be drowsy and irritable. If the restraints were removed, he would get up and wander about his room in a confused state. He was excreta careless. He was completely disoriented regarding time and he could not recall events in the recent past. On a regimen directed toward management of the wet brain, and general support therapy, the patient's condition began to clear. Within 3 weeks of admission he was completely clear except for a partial amnesia for the accident itself. When seen 1 month later, he had gone back to school and seemed to have regained his preaccident level of performance. A typical traumatic delirium is usually occupational in type. These reactions are usually transitory and may or may not produce chronic residuals. These will be discussed under the chronic brain syndromes.

Acute Brain Syndrome Associated with Circulatory Disturbance 000–5

This type of reaction includes patients who show confusion, disorientation, and at times vague paranoid phenomena as a result of brain edema from faulty circulation. These syndromes are most commonly due to cardiac decompensation and are always accompanied by other evidence of circulatory failure.

In some instances this syndrome appears in cases of endocarditis with emboli which may lodge in the brain, producing transitory periods of confusion. Confusion seen in these cases is typical of that in other deliria except that the patient almost always appears ill and is often not disturbed in the motor sphere. The first sign to appear is usually lapse in attention, lapses of recent memory, drowsiness, and transient periods of unconsciousness. Patients may not recognize their physicians or nurses but will usually recognize members of their family. At times they become apprehensive and fearful, and some may become paranoid and belligerent.

Pathology. The pathology is that due to the underlying disorder, usually a wet brain, but if the circulatory deficiency is due to arteriosclerosis, brain emboli, or small thrombi, these conditions would be found on postmortem. Treatment is directed toward improving the efficiency of the circulatory system. It has been our experience that placing the patient in an oxygen tent during the period of circulatory support relieves the delirious state. One should also put these patients on an adequate diet particularly with respect to the protein and vitamin factors. Other items of treatment are typical of those to be discussed for delirium in the section on treatment.

Acute Brain Syndrome Associated with Convulsive Disorder 000–550

Convulsive disorders as such will be classified under the neurologic diagnostic groups, which are not included in this textbook. These convulsive reactions occur in a wide variety of conditions and are usually referred to as *the epilepsies*. Convulsions may occur as a result of almost any type of toxic or organic state involving the tissue of the brain. These states are called *symptomatic epilepsy*. So-called "genuine" or "idiopathic epilepsy" has been conclusively demonstrated to be a "disordered functioning of the rate-regulating mechanism of the brain." Data accumulate, but as yet we do not fully understand what precipitates these paroxysmal dysfunctions of the rate-regulation mechanism of the brain. A history of some type of attack disorder, plus the typical electroencephalographic pattern, is usually thought to be sufficient for a positive diagnosis.

The disease commonly starts in childhood but may be seen in adolescence. At least three-fourths of the cases develop their first "seizures" before the age of 20. Convulsive seizures are usually classified as grand mal or major attacks, petit mal, and psychomotor states. In all there is a disturbance of consciousness. Most patients with convulsive disorders have no symptoms except the attacks or seizures. A small percentage develop personality change, and some of these develop more serious mental disorders. Only the epileptic psychoses should be classified here.

There are several types of epileptic mental disturbance; probably the most common is a *periodic ill-humor* which may last from a few hours to a few days and most commonly follows a seizure. Similar to this and sometimes accompanying it is the *epileptic twilight state* in which the patient is quite confused. This may last from a few minutes to 2 or 3 days following a seizure. Some patients have *furor states* following seizures or as a replacement for seizure. In a furor they become extremely disturbed and during these times are overactive, combative, destructive, and at times homicidal. Patients in a furor state are extremely dangerous and should be handled promptly and effectively by adequate personnel. The *epileptic equivalent state* consists of an attack of mental disorder with confusion and perhaps with paranoid delusions or hallucinations instead of convulsive seizures. They are frequent but are not apt to approach the violence of the furor states. Some of them show transitory states of depression and excitement. Some equivalent states are expressed as visceral equivalents with pains. *Epileptic fugue* states are closely related to twilight states, but the patient may have prolonged periods of amnesia lasting from days to months. These are difficult to differentiate from the hysterical amnesias, and only the history of seizures or periods of unconsciousness or the routine use of electroencephalography will lead one to this diagnosis.

Pathology in the epilepsies is unknown in so far as the structure or the chemistry of the brain is concerned. The above-mentioned electrical dysrhythmia is known to exist and the pathologic EEG can be elicited in nearly all cases, although it is not always present on the first routine electroencephalographic tracing.

Treatment. The treatment of the epileptic clouded states and psychosis consists of supportive care during the psychotic episode, and prompt, vigorous treatment directed toward the convulsive disorder itself. Treatment of the convulsive disorder is not a proper subject for this book, and the student is referred to the excellent texts available in neurology.

Acute Brain Syndrome Associated with Metabolic Disturbance 000-7

A chronic metabolic disturbance may produce disordered functioning of the brain. This may be brought about by faulty metabolism or it may be due to accumulating edema of the brain. The symptoms are essentially the same as those of any other delirium: confusion, fluctuating levels of awareness, and irritability. Certain illnesses such as uremia tend to produce muttering, picking at the sheets, and motor restlessness. Diabetes patients, either in acidotic coma or hyperinsulinism, show stages of confusion and coma, but the physiologic concomitants are such that even though the mental picture is somewhat the same, the differential diagnosis is usually easily made. Hyperthyroidism will produce an anxious, restless, overactive type of confusion. Hypothyroidism or myxedema produces a lethargic, sluggish demeanor and a stupid expression. The mental symptoms in hypothyroidism, if present, will show functional overlay such as paranoid or depressive symptoms in addition to the sensorium changes and the generally retarded dull appearance.

Acute Brain Syndrome Associated with Intracranial Neoplasm 000-8

Some patients with brain tumor after surgery or with impaired cerebral circulation from the tumor's location will develop a wet brain which may produce a delirium. There is nothing in the delirium itself to differentiate this from any other toxic state. In patients with delirium or confusion of unexplained origin, one should do a particularly careful neurologic and electroencephalographic survey to rule out the possibilities of a cerebral neoplasm. Obviously one would consult with a neurosurgeon and a neurologist in case of doubt.

Acute Brain Syndrome with Disease of Unknown or Uncertain Cause 000–900

This is a general classification for grouping patients with psychotic reactions complicating such disorders as multiple sclerosis or other conditions in which the underlying disease has been diagnosed, but the cause of the disease is not known. The acute deliria are not distinct from those of metabolic disturbances or traumas or circulatory disturbances, and they are handled in much the same way.

Acute Brain Syndrome of Unknown Cause 000–xx0

The classification manual includes this number for those cases of delirium for which no cause can be discovered.

CHAPTER 9

Chronic Brain Disorders I

The symptoms and signs of chronic brain disorder are similar, regardless of the etiology. Therefore, the general symptoms will be presented here, and the details and variations will be discussed under the various diagnostic category numbers.

The symptoms and signs common to organic disorders are irreversible changes in the brain and include a history of gradual change in personality with reduction of mental capacity and development of defects in judgment. Behavior changes, best described as habit deterioration, are common.

Physical, neurologic, encephalographic, or spinal serologic findings indicate some destructive process in the brain. There may be increased protein in the spinal fluid and perhaps increased cell count if irritative or infectious phenomena are going on.

Mental-status examination reveals defects in memory, defects in retention, difficulties with orientation, and failure to grasp the niceties of the situation in which the patient finds himself.

Emotional instability most frequently characterized by irritability and rapid shifts in mood is common. This lability is sometimes called *emotional incontinence* because the patient may become tremendously angry or begin to weep for little or no reason so far as environmental events are concerned. Emotional reactions are often of an "all-out" type, such as those seen in childhood, and not regulated in intensity to fit the situation which precipitated the outburst. The behavior changes seen are moral offenses, quarreling, deterioration of personal habits, and poor direction of energy.

Exaggeration of the previous personality occurs. Aggressive persons may become overactive, quarrelsome, and irritable. The seclusive, suspicious individual might become paranoid, and the quiet, shy pessimist may become depressed.

There is decreased tolerance to toxic substances. Patients may have confused or delirious episodes on small doses of alcohol or sedative drugs. In many patients the initial symptoms are precipitated by some inter-current traumatic infection with fever.

Whenever encountered, this constellation of symptoms should suggest some organic disorder of the brain, and appropriate diagnostic study should be performed to determine the etiology. The neurologic evidence of central nervous system damage adds to the conviction that the patient suffers from an organic reaction.

One should not be led astray by either the presence or absence of gran-diose delusions, paranoid projections, or even hallucinatory phenomena. These symptoms are present in some organic cases and absent in others, probably depending upon the person's previous personality pattern and mode of adjustment.

In early organic reactions the sensorium disturbance may be mild, and it may take prolonged and detailed examinations to demonstrate it. In these cases, however, it is improper to state that the sensorium is clear in this organic state; rather, it is proper to say that the examinations of sensorium were not sufficiently detailed to demonstrate the mild changes present.

Organic reactions may be found in any age in life, beginning with birth injuries and terminating with the changes of senility. Of admissions to psychiatric hospitals, approximately 16 per cent are due to senile reactions; approximately 11 per cent due to psychosis with cerebral arterio-sclerosis, and the remainder due to trauma, disease of various types, and degenerating central nervous system conditions. At one time, 10 per cent of the admissions were due to general paresis, but with the advent of penicillin and its more intensive applications this is no longer true.

Chronic Brain Syndrome Associated with Congenital Cranial Anomaly, Congenital Spastic Paraplegia, Mongolism, Prenatal Maternal Infectious Disease, and Birth Trauma 009–0, 009–016, 009–071, 009–052, 009–050

The official classification manual suggests that persons suffering from organic brain changes due to these illnesses should be classified here. Cases of mental retardation, thought to be due to one of these conditions, might be in this category, but in our opinion such cases are more properly classified under the general heading of the mentally retarded which is in a subsequent chapter.

Chronic Brain Syndrome Associated with Central Nervous System Syphilis, Meningoencephalitic (General Paresis) (Parenchymatous Syphilis of the Nervous System) 009–147.0

In studying the various forms of syphilis of the nervous system the student should bear in mind that this is only one of the manifestations of a generalized systemic infection. Why the spirochetes invade the nervous system in some individuals and not in others is not clearly understood. In parenchymatous neurosyphilis it was known that patients improperly treated in the early stages of syphilis sometimes, after long latent periods, suddenly developed symptoms of extensive involvement of the central nervous system. The earlier editions of this book contain prolonged discussions of this latency period and the incubation period. In the seventh edition we pointed out that the use of intensive penicillin therapy had largely replaced all other forms of chemotherapy. At that time we mentioned that statistics were not available to show the effect of penicillin therapy on primary syphilis or on the incidence of neurosyphilis and the other forms of late syphilis. We now know that penicillin therapy of early syphilis has tremendously reduced the incidence of neurosyphilis, or, if it has not, the latent period certainly is more than the 12 years that have elapsed since penicillin came into rather general use for the treatment of primary syphilis.

At one time parenchymatous neurosyphilis made up approximately one-tenth of admissions to mental hospitals. Now it is a rarity in its acute manifestations. Parenchymatous neurosyphilis includes tabes dorsalis, primary atrophy of the optic nerve, and general paresis. It is not within the scope of this book to discuss the first two forms, but considerable space will be devoted to general paresis even though it is now rare. When it does occur, it is a serious mental disorder.

Symptoms. The primary symptoms of paresis are those seen in any organic psychosis: irritability, general slowing of all mental processes, errors in judgment, and capricious defects in memory. Minor behavior disorders and intellectual defects progress and, if unchecked, will become more severe until the patient becomes a "vegetable," displaying little awareness of or interest in events around him.

The physical and neurologic signs are nonspecific and consist of loss of weight, hypersomnia, increase in appetite, pains of a lancinating or stabbing character, gait disturbance, and pupillary irregularities and inequalities in about 70 per cent of cases, with Argyll Robertson pupils in about 40 per cent of these. There are generalized hyperreflexia and pathologic-thumb and -toe signs. The speech is usually slurred, and there is commonly a coarse tremor of the tongue and lips. Writing is frequently tremulous and in more advanced cases words are misspelled and entire phrases omitted.

Secondary Symptoms. The secondary symptoms are determined by the individual's previous personality and colored by his occupation, education, and past experience. The farmer plants, the preacher prays, and the physician discovers new and wonderful cures during the psychotic episode. The affable, aggressive, outgoing individual tends to become euphoric, elated, overactive, and given to many expansive ideas and delusions of great wealth, power, or spectacular talent. For example, one expansive patient proposed to give the physician a gunny sack of diamonds; another had a wife who he stated was more beautiful than any movie star. Another patient worked out a scheme by which he could become the greatest pitcher in baseball and the world's champion prize fighter, and perform all in one evening.

The suspicious, introverted individual becomes sullen, irritable, assaultive, and has many paranoid ideas during his paretic episode. The dour, sour pessimist will show all the signs, symptoms, and suicidal tendencies of a true depression or melancholia.

Paretics may be classified in various ways. Many texts use the Kraepelinian groupings, but it is our impression that these are based more on the secondary symptoms than the basic organic findings. In this textbook we have tried to classify paretics according to the severity of the involvement in the brain itself.

Group A, the most advanced deteriorative group, shows marked confusion, apathy, disinterest, and bewilderment, and is often described as "dirty and deteriorated."

Group B shows an organic psychosis but with less marked sensorium changes and with more pronounced secondary symptoms such as manic excitement, depressions, or paranoid reactions.

Group C consists of patients without marked signs of deterioration or marked signs of paretic manifestations. In these patients the confusion and intellectual changes are minimal and consist of transitory difficulties with retention and short periods of confusion. The patient is often irritable and expansive with mild psychotic symptoms. It is difficult to separate these patients from the typical meningovascular group, but they should be so separated because the involvement is more serious and they can easily progress to the Group B. The vascular phenomena seen in the meningovascular group do not occur in this group.

Pathology. Paresis is an organic brain disease always due to syphilis and marked by serologic findings, which are almost absolute in diagnostic value, by neurologic signs, which are reliable, and by mental findings, which, although often more or less characteristic of organic disorders, have certain distinguishing signs as mentioned above that make one suspect syphilis. It is a most malignant form of syphilis, and prior to the development of modern treatment methods the majority of patients died in 2 to 4 years. The development of paresis commonly comes many years after the primary infection. What circumstances or combination of physiologic functions permit the spirochete to remain dormant for so many years and then to become active in the brain remains unknown. Many cases develop the symptoms as long as 15 and 20 years from the time of well-authenticated primary infections, but others may progress in 1 to 5 years.

There are many theories discussed in the literature, such as "zone of minor resistance" or "neurotropic strains of spirochete," but they do not fully explain why the infection remains without causing symptoms and then progresses to serious pathology. The role of trauma in precipitating the symptoms has been discussed in scientific meetings and in compensation courts. It has been generally conceded that trauma, excessive alcoholism, or other agents which disturb the physiologic equilibrium of the central nervous system may precipitate paresis in a person suffering from asymptomatic neurosyphilis. The evidence upon which this belief is based is far from convincing. Similarity of the symptoms in paresis to those seen in some of the nutritional disturbances of the brain, advanced age, or excessive alcoholism also offers fertile fields for speculation. The role oxygen and carbohydrate metabolism may play in the disorder is unknown but tempts one to think of nutritional disorders and the avitaminosis states as possible priming agents that set off the paretic explosion. The influence of racial and climatic factors was discussed by Kraepelin, but this phase of the problem has been neglected and needs further study.

Serologic findings in paresis are constant. The blood-serology tests for syphilis are positive in about 90 per cent of untreated paretic patients. The Wassermann is positive in high dilutions. This is also true for the other serologic tests for syphilis. The colloidal-gold curve usually has a first zone rise, and the cell count is usually elevated to from 15 to 100 lymphocytes. The globulin reaction is in most instances positive and the total protein content increased. A history of previous antisyphilitic treatment of any type should make one depend less upon the laboratory findings.

Histopathology of the brain in patients who die of syphilis is typical. Grossly the meninges of the brain present a ground-glass appearance and often adhere to the skull, the brain cortex, and to each other. The brain is diminished in weight and usually shows atrophy, which is most marked over the frontal poles but which is also manifest by enlarged ventricles. The microscopic findings are those of any chronic encephalitic process. There is an infiltration of plasma cells and lymphocytes into the meninges and into the perivascular spaces. This perivascular accumulation of cells produces the well-known *perivascular cuffing* described in pathology textbooks. There is a marked increase in the number of small blood vessels, and they appear to run through the tissue in a disorderly pattern. Nerve cells are reduced in number, and the usual cortical layers may not be clearly defined. Many cells are seen in the process of destruction, partially degenerated nerve cells covered with glial cells, like currants on a cookie, are common, and the picture is described as neuronophagia or referred to as "coffin formation." These changes, plus the proliferation of glial cells and elongated microglia or rod cells scattered throughout the cortex, are classic findings in the brain of the paretic patient.

Spirochetes in the tissues of the frontal lobe have been demonstrated in untreated cases, but they are difficult to demonstrate and not essential to the diagnosis.

Treatment. The treatment of paresis is extensive and consists of intensive use of penicillin. A secondary functional change may be present after the organic pattern has responded. If the sensorium is clear, the use of shock therapy, drug therapy, and group psychotherapy is often of great value in these patients. The degree to which these patients recover usually depends on their classification in Group A, B, or C, but many of those in the B and C categories will improve sufficiently to return home. Those in the B group usually show some organic residuals, principally manifest as capricious memory and irritability, but most of them can resume productive work although often at a lower level in the socioeconomic brackets.

A typical case history in a paretic patient would be the man who was brought by his family with a complaint that he would be talking on a subject and forget what it was, that he would develop lapses in memory, that he would seem weak and tired yet could not sleep. The family noticed that he had been telling what they interpreted as lies or exaggerated stories. At other times they felt he was mixed up and "out of his head." Sometimes families complain that the patient has been showing poor judgment in managing his personal or business affairs. Patients often appear bewildered and depressed or overactive, depending on the previous personality pattern. Neurologic findings are usually those outlined in the earlier section. Mental-status examination shows the sensorium changes mentioned earlier and the affect phenomena of irritability and depression. The Wassermann reaction in both blood and spinal fluid is ordinarily positive with the supporting data in terms of cell-count, protein, and colloidal-gold changes. Because a student may not have an opportunity to see a paretic patient, a rather typical abstract of a case history will be described.

The patient, male, age 45, was brought to the hospital by his sister with the complaint, "He brags and talks and tells ungodly lies." The informant stated that the patient always was a rather expansive person and that the family noticed that during the last 20 years he bragged and exaggerated when intoxicated. During the past year they noticed that his bragging and lies increased tremendously and that they lately occurred almost any time, drunk or sober. They mentioned that for the past year he had outbursts of irritability and cited as an example the fact that about a year ago he beat up a neighbor's dog so severely that they had to pay a fine. While walking home from work one night, the patient wrote on store windows with red and yellow crayons and had no explanation as to why he had done so. Two months before admission he quit work without reason. Since then he spent most of his time telling the family stories of his travels to Arabia, South Africa, and other places where he had never been. He apparently had no ability to distinguish between fact and fantasy. He bragged about his ranches and oil wells, although he had none.

His admission to the hospital was precipitated by two events: First, he called the police and told them that there was an old woman in his house whom he had hit with a chair. They investigated and found this was untrue. Then, a few hours later, he was observed taking a neighbor's child down the street. He stopped and took off both his clothes and the child's clothes and then turned and walked away. This resulted in his apprehension and the police, recognizing his mental symptoms, brought him to the hospital. Further inquiry in the family revealed that his memory had become progressively poor. He was unable to play dominoes or cards with his usual skill. The sister thought that he always had an inferiority complex, until the present illness hit him. He showed no unusual habits and had never been in difficulties previously except for the above-mentioned episode about the dog. The family believed that this was a complete personality change and thought he must have been taking some type of drug to act this way. Past personal and family history contained no other information pertinent to the present illness.

Mental-status examination revealed that the patient was pleasant, cooperative, and confused, and had many expansive delusions of wealth, trips, and fabulous organizations he was forming. He had marked defects in recent memory and some disturbance in remote memory. He was oriented for place and person but disoriented as to time.

Neurologic examination revealed some incoordination in the left foot and leg and hyperactive tendon reflexes bilaterally equal in all four extremities. He had Argyll Robertson pupils and paralysis of the right soft palate. The remainder of the neurologic examination was within normal limits. Blood count and urine were within normal limits. The blood serology revealed a positive Wassermann in a 1:320 dilution, and a positive Kahn. The cerebral spinal fluid revealed a Wassermann positive in a dilution of 1:64, and a Lange of 5,553,210 with 30 white blood cells per cu mm, mostly lymphocytes, and 59 mg of protein. (This is high for that laboratory.)

The patient was treated with penicillin, 300,000 units intramuscularly twice a day to a total dose of 10,200,000 units. He improved under treatment, but even after the sensorium seemed relatively clear he remained expansive and overactive. He was given eight electric-shock treatments and during these treatments the expansive delusions subsided rapidly. He improved and was soon able to play skillfully at cards, and his judgment became adequate. He was discharged to his family 52 days after admission, in a good clinical remission. The family felt that he had entirely recovered his previous personality. Follow-up examination shows that he remains well.

JUVENILE PARESIS

This form of neurosyphilis is the most chronic, progressive type of neurosyphilis. It usually appears in infancy but may appear at any age up to the early twenties. The authors are reluctant to make a diagnosis in adults unless there are other signs of congenital syphilis such as malformed teeth and interstitial keratitis. Previously indiscreet young housewives or careless young men often convince the newly acquired spouse that their syphilis was congenitally acquired, when in most instances the "con" is a trimming and the "genitally" contains more of the truth.

William Menninger has written extensively on this form of neurosyphilis, but most authors neglect it. Some juvenile-paretic patients are intellectually retarded from birth, and the diagnosis is often made by the pediatrician or psychiatrist who examines the child because of the failure to show the proper intellectual development. In most instances a child may develop normally and show satisfactory progress in his school and social relations up to the age of 8 or 10 years. Parents then note a progressive dullness, and a loss of interest in play, possessions, etc. This may be accompanied by a slowing or arrest of physical development, convulsions, interstitial keratitis, or atrophy of the optic nerve. The diagnosis is based on the clinical findings plus the uniformly present paretic formula in the spinal fluid. Even the most energetic treatment is usually unsatisfactory because the malformations are present. Newer forms of treatment have been disappointing in the treatment of juvenile paresis.

Treatment of juvenile paresis is the same as that of general paresis and will be discussed in more detail in the section on therapy.

CHRONIC BRAIN SYNDROME ASSOCIATED WITH CENTRAL NERVOUS SYSTEM SYPHILIS (MENINGOVASCULAR) 004–147.0

This is numerically the most common and symptomatically the most heterogeneous form of neurosyphilis. Symptoms may consist of evidence of acute or chronic meningeal irritation plus various types of vascular phenomena that are commonly seen in vascular diseases. In general the symptoms are characterized by headaches, convulsive phenomena, aphasia, cranial nerve palsies of various types, mild defects in memory, and dulling of the intellectual processes. Hemiplegia is a common symptom and may be the initial complaint in the disorder. The hemiplegia often develops slowly as in thrombosis but in some cases is a transitory phenomenon. The general mental picture is like that of any organic mental disease with the addition of neurologic signs.

Of the untreated patients with early syphilis 10 to 15 per cent develop diffuse meningovascular neurosyphilis. The period between primary infection and the onset of meningovascular syphilis varies from 1 to 20 years, although the average patient develops his symptoms in 8 or 10 years after his initial lesion. The incidence of this form of neurosyphilis is greatly reduced by even inadequate treatment of early syphilis. Adequate treatment of early syphilis reduces the incidence of meningovascular syphilis to an insignificant figure. There is little evidence to date that inadequate treatment of the early phase of the infection significantly shortens the incubation period as it is thought to do in general paresis. Moore reported the difference of only 2 years in the untreated and treated group. The pathology varies with the extent and type of involvement. The vascular picture is predominantly one of endarteritis and the brain parenchyma may show areas of ischemia or softening. Hemorrhages are rare and usually small. The meningeal reaction results in adhesions and thickening; the serology in the blood is positive in about 65 per cent of the cases before treatment, and a smaller percentage if treatment has been started before the tests are made. The spinal fluid will be positive in approximately 90 per cent of untreated cases, but any treatment at all of the early syphilis will result in a smaller percentage of positive serology in the spinal fluid of patients with clinically manifest meningovascular syphilis. Each case must be considered individually with careful study of the history and findings in all the physical, neurologic, mental, and laboratory examinations.

Cerebral arteriosclerosis is a disorder which most often obscures the picture. It may be differentiated because meningovascular syphilis usually causes cortical irritation with signs of vascular inadequacy. Cerebral arteriosclerosis develops in a later age group, usually not before 50 or 60 years, but this differential may be misleading if patients contract syphilis late in life, or in younger individuals with a tendency to transitory vascular phenomena of the brain. A spinal-fluid examination and finding definite signs of retinal and generalized arteriosclerosis are the most reliable differential signs.

A typical case of this type of syphilis of the nervous system is the young married female brought to the hospital by her family with the complaint that her habits had changed. She was swearing, was vulgar, and had been running around with other men. Members of the family also stated that she had changed in appearance and manner during the past 5 or 6 months. At times her left arm seemed paralyzed. They reported that she had separated from her husband approximately 5 months before they brought her to the hospital and that her marked irritability was the reason. The family stated that the patient had a very unfortunate earlier life, coming from a broken home. In childhood she suffered from frequent colds but was otherwise well. She quit school in the ninth grade, and worked as a waitress, as a factory worker, and finally as a prostitute. She reputedly acquired syphilis from her first husband and had had numerous miscarriages. At the time of admission the patient was pleasant. While in the hospital she had a convulsion with a Jacksonian onset on the right side. Following this seizure, she had a flaccid paralysis of the left arm and leg. Mental confusion was more marked after the seizure. The patient was excreta-careless, exposed herself, and talked with slurred speech. She was irritable and demanding. The patient showed reflexes (on the left side of the body) typical of internal capsule involvement. The spinal fluid showed a positive serology. There was a paretic-type gold curve and an increased spinal-fluid protein. Because of the severity of the symptoms, the patient was first treated with chemotherapy, then with malaria, and finally continued on chemotherapy in the outpatient department. The symptoms cleared up, including the hemiplegia.

Treatment. Meningovascular neurosyphilis is treated much like paresis, except in the initial stages treatment is more conservative because early energetic treatment may precipitate vascular episodes.

Students should recognize that some forms of neurosyphilis produce no symptoms and are manifest only by positive spinal fluid serology and changes in cells, protein, and gold curve. There are also cases of syphilitic meningitis and cases showing purely vascular phenomena due to syphilis.

CHRONIC BRAIN SYNDROME ASSOCIATED WITH OTHER CENTRAL NERVOUS SYSTEM SYPHILIS 0y0–147.0

This classification is included in the manual to place those types of syphilis showing organic reactions other than the two above groups. Presumably this would include those cases of vascular syphilis with periods of confusion, aphasia, and unconsciousness after an acute vascular episode. This group would also include those cases of gumma of the brain that are reported in all textbooks on syphilis. The mental picture includes confusion, dullness, lethargy, and perhaps some irritability. One of us formerly did extensive research work in neurosyphilis, and during that period saw several cases with glioblastoma and other forms of brain tumor, in addition to neurosyphilis, but has yet to see a well-authenticated case of gumma of the brain.

Chronic Brain Syndrome Associated with Intoxication 009–300

Any chemical poison inhaled or ingested, if continued long enough, may produce symptoms. Most of these patients have a stage of acute toxic reaction as described in the reversible brain syndromes. Some of these patients do not recover, and the brain damage becomes permanent. Most common among these reactions are Korsakoff's psychosis, which often does not clear up. The hallucinosis reactions and the paranoid-type reactions described under the acute syndromes may become chronic and are properly classified in this section.

Perhaps the commonest reaction to be classified here is alcoholic deterioration. This is the common end reaction of all chronic alcoholics who do not recover from their alcoholism or who do not die of some accident or infection. After years of drinking, either continuously or episodically, and after several acute hallucinatory experiences or attacks of delirium tremens, the patient begins to develop a slow but definite change in personality. He becomes ill-humored, irascible, and begins to show deterioration in ethical sense, business judgment, and general moral code. A few individuals develop a rather mild euphoric good humor similar to that seen in many mental defectives and in some posttraumatic patients. They become unreliable, have a tendency to prevaricate, and often are paranoid toward members of their own family. They usually show deterioration in work ability, and persons who formerly held responsible positions become unemployable or have to take jobs of lesser responsibility. Memory and intelligence are usually somewhat impaired in these patients, intellectual changes being of the deteriorative type. Some of these patients become so advanced in their deterioration that their illness resembles a true organic reaction of the nervous system and is frequently dubbed "alcoholic pseudoparesis." The treatment of these patients is detoxification, correction of any physical disabilities noted, and the long, slow process of rehabilitation. Those rehabilitated will usually adjust at a lower level of occupation than they were capable of before the illness.

CHAPTER 10

Chronic Brain Disorders II

Chronic Brain Syndrome Associated with Brain Trauma 009–400

Changes in human behavior that follow traumatic head injuries are becoming more frequent in this mechanized age. The plane, the automobile, and modern mechanized warfare have greatly increased the incidence of traumatic injuries. The expanding industrialization of America has also brought to our clinics many problems incident to industrial accidents which involve injuries to the head. Every physician, whether general practitioner, specialist, or research worker, will be called upon to evaluate the extent of head injuries; usually the patients are involved in legal difficulty over compensation. Although there has been a considerable advance in the technical procedure of examining these patients and in determining the nature and extent of the injuries to the nervous system, there has been little alteration or advance in our fundamental attitude toward the person with head injury. The general attitude of the medical profession, the public, and the courts toward the injured person has remained essentially unchanged through the past several decades.

Traumatic cases are usually divided into three large groups and they have been rather clearly defined by Smith and Solomon. First, there is a large group where the stimulus is largely psychologic or "nerve shock" lesions of the central nervous system. This trauma causes the person to develop symptoms which are largely of a neurotic nature and "bespeak a neurotic personality." Second, there is a small group of patients who are led by treatment to think that they have been more severely and permanently injured than they actually have been. Third, there is an intermediate group.

These authors point out that 90 per cent of the defendants in suits involving so-called "traumatic personality" cases or traumatic neuroses are wealthy corporations. They state, "the purposeful mechanism of neurosis may operate on a subconscious level but the hope of being compensated thrives best when a stout corporation can be looked to as the party defendant." These authors feel that the courts are too lenient in awarding compensation.

Smith and Cobb have also written at some length on the traumatic nervous states. They also feel that in the absence of a definitely demonstrable injury to the nervous system, the development of symptoms in the case suggests predisposition in a particular person and that the symptoms would not have been developed in a person of average constitution.

A person is considered to be a truly traumatic case if the injury that he sustains and the symptoms he shows are those that might be expected in a person of average constitution, no provision being made for the individual's own idiosyncrasies or vulnerability to the development of symptoms subsequent to the trauma. On the other hand, those persons who have been injured severely enough to produce organic changes in the central nervous system that are demonstrable are considered to be the proper candidates for compensation. Methods of determining the degree and extent of this injury will be discussed later.

There are many objections to the present attitude of the courts and the bulk of the medical profession to traumatic problems. Many studies indicate that persons receiving organic injuries to the nervous system or other body segments are "accident habit" or "accident prone," and the injury is due to some neurotic predisposition or to the inadequacy which caused the accident. It is difficult for us to see why a person who receives a severe head injury as a result of his own awkwardness or impulsive act or latent suicidal trend should be compensated any more than the person who, because of somewhat similar trends, receives only a slight injury or none at all but claims compensation and readjustment from the company nonetheless.

From a practical point of view the difference is obvious because anyone could then become compensable, but from an idealistic point of view both individuals have been injured, although the sphere of injury is different, and both have been injured at least partially due to their own actions, through awkwardness, being in the wrong place at the wrong time, or some neurotic tendency. Compensation in either type of case tends to aggravate the symptoms and tends to increase the patient's dependency reaction. Perhaps when our "utopian" period begins, all persons, whether injured in an industrial accident or ill from disease, will be given minimum care by the State. The patient will be provided with treatment by the State, but he will receive no cash compensation, and no distinction will be drawn between persons injured in government service, in industrial accidents, or injured or ill due to their own activities while working for themselves. This will obviate the necessity for hearings to determine responsibility. We know the above statement contains many far-reaching political and economic conclusions and is not practical for achievement in this day and time.

PSYCHOPATHOLOGY

Pathogenesis of Posttraumatic States. There is much work being done on the nature of the changes in the brain in cerebral concussion and the nature of posttraumatic neurosis. Smith and Cobb have written extensively on the so-called "nervous changes" following head trauma and they discuss fully the concept of nervous shock. They find that most cases of nervous shock are not related to the injury per se but are merely the effects of the injury on a person of previous inadequate or vulnerable constitution. They stress the importance of further studies on the effect emotions may have on structure and structure may have on emotions or the so-called "psychosomatic approach" to these problems.

Denny-Brown and his coworkers have reported rather extensively on work in experimental cerebral concussion. They found that in certain cases the injury becomes more severe if the head moves with the impact of the injury. They have studied the effects of concussion and other mild cerebral injuries rather extensively. For example, the rise of intracranial pressure is not an essential feature of concussion, at least, in so-called "acceleration concussion." They find that the symptoms of acceleration concussion are due to failure in the blood pressure. It may arise from failure of the vasomotor center during the paralytic phase of severe injuries. The failure of recovery arises from the effect on the vasomotor mechanism induced during primary shock. Death from vasomotor paralysis may occur as a delayed effect after recovery. The vasomotor paralysis of concussion is immediate whether it is associated with experimentally increased blood flow through the brain stem or not. There is no evidence of vascular spasm of the brain during or resulting from acceleration concussion. Contusion in the cerebral hemispheres has no effect on the bulbar centers unless a great increase of intracranial pressure is developed as a result of hemorrhages into the bruised area. This effect is delayed in onset and reaches a maximum in from 1 to 4 minutes after the injury.

Lindquist and LeRoy also made studies on the pathogenesis of cerebral concussions. In experimental animals they have found that immediately after concussion there is a decrease of 17 per cent in cerebral blood flow and of 24 per cent in cerebral oxygen consumption. In 24 hours there is a decrease of 19 per cent in cerebral blood flow and 21 per cent in cerebral oxygen consumption. They have found that 50 per cent sucrose or glucose increases the oxygen use from 45 to 100 per cent in the case of sucrose and from 90 to 130 per cent in the case of glucose. They found that cisternal drainage also improves the blood flow and oxygen utilization in the acute phases. Their work indicates that the symptoms from posttraumatic states are due to prolonged anoxia and decrease in the cortical metabolism.

Traumatic states in the acute phases almost all show electroencephalographic abnormalities. This has usually been assumed to be due to increased intracranial pressure, but Stewart, in 1941, showed that it was not the cerebral edema but internal hydrocephalus that produced the slow waves. This work has neither been confirmed nor refuted, so far as we know, but it was carefully done and may be assumed to be accurate. There is one observation in this paper, however, that we cannot accept. Stewart suggested that slow waves are the resting rhythm of the anterior portions of the brain. It is not clear from his work upon what facts he bases this statement, and it is certainly not confirmed by the work of other authors in this field.

Research on the pathogenesis of head trauma is now being financed by the Office of Scientific Research and Development. According to verbal reports emanating from this work, the best method of determining the nature and extent of brain injury still remains the case history, which includes facts on the duration of the period of unconsciousness following the injury. The nature and severity of the posttraumatic changes seem to be more nearly in proportion to this than to any other one item in the examination of these cases.

Some workers in Boston found that with patients where compensation is involved there is a much higher incidence of posttraumatic headaches and the patients take a much longer time to recover from head trauma than those who have no hope of compensation. This study was very carefully done and confirms the idea of many authors that most so-called posttraumatic states are actually functional conditions superimposed on severe or minor organic damage and motivated by the desire for personal gain.

Pathogenesis of Posttraumatic Neurosis. This was alluded to somewhat briefly in one of the earlier chapters. We believe that individuals adjust to life situations in terms of their own basic potentialities as determined by their constitution, education, previous experience, and ego strength. Many individuals meeting severe situations in the environment of a more purely psychologic sort find themselves unable to adjust. Other persons meeting equally severe situations, but of an organic sort, also find themselves unable to adjust.

Thus, one comes back to the old I plus S formation. An individual confronted with a situation in his environment will adjust or not, depending on his total potentialities in terms of his constitution, heredity, previous experience, and degree of integration. Meeting a certain situation in the environment, which may be psychologic or may involve organic trauma or disease, he will react with adjustment or maladjustment, depending on whether his potentialities are sufficient to handle the environmental situation. Thus, a person of great potentiality may handle situations which would be overwhelming to a brother made of lesser stuff.

Posttraumatic neuroses are only special instances of this general psychopathologic equation. An individual of high potentialities sustaining some minor head injury may suffer the usual symptoms from it but adjust to it and carry on his work without handicap or without taking particular notice of his symptoms, his reserve being sufficiently great to compensate for any shortcomings that may have been brought about by the trauma. A person of lesser endowment meeting the same situation may fail to adjust to it because he does not have enough reserve to compensate for the minor and usually temporary changes in function incident to the trauma itself. This applies, of course, in great measure to the person who has had an organic injury from his trauma. If he is originally a person of superior potentiality, he compensates readily for organic injury unless it is very extensive, while the person of lesser potentiality cannot adjust to loss of function in an organic sense as well as can his better-endowed brother. If one adds the factor of compensation, which makes these difficult situations gainful, there is a tendency to prolong the symptoms.

Symptoms of a posttraumatic neurosis vary considerably. The chief symptoms, however, are recurrence and persistence of headaches, backaches, and pains in the neck and other body segments. These are usually accompanied by more or less transitory attacks of dizziness. These attacks of dizziness may vary from a few seconds to many weeks in duration, depending upon the patient. There also frequently is complaint of great fatigability, particularly associated with any type of constructive effort such as work, running to catch a bus, or anything that is not pleasure producing. Many of these patients who complain of great fatigue on reaching down to pick up something or upon running up steps report that they can have sexual intercourse without any difficulty, although in some instances this must require effort on their part. We have found this to be a rather valuable differential point, but the two factors must be determined at different levels of history taking. Patients also complain of various other pains and symptoms such as aches, indigestion, belching, gas on the stomach, blurring of vision, impotence, roaring in the ears, and many other symptoms, many of which may be suggested by the physician during the examination if the questioning is not done skillfully. We have found it best not to ask the patient leading questions but merely to request him to describe his symptoms and to give him ample opportunity to do so. Perhaps the outstanding feature of all these symptoms in the posttraumatic neurosis is the fact that they all become greatly exaggerated and aggravated when a patient attempts to do any type of work, and yet they are intermittent and do not bother the patient when he is pursuing his own desires and amusements.

SYMPTOMATOLOGY

Workers on this subject divide the cases into three large groups: (1) Those in which the symptoms are predominantly organic and due to injury to the brain, (2) those which are mixed with some organic damage to the brain but the organic lesion is aggravated by neurotic or other personality-determined factors, and (3) those in which the symptoms are predominantly functional. The functional group may be subdivided into (a) cases involving posttraumatic neurosis, and (b) so-called "malingerers."

Examples of Direct Injury. Under this first category come patients who have had a severe concussion, contusion, or laceration of the brain with symptoms that are predominantly organic in origin. In practically all these cases there will be a history of prolonged unconsciousness with amnesia for the entire period. The symptoms are colored heavily by the patient's previous personality, but they all contain the configuration of symptoms common to all organic impairment of brain function.

A typical case is a male who became irritable, paranoid, and fearful following an auto accident in which he was injured severely and was unconscious for 24 hours and stuporous for 2 weeks. The mental symptoms developed over a period of 5 months. He became careless of his appearance, took long trips in his car, had periods of amnesia, and seemed bewildered.

Examination revealed signs of a subdural hematoma which was successfully evacuated. Following this, he was less confused and no longer had amnesic periods, but he remained paranoid, irritable, and difficult until his death several years later. Death was due to cardiovascular disorder.

Posttraumatic Personality Change. This second group is a mixed type in which the patient has received some definite brain injury with history of a period of unconsciousness of varying length but of sufficient duration to make one certain that there has been some injury to the brain. In these cases there is also demonstrable evidence of some organic brain pathology. In addition to the organic symptoms, there are signs of personality change often manifest by irritability, weakness, headache, and insomnia. Many of these patients, as a result of repeated examinations and trips to various consultants' offices, develop a marked elaboration of their symptoms. A person who may be having posttraumatic convulsions or perhaps occasional posttraumatic headaches may become a weak, chronic invalid, have a marked effort syndrome, and be completely unable to carry on with ordinary activity even though there is nothing in the residuals of his injury to account for this tremendous incapacity. A case of this particular type is as follows:

A patient claiming an injury was referred for a neuropsychiatric evaluation. The physicians previously managing the case had submitted different opinions. The patient had in the meantime retained a lawyer and was contemplating bringing suit against the company for a fantastic sum of money. The patient was employed in a small hospital. In the course of her duties she had been attacked by an alcoholic patient who had struck her with a bottle. In attempting to avoid this blow, the patient slipped on a polished floor and struck her head. She states that she was unconscious for only a few moments, but when she came to, she noticed that there was a little blood on the floor and that her glasses were broken. Apparently, she was not fully conscious at this time because it was not until the relief nurse came on and pointed out to her that her uniform was bloody that she discovered that she had a cut on the forehead. After resting a while she awakened and found that she had a very severe headache. She then contacted her employer who referred her to a doctor who worked in that hospital.

The doctor, after a very superficial examination, drew the wound together with adhesive tape and advised cold compresses. The patient carried out this treatment with very little relief, and as a result the wound healed with considerable disfiguring scar formation. She also noticed numbness over the frontal area. Between the numbness and the disfigurement, the patient's attention became focused on this part of her anatomy. She then began to develop severe headaches and dizzy spells. The patient consulted a physician on her own initiative who informed her that a small nerve running to that part of the scalp had been involved either in the cut or in the scar that subsequently formed. He also gave her some deep x-ray therapy to reduce the scar formation. The patient was then referred to another physician who advised an operation to relieve the puckering and to relieve the pressure on the small nerve that was thought to be involved in the scar. Throughout all this the patient was unable to get any satisfactory response from her employer or from the insurance company because the first physician on examining her had assured her that it did not amount to anything and was not serious. The insurance company, going on this basis, apparently assumed that the patient was malingering. The employer apparently took a similar attitude, and the patient was not allowed to return to work. As a result of this, she became very hostile and resentful because she was losing time from her work, her doctor bills were mounting, and she was obtaining no satisfaction and little relief.

The patient was referred to us and seemed to be a very reasonable person. She was cooperative through our whole examination. The examination revealed that she had received a definite injury to the supraorbital nerve. She had a scar approximately 5 cm. in length over her forehead which presented some aspects of disfiguration. A careful check revealed that there had been some damage to the underlying brain tissue, as manifest by the electroencephalogram and clinical studies. Our recommendations, therefore, outlined the difficulty and advised a lump-sum settlement with the patient to compensate for the expense of her care and the time lost from work. The patient agreed to accept this.

The above case is presented because we feel that if this patient had been properly handled at the onset, with proper suturing of the wound and good care for her concussion, and if her employer had allowed her to return to work, the total sum of the settlement would have been much less; the patient's attitude toward the physician, the insurance company, and her employers would have been much better; and a great deal of difficulty could have been avoided by all. The patient's desire to get something or "make them pay" came from her feeling that she was mishandled and neglected, an opinion which we shared.

A similar case was that of a Negro man who received a head injury while at work:

It is interesting that this man had had a series of injuries, and that the present one was obviously from his negligence, or, perhaps, the negligence of his foreman, who allowed him to attach some equipment to a building in an unsafe manner. The result was that the equipment came undone and hit him on the head. The patient received a concussion which was followed by a period of confusion and then irritability, headaches, and weakness after exertion. At the end of the usual 60- to 90-day period, the patient was eager to return to work, but not to the heavy work he had done. His former employer offered him light work, but the pay was accordingly light. The patient bitterly resented this, feeling that he should have been allowed to work during his convalescence and that he should have been paid a more equitable salary. The employer informed him that if he was going to get heavy pay he would have to do heavy work. The patient, accordingly, did not go back. He spent another 90 days drawing compensation from the insurance company because he was unable to return to his original job. At the end of the second 90-day period, the patient was extremely resentful when told that he was completely well and could do any type of work. He expressed great doubt about his ability to do so.

We do not believe that this man will ever entirely recover from the sequela of his accident. The headaches have carried over from an organic phase into a type of behavior reaction as an expression of his resentment toward the employer and toward the insurance company. It is believed that a more tolerant attitude toward the patient when he first returned to work would have saved at least 90 days of compensation and perhaps many years of resentment and symptoms.

Predominantly Functional Symptoms. The third group is one in which the symptoms are predominantly functional. In these cases there may have been some trivial head injury of an organic nature or no organic injury at all. The injury, if any, clears up and the patient's residual symptoms are completely functional.

Posttraumatic Neurosis. In these patients the neurotic symptoms follow the general pattern of the ordinary neurosis. Most of the cases show evidence of anxiety psychoneurosis, although in some instances there are full-blown hysterical reactions. Other than the history of trauma and the fact that a large part of the gain of hysteria is to be found in the desire for cash compensation and the wish to hit back at the offending company, these cases show little to distinguish them from other types of neurotic reaction. The statement made by some authors that these patients respond miraculously after receiving compensation has not been true in our experience, and one suspects that such cases belong in a subgroup commonly called malingering. The following case is an example of a posttraumatic psychoneurosis:

A patient was referred to the clinic by his insurance company and also by his private physician, whom he had consulted, both suggesting the name of the particular clinic in which he was examined.

According to the patient, he was very "nervous" and had convulsions. According to the informant, the patient had been a chronic invalid since an injury which occurred in June, 1944, approximately 2 years before his examination by the senior author. In June, 1944, the patient is said to have suffered an electric shock from a 12,000-volt current while working for a large utilities company. According to the patient, the current entered one hand and went out the other, leaving both burned to a slight extent. He states he was knocked down, struck his head, and was unconscious. He was able to return to work in a few days as a lineman, but immediately after the accident he began to experience a constant, poorly localized, dull aching pain in the back of his neck and head. He was extremely tense and irritable, had much difficulty in sleeping at night, and had a definite decrease in his appetite. These complaints became much worse when some situational incident occurred which upset or irritated him. His episodes of tenseness lasted from a few days to a week, and then he seemed better from a few days to a week or so.

It was not until about 3 months after the initial accident that the patient's wife became aware that anything was wrong. At that time he returned home from work during a period when she was ill in bed. On this particular day he came to her room, sat on her bed, and spontaneously began to cry. When asked why he cried, he merely stated that he was somewhat upset because none of the family or friends had come to see his wife during her illness. A few days later (early November, 1944), while he was on the job, he complained of marked dizziness right after he had climbed a pole. He immediately descended, complained bitterly of his head swimming, and is said to have lost consciousness and to have remained in that state for 2 days. During his periods of supposed unconsciousness he had almost continuous writhing and jerking movements of all extremities and at times required restraint. At the end of 1 week he was discharged from the hospital and had no further episodes of syncope until March, 1945. In this interval he was able to work. He seemed to get along fairly well except for the previously discussed episodes of restlessness and irritability which lasted from a few days to a week. Between these periods he seemed much better but "never got back to his former self." At this time he was receiving liver and iron shots from a local physician in order to "build him up." In March, 1945, he had a similar apparent syncope and is said to have been unconsious for 12 hours and hospitalized for 1 week. He did not return to work for 1 month and when he did go back, could not continue to climb poles. He seemed slightly improved to the informant and his periodic spells of tension and restlessness were somewhat less. His headaches at times seemed much better also.

In the latter part of August, 1945, the patient again began to climb poles, and in less than a week the informant noticed that he was much more tense and irritable, and that his insomnia and loss of appetite became more severe. On October 11, 1945, while attempting to raise a line, the patient was pulling on a rope attached to a block and tackle. The pulley broke and the patient fell backward and struck his head on the ground. The informant states he was again rendered unconscious for a period of about 24 hours but was hospitalized for only 6 hours and then sent home. He again experienced writhing and jerking movements of all extremities during this "coma." After a week's time he was able to be up and about the house, but his headaches were much worse and were present constantly. The insomnia again became severe, his tenseness and restlessness more marked, and at times he seemed unable to sit still at all. Since this episode he has been unable to work and the condition has run a fluctuating course.

On December 1, 1945, the patient was told that he should go back to work, but when he went to the company, he learned that all that was available was a job as night watchman at $0.75 an hour, whereas formerly he had made $1.25 an hour. He left the office and met his wife at their car a few minutes later. When she saw him he seemed quite tense, his hands were shaking, and she states that he seemed to be in a "nervous jerk." They went to the office of a chiropractor who had been treating the patient for some months for a supposed "dislocation of the neck and edema around the base of the brain." There had been no diminution in sexual desire or ability. During none of the periods of unconsciousness and jerking movements had the patient been incontinent or bitten his tongue.

The information received from the patient's fellow workers, as supplied by the insurance company, revealed that none of these injuries was quite as dramatic or severe as the patient had suggested in his history. Apparently he did fall but was not severely injured, and apparently the burns he sustained were very superficial ones. The episode occurring on the pole, according to the eyewitness description, was merely a slipping with his catching himself on the safety belt of the man working immediately below him. The patient had been unable to work at his occupation as a lineman since the last injury, and he had some difficulty with the insurance company over compensation. He had been getting about $20 per week as compensation, although his earnings prior to injury were about $250 per month. He stated that at one time he offered to settle with the insurance company for $6,000 but they offered him only $100. This was unsatisfactory and he continued on compensation.

Our detailed examination of the patient revealed no evidence of anything in the way of organic neurologic disturbance. He was physically quite sound.

The neurologic status was as follows: the cranial nerves were intact. In sensory status there was a moderate diminution of pain perception, glovelike in distribution, in both arms below the level of the elbow. A similar defect was found in both legs below the level of the knees. The position sense was intact, and the touch perception was normal. There was an area on the forehead extending from the eyebrows posteriorly to the vertex and laterally to the ears and malar eminence in which the patient was completely unable to perceive vibratory stimuli. Vibration was normally perceived in the area of the occiput, the mandible, and the maxillary area, as well as on the extremities. In the motor system there was no weakness in any muscle group of any extremity. There was no atrophy or abnormality of tone and the finger-nose and knee-heel tests were performed without difficulty. No tremor was noted unless the patient was in the upright position, and skilled movements were well done. When standing, there was a gross, rhythmical tremor of both hands which consisted of a rapid, slight, alternate pronation and supination of each hand. Deep reflexes—biceps, right plus 1, left plus 1; radial, right plus 1, left plus 1; knee jerks, right plus 2, left plus 2; ankle jerks, right plus 1 (reinforced), left plus 1 (reinforced).

The corneal and abdominal reflexes were bilaterally present. Hoffmann, Babinski, Chaddock, and Oppenheim reflexes were bilaterally negative. Kernig and Brudzinski signs were negative. The Romberg test elicited a marked swaying movement principally from the waist up, but at no time did the patient fall. The gait was somewhat wide based and shuffling and the hands were held rather stiffly at the side, and at this time the previously discussed tremor of the upper extremities was marked. The patient was observed walking down the hall when he did not know he was being examined, and his gait was entirely normal.

A Rorschach test revealed the patient to be rather tense, neurotic, and of no better than average intelligence. It showed no evidence of organic disease of the brain. The Minnesota Multiphasic test also confirmed our opinion that there were many neurotic changes present and showed no evidence of an organic reaction. The nature of these reports was explained to the patient, and he was allowed to read the letter to the insurance company which set forth the recommendation that the patient get his difficulties with the insurance company straightened out; that if there was any further compensation due him, it be paid at once; and that he be permitted to return to work. Both the patient and the insurance company apparently agreed to accept these terms. At least to date we have not been summoned into court for further testimony concerning the patient's difficulty.

Malingering. The question of malingering often produces a great deal of argument in compensation cases and other types of traumatic reactions. Detailed examination of malingering patients usually reveals that they have for many years been unable to adjust to ordinary life situations, and a great many of them fall within the group commonly dubbed the "constitutional psychopaths" or "sociopaths." While it is true that such persons do not deserve compensation, in a broad psychiatric sense they are ill to the same extent as the neurotic or the organically injured person. It is merely that the company or party involved in the compensation suit is in no manner responsible for the patient's difficulty. These persons should not be considered traumatic cases in the ordinary sense of the word but are rather persons whose inadequacy is manifesting itself by attempting to be dishonest and obtain money under false pretenses from an insurance company or corporation or some individual whom they accuse of wronging them. These cases should be properly diagnosed and considered in terms of the material contained in the chapter on personality disorders. All the theoretical aspects and all the symptoms and signs contained in that chapter apply equally well to patients who are attempting to receive compensation, pretending to be injured. The neophyte is warned to study these patients very carefully and not to confuse patients with a hysteric neurosis or an anxiety state following trauma with patients who are being dishonest to obtain compensation.

METHODS OF EXAMINATION

Very detailed examination is always required in handling any type of traumatic or insurance case. The successful handling of traumatic patients, particularly where compensation is involved, begins the moment that one is first introduced to the patient. In general, traumatic cases will be seen under the following circumstances by the neuropsychiatrist. In the first circumstance the patients themselves or their representatives ask the psychiatrist to examine them to determine the extent of injury, with the view of obtaining treatment, and in many cases with the view of establishing a claim for compensation. In the second circumstance the insurance company has asked the patient to report to the physician for an examination and consultation to determine the nature and extent of the injury and the appropriate treatment. The physician's attitude toward the patient should be the same in both instances, and it should of course be the same toward the referring agent. The physician should assume, which is usually the case, that both the individual and the insurance company want a true evaluation of whether any injury has been sustained, its nature and extent, and what may be done to improve the condition. One should not approach the patient in terms of trying to find out something to keep him from getting compensation. When the physician is hired by the patient himself, the patient usually assumes this to be his attitude. When, however, the consultant is called by the insurance company, it is sometimes necessary to explain to the patient the consultant's status in the case before any successful rapport can be established with the patient. It is our policy to tell the patient frankly that the insurance company has asked us to examine him; that the companies sometimes do ask us to examine patients in an effort to determine honestly the nature and extent of their injuries; and, if there has been no injury, what might be causing the patient's present symptoms. Most patients accept this. If the interview is properly handled, one can usually win the patient's cooperation and appreciation of the unbiased point of view.

The first step in obtaining a fair evaluation of any traumatic case is to get a history. One should be especially careful to obtain the patient's account of the time of the injury, the exact circumstances in which the injury was sustained, whether he was unconscious or merely dazed by the injury, and how long either state persisted. He should be quizzed carefully as to what things he recalled when he first began to come to. He should then give a detailed recital of the evolution of his symptoms since the injury. These particular items are extremely important in getting a history in compensation cases. One should also obtain in great detail the history of any previous injuries and previous contacts with compensation commissions or courts. The rest of the history should be the same as that obtained from any other patient but should be in great detail. Careful records of these histories should be kept and, where possible, the patient's account should be made verbatim. One of us has found it useful to use a recording device for getting the patient's history in exactly his own terms. In addition to the patient's history, it is extremely important to get his family's version of the symptoms and the change in the patient since the injury. This should be obtained from as many members of the family as possible, and preferably one should interview the members individually, because their stories will sometimes conflict if they are interviewed separately. A copy of the record of the patient's care in the emergency station or the emergency room should be studied with particular attention to the duration of unconsciousness, the depth of unconsciousness, the presence or absence of convulsions, the condition of the spinal fluid, and external injuries.

Another important factor in evaluating the nature and extent of the patient's injury is the so-called "eyewitness accounts" to the accident. It is usually possible in industrial cases to obtain this material from the foreman or supervisor and from fellow workers. In most cases the company physician or safety supervisor of the company will have this information, and they are usually cooperative about submitting a copy of it to the physician. One frequently finds marked variations between the fellow workers' description of the accident and the duration of the unconsciousness as compared to that of the patient's version. These items are of great importance in evaluating the symptoms. The history of any traumatic case should carefully survey the patient's record of adjustment prior to his injury. The two items that are particularly pertinent in distinguishing a person who is well adjusted in his occupation from one who is not are the patient's previous work records, including changes of occupation, and his marital history. A large number of these patients will give a history of very poor adjustment to occupation and to marriage, with nomadism from job to job and wife to wife. There is also an amazing record of previous injuries in many of these cases. The incidence of previous injuries has been rather extensively reported in the literature. A small percentage of workmen have most of the accidents.

After obtaining the history, the next step in the evaluation of one of these patients is a very detailed physical and neurologic examination. Patients are resentful if they are not examined carefully and the physician gives an opinion without fully evaluating all the factors in their case. If the physician's examination is skillfully performed and done in great detail the patient begins to develop considerable respect for the physician, believes that the physician is genuinely interested in his welfare, and is more apt to follow the physician's recommendation.

At the conclusion of these preliminary examinations the patient should have a number of complementary examinations, most of which involve laboratory procedures. It is our policy to carry out these procedures irrespective of what our clinical findings may have been, for the simple reason that it makes the patient feel that our investigation has been thorough and our interest in him genuine, even though our clinical findings may have been completely normal so far as somatic pathology is concerned. In cases of head injury laboratory studies such as blood, urine, and Wassermann examinations are made. In addition, all such cases should have spinal puncture performed, unless this was already done in the emergency room and reported as normal, and all cases should have blood-chemistry studies, both sugar and N.P.N. (nonprotein nitrogen) performed. The accumulation of nitrogen metabolites or a low blood-sugar level may produce symptoms that are frequently associated with so-called posttraumatic reactions. Skull x-rays are in general noninformative, so far as any injury to the brain is concerned, but the concepts of the lay public, the attorneys, courts, and judges are such that any patient who is claiming a head injury who has not had a skull x-ray is not considered to have been adequately examined. Many patients informed that the x-ray of their head is entirely normal conclude that the brain is not injured, which is a help in the neurotic patient. It is our policy, therefore, to order skull plates routinely in all patients for their own satisfaction even though they contribute little information about brain injury. If there is evidence of a space-occupying lesion or loss of cortical tissue, we recommend that the patient have a ventriculogram, arteriogram, or pneumoencephalogram, as indicated. It is our policy in all head injuries to have an electroencephalogram made starting with the standard 6-lead test. If any pathology is detected in this test, the patient is then given a multilead test, in most instances a 16-lead one, to determine whether there is any localization present. The use of the electroencephalogram in posttraumatic cases is helpful in many cases, but confusing in some as the exact meaning of the presence or absence of abnormal findings is still open to debate.

Williams studied the electroencephalogram in head-injury cases in both acute and chronic conditions. He found that the electroencephalographic changes usually parallel the clinical progress of the case and the electroencephalogram is of value in determining the presence of injury and in following the course of the patient's clinical improvement. He reports that when the clinical course and the electroencephalographic changes parallel one another, recovery is the general rule, but when the electroencephalograph shows recovery and the clinical symptoms persist, the patient's symptoms tend to become chronic. Most of the posttraumatic cases have some type of focal abnormality in the electroencephalogram rather than the diffuse abnormality seen in convulsive patients or patients with so-called "normal abnormalities."

Jasper and Penfield found that 90 per cent of posttraumatic epileptic patients show some type of focal epileptic discharge. The waves are a combination of small slow waves with random spike and sharp waves.

They report that complete excision of the focal area in their cases brought about recovery in most instances. If the slow waves persisted after the operation, it was considered to be a bad prognostic sign.

At present one may state that when the electroencephalographic tracings show evidence of abnormalities, particularly of a focal type, in a patient who has a history of a definite head injury, this is evidence in support of the patient's claim of injury. If, on the other hand, the history and clinical findings do not closely correlate with the electroencephalogram in either direction, the electroencephalographic tracings become less significant. If the patient gives a history of minor trauma and the electroencephalographic tracing is normal, we in general interpret this as being further evidence that the patient has not had a severe cortical injury. More detailed work is necessary in the use of the electroencephalogram and its correlation with clinical states in the traumatic reactions. At present, it offers a valuable complementary examination, and in most instances yields far more information than such standard procedures as skull x-ray or spinal-fluid examination.

Psychologic tests in skilled hands also give aid in determining whether the patient has received an injury. Probably the outstanding test among these is the Rorschach test. Russel, Grassi, and Melenkier report a series of military cases studied for posttraumatic changes by the Rorschach method. The Rorschach test distinguishes easily between predominantly functional and predominantly organic reactions. In posttraumatic cases a predominantly organic configuration is usually assumed to be due to the trauma, if paresis, arteriosclerosis, and tumor are ruled out. The test is also valuable in separating the malingerer, the posttraumatic neurotic case, and the posttraumatic organic case from each other. I wish to emphasize that this test is valuable in the hands of a skilled operator. The neophyte or amateur in the Rorschach method is not competent to perceive these differentials, and such persons will only confuse rather than clarify the issue.

Another series of tests that is becoming of increasing importance in detecting evidences of brain trauma is the so-called Halstead test. This is a series of rather complex test situations in which the patient's ability to organize things into categories is measured. It is probably the most sensitive test for detecting minor organic changes in cortical function. Unfortunately, the test as presently constituted also requires a skilled operator and a special machine.

It is our practice, when we obtain the evidence from the above methods, to bring the material together in a brief formulation which is then presented to the patient. If we find the patient is suffering from organic damage, he is told so, and we tell him almost verbatim what our brief letter report to the insurance company will be. It is also our policy to send a copy of the clinical records substantiating our opinion to the insurance company. We obtain the patient's permission to do this, and in almost all instances this is granted. In the event that we find the patient is suffering from a posttraumatic functional disturbance, this is also explained to the patient. We are careful in explaining the symptoms to the patient. We state that we realize he really has symptoms, but that their cause is not from the trauma itself but rather from his reaction to the traumatic situation. The symptoms are then explained to him in terms of anxiety and autonomic phenomena or in terms of hysteric conversion phenomena, depending upon the reaction type. The importance of understanding the nature of his symptoms so that he may be rid of them and go back to work is stressed. Nothing belittling is said, and the material is presented to the patient in a manner which makes it easy for him to accept a functional diagnosis. We usually tell him he is fortunate to have a functional disturbance from which he can entirely recover rather than organic damage to the brain which is irreversible.

If the patient is pretending to be injured for some gain to himself, he is informed that we find no evidence of injury and that we believe he is exaggerating whatever symptoms he may have. Many of these patients accept their detection without too much resentment. Some become very indignant. A number of these patients drop the claim after having been examined and told that the report to the insurance company will be that they are not entitled to compensation.

During this formulation to the patient the physician's attitude should be that of an explanation, on the assumption that the patient really wants to know the facts. The physician should not be on the defensive about his findings. Nor should the patient be given any reason to have to defend his symptoms. If the physician attacks the patient's symptoms in an aggressive manner, the patient will often be irritated and feel it necessary to defend his various complaints and symptoms in order to keep from considering himself dishonest. The patient often imitates the physician's attitude of attempting to understand the nature of the illness, and in most instances will cooperate.

Patients who have organic handicaps as a result of their injury should be given a very frank evaluation of them and what they will mean in terms of future usefulness. It is important that the physician consider not only what the patient's injuries have been but also what his remaining capacities, potentialities, and abilities are and what ways there are in which the patient can use them. For example, a patient who loses an extremity can often be put to work in the same factory doing a job which does not require two extremities.

In the case of a severe head injury, it is sometimes more difficult to find duties to which a patient can adapt himself. Posttraumatic convulsions can be controlled in most instances by medication and, where focal abnormalities are detected, they may be relieved by operation. These patients should be placed on jobs where it makes no difference if they have an occasional seizure. We have placed many of these people in industries where they work faithfully. Patients who show symptoms of recurring headaches, dizziness, and forgetfulness are more difficult to manage, and they usually have to be placed at occupations of greatly reduced responsibility. Many patients with severe posttraumatic symptoms cannot work for long periods in the sun nor can they do heavy work. On the other hand, they frequently can do such things as cleaning up, janitor work, or clerking in a storeroom. Their irritability is a problem in their adjustment to their fellow employees, but they do much better if employed than if they are dependent on compensation allotments from the insurance company.

No mention has been made of the care of head injuries during the immediate posttraumatic period because this is a problem for surgeons and neurosurgeons, and the psychiatrist or neurologist is called in to see the patient late in the course of his illness to determine the nature and extent of the previous injury. None of the authors of this book do emergency work and they therefore do not consider themselves competent to describe the emergency care of head injury.

CHAPTER 11

Chronic Brain Disorders III

Chronic Brain Syndrome Associated with Cerebral Arteriosclerosis
009–516

The mental symptoms in this syndrome are similar to those of senile dementia, and at times a differential diagnosis is impossible. Autopsy findings will usually sweep aside theoretical clinical considerations. In general, arteriosclerotic brain disease occurs somewhat earlier in life. Peripheral blood pressure is not a safe index because it is not necessarily high. We feel that the diagnosis of psychosis with arteriosclerosis is best reserved for those cases showing evidence of headache, dizziness, fainting attacks, and perhaps focal symptoms such as aphasia or paralysis in addition to the general mental symptoms. These patients share with those who have other organic diseases, emotional lability and sensorium defects, but, different from others, they may show fluctuation in memory. This fluctuation or "spotty" sensorium is perhaps the most characteristic defect of arteriosclerotic brain disease. Patients will remember certain events from the remote or recent past at one time and forget them at another. This is distinguished from the typical memory pattern in senility where recent memory fails first but recollection of events in the remote past remains strong. Similar to this capricious memory are fluctuations in the degree of irritability, emotional lability, and judgment defects. As in other types of organic disease of the brain, the past personality pattern of the patient colors his psychotic picture, so that we may have overlaying the organic symptoms, overactivity, depression, or paranoid delusions in different cases. The course of the illness is one of steady deterioration. As the condition progresses the clear episodes become less frequent and the confused, disturbed periods more prolonged.

In the advanced stages, the patient stabilizes into an organic type of psychosis indistinguishable from that of an advanced senile or general paretic patient, in so far as the mental symptoms are concerned.

The other important feature in diagnosis is the evidence of neurologic complications and of vascular sclerosis on examination of the retina. A typical case is a 57-year-old man who was brought to the hospital by the police for observation. He complained that he had weak spells and dizziness, and that at times his mind seemed to give out on him. He also stated that his family upset him. The family complained that the patient had been growing increasingly irritable over the past 4 years and had developed paranoid ideas principally involving his wife's fidelity. For about the last 12 months he had shown evidence of emotional instability manifest by periods of weeping and outbursts of rage. On one occasion he threatened the family with a knife. His background revealed a person who had supported his family on a farm; he had only 6 grades of education but was of normal intelligence. His mother and one sister died with "apoplexy." Examination on admission revealed emotional lability, manifest by weeping with shifts to irritability. He admitted that he was irritable, but had no insight concerning his wife's supposed infidelity. He also felt his children wanted to get him out of the way and did things intentionally to antagonize him. He had no hallucinations. He was oriented, but at the time of the examination was having difficulty with remote memory such as the age when he left school, year in which he was married, years he had been married, and similar facts usually recalled by the average person. The patient did not have hypertension. He showed marked tremors of the fingers and hands and had an advanced degree of retinal sclerosis. This man was thought to be chronically ill. He did not respond to treatment and was ultimately committed to a state hospital.

Treatment. Various measures to improve cerebral circulation are sometimes used in these patients with some success. Group psychotherapy and rehabilitation with attention to teaching the patient to live within the limitations of his illness sometimes succeed in getting the patient back home. If the depressive or paranoid symptoms are advanced, the use of the new drugs or shock therapy is helpful.

At autopsy the brain is lighter than average and advanced cases show atrophy of the convolutions, particularly over the frontal lobes. In advanced stages there is a loss of ganglion cells from the cortical layers, and the remaining layers show varying degrees of deterioration. There are small areas of softening scattered diffusely through the cortical areas.

Chronic Brain Syndrome Associated with Circulatory Disturbance Other Than Cerebral Arteriosclerosis 009–5

Cerebral embolism, small cerebral hemorrhages, and arterial hypertension without marked sclerotic changes may produce mental symptoms in some patients. In patients with these conditions the predominant symptoms are those of the underlying vascular disease. The symptoms, in so far as the psychiatric examination is concerned, are indistinguishable from those of other organic states and are particularly similar to those of cerebral arteriosclerosis.

Chronic Brain Syndrome Associated with Convulsive Disorder 009–550

Patients with idiopathic epilepsy who have chronic mental symptoms are classified here.

Any organic condition of the central nervous system may produce seizures, but seizures associated with known brain pathology are properly classified under the cause of the basic pathology such as neurosyphilis, cerebral arteriosclerosis, etc. A few patients with epilepsy may deteriorate and develop symptoms of a chronic brain syndrome. More common are the acute mental findings reported under the acute brain syndromes, and the student should bear in mind that any type of psychotic reaction in an epileptic patient is the exception rather than the rule. Certain severe idiopathic epileptic patients develop chronic organic symptoms usually referred to as "epilepsy with a psychosis" or "epileptic deterioration." There are few distinguishing characteristics between these symptoms and those of other organic disorders. There is the history of epilepsy and the history usually reveals the patient has had prolonged and frequent grand mal attacks that have been improperly or incompletely controlled by medication. An occasional case will give a history of few seizures, but careful inquiry reveals a history of outbursts of rage or irritability that may have been equivalent states or transitory furor reactions of some type.

The mental symptoms of this syndrome are irritability, outbursts of rage, and combativeness. They may be precipitated by environmental events or may occur spontaneously. Many of these patients have paranoid ideas and become extremely suspicious and unpleasant. Some are overactive, while others show a general lethargy and disinterest in their surroundings. Most of these patients have periods of amnesia during their more violent outbursts, but remember the paranoid and irritable attacks. The deterioration of the intellectual processes varies in severity but usually progresses slowly. This form of convulsive disorder responds less well to treatment than the other forms. Some centers report momentary clearing following electroshock treatment, but in our experience this has not been successful in the chronic deteriorated case, although it may be spectacular in those showing acute psychiatric reactions. Anticonvulsive drug therapy, particularly the use of Dilantin, although other drugs should be tried, seems to be most helpful. There is some evidence that the new drugs, particularly chlorpromazine, controls the overactivity, paranoid delusions, and irritability in some of these patients. Physical and neurologic examinations show nothing specific for this disorder. Practically all these patients show electroencephalographic changes typical of a convulsive disorder.

The treatment is anticonvulsive medication, custodial and rehabilitation programs, and the use of chlorpromazine. These are discussed in more detail in the treatment section.

Chronic Brain Syndrome Associated with Senile Brain Disease 009-79x

Mental changes incident to aging are becoming an increasing problem in our large state hospitals and in the private practice of psychiatry. People are living longer and the population is growing. These two factors combine to bring increasing numbers of persons into the older age group. There is also some reason to believe that urbanization of our population and the increasing tempo of daily life make adjustment difficult for older persons showing mild degrees of senile change. In Massachusetts and other states, special facilities are being created for these borderline senile patients.

Literature is full of references, humorous and sad, to the mental deterioration seen in older persons. In *Gulliver's Travels*, Swift describes typical senile changes in the Struldbrug. P. G. Wodehouse's fine character, Lord Emsworth, shows mild and benevolent senile changes.

A well-developed case of senile deterioration offers no difficulty. However, the early recognition of senile changes is of great importance, in view of the fact that patients are readily victimized by designing individuals, and may bring disgrace to themselves and family or waste their resources. There is a prodromal period of many months during which the patients are irritable, sleep poorly, and complain of malaise, muscular weakness, and anorexia. They tend to become seclusive; mental powers may show impairment; recent memory becomes uncertain; and faulty recollection is covered by crude fabrication. The patient wanders about and may lose his way. The emotions deteriorate and sympathy is often lacking. Some become quite stubborn and obstinate, show a narrowing of interests, become selfish, and have outbursts of temper. The previous personality pattern is accentuated. They are often extremely stingy.

Signs of physical decay are usually obvious. The patient may lose his way on the train because he forgets where he is going. In one instance a patient was reported to the police as lost because he had gone to town with his wife and agreed to meet at the parking lot where they left their car. When he failed to return in 3 or 4 hours, the wife became quite concerned. She finally went home, pending a police search for him, and found the old gentleman at home, furious because his wife was not there. Having forgotten that he went to town with her and had driven the car, he had taken the subway home.

The first mental symptoms may develop in situations of stress produced by illness or strange situations. Some patients may develop rather pronounced paranoid delusions. For example, a patient became paranoid toward the director of the nursing home in which the patient stayed and he killed him. Another patient married a younger woman, had delusions of infidelity about her, and killed her while talking to her and her attorney about a divorce settlement. In some cases the symptoms progress until the patient becomes completely disoriented and has gross defects in the sensorium and gross defects in judgment. Most of these cases progress. The brain shows atrophy and a predominance of senile plaques. A touching story of the confusion shown by a person beginning senility in situations of stress is "No Enemy but Time," by Maurice Rowdon, published in *Harper's Magazine*, April, 1954.

Many senile patients show evidences of functional disturbance in addition to the organic phenomena. Depressive symptoms are the commonest, but paranoid reactions are also frequent. In this group of patients we feel that the functional part of their disorder is a complication of the organic factors and arises because an individual of a particular character organization is unable to adapt to the loss of cerebral function due to the organic disturbances. Thus one would think of the senile changes as being a combination of biologic, sociologic, and psychologic processes.

Pathology. The senile brain shows a loss of weight, principally due to atrophy over the cortical areas, especially in the frontal lobes. In addition there are characteristic areas of softening and the typical senile plaques described in all standard textbooks of pathology. Recent work shows that these senile plaques occur with the same frequency in nonpsychotic old people as in those showing senile mental changes, and the exact role such plaques play in the production of symptoms is not clear. The course in these cases is usually chronic and progressive, although some may improve temporarily, particularly if there are many depressive symptoms present.

Treatment. The treatment is supportive. Some with depressive or paranoid symptoms benefit from electroshock treatments. Some of those who

tend to be agitated, paranoid, and overactive benefit from chlorpromazine, and if they have hypertension, from reserpine. Many patients improve remarkably with attention to intercurrent infections or treatment
of cardiac decompensation when present. It has been our experience that
many of these old people come to us showing dietary deficiency, particularly low vitamin and protein intake. Correction of these dietary deficiencies will often produce a pronounced increase in physical vigor and
an improvement in mental function. The patient should be protected
from the consequences of his psychotic behavior. To be kept in mind are
the liability to physical injury, sexual offenses against youngsters, and
disgraceful marriages. Some carelessly set fire to themselves and others
or cause explosions by turning on gas jets and forgetting to apply a
match immediately afterward. Some of these patients commit suicide.
Institutional care seems inevitable for some.

Special institutions to care for the problems of the aged and the infirm
are to be preferred and should provide special facilities for recreation,
sunning, and other types of activity within the limit set by the physical
condition of the patient. There should be facilities for visiting in privacy
with family and friends. Provision should be made for the patient to have
about him some of his personal possessions which have sentimental value.
The provision of facilities away from urban areas rather than in the centers of population may be preferable for these patients because they can
be allowed more freedom within a semirural environment. While medical
supervision is necessary in these cases, the patients do not need the active
psychiatric care required for those with acute mental problems. Recreation, occupation, and rehabilitation services succeed in getting a surprising number of these patients back into the community. Preventive management is more effective in these cases than treatment of the psychosis
after it develops. Attention should be given to preparing older persons
for retirement. Work should be made available to individuals as long as
they can stay constructively occupied and wish to do so. It will be necessary to modify schedules and salary scales in keeping with the amount of
productive work they can carry on. Recreational activities for these patients of types suited to them should be provided in the community, and
local physicians or hospital clinics should be interested in them. Some
centers provide special geriatrics clinics; others merely give older people
special attention in the regular clinic. Neither method has all advantages,
but one or the other should be worked out so that these older patients are
not neglected from a physical and psychologic point of view.

Many states now have councils or commissions on aging as a part of
public and state government activity. The physician should get in touch

with these agencies for information on community resources for the rehabilitation of elderly patients.

Chronic Brain Syndrome Associated with Other Disturbance of Metabolism, Growth, or Nutrition 009-700

A variety of disorders is included here. One stipulation is that the patients should have organic mental change.

Alzheimer's disease should be classified here. Alzheimer's disease is an early presenile deterioration which usually leads to dementia. Cases have developed in persons as early as the age of 40 years, usually with marked emotional disturbance, and with aphasic and apractic symptoms. At autopsy approximately one-third of the nerve cells in the cortex are destroyed, and replaced by dark-staining fibril bundles in the form of plaques, called Alzheimer's plaques. These plaques are the result of the degeneration of nerve cells and thickening of the glia elements and are regarded as pathologically diagnostic. A pneumoencephalogram in these cases will usually show a dilation of the ventricles and often severe cortical atrophies somewhat like that seen in paresis or advanced senile states. Pathologic examination with demonstration of Alzheimer's plaques confirms the diagnosis.

Patients showing organic symptoms following pellagra, cretinism, or other disturbances in metabolism are properly classified here. The mental symptoms are indistinguishable from those of other organic disorders, and the differential diagnosis will depend upon the other findings from the physical and laboratory studies.

Chronic Brain Syndrome Associated with Intracranial Neoplasm 009-8

An occasional patient suffering from a tumor of the central nervous system will show organic mental symptoms. Typically these symptoms are a gradual dulling of the sensorium, a lowered level of awareness, and at times some irritability. Frequently there is aphasia. Silliness, euphoria, and impaired judgment may be seen in patients with frontal-lobe tumors. Patients in this category will show mental symptoms like those of other organic cases, and the detection of an organic mental reaction should lead to careful neurologic, physical, and laboratory investigations. Such studies will usually demonstrate the cause. The tumors of the brain producing these symptoms may be primary or metastatic.

Chronic Brain Syndrome Associated with Disease of Unknown or Uncertain Causes 009-900

The mental picture in these cases is also typical of organic findings. Cases are classified here because the disease productive of the organic change is diagnosable and of known clinical symptomatology but the cause of the disease is unknown.

PICK'S DISEASE

This disease is characterized by a slowly progressing dementia and marked atrophy of the frontal lobes which is demonstrable by pneumo-encephalogram. The brain often appears to have been scooped out. It occurs most often in women, but may occur in either sex, and sometimes develops as early as 30 years of age, or as late as the sixties. It is a rare disorder. We have seen two cases of Pick's disease, originally diagnosed as schizophrenia, but a mental-status examination at the time of consultation demonstrated obvious organic changes in addition to the schizophrenia-like delusions and hallucinations. The new diagnosis was confirmed by pneumoencephalogram and in one of the cases by subsequent autopsy.

HUNTINGTON'S CHOREA

Huntington's chorea is more common than either Pick's or Altzheimer's. It is a disease of middle life, progressive and degenerative, and is associated with gradual intellectual deterioration. Both sexes are equally affected, and heredity is the chief etiologic factor. It should not be confused with Sydenham's chorea. The neurologic findings of choreiform movements and marked ataxia, with the "skater's gait," are so pronounced that the diagnosis is rarely missed. The mental picture is not different from that of any other chronic progressive organic reaction. It usually starts with irritability, emotional lability, and sometimes mild paranoid changes, and progresses to severe intellectual deterioration. A typical example is a 60-year-old married physician, who had noted twitching and mild choreiform movements in himself 10 years before. These progressed slowly for about 7 years, then more rapidly, and made it necessary for him to give up practice. He reported that he began to have difficulty recalling what he had prescribed for patients, and at times he became so confused he could not see patients. His speech was markedly impaired, he could not feed himself, and for 6 months prior to admission his mental symptoms had progressed. These mental changes were described as explosive outbursts of temper and paranoid delusions. The patient's mother died of Huntington's chorea at the age of 68. A maternal aunt died from it, and a niece at the age of 19 had Huntington's chorea. Examination of the patient showed typical neurologic findings of advanced chorea plus the mental-status changes of marked organic deterioration in the intellectual fields.

CHAPTER 12

*Mental Deficiency 000–x90**

During the past few years, there have been many note-
worthy and encouraging advances in the medical aspect of the field of
mental subnormality. Investigations in pathology, neuropathology, em-
bryology, and embryologic pathology have thrown much light on the
etiology of subnormality and have offered many practical suggestions as
to its prevention. In addition, the application of psychodynamic principles in this field has extended the benefits of psychotherapy to the
mentally subnormal. In general, there has been a more enlightened attitude on the part of the public. This is doubtless owing, in large measure,
to the organization of parent groups which are encouraging both profer-
sional and lay interest in the field. These facts, in addition to the shees
weight of numbers of afflicted individuals, are forcing professional
workers to reexamine their attitudes toward the entire problem of mental subnormality.

Probably no other field of medicine and psychiatry has suffered from
so many professional misunderstandings and misconceptions. Until recently, one of the great stumbling blocks in the way of better understanding and investigation has been the almost universal notion that
mental subnormality is hereditary in origin. Because no immediate and
direct cause could be found, it was easy to blame heredity and to say
that nothing could be done. Many professional people thought of mentally subnormal persons as comprising a stereotyped group of individuals
so limited in understanding that they could not be taught even the rudi-

---

* By MALCOLM J. FARRELL, M.D. Superintendent, Walter E. Fernald State
School, Massachusetts Department of Mental Health; Instructor in Psychiatry,
Boston University Medical School; Instructor in Psychiatry, Tufts University Medi-
cal School.

153

mentary care of themselves and their bodies. They were regarded as being
in a hopeless condition for which little if anything could be done. Such a
belief is far from the truth. It is generally recognized that in the concept
of physical health there is acceptance of the fact that interferences may
vary in severity, from a mild head cold, for example, to a severe illness
such as terminal lobar pneumonia. The traditional consideration of mental subnormality, however, regarded it as black or white, and the possibility of anything in-between had not been considered. Actually, of
course, mental subnormality like physical ill health ranges all the way
from mild to severe. Also, many physicians thought of mental retardation as a subject outside the realms of psychiatry and medicine. To complicate the picture further there has been much confusion in terminology
and definition. A glance at the classifications of mental defects now commonly used reveals a most amazing and inconsistent table of clinical
entities based on entirely different descriptive and etiologic categories.
Many of the classifications would appear to deny the fact that a medical
or biologic approach is basic. Until relatively recent times, most of the
studies in this field have been along statistical and descriptive lines. Only
now is this field emerging from the level of description characteristic of
psychiatry in the days of Kraepelin.

Definition

Many attempts have been made to arrive at a definition which covers
all aspects of mental subnormality. The American Association on Mental
Deficiency has adopted the following definition: "The term 'feeble-
minded' is used generically to include all degrees of mental defect due
to arrested or imperfect mental development, as the result of which the
person so afflicted is incapable of competing on equal terms with his normal fellows or managing himself or his affairs with ordinary prudence."
The Committee on the Mentally Subnormal Child of the World Health
Organization uses the term "mental subnormality" to describe an incomplete or insufficient general development of the mental capacities.
This author suggests the following as a possible workable definition:
"Mental subnormality is an irreversible, pathologic condition existing
from an early age involving intellectual, emotional, and social immaturity, which is responsive to appropriate methods of education, training,
and treatment."

Incidence of Subnormality

At present, no country has compiled a complete and exact census. The
Committee on the Mentally Subnormal Child of the World Health Or-

ganization offers a few statistics which they recognize as estimates based on figures which vary greatly according to the criteria employed in the various countries. Dutch estimates, based on eight large cities, give a mean rate of 2.6 per cent. French estimates vary from 1.5 to 8.6 per cent, depending on age. It is the educational practice in England to make provision for 1 per cent of school children in special schools, while a further 8 or 9 per cent are considered to require special educational provision. Varying estimates have been made in different states in the United States and in Switzerland. The National Association for Retarded Children, Inc., reports that 3 per cent of the population are affected and that there are 1,500,000 mentally subnormal individuals in the entire country. In New York State alone it is estimated that there are 400,000 subnormal individuals, and in Massachusetts approximately 140,000.

A few pertinent facts bear upon the question of a possible increase in the incidence of subnormality. With improvement in medical techniques, the survival rate of infants with severe developmental abnormalities has increased markedly. This seems to be borne out by the infant-mortality statistics of the City of New York, which show that in 1920, among the causes of death, congenital debility and malformations ranked first with a rate of 35.3 per thousand live births. In 1949, the mortality rate for malformations fell to 16.8 per thousand. Thus, out of 1,000 newborn infants, 19 survived in 1949 who as late as 1920 would have died of congenital factors. Concurrent with these developments the greatly increased birth rate of the years following World War II has increased proportionately the number of such individuals in the population. These considerations suggest there has been a real increase in the incidence of mental subnormality.

Nomenclature and Classification

As indicated earlier, there has been much confusion in the use of terms in the field of mental subnormality. As a member of the Joint Expert Committee on the Mentally Subnormal Child convened by the World Health Organization, this author offers the nomenclature and suggestions made by the World Health Organization in 1952 (Table 1).

The Committee suggests the term "mental subnormality" to describe the intellectually inadequate child. It proposes the replacement of the terms "idiot," "imbecile," and "moron" with the terms "severe subnormality," "moderate subnormality," and "mild subnormality." These designations are proposed because of the confusion in the use and meaning of terms throughout the world. In the United States, for example, the term "mental deficiency" has replaced terms like "feeblemindedness"

TABLE 1. CURRENT AND PROPOSED NOMENCLATURE OF MENTAL SUBNORMALITY*

Recommended terms	Current usage				IQ (children)	Mental age in years† (adults)
	British	American	French	German		
Mild subnormality	Feeble-minded	Moron	Débile	Debil	50–69	8–12
Moderate subnormality	Imbecile	Imbecile	Imbécile	Imbezill Schwach-sinnig	20–49	3–7
Severe subnormality	Idiot	Idiot	Idiot	Idiotisch Blöd-sinnig	0–19	0–2
All grades of mental subnormality	Mentally defective Amentia	Feeble-minded Mentally deficient Mentally retarded	Arriéré Oligo-phrene	Geistes-schwach Oligo-phren	0–69	0–12

* From "The Mentally Subnormal Child," p. 8, Table 1, World Health Organization Technical Report Series No. 75, Geneva, April, 1954.

† From "Manual of the International Statistical Classification of Diseases, Injuries and Causes of Death," vol. 1, p. 114, the World Health Organization, Geneva, 1948.

and "idiocy" which were used for many years. In England the term "feeblemindedness" was reserved for the group called "moron" in the United States. In some countries the term "mental deficiency" is used as a descriptive term for an incomplete emotional development with normal levels of intelligence. In some countries the term "mental deficiency" includes also the "moral defective."

Psychiatric Considerations

Only within the past few years has any attempt been made to apply the principles of psychodynamics to the field of mental subnormality. This is in a large measure due to the widespread belief that most, if not all these cases, are due to heredity, and that as a group, mentally subnormal individuals constitute a homogenous population in terms of their psychologic needs. These views led to a feeling of hopelessness as far as therapy and other investigations were concerned.

It must be emphasized that mentally subnormal persons have feelings, emotions, and the same emotional needs as persons of normal intelligence and use the same varieties of defense mechanisms. The two groups differ only in the fact that personality development in subnormal persons is much slower and that without suitable therapeutic attention they are less able to achieve a well-integrated personality structure than persons with normal intelligence. The lower the intelligence, the more the individual is motivated by the id. As the mental level increases, ego development increases. Because of retardation in the development of the ego, a rather superficial superego will develop. It is now generally accepted that mentally subnormal individuals develop the same personality patterns as are observed in individuals with normal intelligence and can be classified according to the usual categories. Like his normal fellow, the mentally subnormal individual who develops a psychosis will usually develop one based on his personality make-up. He may develop schizophrenic reactions, manic-depressive reactions, or other reactions observed in the so-called "normal" group. In such a case, the correct psychiatric diagnosis should be made and the treatment proper for the condition instituted. In view of these considerations, present-day psychiatric concepts of the mentally subnormal individual must be revised and the term "psychosis with mental deficiency" dropped completely.

Role of Emotional Deprivation

In recent years, considerable attention has been directed toward the role of emotional deprivation, particularly in the early years of a child's development. There is much evidence that when a child is emotionally deprived at an early age, he may suffer not only emotionally but intellectually as well. Fundamental contributions in this area have been made by Skeels, Bowlby, Kardiner, L. Bender, Gesell and Amatruda, and Spitz and Wolf. Recently Goldfarb has contributed significantly to the understanding of the consequences of psychologic deprivation in infancy in his critical review of the literature on this subject. Excellent work has been done by Thompson who points out that early environment in which an organism grows is a crucial determinant of later behavior and he supports his conclusions by a careful review of animal experimentation in this area. Farrell's strong convictions about this matter have been stated in a paper calling attention to the serious and far-reaching implications of the indiscriminate and almost universal advice toward the early institutionalization of mentally subnormal children, with particular emphasis on the adverse effects of advising parents to admit children to an institution shortly after birth. Not only is the emotional and intellectual development of the child involved, but also the emotional health of the parents.

As long as mental illness was considered mainly a condition of adult life, childhood psychoses being practically unknown, most children with mental anomalies were considered mentally defective. Since childhood

schizophrenia, childhood autism, Heller's disease, and other mental illnesses have become known, the differential diagnosis between mental illness and mental deficiency in children is often difficult.

Mental illness in children is discussed in another chapter of this book.
It may be stressed at this point, however, that the diagnosis of mental
subnormality is a psychiatric medical diagnosis and should not be based
on psychologic tests alone. Children with childhood schizophrenia or emotional disorders may do poorly on psychometric tests because they lack
motivation and interest in the test procedures or live so much in their
own world that they do not use speech as a means of communication. In
these instances, mental capacities have to be inferred by bits of circum-
stantial evidence and by observing the behavior of the child in general.

A low psychometric rating is not proof of mental subnormality. The
psychiatrist must be extremely careful in the evaluation of low IQ ratings in infancy and early childhood because children normally show a
wide range in developmental rates. Some children are slow starters, are
late in talking, have reading difficulties and other signs of slow development, and yet turn out to be normal, occasionally highly intelligent, persons. Neglect, psychologic deprivation, malnutrition, and other factors
have a detrimental effect on IQ ratings in infancy and early childhood.
The situation is especially complicated in instances of cerebral palsy or
brain injury, where the slow mental development usually seen in the first
years of life is often mistaken for a definite mental subnormality, while
the brain-injured child frequently has intellectual potentialities which are
obscured by the neurologic lesions.

The term mental "retardation" is widely used nowadays by parent
organizations, psychologists, and psychiatrists, and is identified with the
diagnosis of mental subnormality. When psychologic tests indicate a slow
development and that a child is "retarded," many parents conclude from
the use of the word "retarded" that their child is definitely mentally subnormal. It must be pointed out that the test may indicate a slower development than average up to the time of examination, and that the child
has not yet reached the mental level which is expected at that certain age.
In the literal sense of the word, such a child is "retarded" but not necessarily mentally subnormal.

It may be summarized that the field of mental inadequacy and subnormality covers a wide range of conditions. One may generally distinguish
between the milder forms of mental subnormality—roughly, the IQ ratings above 50—and the more severe conditions which compose the range
of severe mental deficiency or the IQ ratings between 0 and 50.

Oligophrenia

In any given population, the group of highly qualified and superior persons is counterbalanced by a group with less intellectual endowment who have a dull-normal, marginal, or an actually inadequate defective intelligence. This group could be considered the minus variations in the population sample. Genetic studies by Roberts, Norman, and Griffiths indicate that certain intelligence factors are of a genetic nature, and subnormality in the marginal group is determined primarily as of a familial type. The milder forms of subnormality are composed of about 80 per cent of familial cases while 20 per cent are due to accidental factors like brain injuries, infectious diseases, nutritional deficiencies, emotional deprivation, neglect, and other factors. These so-called "clinical" cases come from average and superior families, and if one child in an intelligent family is of subnormal intelligence, one may suspect that some extrinsic factors interfered with mental development. A thorough family history and a neurologic examination will usually produce evidence of asphyxiation at birth, brain injury, postinfectious diseases, or some illness of the mother during pregnancy.

In the familial form of subnormality, the conditions are complicated since genetic and environmental factors are interwoven in a very complex manner. Since at least 3 per cent of the population is of subnormal intelligence, persons with limited intelligence form an intrinsic factor of each social group and are not subjects of special attention except from an educational point of view. The subnormal group needs special education, and all school systems and communities should provide facilities for the education and recreation of the subnormal group. However, social difficulties play a considerable role in families of subnormal intelligence because subnormal intelligence is associated with poor planning, poor management, poor earning, and little ability to cope with the conditions of a highly industrialized modern society. Children with subnormal intelligence need not be admitted to state institutions on account of their subnormal intelligence except when environmental factors in the family make a long stay in the community impossible for the child.

A study of a moron group at the Fernald School (not yet published) indicates that institutionalization was primarily for social reasons: 80 per cent of the male and 58 per cent of the female patients of this group came from broken homes; 24 per cent of the male and 16 per cent of the female patients were illegitimate; in 7 per cent the father had deserted the family, in 4 per cent the mother; in 4 per cent either the father or mother was in prison, and in 1 per cent both parents; 3 per cent of the mothers were institutionalized in a state school and 3 per cent in mental hospitals. Abuse of alcohol by the parents was found in 36 per cent, and sexual promiscuity and low moral standards in at least one of the parents in 44 per cent of the case material.

These figures give only a vague idea of the social implications of subnormalities. Emotional neglect, physical neglect resulting in malnutrition, infections, and general ill health, lack of ego development, subnormal standards, and emotional disorders were present to such an extent that most of the new admissions on a moron level were psychiatric problems in addition to having mental limitations.

It is in this area that modern psychiatry has paid too little attention to the welfare of the subnormal group. Mental-hygiene clinics, child-guidance clinics, and many outpatient departments do not accept children with IQ ratings below 85 because a child with limited intelligence is regarded as not worth the bother—he should be institutionalized. It has to be recognized that the marginal group lives in a pyschiatric and social no-man's land. They need much more attention since this group is especially responsive to educational and psychiatric proceedings and, if neglected, contributes largely to the minor forms of delinquency, misdemeanors, and social disturbances.

The Severe Forms of Mental Subnormality

In contrast to the milder forms of mental subnormality, the severe forms are actually identical with the "organic brain syndrome," and newer neuropathologic studies have provided evidence that pathology of the brain is always present in the severe forms of mental subnormality.

Previous classifications have not given sufficient attention to the etiologic factors and the time at which the pathology underlying the mental subnormality developed. Benda has offered what appears to the author to be the most satisfactory classification from a medical point of view. His classification indicates that mental development has been interrupted before birth, at birth, or after birth because of some noxious factor. He points out that the differentiation of these disorders according to time has a great value for diagnostic and prognostic purposes. He offers a classification according to time as follows:

A. Antenatal
B. Paranatal
C. Postnatal

Benda also suggests a classification according to causes, as follows:

A. Endogenous (genetic-metabolic) disorders

B. Exogenous (extrinsic, accidental) disorders

    1. Traumatic

    2. Vascular

    3. Infectious

    4. Metabolic

    5. Degenerative and unknown

It appears to the author that this classification demonstrates that it is possible to introduce a classification which offers a more satisfactory understanding of the different conditions involved. Even more important, it provides a classification in agreement with experimental data which indicates that many of the severe cases of mental subnormality are due, in fact, to the production of some type of malformation caused by an exogenous factor. This classification includes the two more severe groups, formerly designated as idiot and imbecile.

Benda has collected material of 267 cases in which it was possible to obtain fairly adequate histories and clinical observations and perform autopsies (Table 2).

TABLE 2. MATERIAL OF THE STUDY*

		No. cases	Per cent
Total material............................		267	
Questionable material, excluded............		9	
Total material analyzed...................		258	100
Prenatal disorders.........................		91	35
Congenital malformations...............	36		14
Mongolism............................	55		21
Paranatal cerebral palsies.................		61	24
Postinfectious cerebral palsies..............		37	14
Metabolic disorders.......................		17	7
Neoplastic disorders......................		12	5
Oligoencephaly............................		40	15

* Reprinted by special permission from C. E. Benda and M. J. Farrell, Psychopathology of Mental Deficiency in Children, in "Psychopathology of Childhood," edited by Paul H. Hoch and Joseph Zubin, Grune & Stratton, Inc., New York, 1955.

Prenatal Disorders. Benda points out that it is possible to determine the stage in which a developmental disorder occurred by comparative studies, even if the patient died many years after birth. Experimental

162 Practical Clinical Psychiatry

teratology and comparative pathology have enabled investigators to establish almost an exact timetable in which specific human malformations occur in the first 4 or 5 months of the gestation period. Although Benda emphasizes that mongolism is clearly a prenatal developmental disorder, the treatment of mongolism as a specific entity is justified by the large percentage of mongoloid patients in this group. Referring to Table 2, it is evident that congenital malformations including mongolism occurred in 91 cases, or 35 per cent of the total. Congenital malformations such as agyria, microgyria, microcephalia vera, and the Arnold-Chiari malformation accounted for 36 cases, or 14 per cent, while there were 55 cases of mongolism, or 21 per cent.

Experimental teratology and pathologic studies demonstrated that there may be considerable interference with normal development by a variety of noxious factors. Some of the prenatal developmental disorders are of a genetic nature, and the psychiatrist must evaluate the situation thoroughly because he may be asked for advice in regard to further offspring. Certain forms of microcephaly are genetic, and families with as many as 5 to 7 microcephalic children are on record. However, microcephaly may also be due to vascular factors, asphyxiation, and other environmental agents, and a differential diagnosis is needed between the genetic and the accidental type. Some forms of hydrocephaly, cleft formations, and neoplastic malformations (tuberous sclerosis, von Recklinghausen's disease, megalocephaly) are genetically determined. Mongolism is definitely not a genetic disorder, while gargoylism and phenylpyruvic oligophrenia are highly genetically determined.

The majority of developmental disorders of the prenatal period are due to interference with normal development, and experimental teratology has provided convincing evidence that most prenatal disorders can be produced experimentally. The role of infectious diseases, such as German measles and other virus diseases in the mother, is scientifically established beyond doubt.

Benda's material appears to provide ample evidence that mongolism is a congenital acromicria in which the growth of the embryo has been decelerated between the sixth and twelfth weeks of pregnancy. The mongoloid newborn infant shows many characteristics of *fetalism*, but most important in this respect is the immaturity of the nervous system.

Experimental teratalogy has provided a wealth of evidence that malformations are correlated with the time of development when a specific noxious agent was operative. Poisons, changes in carbon dioxide concentration, asphyxiation, mechanical traumas, vitamin and nutritional deficiencies, and radiation can be used to produce a specific malformation.

The type of malformation depends on the developmental stage of the embryo during which specific tissues are showing the highest rate of developmental metabolism and are, therefore, most susceptible to any noxious interference. It would appear that tissues which have reached a certain degree of maturity or are still in a dormant condition are affected slightly or not at all.

The classic experiments of Hicks and Russell, using x-ray radiation on pregnant animals on specific days of gestation and examining the surviving embryos at full term, present a perfect timetable of developmental variations. They have shown that x-ray radiation of rats, for example, on the twelfth or thirteenth day of gestation produces a stunted growth and an underdevelopment of the visceral skull and the skull basis. The specific stage through which a rat passes at the twelfth day can be compared to the seventh to the ninth week of development in the human embryo. The application of this information to mongolism is obvious.

Ingalls and his coworkers at the Harvard Graduate School of Public Health have been able to expose pregnant animals to varying degrees of oxygen deficiency using a low-pressure chamber. The timing and degree of this maternal stress could be varied at will. Pregnant mice, for example, could be placed in a low-pressure chamber on any day of pregnancy, and it was found that both timing and degree of stress profoundly influenced the type and number of congenital deformities found in the young. Ingalls' experiments led to the construction of an integrated theory of congenital anomalies. This work suggests that normal human embryos are potential candidates for cyclopia around the first week of life, conjoined twins about the second, ectromelia around the third, tracheoesophageal fistula at the fourth, nuclear cataract of the lens around the fifth, harelip at the sixth, cleft palate around the seventh, mongolism at the eighth week, and so on. He points out also that at 8 weeks, for example, the embryonic hand has formed the primordium of the middle phalanx of the little finger and suggests that this may explain why this structure is stunted in most mongoloid patients. The practical implications of Ingalls' experiments include the possibility that mothers should allow their small children to get the ordinary childhood infections naturally, so that future mothers would have developed natural immunities. Other implications are that pregnant women should not take airplane trips, that elective surgery involving prolonged general anesthesia should be deferred, and that all precautions should be taken to guard against infectious diseases, dietary or vitamin deficiencies, or any condition which might impair the health of the mother and thus produce a developmental defect on the part of her unborn child. Ingalls makes a forceful plea that the understanding and control of environmental stresses take precedence over genetic considerations in the critical stresses of pregnancy. Every effort should be made to prevent damage to the developing embryo since there is ample evidence that malformations are acquired, not inherited.

Paranatal Disorders. The largest single group in Table 2 is composed of paranatal disorders, which at the same time constitute the bulk of what is commonly known as "cerebral palsy." It must be mentioned that *cerebral palsy* is a clinical term which indicates some form of paralysis connected with cerebral lesions. Since cerebral lesions are actually almost always associated with some forms of motor disorder, danger exists that the term *cerebral palsy* would lose its meaning and become identical with cerebral pathology, which would also include prenatal disorders, metabolic disorders, and others. Benda has therefore attempted in his book to restrict the term *cerebral palsy* to the paranatal disorders in which brain development was normal up to the time of birth and to the cerebral palsies due to infectious diseases and the Rh factor (kernicterus).

The term *paranatal disorders* connotes pathology due to a variety of factors of a noninfectious nature operating shortly before birth, at birth, or after birth. These factors are asphyxiation due to a cord around the neck of the embryo, placenta previa, placental thrombosis, toxemia of the mother, prematurity, bleedings during birth due to immaturity of the vascular and nervous system of the newborn, bleedings due to anomalies in size of the maternal pelvis, actual traumas due to the application of forceps, and precipitate birth or long-lasting deliveries associated with severe changes in pressure and asphyxiation. Venous bleedings often occur, even several days after birth, when the actual birth process had been completed.

The effects of paranatal disorders range from mild palsies with little involvement of mental functions to most severe conditions of quadriplegias, Little's spastic rigidity, decerebrate rigidity, and diffuse cerebral lesions which paralyze the child completely and are associated with most severe mental disability. Patients with cerebral palsy range intellectually, therefore, from high intelligence to the lowest levels of mental functioning. The different forms of neurologic disorders represent a great variety of clinical pictures, of which the choreoathetosis, hemiplegias and paraplegias, spastic rigidity, and ataxias are the main types. The child with aftereffects of severe asphyxiation resembles in many ways the autistic child, being weak in its contacts with the outside world, unable to talk, and often completely unaware of its surroundings.

Infectious Diseases. Infectious diseases of childhood appear to play an important part in the causation of mental retardation. Referring again to Table 2, there were 37 cases (14 per cent) in this group with a definite history and histopathologic evidence of infection of the central nervous system at an early age.

For a long period of time, it has been well known that infectious diseases, particularly at an early age of life, could result in severe damage in the young brain. Congenital syphilis is gradually disappearing as a factor in mental deficiency whereas toxoplasmosis seems to be gaining in importance. This condition may affect the child prenatally, and the histopathologic examination reveals a granulomatous encephalitis with severe scar formation. It is sometimes possible to establish the diagnosis by findings of toxoplasmic "cysts." Among the postnatal infectious bacterial and virus diseases, whooping cough, measles, influenza, meningitis, pneumonias, and others may cause an encephalomyelitis with resultant damage to brain tissue. Bruetsch has called attention to the significance of rheumatic encephalitis.

Table 3 shows the number and types of cases due to infectious diseases in a total of 3,130 seen in the Walter E. Fernald State School Outpatient Clinic during the 7-year period, Jan. 1, 1949, to Dec. 31, 1955.

TABLE 3. ENCEPHALITIS AND MENINGITIS AS CAUSES OF
MENTAL SUBNORMALITY

No. cases

History of encephalitis in infancy or early childhood
Forms of encephalitis:

Measles	18
Pneumonia	9
Whooping cough	8
Tuberculosis	1
Scarlet fever	3
Meningoencephalitis	1
Unknown type	25
Total encephalitis	65 (2.0%)

History of meningitis in infancy or early childhood
Forms of meningitis:

Influenza	6
Tuberculosis	1
Pneumococcus	2
Meningococcus	2
Otitis media	2
Unknown type	8
Total meningitis	21 (0.7%)
Poliomyelitis	2 (0.05%)
Toxoplasmosis	2 (0.05%)
Total, all cases of postinfectious subnormality	90 (2.8%)

Metabolic Disorders. While the group of metabolic disorders in Table 2 was small—17 in number (7 per cent)—the term is used as a common denominator for such conditions as gargoylism, phenylpyruvic oligophrenia, amaurotic idiocy, leukencephalitis, and other forms of disorders of lipoid, sugar, or protein metabolism.

The contributions of biochemistry to the field of mental subnormality are rapidly growing. When one considers the tremendous number of amino acids involved in brain and body metabolism, one may safely assume that as adequate histochemical and biochemical methods are established, a larger number of metabolic disorders will be discovered. Phenylpyruvic oligophrenia or Foelling's disease is a well-recognized disorder of protein metabolism which may be readily identified by simple chemical examinations of the urine. Bickel, Woolf, Wilson, and Armstrong, and Hsia and associates, among others, have studied the effects of diets low in phenylalanine content on the mental development of children with phenylketonuria.

Lipoid metabolism is now much better understood, and much attention has been given to amaurotic idiocy. Gargoylism, recognized in 1917 by Hunter and in 1919 by Hurler, is a complex metabolic disorder of fat-protein-glycoside metabolism, the exact chemistry of which is not yet fully understood. However, gargoylism is not rare and the very distinct clinical features of gargoylism, which previously had often been confused with mongolism or cretinism, now make it possible to establish this diagnosis with great accuracy.

Neoplastic Conditions. Twelve cases (5 per cent) of neoplastic conditions were included in Table 2, such as tuberosclerosis, neurofibromatosis, Sturge-Weber disease, and other similar conditions. Benda also discovered among this group 3 new cases of megalocephaly or macrocephaly, which appears more important than previously realized.

Therapy of the Subnormal

Psychotherapy. The misconceptions discussed earlier in this chapter have interfered with progress in psychotherapy of the subnormal, but although the literature on the subject is still meager, it already presents an encouraging awareness of the necessity for including psychotherapy in an adequate program for the mentally subnormal, particularly the oligophrenic group. There are difficulties involved, since most psychotherapeutic procedures require verbal communication between the patient and the therapist, and it is in this skill that the mentally subnormal patients are least adequate. There is the additional problem of the development of insight, though it should be pointed out that this need not necessarily be complete. Thorne has stated that much can be accomplished through the flexible use of suggestion, persuasion, advice, or reassurance consistent with the patient's changing psychologic needs. Within the past few years several authors have called attention to the beneficial results of both individual and group therapy. Notable contributions have been made by Sarason, Ringelheim and Polatsek, Astrachan, Wiest, and Kugelmass. Depth therapy may not be possible or even essential in all cases, but this is no reason why psychotherapy in some form should not be attempted. The condition of mental subnormality itself may limit the selection of appropriate techniques and modify the therapeutic goals, but this should serve only as a challenge to the therapist to refine his therapeutic procedures in terms of his patients' potentialities, both intellectual and emotional. Such refinement must include nonverbal means of determining underlying conflicts.

Occupational Therapy. In recent years the increasing use of occupational therapy has been made in the treatment of the mentally subnormal. This activity, particularly when used under the direction of experienced and qualified occupational therapists, can create a most satisfying and favorable adjunct for these individuals.

At the Walter E. Fernald State School, the goals of this form of therapy provide a socially acceptable release of emotions for those with or without physical handicaps. The subnormal patient can be aided to develop good working habits and skills in handwork either in preparation for or to supplement vocational training. In addition, good socialization may be encouraged. Also experience is provided which students may use in leisure time on the wards.

Anderson and Watkins call attention to the paucity of literature dealing with techniques, the possibility of professional growth, and the rewards inherent in developing this new area of occupational therapy.

Drug Therapy. Recently, much attention has been given to the effect of the tranquilizing drugs such as Serpasil and Thorazine in the mentally subnormal. Noce, Williams, and Rapaport reported extremely good therapeutic results in using Serpasil on a group of 13 female patients who were noisy, untidy, intractable, resistive, and destructive. They used 1 mg daily by the oral route. After 3 months of treatment there was marked improvement in this group. At the Walter E. Fernald State School, Timberlake, Belmont, and Ogonik are studying 200 similar patients. Half the group is being treated with Serpasil, 1 mg daily for a period of 2 months, during which the control group is receiving a placebo. The patients included vary greatly in both age and psychometric level, and at the moment the results of the medication are encouraging, particularly in the youngest members of the group. Improvement has been observed, also, in the care of certain older, mildly mentally retarded individuals whose difficulties in adjustment appear to be psychogenic in origin. These individuals are described as more responsive to direction and better able to discuss their problems realistically. Further investigation is needed to determine whether increased dosage will produce these desirable results in the older age group whose mental subnormality is more severe.

Beneficial results, using Thorazine, have been reported. Flaherty gave 10 to 250 mg a day to 16 disturbed children who were hyperactive, intractable, hostile, and aggressive. He reported a marked diminution of aggressiveness and hostility. The children were more approachable and became aware of their ability to control their impulses. Better hospital adjustment was the result. Bonafide used Thorazine in 78 epileptic patients, all but 3 being mentally retarded. He found that the drug was highly effective in controlling behavior disturbances and did not increase the number of seizures. Additional favorable results with Thorazine have been reported by Brooks, Adamson, and Brill. Bair and Herold noted similar good results in a group of 7 male and 3 female patients. In addition, they reported a phenomenal rise in IQ, attributed by them to the removal of severe emotional and nervous states which, they felt, prevented their patients from functioning at their true level of mental ability. The use of tranquilizing drugs has placed in the hands of the physician a means of controlling the severe behavior disturbances of the more severely retarded individuals who have been refractory to ordinary treatment.

Glutamic acid and its effect on mental functioning has been given a great deal of attention since it was first recommended by Zimmerman and his associates in 1946. The pros and cons of the value of this drug have been discussed in numerous articles. At the present time the findings of Lombard, Gilbert, and Donosrio, who concluded that the feeding of glutamic acid to high-grade mentally retarded children resulted in no improvement in general intelligence, performance rating, or social maturity, are representative of the general feeling about the use of this drug. Zabarenko and Chambers also found that glutamic acid did not produce significant changes in mental functioning.

Shock Therapy. Shock therapy has been utilized in the treatment of some of the emotional disorders of mental subnormality. Although this method of treatment may be beneficial in many cases, consideration must be given to the danger in utilizing this therapy where there is underlying cerebral pathology.

Specific Therapy. Specific therapy of an underlying or accompanying medical disease is, of course, desirable. For example, in the case of cretinism thyroid extract must be given early and in sufficient dosage, since the young untreated cretin will not develop intellectually without adequate treatment.

Therapy of Parents. When a physician is consulted by the parents of a retarded child for advice, that physician has a responsibility not only to the child but to the parents as well. Owing to the tremendous emotional investment which both parents have in any pregnancy, the birth of a subnormal child is, without a doubt, a most serious matter. In his relationship with the parents, the physician must give careful and thoughtful advice, weighed in terms of its possible effect on the parents, on the child, and on other members of the family. The discovery by the parents that they have a subnormal child comes as a profound shock. They experience groundless personal guilt or perhaps half blame their marital partner. They need an opportunity for consultation with an expert in the field of mental subnormality or mental health for frank discussion and reassurance that most of their feelings of guilt are groundless and that many of these conditions are not hereditary in nature. It is hardly necessary to point out that more than one conference with parents may be necessary. Such matters of strong emotional significance cannot be understood and faced after a single interview. Parents should be given accurate information, and their questions should be answered fully and frankly. They should be told what to expect of the child and be helped to guard against expecting too much or demanding too little of him.

Sooner or later the major decision must be made as to whether the child can be cared for at home or whether he should be placed in a foster home or an institution. In reaching this decision three aspects must be carefully considered. These are: the actual condition of the child; the mental health of the family, including the condition of the mother, and the possible effect on the family of retaining a subnormal child in its midst; and the home conditions and financial circumstances of the family. It is obvious that home care is to be recommended in the light of the above discussion of emotional deprivation unless serious family problems might result. Even severely handicapped children can be cared for at home if the parents take a realistic view of the situation and make the use of available child-health services. It is denied catagorically that all subnormal children should be institutionalized. The decision to place a child in an institution should be based on the needs of the individual child and his family. It must be borne in mind that early institutionalization not only fails to relieve the stress, but may intensify it. Early placement can easily be interpreted by troubled parents as a confirmation of their own guilt feelings and an irrevocable rejection of the child. Even a good institution is no substitute for the essential emotional interplay between parents and child.

Professional workers in institutions for the mentally subnormal often witness the distressing experience of a mother who for the first time sees her mongoloid child. Often this meeting is a few years after the birth of the child. In instances where the infant is to be institutionalized, the parents have often been advised not to take the baby home from the maternity hospital for a variety of reasons, including the possibility that they would become overattached to the child. However, the parents, especially the mothers, do not forget the child. The mother wonders how it looks, how it behaves, and has the thoughts common to all mothers. The time eventually arrives when she just has to see the child, and what she sees is not the distressing little creature she had been led to expect, but a lovable child capable of returning parental affection. The emotional reaction of the parent to this discovery is often terrific and potentially pathologic.

Much has been done to ease the burden of retaining a child in the family setting. In most instances only ordinary pediatric care is necessary. When the time for education and training arrives, Massachusetts and other states have provided subspecial classes for those who are too immature mentally and socially to attend the traditional special classes. Studies are being made of the possibility of providing sheltered workshops for the handicapped person who has finished his formal education and training. In short, many facilities either have been provided or are being planned to make it possible for these handicapped people to remain at home. Even in many places where such opportunities are not available there are numerous instances of such individuals making a satisfactory adjustment in the community where they are accepted by their families and neighbors. In large measure the adjustment of these children, the acceptance of them in the community, and the attitudes of siblings depend on the emotional reactions of the parents and their ability to resolve their inevitable guilt feelings and disappointments. A book by the Pollocks entitled *New Hope for the Retarded* can bring explanations and encouragement to parents.

It is recognized that at some time institutionalization may be necessary. If such need occurs, the retarded child who has the advantages of family and community acceptance will find adjustment to the institution easier because of appropriate education and training, especially in the realm of living with others. It is the right of parents to assume the responsibility of deciding the future course for their children. It is the duty of the physician to guide them through the many ramifications of the problem in arriving at a decision.

Conclusions

From the foregoing it should seem obvious to the reader that mental subnormality is a legitimate part of medicine and psychiatry, that advances in this field are only beginning, and that continued investigations in this area will be fruitful and rewarding. Investigations in the field of neuropathology and experimental teratology are giving greater understanding into the nature and prevention of the severer disorders. The application of psychodynamic principles in programs designed for the oligophrenias or milder disorders holds great promise in the field of psychotherapy, while the tranquilizing drugs show great promise as useful pharmacologic agents in therapy for all levels. Few fields offer greater opportunities for scientific research and new contributions.

In this presentation, emphasis has been placed on the medical aspects of mental subnormality with full recognition of the fact that other disciplines have made important contributions to the field, particularly in the areas of psychology, education, and sociology. These advances are of such significance that they merit more detailed discussion than is possible in a single chapter.

PART TWO

Disorders of Psychogenic Origin or without Clearly Defined Physical Cause or Structural Change in the Brain

CHAPTER 13

Psychotic Disorders (The Psychoses)

This group of illnesses is often referred to as the *functional* psychoses and are those which the lay person typically associates with the mentally ill or the "insane."

The division of the mental states into those with and those without demonstrable changes in the brain is a wholly artificial one, and the student should understand that they are divided so at this time because of common usage and because the present state of our psychologic, chemical, physiologic, and histologic techniques is such that no consistent and persistent changes can be found in the disorders included in the following chapters. As we have attempted to point out, all disorders show a combination of somatic and psychologic phenomena. It remains true, however, that in some disorders the somatic phenomena are best understood, and in others, the psychologic. As research and techniques advance on all fronts, these differentials into organic and functional become less meaningful.

Involutional Psychotic Reaction 000–796

Some individuals without previous history of serious psychiatric illness develop a psychosis during the so-called climacteric or involutional period. There is a group of disorders that seems to share common factors in etiology and symptomatology, which can with justification be diagnosed in this category. But recurrences of manic or depressive episodes, the development of paranoid schizophrenic psychoses, the first phases of organic reactions due to cerebral sclerosis, or some of the degenerative disorders should not be confused with or classified in this category.

Symptoms. Typically, symptoms in these cases are difficulty in sleeping, loss of appetite and weight, appearance of aging, feelings of uselessness and a conviction that life is over, and, in some cases, suspiciousness.

172

In many cases the symptoms evolve through these initial stages rapidly, and in well-developed cases one sees marked depressive symptoms with delusions of hopelessness, fears of death, and, in those with paranoid coloring, belief that family, friends, or unspecified persons are attempting to kill them. Somatic delusions of needle pricks and electric shocks to the genitals, the anus, and the extremities are quite common. There is often a wringing of the hands, muttering of hopeless phrases, and picking at hands, feet, or face. The self-inflicted lesions must be treated because secondary infections may progress rapidly in these patients. Patients in this state are suicidal and homicidal, and homicides followed by suicide or suicide attempt occur.

Etiology and Psychopathology. This reaction occurs more commonly in women than men and at a little earlier age. In females it comes on during the middle forties and in males during the middle fifties. In the female the onset may be coincident with the menopause. At one time it was believed (and such opinions are still held by some) that the involutional reactions were precipitated by the endocrinologic changes. More detailed study of these cases and the poor results obtained from endocrine-replacement therapy have led to a reevaluation of these concepts. We now think of the involutional melancholias as due to a combination of the physical and psychologic changes of the climacteric, with the sociologic implications these changes carry in persons who have previously been rather rigid and compulsive-like in character. These people with rigid, meticulous, or compulsive personalities are known to have had some psychologic difficulties with repression at the anal sadistic level. Throughout life, by the mechanism of repression and reaction formation, with the development of a cautious, meticulous, neat, and obsessive character, they are able to adjust satisfactorily. With the sociologic, physiologic, and psychologic stresses incident to the menopause, the reaction formation is no longer sufficient to hold these earlier impulses in check. The situation is solved by one of two methods in these patients: In some patients the hostile impulses are projected onto the environment, and the patient believes that those around him wish to carry out the sadistic impulses on him. This relieves him of the responsibility for these thoughts, thus further serving the ego defense, and at the same time, by making himself the object of the threat, he works out some of the unconscious guilt mechanisms. In some cases these paranoid projections work reasonably well, and the patient's conduct other than the behavior incident to the paranoid delusion remains reasonably good. The delusions serve a useful purpose and they are held onto tenaciously with little possibility of reason or expected success from explanation or psychotherapy.

The failure of psychotherapy in some of these cases is due to the fact that to take away this paranoid defense leaves the second or more common picture in the involutional disorders. In some patients, due to the strength of the repressed hostility, and in others, due to physical deterioration and loss of ego strength, the ego defenses are overwhelmed and the patient is flooded with guilt and delusions of self-destruction. This state may be precipitated by beginning brain changes from cerebral sclerosis, prolonged use of sedative drugs or alcohol, or by the death of a spouse or a child. These patients are dangerous and suicidal. Cultural forces working on these patients are chiefly responsible for the crisis at this period. In women, the cessation of the menses signals the end of the reproductive period, and to some women this symbolizes the end of their sexual attractiveness. For married women at this age, the menopause is often associated with the growing independence of the children and their leaving home. For the spinster or childless couple, hope of procreation is terminated.

In males, the psychologic picture is somewhat the same but with a masculine twist. The sexual drives are no longer as frequent nor as ardent as before and signal the inevitable loss of youth. The physical resources, athletic prowess, and other secondary sexual characteristics begin to decline. For those with some doubts about their masculinity, who have compensated for years with trimness of figure, physical dexterity, and skill at aggressive sports, this decline is threatening and often blindly rationalized. At this age in life a man must recognize that his future has now become the present, and that he has probably realized the top status in life which he can hope to achieve. Also the odds are greater against showing much more progress in his professional or business career and his employability is less.

These psychologic factors for the male and female cannot be escaped in our culture, and if they are not accompanied by too marked a physical deterioration, and if the ego has not been under too much stress adapting itself to pregenital difficulties, most people survive this period by a combination of physiologic and psychologic reorientation. As stated above, some persons cannot summon the resources to meet this new stress in life, and there is the development of a typical involutional reaction; or if the fixations have been different or the life experience of another type, other forms of psychiatric reactions may develop at this stage.

Illustrative of some of these features was a 56-year-old female who came for treatment with a statement that her family was against her. The family stated that she had been agitated, delusional, and had upset the whole neighborhood and the family for about 6 years. The symptoms started coincident with the onset of World War II, when the patient felt that her older son would be drafted. She developed the idea that Germans were in her home town trying to trap him and other members of the family as they went out. This boy was in fact drafted, making the patient's symptoms much worse, and when he was subsequently killed in combat, her agitation and delusions became still worse. Her other children and husband supported her through this period, but finally the family physician convinced them that something would have to be done. Hospitalization was precipitated by the return of her son's body to the home town for burial. Following this event the patient became so upset and agitated, refusing to eat, that the family feared she would commit suicide or starve and brought her to the hospital. From the case history it was revealed that the patient and her husband got along reasonably well. They had 7 children. One child died in infancy and 1 was killed in service. The others were all adults, healthy and productively employed at the time of the patient's admission. The patient was described as being a sober, jealous, suspicious person, with little sense of humor. She was known to be rather quick-tempered and stubborn, very orderly, overly tidy, and stingy with her money. In spite of this, the husband felt she had been a good wife, and the children were obviously fond of her. On admission the patient had a mild hypertension and no other gross physical abnormalities, although she had lost weight and was having great difficulty in sleeping. The patient was placed on treatment with subshock insulin and had eight electroconvulsive treatments. The symptoms cleared up within 37 days of admission. During the latter 2 weeks in the hospital and after discharge, she was given superficial supportive and explanatory psychotherapy. There have been no recurrences of this illness.

A similar case, but without the paranoid projection, was that of a 63-year-old male professional person who, with the development of cardiac and cerebral sclerosis, and the increasing responsibility of his professional job, became moderately confused and developed marked motor agitations, sleeplessness, loss of appetite, loss of weight, and loss of interest in his work. He became mildly suspicious of his colleagues, but there were no well-developed paranoid projections. His family and physician felt that his mental changes were due to the cerebral sclerosis, and that he should be institutionalized for the balance of his life. Because he was a prominent person he was brought to the university hospital for a consultation and final evaluation. It was felt that the organic factors played a role in breaking down the ego defenses, but it was also noted that the patient was approaching retirement, and he resented the physical symptoms which kept him from turning out his previous volume of work. The history revealed that he has always been a very rigid, meticulous, conscientious person, who worked compulsively throughout his life. He felt that since he could no longer produce, he should commit suicide. He felt helpless, and, while grateful for the attention shown by the physicians, thought they were foolish to waste their time. Because of his agitation it was felt that the patient produced a crisis in his cardiovascular state, and after careful consideration by the cardiologist it was decided to place him on subshock insulin and electroshock treatment, with the use of atropine and oxygen as added support during the treatment. The patient cleared up under this treatment within 41 days. At the time of dismissal from the hospital he had arrived at some understanding of the nature of his illness and was determined to seek gainful employment at a lower level of responsibility. He still showed minor defects in memory from the cerebral sclerosis, and, of course, the cardiac damage was still present. This man has had no recurrence of the mental symptoms.

Treatment. The goal in management of these patients should be prevention. Because these individuals tend to be rigid, meticulous, orderly, and often successful, they rarely come to the attention of psychiatrists early enough for one to recommend analytic therapy in their late adolescent or early adult life. The family physician can in his general concern for his patient's health note these rigid, compulsive people as they approach the menopause. Such persons should be encouraged to take up new careers or new active and absorbing hobbies. The choice should be directed so that they provide a suitable outlet for the sublimation of the aggressive urges, an outlet that is acceptable to the usually rigid superego of these patients.

Riesman, in commenting on the deterioration of some persons in the aging process, speaks of the "deterioration and change in some persons as opposed to others." Those who retain their vigor and vitality are often people in the professions or businesses where the business or profession offers an outlet for the constructive use of aggressive energies, where increasing responsibilities may call upon a greater use of these resources. The preparation for retirement will often go far toward preventing the occurrence of these types of illness. At least that is our present impression. If the disorder develops, the treatment is physical support and the correction of minor or major physical deterioration where possible. The use of endocrine preparation should be limited to those cases where it will give needed physical support. A combination of supportive psychotherapy and electroshock therapy has been of great value in our experience. The newer drugs are also of value to patients with a great deal of agitation but must be used with careful supervision of the cardiovascular system, as patients with hypertension do not tolerate the sudden lowering of blood pressures. The supportive psychotherapy should contain a good measure of environmental manipulation by explanations to the family and through attempts to provide the patient with constructive outlets for his energies.

CHAPTER 14

Psychotic Disorders: Affective Reactions 000–x10

The affective disorders are psychiatric reactions grouped together because the primary and principal symptomatic display is found in the fields of emotion, and clinically there is a domination by the emotional processes of thinking and behavior. Kraepelin first described the emotional disturbances as a group under the name of "manic-depressive psychosis." Kraepelin felt that this group of disorders was a definite disease with a hereditary and constitutional basis.

In modern psychiatry many patients are observed with various types of mild disturbances with either a depressive or euphoric symptomatology which does not exactly fit the original description of Kraepelin, and which is obviously due to psychogenic causes. There is no general agreement as to how these disorders should be classified other than the general division of affective disorders. The official classification manual which we are following in this edition of the textbook describes the affective disorders under the headings of the *manic-depressive reactions* and *psychotic depressive reactions*. For the student's convenience we shall describe the symptomatology under these headings, but from a psychopathologic point of view there is little justification, other than different utilization of defenses, for separating a manic-depressive, depressed type from a psychotic depressive reaction. We believe it will be more enlightening for the student if we discuss the etiology and psychopathology of the affective disorders as a unit so that he may have a picture of the clinical syndrome of the affective disorders. Then, for his convenience, we shall describe the symptoms in order that he may properly classify his patients in the record library under the official classification manual.

Incidence of the Affective Disorders. The exact incidence of the affective disorders is not known because many of them are so mild that they

178

are cared for by the general practitioner, and the majority of those seeking psychiatric aid are cared for on an outpatient basis. Public mental hospitals contain over 40,000 individuals classified as suffering from manic-depressive psychosis, and the annual admission rate is about 11,000. The disorder seems to occur more frequently in females than in males and is reported more commonly in city dwellers than in country folk, but inasmuch as the true incidence of the disorder is not known, it seems unwise to draw a far-reaching conclusion from these data. It is accurate to say that of the hospitalized patients, more of them are females than males and more of them come from the city than from the country. Most authors agree that the symptoms of an affective disturbance are manifestations of the patient's attempt to cope with situations in the environment caused by external circumstances or difficulties within himself.

At one time the manic-depressive disorders were thought to be predominantly physiologic or genetic in origin, and many people maintained this belief. In more recent years, however, increasing evidence accumulates to support the belief that the psychologic causes of this disorder are the predominant ones. At least it may be said that the psychologic pictures are much more persistent and recurrent and appear much the same in all cases, while the genetic, constitutional, and physiologic changes vary a great deal among patients. It is our opinion that the psychogenic factors with genetic predisposition are basic and that the physical changes, when present, merely add to the ego load which the individual tries to carry. Vogt, Kraepelin, Reese, and others have shown a marked familial tendency in their patients with manic-depressive reactions. Bellak, after an exhaustive survey of the literature prior to 1952, concluded that there was no single cause for manic-depressive disorder and proposed a psychosomatic etiology.

Pollock, Malzberg, and Fuller state, "There appears to be therefore a familial basis for the development of mental disorders in many cases, though the underlying laws of their manner of transmission are not yet understood." (They are referring to the manic-depressive psychosis.)

All these statistical studies appear to have been carefully made, and we do not doubt their authenticity for the cases upon which their studies were based. It must be pointed out, however, that these studies concerned small segments of patients in institutions and have no validity for the large numbers of milder reactions in persons not in mental institutions, who may not even be seen by psychiatric specialists. Furthermore, the psychologic investigations of the cases they reported (these were not done by the authors of course) did not include deeper psychoanalytic investigation which seems necessary to demonstrate the basic psycho-pathology seen in these cases.

Psychopathology. The original descriptions of Kraepelin and many other authors of descriptive textbooks, including earlier editions of this one, speak of the *dispositional deviations* in individuals who later developed frank manic-depressive psychosis. It appears that approximately one-fourth of these patients show a type of cyclothymic personality pattern, but the fact that the other three-fourths do not indicates that this is a symptom and not a prerequisite of the development of the disorder. Early beliefs that the overactive, energetic, bright, euphoric person tended to develop a manic reaction and the sour, dour, pessimistic one to develop depressive reactions are not borne out on careful statistical analysis of cases in the hospital or clinic. Variations in statistics reported perhaps may be due to confusion and the lack of a clear differentiation between some manic-depressive and some schizophrenic patients, one clinic tending to diagnose them in one category and one in the other. Some of this confusion is explained by the evolution of the disorder in some cases.

White presented the psychopathology of the manic reactions as a "flight into reality," instead of an inward turning. The great activity of the manic patient could be best understood, according to White, as a defense mechanism. The patient appears, by his constant activity, to be covering every possible avenue of approach which might by any possibility touch a sore point or complex, so he rushes wildly from this possible source of danger to that, meanwhile keeping up a stream of diverting activity. White stated:

The manic-depressive psychosis is seen, therefore, not to be characterized so much by the nature of the difficulty with which the patient has to deal as by the way in which he deals with it. This method I have described as a "flight into reality," which is the characteristic of the manic phase, while the failure to deal adequately with the difficulty is manifested by the depression of the depressive phase. In depression the defenses have been broken down, and the patient is overwhelmed by a sense of his moral turpitude (self-accusatory delusion).

Lewin points out that elation is a defense or denial against depression.

Cohen et al. in a detailed analysis of 12 cases confirm the statements of Lewin, Freud, and White that, dynamically, manic behavior is a defense used by the patient to avoid experiencing the underlying depression. Cohen noted that in some cases, prior to the depression, there was a transitory manic episode, but in some patients this defense failed, and the patient developed a full-blown depression. They conclude that manic and depressive attacks are differentiated psychodynamically only on the basis of what makes the manic defense available to some patients and not to others. They point out that some investigators use this difference in a patient's response as an argument for constitutional or metabolic factors, but they correctly point out that this is a matter of opinion and not supported by data, and that further study of the manic defense in the depressive constellation is needed.

Rowe and Daggett made a study of the personality traits of patients with manic attacks, manic and depressive attacks, and depressive attacks, as to their personality traits. Detailed charting shows that all three groups are much alike in that they are frequently sociable and religious. In addition, the manic and depressive groups are alike in that they are fairly often described as reliable, ambitious, and meticulous. The depressive patients differ from the manic ones in that the latter are frequently described as active and egocentric and are commonly considered intelligent, but rarely conscientious. In contrast, the depressive patients are frequently conscientious, usually not active, and rarely considered intelligent or egocentric.

Freud stressed an analogy between normal grief and mourning and pathologic depression, the chief difference being that in pathologic melancholia the loss of the love object is unconscious.

In mourning the attempts to distract the libido from the lost object are made in the unconscious. In pathological depression the conflict of love and hate, in which the one seeks to maintain the other—to break off the libidinal objectives, takes place in its same mental system. But in mourning the road to consciousness is open, while in melancholia, due to a concatenation of factors that invoke repression, this path is closed. It is only after the conflict has taken its repressive turn that the repressed enters consciousness in that form which descriptive psychiatry has considered the disease itself, but which psychoanalysis has proven a restitution attempt on an oral narcissistic basis.

In later writings Freud pictures depressions or melancholia as a conflict between the ego and the superego.

In enlarging on this concept, Oberndorf stated, "The superego has taken possession of the entire sadism of the individual, rages against the helpless ego, which acknowledges its guilt and submits to punishment."

Edward Bibring states that depression is not determined primarily by a conflict between the ego on the one hand and the id, the superego, or the environment on the other, but stems primarily from tension within the ego itself, from an inner systemic conflict. "In other words depression represents an affective state which indicates a state of the ego in terms of helplessness and inhibition of functions." Bibring goes on to state that "The basic mechanism of the depression is the ego's awareness of its helplessness in regard to its aspirations." It is assumed that this represents the core of neurotic and probably psychotic depressions. He assumes that the traumatic experiences occur in early childhood and establish a fixation of the ego to that state of helplessness present at that time. The state is later on regressively reactivated when external situations arise which resemble the primary state. He suggests that the child in its oral phase is exposed to traumatic impressions of helplessness, since it is really helpless, and that reactions of this type may be established by any severe frustration to the little child's vital needs in and beyond the oral phase, especially his need for affection and attention from the parents, or by failure in the child-mother relationship. He feels that other factors which determine the differences in the clinical picture in depressions represent complications or other conditions.

Cohen and her group also comment on the fact that depressions basically represent symptoms stemming from overindulgence or frustration during the oral phase, and they attempt to determine as far as possible the experiences with the parent or other significant people which made it necessary for the prospective manic-depressive individual to develop a pattern which laid down the character, which, in turn, faced with environmental stresses, would develop manic-depressive psychosis. Cohen mentions that the potential depressive person is conventionally well-behaved and frequently successful and hard-working. At times he is so overconscientious as to be called obsessional. Typically the prospective manic-depressive patient is involved in at least one relationship of extreme dependence, his inner need being one of emptiness, and his desire to control the other person is in the sense of swallowing him up or monopolizing him. Cohen et al. found that the family of manic-depressive individuals is typically socially isolated in some way, either from being in low prestige situations or from membership in some special group different from the majority of neighbors. They note that the chief interest in the child by the family is his usefulness in improving the family's position or meeting the parent's prestige needs. They also found that in most families one parent (usually the father) is a failure and is blamed for the family's plight, and that the other parent attempts to use the child to remedy the situation. They stress the importance of the further investigation of these family constellations.

According to some analytic concepts a mild depression or a neurotic depression represents the reactions of a patient to an environment which refuses adequate emotional satisfaction. The illness represents the attempt of the patient to force some object or person in the environment to satisfy these basic needs. The more severe states or so-called "psychotic depressions" represent an accentuation of the above picture in which the patient feels that there has been a complete failure of the environment to provide the needed emotional support, and the psychosis is the patient's attempt to distort the environment so that these needs are supplied on a psychologic level. In the psychotic states the patient turns upon himself his hostility toward the environment or the frustrating objects which will not satisfy his needs. Thus, depressions result when certain persons find their surroundings unable to supply their basic needs for love and self-esteem. The situation may be one in which anybody would feel some lack of self-esteem, such as loss of money, loss of job, some failure in personal or professional relationships, or the loss of some loved person.

There are cases in which success produced a similar feeling. Fenichel describes it, "Paradoxically, even experiences that for a normal person would mean an increase in self-esteem may precipitate a depression, if the success frightens the patient, as a threat of punishment or retaliation, or as an imposition for further tasks, thus augmenting his need for supply."

Cohen, Baker, et al. also comment on this:

In some it has seemed that a depression occurred at the time of promotion in job or some other improvement in circumstances. On scrutiny it can be seen that in those patients where a depression has occurred without an apparent change in circumstances of living, the change which has actually occurred has been in the patient's appraisal of the situation. The patient incessantly hopes for and strives for a dependency relationship in which all his needs are met by the other.

Fenichel further calls a neurotic depression a warning. The person, failing to find satisfaction from that situation in which he finds himself, develops some hostility toward the frustrating object and some feelings of guilt or retaliation. At this stage, however, he clearly distinguishes that which is within himself and that which is the external world, and such depressions are often called reactive depressions, both the patient and the physician realizing that he is reacting to something in his environment. In more severe states the hostility may be greater or the environment less satisfactory, and the patient regresses to an earlier phase in his development in which there is no clear distinction between himself and his environment. As a result he begins to distort the environment, and all the hostility which was originally directed to objects about him, because they refused to satisfy his needs, is now introjected or turned upon himself, and he goes through the sequence of: "You don't satisfy me, I hate you." "You don't satisfy me, I hate me." "I don't satisfy me, I hate myself." This leads to suicidal preoccupations, ideas of self-depreciation and self-condemnation. The patient, having lost the clear distinction between that which is he and that which is the world about him, is psychotic. It is in this state that the patient will attempt to punish himself and become suicidal in his reaction to his original frustrations and loss of esteem. In his zeal to punish himself and also satisfy the hostile urges originally directed toward the environment, the patient usually succeeds in making the persons around him miserable. By his groanings, moanings, and general agitation he reduces the family to a state of turmoil and disorganization that gives some satisfaction to his original externally directed hostile urges.

The story of *Oedipus Rex* is famous in analytic psychology. The sequel to this, *Oedipus at Colonus*, contains beautiful illustrations of self-punishment and projection of hostility onto persons in the environment. In the famous legend, King Oedipus in self-punishment blinds himself, but in *Oedipus at Colonus*, he reduces his daughters and all those around him to a miserable state by continual ranting and self-depreciation.

Publications by psychiatrists in the past 3 or 4 decades suggest that patients fail to find satisfaction in the environment and react with depressive symptoms. Other individuals develop a compulsion neurosis, and still others manage to adjust successfully as a result of differences in constitutional or hereditary predisposition. With each edition of this book we become further impressed that it is the socioenvironmental and psychologic situation which precipitates the illness, and that this situation in some manner either directly or symbolically reactivates earlier experiences and frustrations which were associated with guilt feelings. This failure of the environment to supply satisfaction and the consequent kindling of old guilt feelings causes the patient to react with frustration and hostility, which in the face of the old guilt feeling are introjected and bring about the feelings of guilt, self-punishment, and depression.

Many patients after several recurrences of their manic-depressive reaction progress to a more serious type of disorder, usually diagnosed as schizophrenia. Cohen et al. believe that at the onset of a depression the symptoms and helplessness are an exaggeration of the type of appeal which the patient makes to the important figures of his life in healthy intervals. When they fail to give these satisfactions or reject him, the patient becomes ill. He is left with his severely depressed feeling. "At this point, where the feelings of depression and emptiness are acute, the patient may follow one of three courses. He may remain depressed, he may commit suicide, or he may regress still further to a schizophrenic state."

Helena Deutsch believes that mania and paranoia are alternate defenses against the intense danger to survival of an ego oppressed by melancholia.

There have been many studies of the biologic features in the affective disturbances. The results of biochemical and physiologic studies have been inconclusive. Many variations from normal and the physiochemical state of the body have been recorded. Most of these, however, can best be explained as due to autonomic imbalance engendered by the anxiety and tension accompanying this disorder. Differences in sugar tolerance, blood-calcium levels, lipoid levels, metabolic rates, pulse rates, differential blood counts, etc., are numerous, but these, as in the schizophrenias, occur only in certain of the cases and not in all. One suspects that these are physiologic concomitants of the psychologic disturbance. The basic disturbance in manic-depressive reaction, if not psychologic, remains unknown.

One of the major objections to a predominantly psychologic explanation of the cause of the manic-depressive or affective disorders has been the fact that in some cases there is a definite periodicity to the attacks and in others there is a definite circular quality, patients alternating between manic and depressive states. This circular quality is amply explained by more recent knowledge in psychopathology. Some authors, however, believe these cycles and recurrences are explained in some manner by biologic rhythms, common in other types of illness. It has been demonstrated, however, that psychologic rhythms are as well known and as ancient as the history of man. Ancient writings are full of pagan festivals followed by pagan rites of expiation, and these have their modern Christian counterparts in the Mardi Gras preceding Lent.

Even student behavior shows a gradually increasing crescendo of academic activity culminating in examinations and followed by release of stress and tension by the traditional student binge. It is possible that biologic rhythms have their counterpart in the psychologic functions of certain patients, and that overreaction in either the depressive or manic sphere must bring about its compensation before the person finally levels off to what we interpret as normal emotional activity. At this stage of our knowledge one cannot be dogmatic about the cause of the affective disorders. At the moment, the evidence supporting the psychologic explanation of the disease, including its periodicity, exceeds that supporting the biologic factors. Further research in both spheres is of the essence.

Manic-Depressive Reaction 000–x11, 000–x12, 000–x13

Under this heading go the affective disorders that have been discussed in some detail before, plus possibly a separate type of depressive reaction. This group of disorders is variously called manic-depressive psychosis or manic-depressive disease.

Manic-Depressive Reaction, Manic Type 000–x11

The manic states are usually divided into hypomania, acute mania, and delirious mania, according to the severity of the symptoms. There are innumerable gradations.

Hypomania. Hypomania is manifested by a push of speech and motor activity. Productions are usually coherent and relevant but greatly increased in verbal quantity and often tinged with facetiousness. Patients are usually boastful, optimistic, and aggressive. Attempts to curb their enthusiasm or dilute their expansive plans bring outbursts of irritability. In spite of this behavior many of these patients get along outside an institution but are a source of annoyance to their families and fellow workers. In our experience we have seen a few patients who have successfully launched business enterprises or charitable organizations, or who have sold large quantities of material during the early stage of their hypomanic reaction. Some of these patients subside into a chronic irritable state with frequent complaints directed toward an environment which refuses to cooperate in their schemes and withholds recognition of their true worth. Many develop paranoid tendencies because of the world's failure to accept them at their own evaluation. Still others develop chronic, diffuse, frequently shifting hypochondriacal complaints. Many patients of this group show a hypomanic swing as a precursor to an acute manic episode.

Typical symptoms were shown by a 29-year-old male patient who was brought for observation because of repeated quarrels with employment bureaus, relief agencies, the police, and the judge. The patient's parents were continually bickering and had separated when the patient was a small child. Whenever brought together to discuss the patient's welfare, they used the patient as a weapon against one another. In addition to this family situation, the patient had poliomyelitis, which left him with a deformity in a leg which required prolonged orthopedic attention. He compensated for this by becoming proficient in swimming and horsemanship. It was revealed that he had been sexually promiscuous since the age of 14, and that he had been continually overactive, quarrelsome, and aggressive with the people in his environment. At the hospital he submitted to examinations but refused any form of therapy or attempts to understand his long series of difficulties with his environment. He left the hospital full of plans to succeed on a large scale. He was followed for several years. During this entire period he continued to wander about the country in a restless fashion, never adjusting to any situation or person. When last seen, he was beginning to formulate paranoid ideas centering about one of the social agencies.

Acute Mania. Patients in an acute manic episode require hospitalization as a protection to themselves and the community. They are overactive, combative, and destructive. They frequently disrobe and are quite erotic. If allowed to be at large in the community they often indulge in alcoholic and sexual excesses, unwise investments, and large purchases of useless objects or of junk. They frequently destroy their clothing and furniture, often using portions of the debris to decorate and festoon themselves and their rooms. Feeding becomes a serious problem because they are too busy to eat, and the food is usually utilized for smearing themselves and their surroundings. Forced feeding may be necessary. Sleep is held in abeyance by the hyperactivity and chemosedation in large doses is usually ineffective. The stream of thought is speeded and the patients complain of a crowding of ideas and a pressure of thought. They are distractible, and there is an almost continuous stream of conversation and the progression of thought shows rapid shifts from one topic to another. The shifts are in terms of events in the environment distracting them from their original theme. This rapid shifting is called "flight of ideas." They are often obscene, profane, and their remarks are tinged with eroticism. They laugh uproariously at their own jokes. The mood is one alternating between elation and irritability. When thwarted in their activities, they can show spectacular outbursts of rage but can be easily distracted again to a good-humored vein. There is a progressive weight loss due to the hyperactivity and faulty feeding. The excretory systems function normally, but the excreta are passed promiscuously and are often used for decoration. Sleep is postponed in terms of their hyperactivity, but if put to sleep by prolonged continuous baths or by a large dose of some quick-acting hypnotic drug, they will often sleep from 2 to 5 hours. Hallucinations and delusions occur but are usually not firmly held, and are often of an expansive, wish-fulfilling type. These patients tend to be hyperoriented and within a few hours will have an unusually detailed knowledge of their fellow patients, ward personnel, and the general policies of the institution. Their criticisms of the institution, its management, and its personnel are offered freely, frequently, and in great detail. Elaborate schemes for reorganization and rebuilding may be tendered daily. The patient's grasp of general information, memory, retention, etc., is preserved, but examination of these systems is difficult because the patient is usually distracted from his task to some casual but more interesting environmental activity. Insight is often present to the degree that the patient realizes he is overactive and stimulated, and the patient may state flatly that he is "a manic."

A typical case was a 25-year-old white female, who was brought to the hospital because she was running up excessive bills at a department store for useless objects, was drinking excessively, and was behaving in a profane and vulgar manner in a local hotel. On admission to the hospital she was overactive, elated, and erotic. She would disrobe, destroy her clothing, and break windows at the slightest opportunity. She would demand special privileges and fly into a rage when they were denied. She showed push of speech and flight of ideas. A verbatim example was, "They are all perverts. I caught my husband and his mother together. Imagine that! I've got witnesses. You know I have had a lot of money. I've put out a lot of money. We are all well known. I think I have sex appeal. What do you think of the body? I am pregnant. I want to be pregnant. I almost hemorrhaged to death. How about you? Are you married? I'm interested." The patient broke a large number of windows in a temper outburst and then wrote a clever and facetious poem about it.

Delirious Mania. This term is used to describe patients who are so tremendously stimulated and distracted that they are unable to talk coherently or complete any initiated act before they are distracted to the succeeding one. There is such a frenzy of activity that they lose contact with their environment, and physical exhaustion must be combated to prevent collapse with complicating cardiac and respiratory difficulties.

Psychopathology. This was discussed in the general section on the affective disorders. The manic phase has not been thoroughly studied, probably because this reaction is much less common than the depressive phase. Manic phases are best understood as a type of defense against a depression. Why some patients have this type of defense available, and others do not, is not clearly understood. Symptomatically the patient seems to escape the hostility of the superego temporarily, and by continual movement from one subject to another for a time evades the depression. He brings punishment upon himself either through social and legal complications in the environment, by precipitating confinement, or by running himself to death. If none of these succeeds, he then develops a depression and must work his way through this, or in some instances he regresses further into a paranoid schizophrenic episode with affective coloring.

MANIC-DEPRESSIVE REACTION, DEPRESSED TYPE 000–x12

There is a large literature on the depressive states, and the classifications are about as numerous as the authors. Depressions of psychotic proportions have many features in common. The so-called "reactive depressions" or "neurotic depressions" will be described elsewhere (see Chap. 18, under Depressive Reaction). They share much of the psychopathology of the affective disorders. It is our opinion that the difference between the depressed phase of the manic-depressive disorder and the so-called "depressive psychosis" is that, in the former, the defense of a manic reaction is available to the person but proves unsuccessful and he develops a depressive phase after the mania. To others, this defense is not available and they directly develop a depressive phase as their only type of reaction in the affective sphere. There are many forms of depression described: autonomous, autogenous, endogenous, tension catathymic, agitated, etc. It is our belief these are merely symptomatic variants in terms of the patient's previous personality, his experience, and the capacity he brings to his defense. The psychopathology of these depressions was discussed under the affective disorders. The symptoms, for purposes of classification, may be divided into three groups in terms of severity, simple retardation, acute depression, and depressive stupor. These are merely differences in degrees and do not require subclassification for statistical purposes.

Simple Retardation. These are the depressions which are thought of as being mild. The patients have objective evidence of sadness and retardation. They describe themselves as depressed, sad, or blue, but the symptoms are not too marked, and are often expressed as being "dejected," "defeated," "exhausted," or "disinterested." The patients tend to blame themselves but feel there is no real explanation for their illness. Sensorium and intellectual capacities are unimpaired although thinking is slow. Some of these patients go for years unrecognized as having affective disorders, and take medications, have useless operations, and use hours of a physician's time with no relief for their suffering.

Acute Depression. In this phase the behavior anomalies are most marked. Patients look sad, dejected, and often move slowly. They have a melancholic, stooped, and often disheveled appearance. They take little interest in environmental happenings, although they seem aware of what goes on about them. Many stand or sit in a hypotonic position, while others will show motor agitation with restless pacing, wringing their hands, and picking at themselves. At this stage of depression suicide is an ever-present danger, and patients often make desperate attempts at self-destruction. Some seem purposefully to select painful methods of suicide such as self-mutilation or setting fire to their clothing. They are usually negativistic. The stream of mental activity is slow. They complain of difficulty in thinking, and spontaneous productions are few and colored by their depressed content. Psychomotor activity is sharply reduced, except for those who are motor agitated. The affect is a fixed mood of depression and hopelessness with appropriate biologic concomitants. There is refusal of food, necessitating forced feeding in many cases. Sleep is disturbed, the patients tending to fall asleep or wake up at 2 or 3 A.M. Constipation is a problem. Sex desire is absent and in many instances there is a cessation of menstruation during the period of depression. Evidences of weight loss and dehydration are present if the nursing care is lax. In some instances there is a lowering of the B.M.R. (basal metabolism rate), blood pressure, pulse, and respiration rate. Patients express feelings of guilt, blame themselves for their troubles, and frequently feel that they are to blame for the troubles of the world. They often express ideas of having committed unpardonable sins, and in some instances will fix upon some minor deviation from morality indulged in many years before. Delusions of incurable disease are common. Patients often believe that various segments of their body are dead, have decayed, or disappeared. Somatic hallucinations are common, and auditory hallucinations of a self-condemning, depreciating type are encountered. Olfactory hallucinations of foul odors emanating from their body are sometimes expressed. Sensorium is clear, but a detailed examination is obtained only with perseverance because of the slowing and the patient's lack of interest in the test. Insight which is good during the initial phase of the illness disappears, and the patient is certain of his degradation and hopeless predicament.

A typical example of an acute depression:

A 47-year-old white female was brought to the hospital following a suicide attempt by drowning. She was described as always having been a stable, hardworking person. Her two children were in their late teens. In her twenties, and shortly after her marriage, the patient had a depressive illness which had responded to rest and nursing care after approximately 4 months. At the time the difficulty appeared to have been precipitated by anxiety over her husband who was a maritime engineer carrying explosive cargo during one of the wars. In addition to the concern over her husband's safety, she also had to manage the finances of the family, which she had never done before. Her daughter, the last child at home, had recently married, leaving the patient alone, and in this setting she began to get tired and fatigued. She consulted her local physician who gave her some thyroid to give her more pep, but this did not succeed in alleviating her symptoms and she finally attempted to terminate them by the suicide attempt.

In the hospital she expressed the feeling that she was no good, that she had sinned, that she had disgraced the family, and that we could do nothing for her. She felt that she had some incurable disease, probably cancer. She had a marked sleep disturbance and refused to eat.

After physical examination revealed no pathology, she was placed on electro-shock therapy. After four shock treatments she was greatly improved, and after the sixth one appeared to have recovered from the depressive episode. After a few days' further observation she was dismissed to the community and returned for psychotherapy in the clinic. After further support from psychotherapy she completed her recovery and was able to carry on her activities in the community without further difficulties. After approximately 6 months of follow-up therapy in the clinic, she was dismissed and not seen until 4 years later.

At this time she came to the physician's office, stating that she was again feeling depressed and suicidal and wanted help before she became too ill. She related that about 4 weeks before this visit her husband had been killed in an explosion aboard ship. This was during a postwar maritime accident. The patient was considerably shocked and again had a lost feeling, believing that she had no one to look to for love and affection. Her married daughter, seeking to supply love and affection in terms of the explanations given to the patient and family during her earlier psychotherapy, had moved the patient into her home. However, the patient felt that she was an outsider there and realized that she must build another life of her own. As the danger of suicide was imminent and because the patient apparently previously received some emotional supply from them, she was given four electroshock-therapy treatments and placed in psychotherapy for approximately 7 hours, distributed over a 3-week period. In this setting the patient became more dependent upon herself and began to look about her for emotional satisfaction in the community. When last seen, this patient was getting along well and appeared to be supporting herself in the community.

Depressive Stupor. A depressive stupor is merely a more marked or severe stage of an acute depression. The emotional reaction increases to the point of complete withdrawal from contact with the environment. The patient becomes self-accusative, mute, sluggish, and apathetic. Voluntary motions cease. The patient usually remains in bed and requires tube feeding. The patient usually responds promptly and rapidly to convulsive shock therapy followed by psychotherapy. These patients are not common, particularly with the advent of the acute treatment of these disorders, but one suspects that the stupor is a form of defense against suicidal drives.

Psychopathology. This has been discussed in detail under the affective reactions. Federn states:

The deepest general theoretical assumption is that this group of psychoses represent abnormal manifestations of the death instinct itself, while all other neuroses and psychoses, including the schizophrenic group, represent abnormal manifestations of the love instinct. By this assumption the difference between the two main groups is precisely defined, and the possibility of a combination of both groups in one person is explained. Reactively, of course, both instincts are involved in both groups of diseases just as they are in normal life.

Federn goes on to state that he believes that family research has shown that heredity plays its role in severe cases. He points out that we do not know which are heredity elements and which are due to psychogenic factors. He states, "However, the unbiased observer might conclude that the emotional mental deviation may express itself in the biochemical state, just as well as the unknown biochemical deviation may express itself in the emotional state."

Jeanne Lampl-De Groot speaks of the aggression in depressive states and the origin of these aggressive drives. In psychotherapy the patient shows aggressive outbursts, but he regains more or less gradually a positive attitude toward the analyst and learns to understand that reaction to dangers that were real in childhood is now inappropriate under the circumstances of his adult life in the analytic situation. She says the more successful the realization of the basic instinctual conflict, the sooner the anxiety over aggressive and destructive urges will be overcome, and the patient then may abandon his hostility and aggression against himself, which means that the depressive symptoms disappear.

MANIC-DEPRESSIVE REACTION, OTHER 000–x13

This classification is included for those patients who fluctuate rapidly from manic to depressive episodes or show a mingling of both during one attack. The symptoms and psychopathology are mixtures and demand no further discussion here.

PSYCHOTIC DEPRESSIVE REACTION 000–x14

This classification includes those patients who have no manic episodes but show only severe fixed depressions. Some authors would classify these groups as autonomous and autogenous depressions, as mentioned under the depressed phase of the manic-depressive reactions. A reason for including this classification is that the patient has had no manic episode, which may mean that this type of defense is not available to him, and there is an absence of a history of repeated or recurrent depressions of any kind, or of cyclothymic mood changes when well. If one believes the manic-depressive reactions to be predominantly physiogenic or hereditary, then this classification is justified, otherwise one doubts that it will be included in future editions of classification manuals. The psychopathology for the manic-depressive types of depression is equally valid for this group, but in general the persons described here will have more precipitating factors in the environment. For guidance of the student, it is perhaps best to make a simple rule of thumb. Patients having their first depression, with no history of previous manic swing, and with some precipitating factors in their environment, are classified here.

Treatment of Affective Disorders. The affective disorders respond promptly to proper treatment. They may be managed in the outpatient department, the general hospital, or the psychiatric hospital, depending on the severity of the symptoms. Manic patients usually do best in a hospital and away from distracting influences. In most instances the prompt and aggressive use of the new drugs, chlorpromazine or reserpine, produces a prompt remission in the symptoms and makes the patients amenable to psychotherapy.

In the depressive reactions the principal features to be watched are suicidal attempts, homicidal attempts with suicide following, starvation, and inanition. Patients who are agitated also respond well to chlorpromazine or reserpine. In these patients the electroconvulsive therapy seems to be the treatment of choice for those patients in acute depressions or in depressive stupors. This should always be followed by psychotherapy because there is no reason to believe by experience or by theory that drug or shock therapy resolves the basic conflict. Patients respond readily to psychotherapy in the interval, and it is our clinical impression that the frequency of recurrence is less in patients thoroughly treated by psychotherapy or psychoanalysis. Reactive depressions or cases of simple retardation may be treated with psychotherapy alone.

Prognosis. With prompt and vigorous treatment most of these patients recover from the acute episode. Without adequate follow-up psychotherapy and aid in managing environmental trauma, a substantial number will have recurring attacks. The typical manic-depressive type may have rather periodic or rhythmical attacks. Other patients may have only a single attack in a lifetime. Some cases having recurring manic-depressive episodes ultimately find these illnesses insufficient solution to their problems and develop what may be diagnosed as a schizophrenic disorder. Theoretically this is possible if one believes in the psychogenic origin of these two illnesses. Patients whose recurrences consist of typical manic or depressive symptoms respond equally well to treatment on second and subsequent episodes as they did during the first one. Rapport and confidence established during psychotherapy in the interval will tend to bring these patients back to therapy earlier, and make the treatment of subsequent attacks less difficult.

CHAPTER 15

Psychotic Disorders: Schizophrenic Reactions (Dementia Praecox) 000–x20

Schizophrenia comprises a group of reactions characterized by apathetic, silly, or unexpected emotional responses, by many varieties of defects in the thinking and associative processes, and by, in
many cases, the presence of delusional and hallucinatory phenomena.

These reactions were originally grouped together, under the term "dementia praecox," by Kraepelin, because he felt they shared the tendency
to chronicity, to deterioration, and to development in early adult life.
The present term, schizophrenia, was coined by Bleuler to avoid the unfavorable prognostic implications in the Kraepelin term, and to describe
more accurately the breaking up of the normal pattern of response, particularly the quantitative and qualitative disruption of the usual emotional ideational congruity. Adolf Meyer proposed the term "parergasia"
as a still more accurate expression of the distortions in the behavior pattern seen in this reaction type.

Freud and the psychoanalytic group have described the clinical manifestations of schizophrenia as regression to earlier forms of emotional
adjustment, in which the person was not dependent upon outside sources
for satisfaction of his basic needs. This is usually referred to, in technical language, as "a regression to primary narcissism."

Characteristically the schizophrenias are classified as the simple type,
the hebephrenic type, the catatonic type, the paranoid type, the acute
mixed type, the chronic mixed type, and the mixed schizophrenic-affec-
tive type. Many people feel that schizophrenia comprises a group of disorders, but since we do not know the cause of the disorders there is no
really accurate way of dividing them. Many of us believe that the usual

194

subclassifications mentioned above are descriptive and distinguish the behavior of patients with little differentiation of causes. Furthermore, the longer one works with a schizophrenic person the more apt he is to classify his patient into the mixed or undifferentiated type.

Bleuler believes that "certain symptoms of schizophrenia are present in every case and at every period of the illness even though, as with every other disease symptom, they must have attained a certain degree of intensity before they can be recognized with any certainty." The fundamental symptoms consist of disturbances of association and affectivity, the predilection for fantasy as against reality, and the inclination to divorce one's self from reality (autism). Furthermore, we can add the absence of those very symptoms which play such a great role in certain other diseases, such as primary disturbances of perception, orientation, and memory. The other symptoms, which he feels are determined by causes other than the basic disease, are referred to as "accessory symptoms."

Incidence. This is the commonest form of mental illness in American culture. About 30,000 persons per year are known to develop this disease. Unless treatment is prompt and vigorous many of these patients will become chronic institutional cases. A substantial proportion of them do become chronic. The age of onset is most often in the late teens or twenties, but cases have been reported as young as 4 years and as old as 60.

Symptomatology—History Summary. One of the most characteristic findings in schizophrenia is the history of the patient's development. In the majority of cases the childhood will be characterized by difficulty in socialization with other children and by the inability to find a workable means of forming friendships, giving and receiving satisfaction in play, winning and losing his own battles, and expanding his contacts with people and resources in his environment. At times these children are described as being unhappy, inadequate, and withdrawing. Others are described as odd and irregular in their behavior. It is wrong to think of the child as always being withdrawn and shy (although many are), because others find their difficulty in socialization by failing to make firm or lasting friendships or by undue aggression or hostility. Basically, they seem to have difficulty in forming firm and dependable emotional ties of an appropriate nature to those around them. Attempts to compensate and find satisfaction in adult approval make some of these children well behaved, quiet, and studious. Some are regarded as precocious or brilliant by their parents. Others are reported by their parents as being completely normal children. However, contact with their classmates and associates often reveals that they are in many instances regarded as somewhat different from the others; such terms as "queer," "a sissy," "an icky," "a square," and similar expressions will be used to describe them. Some children, particularly the more withdrawn type, will be taken from school because of "nervousness."

It is often difficult to determine just when the psychotic phase begins. In some instances the family reports a sudden onset with hallucinations or the free expression of delusions. In many cases, more careful inquiry divulges an in-between period of peculiar and odd ideas or behavior, periods of confusion, or periods of rich and vivid fantasy preceding the time of onset as fixed by the family.

In some instances this type of history is not found. This may be an example of the family's projection of their ambitions rather than fact, but in some instances it is accurate. In such cases, the ability to establish good emotional relationships to the environment early, with the symptoms developing late, is a favorable prognostic sign.

Physical Summary. There are no specific physical or neurologic abnormalities in schizophrenia. Generally the individuals tend to be the slender type with poor vasomotor control, particularly peripheral cyanosis, and a general hypotonia is noticed. However, schizophrenic symptoms are seen in the most versatile and perfectly conditioned athletes, as well as in patients showing advanced physical handicaps and deformities.

Symptoms Manifest by Disturbance in Behavior. The behavior of persons suffering from schizophrenia is usually distinguished by some unusual feature, but the nature of this unusual feature shows substantial variation. Some are shy and withdrawn and tend to stand or sit for long periods lost in fantasy—known to students as "schizing"—and oblivious of the environmental events about them.

In some patients this preoccupation becomes pronounced, and the patient appears to be in a stupor, responding only to painful stimuli. In severe cases, the patients are said to have developed *catatonia,* and some of them may be placed in awkward, uncomfortable, or ridiculous positions, which they will retain for a long time. This state, called *cataleptic* or *waxy flexibility,* is associated with the drooling of saliva, retention of excretions, and failure to take food or fluid voluntarily. Postural edema and a peculiar mottled type of peripheral cyanosis are often seen. At times patients may become overactive, assaultive, and destructive. Many patients are confused and preoccupied, and some are aggressive and quarrelsome.

A few patients become silly and sing, dance, and go through weird and intricate gestures, all of which symbolize or act out portions of their fantasies and delusions. Some of this group will decorate themselves with trash, rags, or jewelry, as part of their symbolization. Other patients draw, paint, carve, or model intricate abstract designs and stylized figures to express themselves.

In the paranoid form of schizophrenia, the patient's behavior may attract little attention. Many paranoid patients carry on their routine activities satisfactorily, but close scrutiny will often disclose bizarre diaries, hidden evidence of their persecution protected by elaborate precautions, such as duplicate copies, locked boxes, etc. These anomalies of behavior may be concealed for long periods by these patients, and they are disclosed with great reluctance. Homicidal assaults may occur, but much less frequently than the general public believes. The aggressive acts may occur during periods of catatonic excitement as part of the acting out of fantasies of a religious sort, as a result of orders and commands received via their hallucinatory experiences, or to protect themselves from imagined dangers, threats, or assaults.

Symptoms Manifest by Disturbance in Thinking. Disturbances in thinking are characteristic of schizophrenia and occur in all cases. Bleuler believes that thinking disturbances are among the fundamental symptoms. Disorders of content are found in most schizophrenic cases and are manifest by delusions, peculiar beliefs, and bizarre ideas. Because of their unusual nature, these ideas are most easily detected and are associated with "insanity" or "mental illness" by the average lay person. Disorders of form and organization are more difficult to detect but are more specific for the schizophrenic group of disorders than the content disturbance.

Goldstein believes that schizophrenic patients show a "concrete" type of thinking, as opposed to the "conceptual" type shown in normal individuals. By concrete thinking, he means the interpretation of words and environmental activity in terms of one's own associations or fantasies at the moment. This type of thinking is normal in a child, prior to 3 or 4 years of age. Adults form concepts of situations in terms of all the known elements present and their own prior knowledge and experience. An example of concrete thinking would be a patient thinking that his fellow patients dislike him when he hears another patient sneeze. Instead of believing that the other patient had a cold or some nasal irritation, the schizophrenic patient may interpret the sneeze as an insulting gesture performed to annoy him.

Bleuler describes the thinking in schizophrenias as primarily disturbances in the association of ideas and disturbances in affectivity. The changes in affectivity are usually a blunting or an inadequate emotional response, the patient seeming apathetic or indifferent to emotion-producing events in his environment. At other times the emotional response is inappropriate, the patient laughing at sad incidents, shifting from anger to happiness, or weeping. The emotional reaction inappropriate to his ideas or thoughts is called a disassociated affect.

All these changes in thinking and emotion are described in terms of the examiner's ideas, beliefs, and feelings. The patient's behavior becomes more understandable if we consider his reasons for it. In this disorder the patient has ceased looking to his environment for either emotional stimuli or satisfaction. He has, in the course of the development of his illness, become almost wholly dependent upon himself for emotional satisfaction. He realizes his ambitions and fulfills his desires on an autistic level, and having found these satisfactions within himself he has no need or desire to please or be pleased by the persons in his environment. This results in seeming apathy and indifference to the people about him. The inappropriate affects are often understandable if one considers that the patient has his own special concept of the situation, and his smile on receiving word of a relative's death may be prompted by his belief that this note is proof of his power and that the death occurred because he wished it.

Other patients seem to be under great emotional strain or tension. This is manifest by sweating, sighing, and motor restlessness. At times the tension is discharged in homicidal or destructive outbursts that are unprovoked by the environment. As a rule one finds the tension is secondary to the ideas and delusions the patient is entertaining, but in others the reason is deeper and eludes detection. Patients with this type of emotional reaction are usually in the acute phase, and these signs are thought to be prognostically favorable. With institutional care and chronicity, most of them develop apathy, failing to respond even to their own fantasies.

Another characteristic symptom in schizophrenic patients is the ambivalence manifest by having mixed feelings or, more correctly, opposite feelings, simultaneously about the same object. For example, the mother may love her child and at the same time have death wishes against it. Ambivalence results from the association and emotional disturbances which are basic symptoms in schizophrenia.

Many patients dwell in a fantasy world and have trouble in separating their own identity from their fantasies and in distinguishing between reality and their fantasies. Hallucinations, delusions, and illusions are called the "accessory symptoms" by Bleuler, and he points out that it is usually the accessory symptoms that bring patients to the attention of the hospital authorities.

Meadow, Greenblatt, and Solomon tested the concept that a looseness of association and an impairment of abstraction were cardinal symptoms in schizophrenia. Their data indicate that this concept is true, and they conclude, "The results are interpreted to suggest that impairment in abstraction and looseness of association are closely linked aspects of thought disturbance in chronic schizophrenic subjects, and probably characterize patients with poor prognosis."

Symptoms Manifest by Special Preoccupations, Hallucinations, and Delusions. These so-called "accessory symptoms" are recognized by the public and are quoted as evidence of the correctness of the diagnosis. It is easy to convince a judge or jury that a patient is psychotic if he has these accessory symptoms, but it is most difficult to explain to them the more important primary or fundamental symptoms. The special trend reactions so frequent in schizophrenia are far removed from normal human experience and their presence is thought by some to be specific for the schizophrenic group of disorders. However, similar delusions and hallucinations are seen in various types of chronic and acute toxic states, in the twilight states, in epilepsy, and in severe neurotic panics.

Many patients suffering from schizophrenia are suspicious and feel they are misunderstood and mistreated. Many have definite persecutory ideas, feeling that various fraternal, political, religious, or family groups are organized to persecute, harass, and harm them. Some believe they are being gassed, poisoned, hypnotized or influenced by radio, television, or God. Others interpret innocent actions of other persons as referring to them specifically, so-called "ideas of reference," and offer an excellent example of the concrete thinking described by Goldstein. Many patients have passivity feelings, believing they must do as the voices tell them and disclaiming any personal responsibility for thoughts, words, or actions.

Hallucinations are common in schizophrenia, being found in 50 to 70 per cent of the patients. Auditory hallucinations are the more commonly encountered, but hallucinations may be in any of the sensory fields. The content of the hallucination is colored by the patient's preoccupations, education, and past experience, and represents a projection of his fantasies and desires. Some patients in this group have weird somatic delusions, believe their organs are gone, feel electricity in their body, or receive sex stimulation by remote control.

Symptoms Manifest by Defects in Intellectual Resources. The intellectual reactions are not seriously impaired in schizophrenia. The changes present are more apparent than real and are due to inattention and indifference rather than loss of capacity. The judgment is impaired in terms of the disturbance in emotion, thinking, and the imaginary experiences.

Most of these patients have little insight, failing to understand that the beliefs and experiences which are so vivid to them are peculiar to themselves and lack meaning to other people.

In the early phases of schizophrenia some patients realize that they are undergoing serious mental disturbance. They may seek aid at this time, and, if they do, it is the optimum time for treatment. In this initial stage some patients become worried over their mental changes, become depressed in reaction to them, and at this time may commit suicide. In most cases, however, the transition to acceptance of a belief in their symptoms is accomplished smoothly, and the delusions, imaginations, and hallucinations represent reality to the patient.

Etiology and Psychopathology. The etiology of the schizophrenic reactions is unknown. The theories and explanations of the causes of these reactions are many, and are notable examples of the verbal dexterity of most psychiatrists, but have contributed little to a more satisfactory treatment of the individuals suffering from schizophrenia. The earlier concept that dementia praecox was inherited has been largely discarded. Pollock, Malzberg, and Fuller state, "It is clear, therefore, that though there is probably a familial basis for the origin of many cases of mental disorder in the family stock of probands with dementia praecox, the observed frequency cannot be described in Mendelian terminology."

Kallman studied many sets of twins and other patients in an effort to prove a strong genetic or constitutional factor in schizophrenia and found a much higher ratio of schizophrenia in patients' families than in control populations. Kallman studied 794 sets of twins and 691 families of twins, which included 2,741 full siblings, 134 half-siblings, 74 step-siblings, 1,191 parents, and 264 marital partners of twin patients. The morbidity rate discovered in this series is in line with a genetic theory of schizophrenia. He found a schizophrenia incidence of 1.8 per cent for the step-siblings, 2.1 per cent for the marriage partners, 7.0 per cent for the half-siblings, 9.2 per cent for the parents, 14.3 per cent for the full-siblings, 14.7 per cent for the dizygotic cotwins, and 85.8 per cent for the monozygotic cotwins. "This morbidity distribution indicates that the chance of developing schizophrenia in comparable environment increases in proportion to the degree of blood relationship with schizophrenic index cases." Kallman continues publishing results of his studies of genetics in schizophrenia, and the student is referred to them.

It is emphasized by Kallman, however, that the genetic theory does not invalidate any psychologic theory of a descriptive or analytic nature and is equally compatible with the psychiatric concept that schizophrenia may be prevented as well as cured. He means that patients inherit a susceptibility and that patients with this basic inheritance confronted with adequate environmental stresses will develop the disease.

The factors of inheritance in schizophrenia must also be evaluated in terms of the environmental change for the patient produced by the illness of the parent. Berry found a surprising number of schizophrenic patients had lost their mothers prior to 8 years of age, and the separation of the mother from the child by the development of a psychosis must be evaluated in any consideration of the possible role of heredity in the production of these disorders. Ruth and Theodore Lidz have published material on a small group of schizophrenic patients, showing a significant incidence of parental separation, other parental difficulties, and emotional disturbance in the parents.

The work of Hollingshead and Redlich demonstrates an association between social class and the presence of schizophrenia in the community. They believe the high incidence of schizophrenia in the lower-class group in their population was due to the fact that class differences reflect in different methods of treatment and rehabilitation, and that the lower-class schizophrenic is less likely to be rehabilitated or to have more than one chance in the community. Further consideration of the family pattern by Wahl suggests that hereditary predispositions may indeed contribute to the disturbances in a schizophrenic patient, but they act conjointly with social stresses encountered by the patient as he grows up. Wahl believes schizophrenia is increasingly viewed as the outcome of a disturbance in interpersonal relations. In his series of 392 patients, only 12.0 per cent had family histories unmarred by parental rejection, overprotection, or parental loss. He agrees with Reichard who states, "A schizophrenic cannot have had a happy childhood."

The literature on theories of the cause of schizophrenia and recommendations for its treatment are so extensive that an author cannot honestly claim to have read them all.

Most theories contend that the schizophrenic disorders fall into two large groups. They claim: (1) that schizophrenia is a functional disorder, a faulty reaction to life experiences with habit deterioration, and that anatomic, chemical, or physiologic variations from normal are explained by the tensions, frustrations, and other difficulties induced by the patient's attempt to compensate for his adjustment difficulties in terms of the personality and environmental problems he faces; and (2) that schizophrenia is an organic disease process of unknown cause and unknown pathology, characterized by a faulty inheritance, by alterations in behavior, and by habit deterioration with a return to more infantile levels of adjustment, not unlike those seen in some of the organic mental states.

Meadow, Greenblatt, Funkenstein, and Solomon believe that schizophrenic patients fall into two large groups that can be differentiated chemically. They believe that there are two "polar" types of schizophrenia. The first is distinguished by poor abstraction, disorganization of personality, and a very slight response to Mccholyl; they believe this group has a poor prognosis. The second has good abstraction, good personality organization, and marked response to Mecholyl; they believe this group has a relatively good prognosis.

Bellak published a review of over 3,500 papers concerned with the various aspects of schizophrenia. This, plus his clinical experience with the disorder, leads him to the formulation of a multiple-factor psychosomatic theory of schizophrenia. He believes the clinical condition of schizophrenia is only a common set of phenomena seen in widely differing diseases with a multitude of etiologic factors. The literature contains possible causal factors including anatomic, biochemical, endocrine, genetic, infectious, neurophysiologic, and psychologic. Bellak believes the different causes, whether they may be primarily one or the other, always contain both psychogenic and somatic factors. Whichever factors, somatic or psychogenic, may be primary in a given case, one must see that each case involves both aspects. Federn also believes that schizophrenia is basically a weakness of the ego of combined psychogenic and somatic causes.

The functional concepts of the etiology of the schizophrenias have distinguished American psychiatry after the stimulus of Meyer, Freud, Hoch, White, and their pupils. The basic view is that certain individuals meeting life experiences, to which they have difficulty in adjusting, withdraw or compromise in an unsatisfactory manner. The person finds his satisfactions in fantasy wherein he says or does the things he wished to do in the original setting. Succeeding difficult situations are handled in a similar manner. As time passes and difficulties accumulate the individual depends to an increasing degree upon himself and his own fantasies for his satisfactions from life. At last a point is reached where these fantasies assume the dominant role and environmental events are interpreted in terms of these fantasies. The patient is said to be living in a world of unreality. His own ideas, wishes, and beliefs are attributed to the people in his environment. This disturbance in ego function is the principal symptom of this disorder.

Analytic work with schizophrenic patients demonstrates that these patients have great difficulty in forming emotional attachments to other persons. The disturbance in the capacity to develop emotional attachments to other people explains much of the pathology in schizophrenia.

In Chapter 1 we said an infant has difficulty in distinguishing between that which is himself and that which is in the world about him. His experience and emotional development have not yet progressed to the point where he exists as an individual separate from other persons and objects in his environment. With growth the infant forms emotional ties to parents and others in his environment, but dependable ties are not formed by the potential schizophrenic person. A high incidence of broken families and other difficulties in forming ego attachments are typical of the histories and the content of the analysis of these patients. In schizophrenia, the person, having found the world around him unsatisfactory for supplying his needs and demands, regresses, as a protective device, to levels where he was in effect emotionally self-sufficient. Fenichel stated:

> The infant starts out in a state of primary narcissism in which the systems of the mental apparatus are not yet differentiated from each other, and in which no object exists as yet. The differentiation of the ego coincides with the discovery of objects. An ego exists insofar as it is differentiated from objects that are not ego. Therefore, the following formula means one and the same thing, only varying in point of view. The schizophrenic has regressed to narcissism; the schizophrenic has lost his object; the schizophrenic has parted with reality; the schizophrenic's ego has broken down.

Federn believes the ego efficiency is constantly maintained by its cathexis of mental energy. He believes that schizophrenia is due to a deficiency of ego cathexis, whether of supply or of apportionment. He states that the causes of this deficient supply are unknown, and it is obvious that in schizophrenia it is the ego that is ill. Hoch, Wahl, Lidz, and others have studied the disturbance of family pattern as a source which may explain in part the lack of ego cathexis seen in the schizophrenic disorders.

Arieti states, "The fundamental concept of the dynamic interpretation of schizophrenia may be summarized in the following sentence: Schizophrenia is a specific reaction to an extremely severe state of anxiety originated in childhood, reactivated later in life. It must be added that this specific reaction occurs when no other solution, no other possibility of adjustment is any longer available to the patient." He discusses the psychodynamic patterns of the schizophrenic patient, particularly in his relation with the parent. Children who have difficulty in relating to their parents because of rejection, because of difficulties between the parents, or because one parent is a weakling dominated by the other may seek to obtain parental love and esteem by complying with requests of the parents. Others find that the parent will yield only if they cry and have tantrums, and they, therefore, fight for what they want and become aggressive and hostile persons. Others learn to avoid their parents by maintaining an emotional or physical aloofness. Arieti believes that "the specific type of personality is determined by the specific type of relationship that the child has with his parents."

Arieti does not believe that schizophrenia is an organic disease, but that the psychologic changes produce alterations of the somatic function, and that these altered somatic functions may produce organic pathology or physiologic changes. He likens the changes to the psychosomatic effect seen in certain neuroses.

Beck reviews briefly the successful psychotherapy of a case of schizophrenia managed as an outpatient, even though showing all the typical signs of schizophrenia, both fundamental and accessory. Such reports, although favoring a psychologic or functional cause of schizophrenia, must not be accepted as proof, because it is theoretically possible that the improvement in the psychic conflicts which we know exist may result in sufficient relief of the ego so it can adapt to the continuing physiologic or chemical disturbance that may be the fundamental cause of the disease. It is also theoretically possible that in certain individuals the physiologic or chemical functions become distorted under psychologic stress, and that this happens because of inherited tendencies. Thus, psychogenic factors might precipitate an organic disorder, and psychotherapy might conceivably treat it. One must maintain an open mind, although at present one strongly leans to the acceptance of a psychosomatic concept.

Organic theories of the cause of schizophrenia have been most popular in Europe, and much material has accumulated. The findings are inconstant, and in most instances the clinical features of the particular schizophrenic patients on which pathologic changes in physiology or chemistry are reported are not clearly indicated. Many workers have reported a correlation between schizophrenia and the linear or asthenic or leptosomatic body type, but every psychiatrist has seen many typical cases with athletic or pyknic body build. One can say that there are more linear than broad persons suffering from schizophrenia, but body type is apparently not essential to the development of one of this group of disorders.

Pathology in the brain has been reported by many laboratory workers. Nissl reports cortical degeneration. Josephy found cellular changes in the third and fifth layers of the cortex and Naito confirmed these findings. Fungeld described lipoid sclerosis in the third cortical layer and lipoid deposits in the optic thalamus. Marcuse found double nuclei and lipoid degeneration in some of the thalamic ganglion cells. Kitaboyashi reports characteristic changes in the choroid plexus. Alzheimer demonstrated ameboid glia cells in some acute cases. Penfield, Elvidge, and Reed have demonstrated a glial reaction in the white matter of biopsy specimens removed from both acute and chronic cases of schizophrenia. Elvidge and Reed believe the symptoms are due to a disturbance of the association pathways, and report similar findings in manic-depressive patients and patients in a postepileptic stupor. They found no such changes in epileptic patients, who were mentally clear, and no such change in the control patients. Goldstein, Nissl, and Orton also found a glial reaction in the white matter and the deep cortical layers, plus an increase in the lipoid content of the ganglion cells. Freeman found fat in increased amounts in the cells of the basal ganglia, and calcareous degeneration of the blood cells in many cases of schizophrenia. Freeman also found a deficiency of iron in the cortical ganglion cells in schizophrenic patients of all types except the paranoid form.

R. Hoskins, probably the world's authority on the endocrine factors in schizophrenia, states, after commenting at length about the inadequacy of any of the studies and the unevenness of the results, "But even so, the conclusion is unavoidable, that although the issue is by no means closed the bright hopes that have been entertained have by no means come to impressive fruition. Some of the reasons for the disappointment may be considered." He then comments on psychiatrists being too busy to do research, how research in the field of therapeutics presents difficulties because psychiatric nosology is inexact, and the concept of schizophrenia not being the same in all institutions.

There is not at present any sound reason for thinking that the endocrines play a primary role in the production of schizophrenia, or that endocrine products, other than insulin used as a form of shock treatment, have an important role in therapy.

Bliss, Migeon, and his associates investigated the concentration of adrenal steroids on the basis of their experiments and found no evidence of impairment of adrenal cortical physiology in the chronic schizophrenic patients. They disagree with Pincus, Hoagland, and associates that significant adrenal cortical hypofunction or dysfunction exists in the schizophrenic patients. Pincus and Hoagland have published a series of articles on what seems to be carefully done work, and report adrenocortical change in schizophrenia. The problem in evaluating such differences is illustrated in work by Pincus.

Stevenson, Metcalfe, and Hobbs studied the circulating eosinophil count in morning and afternoon periods in response to the injection of 0.3 mg of epinephrine or to 25 mg of corticotropin. They found that schizophrenic patients showed a smaller response to epinephrine or corticotropin than the healthy controls. They found that catatonic schizophrenic patients had a relatively normal response and they report that this is further reason for thinking that catatonic and paranoid schizophrenic patients are different. One year later Hobbs, Goddard, and Stevenson reported work that does not confirm their original study, stating that there is great similarity in the daily eosinophil cycle in the same patients studied 3 and 6 months apart. They noticed that there was a classic cycle in body temperature, which was the exact reciprocal of the eosinophil cycle, but that there was no significant difference between psychotic and normal groups, and they concluded that the magnitude of the daily cycle of eosinophils in schizophrenic patients is no evidence that adrenal cortical function is impaired in chronic schizophrenia.

Many authors report impaired glucose metabolism in schizophrenia.

Altschule and Goncz report a lag in the return of the fasting level of true blood glucose, and an excessive elevation in lactic acid, a rise in citric α-ketoglutaric acid, and an increased and prolonged fall in serum organic phosphate in schizophrenic patients. It is their belief that the abnormal intermediary carbohydrate metabolism exhibited by patients with schizophrenic, manic-depressive, and involutional psychoses is evidently not the primary cause of the disease, but it suggests that these psychoses are organic diseases of the brain.

Meduna, Kety, and many other workers report studies on carbohydrate metabolism in schizophrenia. These extensive chemical studies done on brain metabolism in schizophrenia give much information, but results are inconclusive and inconsistent in explaining the cause of schizophrenia. There is an excellent review of the various physiologic studies in the schizophrenias in *Medical Research at Mid-century* published for the American Foundation by Little, Brown & Company, Boston, 1955. However, this review will leave the student confused because no single report shows conclusive changes present in all schizophrenic patients or any group of schizophrenic patients that are separable from the others by present diagnostic categories. Certain psychologic phenomena in both symptoms and psychopathology are found in all schizophrenic patients, but it remains a moot question whether these are due to the basic disorder, or whether the basic disorder is secondary to the stresses induced by these psychologic changes.

The work with d-lysergic acid diethylamide and serotonin referred to in Chapter 3 and its significance to our understanding of schizophrenia cannot be evaluated at this time, but it offers exciting possibilities.

The new field of electrophysiology has been disappointing to date.

Heath and his group at Tulane have found certain electroencephalographic abnormalities consistently present in chronic schizophrenic patients if electrodes are placed deep in the midbrain. Jacobsen, Peterson, and their colleagues found on depth recording that patients showed indications of paroxysmal dysthymia in the EEG with deep intracerebral electrodes. These waves were 2 to 5 per second and were found in patients who had been under observation for many years without seizures. These changes were present during hallucinatory episodes, or acute episodes of psychotic behavior.

Hemphill, Reiss, and Taylor report a special form of atrophy of the tubules of the testes in many schizophrenic patients which they feel is not the cause of schizophrenia but is evidence of a complex central unbalance or general metabolic disorder, of which this is one sign. They do not believe it is related to mental trauma or masturbation. This work has not been confirmed so far as the authors know.

The problem of the possible physiologic or chemical changes in the brain is still the subject of extensive research and study.

Lauretta Bender, who has written much on childhood schizophrenia, states, "In other words no child can develop schizophrenia unless predisposed by heredity; the psychosis is precipitated by a physiologic crisis; the pattern of the psychosis and its defense mechanisms are determined by environmental and psychological forces."

Tietza found that mothers of the schizophrenic patients were tense and anxious and could feel secure only when in control of the situation. Some tried to be openly dominating by being demanding. However, others were docile, submissive, and dominated the situation in a subtle, passive way. Most of these mothers were sensitive, easily hurt, and reported that their marital relations had been strained. They were all dominant in their household, either by overt domination or by more passive, subtle methods. The authors conclude that the dominating mother, particularly of the subtle type, is dangerous to the child. The child, wishing to rebel against such domination, is deprived of any outlet for his aggressive impulses, and he senses the rejection his mother feels toward him.

Hotchkiss and her coworkers studied the mothers of 22 young male schizophrenic patients as they appeared in the mental hospital setting. They conducted interviews with the mothers and also directly observed the mother and son during visiting periods. They found the mothers did not fit into a pattern; they were the oversolicitous, hovering, and domineering type; the sweet and indulgent type; the seductive type; the intent, controlled, and purposeful type; and the remote and nonparticipating type. They felt that the information gained was of value, and they attempted to keep bias in their interpretation from appearing by including observations made independently by social workers and nurses.

Prognosis. With each succeeding edition of this book the authors become more optimistic about the therapeutic potentialities of schizophrenic patients, particularly those managed from the onset of their disorder. Most studies on prognosis are mass studies, and we have no dependable information on the prognosis in patients intensively treated with combined modern methods. There are many studies on those treated with the shock therapies and with psychotherapy. In neither case is there careful delineation of the amount or kind of treatment given. Work by Whitehorn and others indicates that even the person who gives the treatment may be important in the ultimate prognosis.

There is an urgent need for a careful evaluation of the effectiveness of psychotherapy, psychoanalytic therapy, psychotherapy combined with the pharmacologic or physical treatments, and total push therapy. At present one can say that about 60 to 75 per cent of cases treated during the first 12 months of the illness will obtain a remission, and, if properly followed, the majority will maintain this remission for some time.

Bond presented a 25-year follow-up study of patients from the Institute of the Pennsylvania Hospital. There were 393 consecutive schizophrenic patients treated between 1925 and 1934, before the use of shock treatments. In the period 1940 to 1946, there were 440 patients admitted with schizophrenia. The two groups were separated because the second group had insulin and electric shock available for treatment. In the earlier group of 393, 30 recovered and remained well for 5 years; 25 were well when they left the hospital; 5 others recovered in a state hospital; and 1 had a recovery lasting 19 years after living in a primitive fashion in the woods with a cousin. After 5 years 7 relapsed; 1 of these recovered from his relapse. In the latter series, after shock treatments, 67 were well on discharge; 8 recovered later in state hospitals; 2 recovered in private hospitals; and 1 recovered after electroshock therapy given weekly for 1 year. In the sixth year 8 patients relapsed, but 5 of these were known to have recovered again; 1 was improved after lobotomy and 2 were suicides; 1 patient relapsed 10 years after treatment and another 13 years after, but subsequently recovered.

Thus, with the shock treatments, there are more recoveries sustained for 5 years or longer, 22 per cent as compared with 9 per cent for the control group. It is also noted that in the shock series the average stay in the hospital was 2 months, while for the control it was 12 months. Unfortunately, while it is known that all forms of psychotherapy, occupational therapy, and other group manipulations are used at the Pennsylvania Hospital, there was no estimate made of the effect these therapies had on patients or the relative amounts of psychotherapy and other therapies administered to the two series. It is also known that during the period of the second series, the psychoanalytic influence was coming into the ascendancy in the Pennsylvania Hospital, and the effect this had on the series is not evaluated. Even so, it is probably the best follow-up study of schizophrenic patients in this country.

Finiefs reports treatment of schizophrenic patients extending over the 17 years preceding the paper. Only "typical" cases were included. This author also describes his use of terms, which is helpful. Of his 1,009 cases, 446 received no treatment beyond ordinary nursing and hospital care. In this group 34.5 per cent were discharged as "much improved" or "improved"; 82 patients received electroconvulsive therapy, and 39 per cent were discharged; 103 patients were treated with combined electroconvulsive and insulin coma therapy, and 54.3 per cent were discharged; 378 patients received insulin coma therapy, and 54.2 per cent of these were discharged. In this latter group the patients received psychotherapy in the form of suggestions and reassurance. In a group of 156 patients discharged after receiving no special treatment, 14 per cent remained well for 5 years or longer; of 188 patients discharged after special therapy at least 5 years before the study, 62 per cent are known to have remained well for 5 years or longer. The average stay in the hospital for the non-treated patients was 8.3 months, and 5 months for the treated ones. They also found that the prognosis was best during the first year of illness.

Treatment of the Schizophrenic Patients. The treatment of schizophrenia has undergone an interesting evolution in the past 30 years. Treatment prior to the advent of the pharmacologic and electroconvulsive treatments consisted in occupational therapy, hydrotherapy, and environmental manipulation. Insulin shock treatment and electroconvulsive treatment became widely used in the treatment of the schizophrenic disorders with obvious improvement in the therapeutic results. In recent years, interest has been revived in combining active and dynamically planned ward manipulations with drug and shock therapies in the management of these patients. This has further increased the recovery rate in schizophrenia, especially in the chronic cases that were thought to respond poorly to insulin coma alone. Lobotomy for selected disturbed patients proved a drastic but useful treatment for the few in which its special indications are found. In the past 2 years new forms of drug therapy, notably chlorpromazine and reserpine, have been shown to exert powerful therapeutic effect on schizophrenic patients, particularly those actively hallucinating and showing any type of disturbed or aggressive behavior. These drugs apparently do not modify the schizophrenic process itself, but through some action on midbrain areas make the patient tractable and capable of participating in psychotherapy and of taking part in environmental manipulative activities. At present, hospitals are not properly staffed to exploit fully the potentials for therapy that large numbers of chronic continued-care patients show under these treatments. As of this writing one can only say that a powerful new weapon has been added to our therapeutic arsenal. Its full impact on the care of patients has not been evaluated.

Other new drugs such as Frenquil and Miltown are also in experimental use, but they seem to be less potent than the two first mentioned. Nicotinic acid and its variations, glutamic acid and its variations, malononitrile, isoniazide, ACTH, cortisone, and lysergic acid (LSD) have all proved valuable research instruments to study the schizophrenic process, but have brought no lasting therapeutic benfits to the patients.

The use of nonmedical people for group and individual psychotherapy in schizophrenic patients has also been under careful study, and it appears that with proper supervision these people may offer new hope to patients who cannot be reached by our limited group of trained psychiatrists. Nonmedical persons trained in therapy, like Gertrude Schwing, show that detailed psychotherapy by skilled nonmedical practitioners can be successful in very difficult cases of schizophrenia. Work done by trained nonmedical analysts also confirms the earlier finding of Federn and others, that the basic difficulty is to be found in ego weakness. "As the patient's ego develops strength in its ability to love, the patient is led slowly into an identification with the psychotherapist. Only this identification will bring about the quiet disappearance of the undesired guest." Other experiments, some of them in the Massachusetts system, reveal that group therapy is effective conducted as discussion groups or patient-government groups by attendants, nurses, and social workers, providing they are supported and supervised by adequately trained physicians.

The prognosis varies with the symptoms and the treatment available. The presence of a large number of precipitating factors in the illness, particularly if these factors are environmental forces that can be altered, is a favorable sign. An abrupt stormy onset with violent reactions to the hallucinations and delusions is also thought to indicate a favorable prognosis. A history of a previously well-organized and strong ego, with regression in the face of severe personal or external events, is another favorable sign. On the opposing side, a gradual insidious onset, the presence of the so-called "fundamental symptoms" of Bleuler early in the illness, particularly disturbances of association, and apathy and indifference are thought to be unfavorable prognostic signs. The presence of an active, rejecting mother, whether her rejection is an active, hostile one or a passive, subtle one, is also an unfavorable prognostic sign.

Bleuler stated that the subgroups, however chosen, were not really natural subdivisions, but were merely a grouping of symptoms. He also pointed out that symptom combinations are endless. The longer one studies a case the greater is the tendency to classify it as an acute or chronic undifferentiated type. For the student's guidance in classifying his patients and talking to his colleagues, we shall describe the symptoms usually grouped under the various types.

Schizophrenic Reaction, Simple Type 000–x21

These patients show principally the fundamental symptoms of Bleuler, with few of the accessory symptoms. The history is typically one of gradual withdrawal of interest in the world around, beginning apathy, and lower efficiency. Many of these patients will have neurotic-like psychosomatic complaints. The onset is usually so subtle and the patients subside into symptoms so gradually that the family is often unaware that anything seriously affects the patients. These patients frequent medical clinics, hobo jungles, welfare offices, and other social institutions that lend support to the improvidence and inefficiency that result from their symptoms. They comprise the most often unrecognized type of schizophrenic disorder. When their economic circumstances are better, they are often considered unbearable, unreasonable, confused, and inefficient persons. Occasionally, one sees such a patient resorting to alcohol or drugs. Many of them show a downward trend in the social and economic scale. Some are thought to have many secondary neurotic reactions, and Hoch has described some of them as "pseudoneurotic schizophrenias." In some cases the symptoms are present long before anybody recognizes them.

An example was a 20-year-old male brought by his mother because he worried about himself, had no ambition, and could not decide what he wanted to do. The mother believed that his illness started when he was a baby, as a result of colitis which she thought was caused by his eating a pickle. She stated that his illness had been diagnosed as hysteria, schizophrenia, and a combination of physical diseases. The mother was a very active, aggressive, domineering woman, who not only managed the patient but attempted to manage his therapy and the long series of physicians with whom she had contact. The parents separated when the patient was an infant. The mother worked and he was cared for by servants. The mother stated that there have been frequent changes of servants because she was not satisfied with the way they took care of the child.

He was incorrectly diagnosed as having syphilis, sarcoma, and malaria. At times he felt nervous and thought he was losing his mind. The patient described a series of maladjustments to school, to college, to the military service, and to innumerable jobs. He was perplexed, yet answered questions coherently. When alone, he would sigh deeply, groan, and touch himself in various places. He stated that he was short of breath and attempted to explain the origin of his pain, but after a few coherent remarks would go into long, irrelevant, and inconsequential stories. He seemed indifferent to the environment, although when one asked him to do something, he could cooperate. At times he became annoyed and irritable with the office staff or with the physician. Tension was more marked when his mother was present than when she was not with him. He had no hallucinations or delusions. He complained of difficulty in thinking, stating, "Words become stuck in my head." He said he was under great nervous tension, thought he might "blow up" and become uncontrollable, but he mentioned no object for his uncontrollable rage. (The psychiatrist assumed the patient meant his mother, but this represented the psychiatrist's feelings for the mother, and not necessarily those of the patient.)

The mother refused to allow the patient to have more than superficial treatment, and when last heard from, was still shopping from one physician to another, exploiting her hostility for the son by never permitting him any type of working relation with any of the long series of competent physicians to whom she had taken him.

Schizophrenic Reaction, Hebephrenic Type 000–x22

These are the silly dissociated schizophrenic patients whose illness usually begins fairly early in life. They smile, laugh, grimace, and display mannerisms and peculiar and changeable ideas which may be absurd and grotesque. These patients show the "schizophrenic dementia" mentioned by Bleuler. They show the fundamental signs of marked dissociation of the thought processes and dissociation of the emotional processes, with silliness and inappropriate affects. The apparent intellectual changes are due to inattention and the associative difficulties. They also have weird accessory symptoms, particularly in the hallucinatory and delusional field.

A particular example is an 18-year-old boy, brought to the hospital because he had started chopping on the hood of an automobile with a meat cleaver. The boy was confused, frequently grimacing and smiling. He went through symbolic activities with his hands and at times would yawn. He stated he attacked the car because it had been calling him an s.o.b. all day while he worked in his father's store. (The car was parked just in front of the store.) He also revealed that for some time the bakery goods in the store had been making derogatory remarks but others would support him. He felt voices were coming from some pies which called him a homosexual and an s.o.b. Other articles in the store told the patient not to worry about these things, that the pies were only trying to annoy him. He had no organized paranoid coloring, and felt puzzled and perplexed by the whole business. He would answer some questions by gestures or by smirking. It was not possible to get an explanation of all of these for he had worked out a kind of sign language of his own and became annoyed at the physician for being unable to comprehend. It was noted that the yawning was most common when one of the nurses went by, particularly if she was a young and attractive nurse. The patient finally said the yawning was his way of offering to go to bed with the nurse if she felt the need, but he did not seem upset that they failed to understand him or failed to respond to his overtures.

Schizophrenic Reaction, Catatonic Type 000–x23

The typical and differentiating symptom of this particular subgroup is the catatonia mentioned earlier, alternating with periods of overactivity and agitation. Very often the onset may be rather sudden, according to the family, with overactivity, combativeness, and destructiveness. In this stage the patients may be thought to suffer from mania if the examination is not carefully done. These patients will ultimately lapse into catatonia in which they stand or sit in a bowed, dejected manner for hours on end. A few assume odd postures. Some develop a stupor in which they appear to be unconscious. At times these symptoms of preoccupation, posturing, and finally stupor are the presenting symptoms. They usually come on gradually, and often lead the family to believe that the person is being drugged or "doped." Patients classified in this group may or may not have an active hallucinatory and delusional system. Typically, they will have auditory hallucinations and at times these hallucinations order them about. Some patients also have somatic hallucinations. It may be difficult to elicit these symptoms.

These patients present a serious nursing problem, because in the stupor state they do not feed themselves. They do not take care of their excretions, and they drool saliva. If allowed to go untreated, they become the backward, sitting, vegetating patient, who may periodically go through a long period of active, destructive behavior. A typical example was a patient brought to the hospital by the family. The police found him in a field, and the newspapers had written him up as "a scarecrow man." Neighbors had noted this person standing in the field posturing for several days at a time and had the police bring him to the hospital. In the hospital the patient stood near the door to the nursing station, and would stay in whatever position he was left by the attendants. He gave no sign of awareness of what went on about him, and during this acute phase it was necessary to feed him by intubation and move him about from his bed, to his feet, to a chair, to prevent postural edema. A manic patient on the ward was intrigued by this patient's lack of activity and heckled him a good deal. When not observed by the nurses, he would place the patient in grotesque positions. One time while the manic patient was standing in front of the catatonic patient berating him, the catatonic patient suddenly struck the manic patient. This was observed by the nurse, but when the manic patient scrambled back to his feet the patient was again apparently oblivious to all that went on around him. Shortly after this the patient went into a very disturbed overactive period but responded promptly to the newer methods of treatment with combined shock therapy and psychotherapy.

Schizophrenic Reaction, Paranoid Type 000–x24

This is one of the commonest forms of schizophrenia. In the older texts and in the courts, many of the patients referred to as paranoid were actually paranoid schizophrenic. This form of the disorder may come on at any age, but tends to come on at a somewhat later age than the hebephrenic form. The onset is usually gradual although it may be precipitated by toxic or traumatic episodes. Postpartum schizophrenia or schizophrenic symptoms precipitated by head trauma or severe somatic infection are quite often of the paranoid type.

Many psychiatrists believe these patients have the personality constellation necessary for both a paranoid reaction and schizophrenia. Some physicians think this group of the schizophrenias is quite distinct from the others. Here the patients show the fundamental symptoms in less profusion; the general organization of the personality is better preserved and these people may get by in the community for years. There is a marked discrepancy in symptoms. Some stay well organized and preserved for many years in spite of active paranoid delusions. Others deteriorate rather rapidly in terms of thinking, social behavior, and general adaptability to the public. This difference in course is due to the ego strength of the individuals and the opportunities for satisfactory living in the environment, rather than to the disease process itself.

These patients are often thought of as peculiar, irritable, and suspicious. They may seriously disrupt a family or a business organization until their paranoid suspiciousness is detected. Many faulty investigations and legal charges grow out of these paranoid delusions. These patients, above all others, are apt to convince a court or an attorney that they have a legitimate case. Every psychiatrist of experience has had some contact with these patients in some form of litigation. Some are quite well preserved and can be managed on an outpatient level.

An example of paranoid schizophrenia is a young and successful businessman in his early thirties who was quite jealous of his wife. He recognized that this jealousy was unfounded but still felt suspicious of her. At times he had ideas that she was trying to poison him. At other times he felt his business associates were ganging up on him and were gossiping about him. He decided to seek therapy after a country club dance where he developed the idea that several of the people there were whispering that he was a homosexual and that he was pimping for his wife. In the process of therapy it developed that this patient had a very active, aggressive mother, and a passive father who was reasonably successful in the financial world. The mother dominated the home, and "sacrificed herself" for her 5 boys. The patient was her favorite. He stated that he resented his mother's solicitousness but should not resent it because of her great love for them. He stated his father quietly encouraged them to "do as Mama says." His mother had at first opposed his marriage but later selected a socially prominent and well-to-do young lady for his wife. Having selected the girl, the mother apparently felt obligated to dictate the marital life even to the number of children. She became resentful and hurt when the wife apparently had ideas that she should manage her own marriage. In this setting the patient noted he was getting more irritable and suspicious but stated he always had been a reserved and careful person. His wife was attractive and popular, and at first he felt justified in his jealousy as a precautionary matter, although he readily admitted he had no reason for thinking his wife was unfaithful. He began to regard his symptoms seriously when his tension and suspicions became so marked that he spoke to his wife about it and she became very much hurt and upset that he should fail to trust her. The symptoms intensified, and on the advice of his wife and family physician, the patient sought psychotherapy. Long and intensive psychotherapy, with a tremendous amount of ego support from the psychiatrist, kept this patient working, kept him from verbalizing his suspicions to his wife, and kept him reasonably happy. He maintained his ideas, however, but remained ambivalent toward them and succeeded in ventilating them with the physician. This suspiciousness made his business relations more difficult, and the nature of his work was such that this often handicapped him and made him a troublesome person to deal with in terms of his business associates and competitors. It is believed that further prolonged therapy may finally solve the problems of this particular patient.

Other patients are much less well preserved. Some believe that the plots against them are serious and their persecutors are closing in on them, so they must take contrary action. Some have somatic delusions, feeling that they are being influenced by electricity, or that they have worms under their skin. Others feel that people are trying to assault them, to kill or to mutilate them, or to make them carry out some perverted sex activity. These patients become very dangerous and may kill or harm their imagined persecutors. Most crimes committed by mental patients are committed by the paranoid schizophrenic ones in reaction to their delusions. In others the symptoms become still more marked, and these patients develop delusions that they are Christ or some other person with tremendous powers. They feel that they can control the world and become so far withdrawn from reality that they must be confined.

Paranoid schizophrenic patients do reasonably well with treatment. It is our belief that this is due to the relatively good ego preservation in these cases, with fewer fundamental symptoms, and a marked elaboration of the accessory symptoms of Bleuler.

The paranoid delusional systems may be very diffuse and scattered or may be extremely well organized into an almost believable (and sometimes they are believable to courts) series of plots, counterplots, and traumatic events. Some of these patients have auditory hallucinations, somatic delusions, and olfactory and visual hallucinations. Most common are the auditory hallucinations, and, typically, the patients have reasonably well-organized delusional systems, which always contain some imagined harm or insult to the patient. These patients show the thinking disturbance known as projection, where their own thoughts, conflicts, and ideas are projected onto the environment, and what they think is true becomes for them an irrefutable fact.

The psychodynamics of the paranoid systems will be discussed under that heading in the following chapter.

An example of a more seriously disturbed paranoid schizophrenic patient is a man who was brought to the hospital after having shot another man in a grocery store. Investigation revealed that the victim was a stranger who had been passing in an automobile and stopped at the store for a package of cigarettes. The patient was standing with a group of local citizens in this small country store and whipped out a pistol and killed the man. On examination in the hospital the patient stated that there had been a plot by the FBI and the Masons to kill him. He felt that the plot involved accusations that he was a sexual pervert, and that they had planned to mutilate him first and then kill him by slow torture. He stated that he had got "messages" that they were to pick him up any day, and he had been carefully watching for the person who was to come after him. He stated that on the day before a salesman had called at this store who he had thought was his pursuer, but just as he started to pull the pistol out, the voices told him it was not his enemy. When his victim came in and ordered the cigarettes, the patient interpreted this as the signal, so he shot the man to protect himself. This patient was sent to a hospital for the mentally ill with criminal tendencies, where he still resides.

Schizophrenic Reaction, Acute Undifferentiated Type 000–x25

In this category will go those patients who show an admixture of the above groups. Most characteristically they are confused, show auditory or visual hallucinations, and have vague paranoid coloring. The admixtures are most typically those of the hebephrenic and paranoid types, or the catatonic and paranoid types. A student may classify here those patients with acute onset, confusion, and symptoms of depression or euphoria and overactivity who do not fit in any of the above groups. Many patients who are treated in this stage recover and will therefore be classified here. Those not successfully treated or not treated in this early phase may finally resolve into one of the above-mentioned types and, if discharged at that time, should be classified in the proper group.

Schizophrenic Reaction, Chronic Undifferentiated Type 000-x26

Into this group go those patients with prolonged illness who show mixtures or combinations of the above types, usually hebephrenic symptoms with a paranoid delusional system superimposed or catatonic symptoms with much paranoid coloring or a paranoid system superimposed. There are also certain borderline patients who are mild, simple schizophrenic cases, but have vague paranoid delusions and occasional periods of hallucinations that are best classified here.

Schizophrenic Reaction, Schizo-affective Type 000-x27

Into this group go those patients who show episodic symptoms, with a periodicity not unlike that of a manic-depressive reaction. During the first episode the symptoms will be very much like those of a manic patient, but with more paranoid elaboration than is common in the acute manic case. Into this category also go those patients who show beginning schizophrenic symptoms, but with a rather severe depressive reaction in response to the patient's insight about his illness. Before classifying a patient in this category, the student should remember that chronic manic-depressive patients, particularly the hypomanic type, may show fairly elaborate paranoid projections, but these are usually against people in the immediate environment who fail to go along with the patients' expansive plans. If the delusional system is weird and bizarre, if the thinking begins to show the dissociation or other disturbances in progression fundamental for schizophrenia, or if there is disparity in the emotional response and the thinking content, the case is then properly classified in this category. Many of these patients after a time subside into or develop symptoms typical of one of the above standard reaction types. It should be remembered that none of the patients accurately or exactly fits these diagnostic categories because they are based not on etiology or psychopathology, but on symptoms and behavior.

Schizophrenic Reaction, Childhood Type 000–x28

Schizophrenia occasionally comes on in childhood. It has been reported as early as 4 and 5 years. There are some differences of opinion among child psychiatrists whether one should call these patients' illness schizophrenia or whether it should be called "autism." The problem will be discussed by Vaughan in the section on child psychiatry.

Schizophrenic Reaction, Residual Type 000–x29

We do not see the justification for this subclassification. In our opinion, the patients who are to be discharged to the community as recovered, improved, unimproved, or worse should carry the proper subclassification of their diagnosis—they are improved or not improved. It is true that a certain number of schizophrenic patients become "burned out" but still show schizophrenic residuals; they get along at a low level of social and economic adjustment. In our opinion it would be less confusing, however, if these cases were classified in their original category and discharged as moderately improved, or in incomplete remission, or some other indication that would not indicate that they were different from other schizophrenic patients, except in the results.

CHAPTER 16

Psychotic Disorders: Paranoid Reactions 000–x30

This group of reactions contains those cases with rigid, well-organized paranoid delusions without signs of schizophrenia, manic-depressive reaction, or organic illness. They include the rare cases of paranoia and the commoner paranoid reactions seen in some individuals under stress. In some persons these reactions are transitory, and in some prolonged, and they are differentiated from true paranoia by the fact that the delusions are a little more bizarre and not so rigidly organized as in true paranoia. Patients with paranoid schizophrenia or patients with psychosis due to aging with paranoid trends should not be classified here.

Paranoia 000–x31

This reaction is characterized by a well-organized system of persecutory delusions that seem logical enough if one accepts the basic persecution. There must be in addition the patient's refusal to change his mind in spite of ordinary or extraordinary attempts to point out the error of his opinions. Less than 1 per cent of patients admitted to mental hospitals can be properly classified in this category. Cases are more often diagnosed as paranoia by courts or attorneys when they are actually either paranoid or paranoid schizophrenic states that are well preserved. The disease is more common in males than females and usually comes on in the thirties or forties. Aside from the paranoid delusional system, which is well-organized and logical, there are no other mental symptoms. The character of these patients tends to be rather rigid. Adolph Meyer described a paranoiac constitution as being that of an uneasy, brooding, sensitive type of person. This constitution contains an inability to correct notions and to make concessions, which is followed by the appearance of dominant notions and suspicious or ill-balanced aim, then by false interpretations,

219

with self-reference and a tendency to systemization, by retrospective falsification, and, in some cases as an end point, by megalomanic developments.

A typical case is that of a 41-year-old white male, who came to the hospital because he annoyed the officers of a trust company. He was a quiet, serious, intent person. He had always been a brilliant student, had started to work early, and had worked himself up in the banking business. He was married but did not get along well with his wife. He stated that she resented his interest in his mother. He was divorced in 1925, and soon after resigned from the bank in which he worked. He was a person of good habits and had not been in any previous difficulty. The patient developed the idea after resignation from the bank that a wealthy businessman who had obtained him his job in the bank had established a large trust fund with the company for which he worked, and that this trust fund was for his benefit. He believed that the trust company had worked various swindles against him in order to deprive him of his rights. He met objections to the validity of his contentions rather cleverly and pointed out that the daily newspapers contained items that should make us realize that financiers are not always men of integrity, and that in these times a bank is not at all anxious to lose control of a large sum of money. If pressed further, he would smile and say with dignity that there was no reason for him to discuss his private affairs. When asked about hallucinations or other false beliefs, the patient would become indignant and say that these would be signs of a mental illness. The patient refused treatment and was not again seen. In this case his whole line of reasoning was entirely logical, except for the fact that there was no fund in the trust company for him, and the fact that he justified his suspicion of the head of this particular bank by reading accounts of embezzlements by clerks, cashiers, etc., of other banks in various parts of the country. This was coupled with a rigid, meticulous, rather dignified mien and a history of marital difficulties.

Etiology and Psychopathology. These cases are so rare that the real etiology is not provable. Freud presented a theoretical analysis of a German judge, named Schraeber. Freud did not analyze the patient but analyzed a long diary or autobiography published by the judge, in which he went into some details about his paranoid ideas and the persecution against him. Freud postulated that projection was the primary defense mechanism in paranoia and postulated that the projection was utilized as a defense against homosexual trends that were not acceptable to the patient. He felt that the paranoid delusions used to cope with and combat the homosexual threats were the delusions of persecution, erotomania, jealousy, and megalomania. Many persons have confirmed Freud's statement of the homosexual elements in cases of paranoia; other persons have denied them.

Aronson ran a series of Rorschach tests on a very carefully selected group of paranoid patients chosen especially for the presence of the paranoid projections as described by Freud. He used as controls a psychotic group without these paranoid projections and a normal group. The studies show that the paranoid subjects reported an overwhelmingly greater number of homosexual signs on the Rorschach tests than either nonparanoid psychotic or normal individuals. He pointed out that this does not prove that homosexual conflicts have a direct causal effect in the etiology of paranoid delusion, but it does show that they are associated to a high degree.

Waelder discussed the whole structure of paranoid ideas from the psychoanalytic point of view. After reviewing many theories he asked, "Could it be that all these concepts describe various aspects of the total picture? That the clue which permits a jigsaw to be put together is the mechanism of denial, and that paranoid ideas are as much the result of unsuccessful denial as psychoneurotic symptoms have long been known to be the result of unsuccessful repression?" He goes on to state that denial is usually a mechanism to deal with external facts, such as danger, anxiety, grief, or guilt, but not with the instincts. He suggests, however, that projection as a phenomenon indicates that denial could be a method of dealing with instinctual drives. If the denial is unsuccessful and the warded-off instinctual drive returns, and if the defense mechanism had been that of denial, the return "must have the form of an assertion." He believes that this would explain the delusions of persecution as the result of an incomplete return of a denied instinct.

Treatment. Older books recommend that paranoid patients be confined because of their potential danger. We find that most well-organized paranoid patients tend to resort to litigious actions, and only if they begin to deteriorate or show secondary organic changes do they become really dangerous and need confinement. In a broader social concept, these people can disorganize an office and perhaps disorganize larger groups of people if they get into positions of influence or positions where they can influence others. There has been much speculation about the possibility of various prominent and unsavory characters in the world being cases of paranoia. So far as I know there has been no psychiatric examination of any of these persons to make these accusations other than idle speculation or gossip.

Paranoid State 000–x32

The symptoms in the paranoid state are not unlike those of true paranoia except that the delusional system is less well-organized, maybe a little more bizarre, and these patients may often have certain unreal and impossible characteristics in their delusions. Some of these patients may show acute flare-ups of symptoms when under great stress, but the symptoms disappear or quiet down as the patient recovers his equilibrium. These patients' ego is able to ward off the threatening content under ordinary circumstances, but in situations of stress, must call into play the paranoid projection as an additional defense to bolster up the weakened ego.

An example of the paranoid state is an officer of field grade who was seen during the war. He had malaria, and following this was somewhat debilitated. He had great difficulty and was under great stress with his superior officers because they refused to return him to flying status. He had obtained a plane without permission, and in taking a rather wild ride had damaged the plane, but not seriously. He felt that his superiors were completely unjustified in any type of disciplinary action, and when appearing before a board to consider disciplinary action, he became acutely paranoid, accused them of talking about him, and plotting against him, which led to the belief that he was psychotic. At the time he was. With the removal of stress, some reeducation, and a building up of his physical reserves, the paranoid content entirely cleared up, and it was finally possible for this man to return to active duty. Some cases do not respond so favorably.

A female patient who had always been a brilliant, rigid, exacting, and hard-working professional person married a soft, passive, unsuccessful male. Their marital relations were hectic, and the patient was particularly threatened by the husband's desire to practice oral perversions or to masturbate her in lieu of heterosexual activity. She first began to quarrel with his parents, then rejected them, stating that they were not his parents, that he was actually the son of a wealthy person. She then further projected that the husband was kept from success in life by the machinations of his own father, and that his delusional father who had left him large sums of money had left it in such manner that neither the patient nor her husband could possess it. She precipitated a long series of investigations of her husband's real father, as she had convinced the father's employers that he might be dishonest. She had the bank, which she thought held her husband's fortune, on the defensive because she was having them investigated for withholding these funds. Attempts to commit this patient to an institution were unsuccessful as she went before a court and proved that she was well according to their views. When last heard from she was still in the process of filing litigations to acquire her husband's "estate."

Treatment. Paranoid conditions, being less well organized and orderly than the paranoias, and much more common, should be closely followed by the physician. If these patients begin to show any tendency toward violence or develop any passivity feelings in which the voices or influences order them to do things, they should be committed. It has been our experience, however, that commitment of these patients precipitates a long series of difficulties. Preferably they should be handled with outpatient psychotherapy, which should start as a superficial, ego-supporting type of therapy, but which gradually undergo transition to an intensive, dynamically oriented psychotherapy, or psychoanalysis if available. These cases are long and difficult, but because of the preservation of the character, they are worth working on.

Psychophysiologic Autonomic and Visceral Disorders

Into this general category will go those illnesses loosely called *psychosomatic disorders*. In World War II and shortly thereafter, psychiatrists and internists and other specialists became interested in those psychogenic illnesses which accompany and seem to play an important etiologic role in the development of certain forms of organic illness and organic pathology. The term "psychosomatic" has been incorrectly used to describe many physiologic concomitants of psychoneuroses. Properly used, it is meant to describe those forms of coronary disease, hypertension, dermatitis, peptic ulcer, and other somatic pathology which are thought to be partially or largely due to psychogenic disturbances.

Ludwig points out that this term was developed in an attempt to describe objectively, by careful psychiatric investigation, those techniques formerly called "the art of medicine." He points out that the key to this is to recognize that certain neuroses manifest themselves in physical changes in certain organs.

Margolin and Kaufman describe psychosomatic medicine as an operational approach to the theory and practice of medicine in which the structure and function of the psychic apparatus are dealt with as variables in health and disease, just as, for example, are physiology and pathology. Their approach specifically denies the type of thinking in which the psychologic factor is considered as a separate layer or as an afterthought in the evaluation of the patient.

Two excellent books by Weiss and English, and Dunbar, plus many monographs, are devoted to the detailed study of peptic ulcer, mucous

224

colitis, correlations between the ovulation cycle in females and psychosomatic problems, diseases of the skin, diseases of the genitourinary system, hypertension, and coronary disease. For a time it was believed that there were definite personality profiles accompanying each somatic illness. There is still evidence to show that predominant types of neurotic conflict and predominant types of psychologic structure are seen in various forms of organ disorder, but it is increasingly realized that these reactions are also generalized and perhaps the etiology is a little more complicated than originally supposed. The coincidence of certain physical precursors or constitutional patterns and of certain specific forms of psychologic conflict is probably necessary for the production of a specific lesion.

Fenichel reverts to the older Freudian terminology of organ neuroses because he believes the term psychosomatic is too generalized and too misleading. The student is cautioned not to include here the physiologic concomitants of ordinary anxiety or hysterical disorders. Symptoms in this category can probably arise on three different bases and have been called by Fenichel the "affect equivalents." These bases are:

1. The expression of emotional drives by an organ without the person being aware of the drives, which is closely akin to a hysteric reaction, except that the displacement is on one of the organs controlled by the autonomic-humoral system rather than on one of the special senses or structures under voluntary control.

2. Prolonged physiologic and chemical changes brought about by psychogenic conflict, especially undischarged affects. For example, hostility or rage not expressed or sublimated may over a prolonged period of time produce definite alterations in body physiology and, eventually, in body structure.

3. Physical results of unconscious attitudes or behavior patterns, determined by unconscious conflict. This type of symptom results from the behavior of the person, and creates secondary injury or physiologic disturbance. A simple example would be a person who insists on taking long walks in cold, damp weather while improperly clothed to "walk off anxiety." The anxiety is psychogenically determined and of unknown origin, but the physical concomitants resulting from his attempt to cure himself of anxiety may give him blisters on his feet and a cold in his head. Accidents in traffic and in industry result from discharging energy of psychogenic origin through unwise or reckless behavior. This is the discharge of anger or tension, and the injury to the body is secondary in order, as a result of this behavior.

These cases should be distinguished from those in which the primary reason for the action is a self-destructive trend. Any combination of the above three forms of psychosomatic disturbance may be seen. In particular cases all three exist to varying degrees.

Psychophysiologic Skin Reaction 001-580

The symptoms of this reaction are skin lesions thought by dermatologists and psychiatrists to be due to a combination of psychogenic and physical causes. They are sometimes called neurodermatitis and are often characterized by localized or generalized redness, itching, and at times weeping of the skin. Certain forms of pruritus, eczema, excessive sweating, and some cases of psoriasis belong in this category.

Etiology. The skin often serves as a medium of emotional expression. In early childhood it may be a source of neurotic expression due to the caressing, stroking, and petting on the part of the parent. The skin's rich supply of autonomic nerves makes it susceptible to physiologic disturbances caused by tensions and this is easy to observe. All humans express some emotion through the skin. Nervous chills, blushing and flushing, prickling of the scalp in dangerous situations, and the "crawling" of the skin after prolonged emotional stimulation are symptoms of cutaneous sensations secondary to inner tensions. In many cases the skin about the genital organs or about the anal orifice is used for discharge of these tensions.

There are cases reported in which the dermatitis is thought to be due to suppressed rage reactions in which the sadistic impulses are turned on one's self and expressed through abrasions of the skin. There are also cases in which the skin manifestations are displacements of erotic impulses unacceptable to the individual. One occasionally sees extensive eczematous lesions in children, and it is thought that these are secondary to anxieties due to deprivation and the autonomic concomitants of fear and rage at the deprivation of love.

Treatment. In the authors' experience these psychophysiologic skin reactions are best handled in conjunction with the dermatologist who understands psychogenic factors. In the advanced cases, local temporary relief is often needed. In patients with eczematous lesions it is essential that the allergic factors be carefully studied and, when present, properly handled. The patient should be kept informed that these are complications to the basic psychogenic conflict, when such is the fact. Treatment will consist principally of psychotherapy and, in really persistent cases, of psychoanalysis, if available. In small infants the treatment consists of working with the parents, who may require superficial or prolonged psychotherapy as the case may be, and in helping supply the youngsters' need for love and security during the period of work with the parents.

Psychophysiologic Musculoskeletal Reaction 002–580

In some patients backache, joint soreness, and other symptoms due to increased tensions in the muscular system may be used for emotional discharge. Prolonged tension and anxiety may produce muscle spasm, which after long periods of time may begin to produce aches, pains, and other changes. Probably one of the commonest manifestations of this form of expression is the chronic backache and the chronic occipital headache, both of which seem to be produced by prolonged states of muscular tension. It is certain that muscular tension over a prolonged period of time aggravates and exaggerates the symptoms of arthritis of the deformans type, and it is possible that tension may play some role in the etiology of these disorders. These patients have some desire to express rage or hostility through movement. The inhibition of these movements, with the continuation of the chronic muscular tension, seems to bring about the changes secondary to muscle dysfunction. Some patients with torticollis, fasciculations, and other muscular movements show similar psychopathology.

Treatment. The treatment of these cases consists almost entirely of psychotherapy of an intensive type and psychoanalysis, when available. In an occasional case superficial psychotherapy augmented by physical therapy may bring about an alleviation of the symptoms.

Psychophysiologic Respiratory Reaction 003–580

The symptoms of this reaction vary from respiratory tics, rapid respiration, and periods of apnea to severe bronchial asthma. We believe that these symptoms have their origin in conflicts originating in the earliest phases of libidinous development, in the so-called narcissistic or pregenital phases. An earlier chapter described how youngsters receive their initial gratification through the oral passages, the first of which is associated with breathing. In certain individuals deprivations or overstimulation at this oral phase may cause the breathing function to be associated with pleasurable and erotic sensations.

French and Alexander have made a detailed study of the psychogenic factors in the disturbances of the respiratory system. They believe asthma is a reaction to the danger of separation from the mother and that the attack is an equivalent of a repressed cry of anxiety or rage. Persons so conditioned during infancy may in later life react to situations of danger, anxiety, or threatened loss of love by such an inhibited cry for help.

It should be stressed that many cases of asthma seem to be allergic in origin, but these, too, may be aggravated and exaggerated by the presence of anxieties and other psychogenic tensions. In those cases thought to be almost purely of psychogenic origin, secondary physiologic changes due to the prolonged disturbance in respiration and concomitant secondary infections will need the conjoint management of the allergist and the psychiatrist.

Treatment. The temporary alleviation of symptoms must be handled by a competent allergist if the patient is in analysis. If the patient is in psychotherapy the therapist himself may be able to handle the respiratory disturbances. These cases can terminate fatally or can produce permanent changes in the lung structure if not handled symptomatically during the exacerbations that inevitably occur during a period of prolonged therapy. Psychotherapy in these cases, either of the deep eclectic or the analytic type, is long and difficult. Therapy of asthma in children is extremely difficult. The other respiratory symptoms are usually less well set, have fewer physical concomitants, and are more simply managed.

Psychophysiologic Cardiovascular Reaction 004–580

Cardiovascular syndromes are ordinarily thought to have some element of psychogenic conflict in their etiology, especially anginal syndromes, coronary disease, and hypertension. The interrelation of the emotional strivings, body and temperament type, and the physiologic and chemical changes in the body that finally result in the atherosclerosis and vascular crises, including coronary disease, is still imperfectly understood. Each year further studies show more details concerning the influence of genetics, constitution, and dietary factors on the development of these disorders. In a similar vein there is more evidence and general acceptance of the fact that psychogenic tensions somehow play a concomitant role with the above factors in the final production of symptoms.

The general psychogenic pattern is one of frustration: a failure of the environment to offer adequate outlet for the tremendous amounts of aggression and hostility that the individual shows. The damming up of these tensions apparently produces chemical and autonomic changes which after prolonged periods of time, joined with certain constitutional and dietary anomalies, begin to show changes in the vascular coats of the cardiovascular systems. Some studies show important psychologic differences between those who suffer from coronary disease and those with hypertension, but other studies show less marked distinction between these two groups. However, research in these fields will undoubtedly bring more knowledge as to how such disasters may be prevented.

Treatment. These patients are conjointly managed by the internist and psychiatrist. Some of these patients respond well to a fairly superficial support type of psychotherapy if it offers outlets for the patient's hostilities which are acceptable to him. Often, suppression of the patient's hostilities and a lack of opportunity for working them out due to prolonged bed rest or enforced invalidism because of the cardiovascular disturbance may result in deep depressions after coronary attacks. These depressions may be more disabling than the heart disorder itself. Whether the psychogenic factors are primary in the illness or are merely aggravated symptoms due to dietary, chemical, or other causes, support psychotherapy and deeper psychotherapy in selected cases are of great help to the internist in managing these cases.

Psychophysiologic Hemic and Lymphatic Reaction 005–580

There are no well-authenticated cases of a psychogenic cause for lymphatic system reactions. Emotional factors may, however, complicate and aggravate the symptoms of patients suffering from disorders such as Hodgkin's disease and various malignant conditions of the blood and lymphatic systems.

Psychophysiologic Gastrointestinal Reaction 006–580

There has been a great deal of study done on the psychogenic factors in the production of these disorders, particularly peptic ulcer, ulcerative colitis, and mucous colitis. After much investigation has been made on the causes of peptic ulcer, particularly in the duodenal area, it is now generally considered that the gastrointestinal reactions have a psychogenic element in their causation.

Fenichel sums up the etiologic picture of peptic ulcer as follows:

Persons with a chronically frustrated oral receptive demanding attitude who have repressed this attitude and often manifest very active behavior of the reaction formation type are unconsciously permanently hungry for love. It would be even more exact to state that they are hungry for necessary narcissistic supplies and the word hungry in this connection has to be taken literally. This permanent hunger makes them act like an actually hungry person does. The mucous membrane of the stomach begins to secrete just as does that of a person who anticipates food, his secretion having no other specific psychic meaning. This chronic hypersecretion is the immediate cause of the ulcer. The ulcer is the incidental physiologic consequence of a psychogenic attitude. It is not a distorted satisfaction of a repressed instinct. It may be questioned whether this etiology is valid for all cases of ulcer. It is possible that the functional changes which in some cases are brought about by repressed oral eroticism may be determined in others by purely somatic causes.

We believe that these same persons in their anxiety and driving reaction formation to their passive tendencies produce pylorospasm. The work of Wolff and his associates and Alexander and his colleagues tends to confirm this.

We agree with the findings of Grace, Seton, Steward Wolf, and Harold G. Wolff that mucous colitis, spastic constipation, and chronic diarrheas of some types are due to frustrations and fixations in the anal erotic spheres. According to them the normal person's concentration of lysozyme increases during periods of anger, hostility, and resentment. In subjects with ulcerative colitis, however, these exacerbations produce sharp rises in stool lysozyme. They correlate the onset of ulceration with this increase. They conclude that this increase of lysozyme in the bowel secretions is highly relevant to the occurrence of ulceration and they believe that variations in the production of this enzyme fluctuate with feelings of security of the patient.

Margolin made careful studies on a patient with gastric fistula under psychoanalytic observation. She showed additional increase of gastric activity in association with conscious emotions, anger, guilt, and anxiety. The unconscious mental content provoked by stimuli in the physiologic observation situation appeared to be an essential determinant in the psychophysiologic reactions manifest.

The unconscious is a potent determinant of organ functioning. This fact must profoundly influence physiologic and pharmacologic experimentation in human beings. Every situation involving manipulation and instrumentation by an observer invoked psychic stresses of varying intensity. The psychological responses of the subject, as in this case, can significantly and meaningfully influence the physiologic data. The application of the technique of psychoanalysis made it possible to control what would otherwise act as an uncertain variable. In other words, the conditions under which an experiment is performed can enter into the data to an undetermined degree.

The careful observations in this case have widespread significance for all attempts at correlating psychologic and physiologic data and perhaps can explain the many inconsistent and varying reports made by different authors. Expressed another way, it is not enough to say that tensions, frustrations, or psychogenic phenomena increase or decrease a given function. Rather, one must say that in a given person under certain circumstances psychogenic functions may alter physiologic function in one direction or another depending on the psychologic meaning of the psychogenic stress to the particular individual. Ideally, persons who are to be subjected to physiologic studies should also be under psychoanalytic observation.

Treatment. These disorders (particularly peptic ulcer and ulcerative colitis, because they can result in perforation and death) must be handled simultaneously by the internist who is psychogenically oriented and the psychotherapist. The psychotherapy will either be of the supporting type, the detailed uncovering kind, or psychoanalysis, depending on the availability of the treatments in the area and the total picture in the patient.

Psychophysiologic Genitourinary Reaction 007–580

Certain menstrual disturbances, difficulty in urination, and some sexual disturbances may be classified here. Other sexual disturbances will be classified under the psychoneuroses. For instance, some forms of impotence might be properly classified here, but if they are part of a hysterical or anxiety reaction or latent homosexuality, they should be classified in the proper category. Some situations of anxiety or fright may bring a cessation of menstruation. Dysmenorrhea is thought to be due to repressed hostility and suppression of sadistic fantasies directed against certain males.

One observes the male who has difficulty in surviving the oedipal conflicts, and runs from woman to woman finding none satisfactory because none is actually his mother. His difficulty in navigating the oedipal area is thought to be due to pregenital complications, particularly in the oral-incorporative stage. This striving for sexual satisfaction, yet always failing to receive the needed narcissistic supplies, results in a sadistic reaction toward the partner for failure to give these satisfactions. Thus, the Don Juan drifts on to another woman without thought to the harm or trauma he may have precipitated on his original object. His series of conquests tends to keep out of consciousness this feeling of inferiority and lack of love. Nymphomania in the female is based on somewhat similar psychologic structure.

The management of genitourinary reactions should be by psychotherapy of an analytically oriented type and, when available, by psychoanalysis. These cases are usually complicated and difficult to treat.

Psychophysiologic Endocrine Reaction 008–580

Ham, Alexander, and Carmichael postulate a psychogenic cause of thyrotoxicosis. There is need for much further study of the specific role psychogenic factors play in the production of endocrine disturbances.

Disorders thought to have psychogenic factors as complications or components of the etiology should be managed conjointly by the internist and the psychiatrist. Psychotherapy in these cases may be of a superficial supporting type, but this will usually be inadequate. Real improvement will come only with detailed and skillfully done psychoanalytic therapy.

Psychophysiologic Nervous System Reaction 009–580

Most texts include this particular group of disorders under the psychoneuroses and under the heading of neurasthenia. Because the classification manual presently in use classifies it here, we shall discuss this disorder under this category.

This term is used to describe patients whose principal complaint is one of chronic fatigue. Typically, these individuals drag around on a low level of social adjustment, reacting to any increased physical or emotional effort or demand with palpitations, headaches, sinking spells, and general muscular weakness. Typically, this fatigue is not associated with pleasurable activities such as discussing symptoms, going for rides, going to see doctors, etc., but is selective in its nature, prohibiting the patient from carrying out gainful pursuits and unpleasant tasks.

Weir Mitchell believed these cases resulted from exhaustion or debilitation of the structure of the nerves themselves, and the cases were treated with prolonged bed rest.

Freud originally taught that they were due to faulty expression of the sexual impulses, and particularly due to chronic masturbation, coitus interruptus, and similar unsatisfactory and incomplete methods of achieving sexual satisfaction. Most of these patients do show faulty sexual expression. Increasing experience, however, indicates that the faulty sexual expression is but another symptom of a deep-seated neurosis rather than the cause of the chronic fatigue state. Many cases of what at first examination appeared to be typical neurasthenias later turned out to be beginning reactive depressions or early phases of a simple schizophrenia.

Some authors classify in this category certain convulsive phenomena precipitated by noises or by psychogenic factors in which the convulsion itself is of true organic rather than hysterical type, i.e., accompanied by typical electroencephalographic changes during these seizures.

Treatment. Treatment of these cases is not rewarded with a great deal of success. Most patients lack the energy and the affect to participate actively in analytic therapy, although when transference is developed, it offers the greatest prospect for good results. Some of these patients respond with some relief of symptoms to supportive psychotherapy in which the patient seems to ride on the therapist's ego and over a period of many years retains a semidependent relationship with the physician.

Psychophysiologic Reaction of Organs of Special Senses 00x–580

Freud described organ neurotic symptoms of the special sense organs using eye symptoms as an example. If eye symptoms, such as refractive error, might be said to be due to psychogenic causes, it would be on the basis of the autonomic concomitants of tension-producing prolonged muscle tension and pull, which might elongate or shorten the eyeball, depending on the mechanics involved. Myopia due to psychogenic causes has been discussed, but in our opinion much more work needs to be done before one can make conclusive statements.

General Discussion

The most fruitful areas for the advancement of medicine are those of the interrelationship of psychologic symptoms in healthy and ill human beings. Since man exists as a unit, it would be impossible to have any type of psychologic reaction without physiologic components, and each physiologic reaction is accompanied by some type of psychologic component, conscious or unconscious.

A simple example would be the anticipation of food which brings on the secretion of hydrochloric acid in the stomach. Since man tends to be a creature of habit, a busy person who does not note that the clock has reached the lunch hour may be reminded of this by a certain sensation of discomfort due to hunger contractions and acid secretion in his stomach.

Further conjoint studies by chemists, physiologists, internists, and psychiatrists are essential to a better understanding of the interdependence of the soma and the psyche. One believes that the whole subject of susceptibility and immunity may be influenced by psychologic differences in reactions to environmental situations. Research suggests, for instance, that patients ignore or avoid diagnosis of cancer in early, treatable stages because of deep psychologic conflict. The student should avail himself of the current literature in this field and, as we have repeatedly stressed, regard the individual as a whole, with both psychologic and physiologic components to each and every reaction.

CHAPTER 18

Psychoneurotic Disorders

The psychoneuroses are mild or minor mental reactions which represent attempts to find satisfaction in life situations rendered unsatisfactory by faulty attitudes or by faulty emotional development. These attempts are manifest by various physiologic reactions, complaints of bodily discomfort, or recurrent mental trends recognized by the patient as being faulty or unusual. Practically, they are somewhat artificially divided into various etiologic entities because the etiology varies in different cases. They have in common, however, the inability to meet life situations, and all of them represent substitution efforts or a symbolic gratification of urges not recognized or accepted by the individual.

The neuroses are the commonest of all mental illnesses, but most of them are treated in the general medical clinic or by the family physician, and only the more severe or persistent ones come to the attention of the psychiatrist.

Because the behavior is not unusual, and because the conflict situations are manifest only in the above-mentioned somatic complaints, these patients rarely come to hospitalization in psychiatric institutions. It has been estimated that as many as 50 per cent of the patients coming to the general practitioner's office have a psychoneurosis as the major cause for seeking treatment. However, all individuals who are sick have both physical and mental components to their illness. The psychoneuroses represent those illnesses whose major pathology is in the mental and emotional sphere and whose physiologic changes are secondary and concomitant to the emotional illness.

The neuroses are distinct from the psychotic reactions for two reasons. First, the etiologic mechanism is clearly psychologic and takes place according to well-understood psychologic mechanisms. Second, the be-

234

havior disturbances in the psychoneurotic patient take the form of unusual concerns and worries about one's self, but they do not interfere with the individual's ability to appreciate the rights of other people (within limits) and do not interfere, as a rule, with the ability to conform to social custom. In fact, the neurosis itself may be understood as an attempt to transmute desires which might not be socially acceptable into some form of behavior which does fit into the patient's concepts of morals and ethics.

There is some disagreement concerning the etiology of the psychoses, and they are by no means as well understood as the neuroses. Behavior in psychotic patients is often unpredictable and frequently antisocial to the extent that the patient becomes a nuisance or a danger to himself or to persons around him. The psychotic patient is not always able to appreciate the rights of other persons and may have difficulty in conforming to the demands and mores of the group in which he lives.

In a few words, a neurotic or psychoneurotic patient generally is in much closer contact with his environment than the psychotic patient. It is usually true that fewer phases of his personality behavior are in disharmony with the responsibilities and expectations of everyday living.

The psychogenic mechanisms will be discussed under each subgroup of the psychoneuroses. All of them, however, have some things in common. Each person has certain basic needs or desires which must find satisfaction if he is to survive in a manner which is satisfactory to him. The environment or culture in which an individual lives makes certain demands upon him. These demands vary from time to time and from one community to another, but to some extent they are in the category of social checks demanding behavior restraints, inhibitions, and suppressions. Patients, owing either to the shortcomings within themselves or to some difficulty imposed by the environment, find it necessary to reach some compromise with the environment, because they are unable to find satisfactory solutions to their problems under the circumstances present at the moment. Much of our normal activity in social functions and customs is an example of this type of adaptation on a so-called "normal" scale.

For instance, there is our institution of marriage. We surround marriage with religious and civil ceremony, and by these means attempt to control heterosexual expression, in keeping with our monogamous type of marriage and for the social weal. By stigmatizing the extramarital sex act as sinful, and by placing it under civil control, we are able in some instances to persuade people to control these urges and to express them only in marriage. The adaptation of drives to fit the moral concepts of right and wrong according to our culture is a type of ego adaptation.

In some individuals these social pressures are so strong that the marriage ceremony fails to remove the patient's sense of guilt when engaged in the sex act and may result in frigidity, dyspareunia, or in running away from the sex act through pelvic complaints or impotence.

There is no gross or microscopic pathology of the nervous system demonstrated in the psychoneuroses. Freud has postulated, "Because of the essential unity of the two things that we divide into somatic and psychic, one may prophesy that the day will come when the avenue from biology and chemistry of the phenomena of neuroses will be open for our understanding, and we hope, for therapy."

Freud also described all the psychoneuroses as sharing a basic conflict between the ego and the id. Neuroses have been described as symptoms which protect the organism from a flooding of the ego with anxiety.

Before proceeding to a detailed discussion of the various subgroups in the neurotic reactions, some remarks concerning the general nature of anxiety are pertinent.

We have stated that the neuroses represent a patient's attempt to find satisfaction in the environment. The analytic group postulates that the beginning roots of neuroses rest in infancy. Work in other spheres supports this. The infant attempts to find satisfaction for his instinctual strivings from the environment about him. Meeting rules, taboos, and frustrations in his attempts to satisfy these drives, he may develop ideas that the satisfaction of these drives will lead to dangerous conditions or to deprivation and other situations threatening to him. The affect produced by a fear that gratification of the instincts will be refused or will result in personal danger to himself is described in analytic terminology as anxiety.

To understand neurotic disturbances and human behavior in general, it is imperative that the student first understand anxiety. Anxiety results whenever the person fears a traumatic state in either the psychologic or physical sense. These fear reactions result in much tension. The unmastered tension or, if you like, unused energy manifests itself as anxiety. Fenichel has written, "Thus in the last analysis all anxiety is a fear of experiencing a traumatic state or the possibility that the organization of the ego may be overwhelmed by excitation. However, after the ego has developed enough to control instinctual actions and to bring about gratification, the instinctual impulses ought not to be frightening any more. If they still are, it is due to the fact that fears over loss of love or castration have induced the ego to block the normal course of its excitement, thus creating an insufficiency of discharge."

Persons subjected to dangerous situations are more apt to be free of anxiety or suffer from less anxiety if a certain amount of action of a constructive sort is possible. Thus, in combat, soldiers who are able to carry out aggressive acts against the enemy are less prone to develop anxiety reactions than those who are holed up in forts, foxholes, or otherwise immobilized and compelled to "take it" without an opportunity to "dish it out."

Fenichel states that anxiety may be stratified. The first phase is that of trauma in which the anxiety results in an automatic and unspecified way. Second, in situations of danger anxiety serves the ego and the anxiety is created by the anticipation of fear. This is the realization that danger is impending; the anxiety is well controlled and warns the organism in an attempt to get ready for "fight or flight." The third phase is called panic, in which the control fails and the anxiety becomes overwhelming, causing the individual to regress to a more primitive state of adjustment in which the anxiety can be relieved or fixed. This latter results in neurotic activity, and a classic example is the so-called "anxiety hysteria" or "phobic state."

Many of these earlier anxiety reactions occur in infancy. A child deprived of love and affection or prematurely deprived of the satisfaction of the breast may develop severe frustration or fear, an anxiety reaction. The anxiety states produced by castration fears encountered during the oedipal epoch are classic examples of the etiology of anxiety. These anxiety reactions may repeat themselves in adult life. Situations of fear may be reacted to with anxiety and preparedness for protective action or may result in panic with regressive phenomena. A classic example of panic is the patient who has repressed latent homosexual trends but who in certain situations is threatened with their reappearance in consciousness. If all other attempts at repression fail, the patient becomes extremely anxious. This results in a panic reaction with regression to psychotic behavior which may be on a temporary or permanent basis. In these states the patient may experience hallucinations, loss of sphincter control, or long amnesic attacks.

There have been many attempts to classify the neuroses in a manner satisfactory to all working in the field. The original effort was to classify the cases according to a description of symptomatology. This has resulted in the commonly used classification of today. Attempts to classify the psychoneuroses into groups according to the psychopathology of the psychodynamic structures have not been altogether successful because of the overlaps among the many subgroups. Original examination of the cases often places them into one category or another but, with detailed analysis, a great many of them end up in the mixed psychoneurotic reaction. To avoid confusion the present discussion will be organized according to the official classification of the American Psychiatric Association, but with a warning to the student that many individual cases seen on the ward and in the clinic will show mixtures because the psychopathologic features producing two or more types of symptoms are present.

Anxiety Reaction 000–x10

In anxiety reaction the patients have symptoms of uneasiness, apprehension, and a vague sense of impending disaster. They often have symptoms of inner tension manifest by hyperacidity, attacks of diarrhea, sweating, and other signs of stimulation of the sympatheticoadrenal system. In the typical case the anxiety remains unobjectified, and the patient states that he is fearful but does not know what he is afraid of.

Freud originally taught that the anxiety states were due to some toxic product secondary to incomplete orgasm during sex relations or other unsatisfactory modes of sexual expression.

Some patients apparently react to rather simple external situations which symbolize the deeper threats to the person, and this threatened loss of love or of other supplies necessary for existence produces the anxiety reaction. In many cases the reaction may be a rather normal one to some immediate environmental stimulus but is of such degree and for so long that definite changes in physiologic functions occur, and symptoms are produced. Depending on the individual's past history and his ego strength it will take greater or lesser degrees of environmental trauma to produce a typical anxiety reaction. In spite of this variation in past experiences and ego strength of a person, even the most stable individual has a point beyond which he cannot tolerate environmental stress without symptom formation. One must not only seek to explain the differences in the personality but also consider the anthropologic and genetic backgrounds. During combat we see many soldiers who respond to battle situations and threats by tremendous anxiety reaction; others respond with the same reaction to the homosexual threat of the "gang shower" room.

Patients with a low ego reserve and a psychologic constellation which makes them susceptible to anxiety first begin to show an exaggerated response in the autonomic sphere. Having physical sensations and ruminating about them, they decide they are ill. A consultation with neighbors or a review of the family history will often reveal that the patient's symptoms are similar to those of someone in the family who perhaps had some serious organic illness. The patient begins to fear that he or she is also ill and becomes increasingly concerned over health, which adds to his burden of worry and increases the symptoms. The symptoms multiply. A consultation with the family physician or some specialist in an effort to reassure one's self may give the patient a diagnosis of a "mild anemia," "leakage of the heart," or "malposition of the uterus." The doctor may give such information in honest error in an attempt to impress the patient with his own acumen and to increase his own confidence in handling the patient. The patient, now having the doctor's opinion to bolster his own belief that he is ill, begins to dwell upon his bodily complaints to the exclusion of other interests.

Many such patients may be handled by the family physician by simple reassurance, by detection of the environmental situation producing stress, and, where possible, by removing it or explaining it away. The patients then revert to their normal situation, which is that of a person with anxiety potential but, in ordinary circumstances, symptom-free.

In our opinion this kind of person should be handled by the family physician without the assistance of a trained psychotherapist. A typical example is a patient who lacked the ordinary intellectual, social, and financial attributes necessary for prolonged psychotherapy but who, with or without her basic conflicts, had adjusted well until she became ill because of a threatening situation in her environment. The goal in therapy was to get rid of the present environmental stress so that the patient could carry on as before.

This patient was the obese wife of a tenant farmer who entered the hospital complaining of a "goiter." The symptoms of the goiter were attacks of choking and the feeling of suffocation plus fluttering of the heart, weakness, and fear of death. The attacks were most severe in the evening and at night. She noted that when she was busy working she did not have them. The patient's symptoms first occurred when she was helping her husband push a light truck that had become stuck. They recurred the following day and when discussing them with a neighbor, she was told that they "sounded like a goiter." After repeated attacks she consulted her family doctor who referred her to the University Hospital for diagnostic studies. Discussing the symptoms further with the patient it developed that the first attack came when she feared she was losing her husband. She had noted that he was no longer affectionate toward her and the children and had not contacted her sexually with his accustomed regularity. She was helping him start the truck so he could go to town for the evening, and she suspected he was seeing a lady friend there. She felt that her whole married life and security were being threatened. She based her suspicions of infidelity on the above incidents, plus the fact that she had actually observed her husband in the company of a younger and more attractive woman. Prior to entry into the hospital, she and her husband had reviewed his indiscretions in a few stormy sessions, and he had promised to forego such pleasures in the future and had in fact resumed his previous affectionate behavior toward her and the children. The patient still felt trouble in swallowing her pride, and was undecided as to the desirability of continuing as his wife. The treatment was rather superficial. It consisted of explaining the desirability of giving her husband another chance and arranging interviews between husband and the wife. After reconciliation her symptoms rapidly subsided, and she was discharged to return home.

In many other patients the anxiety is on a deeper basis because of completely repressed material. Patients in this group will get some relief from an explanation of their worry and the explanation that some of their somatic symptoms are due to autonomic stimulation. In spite of this, however, in most cases the anxiety recurs and the symptoms return. Even though the patient now accepts the symptoms as being due to "nervousness," he still suffers from them. Such patients require the services of a skilled psychotherapist.

In many patients the anxiety remains diffuse but may result in dysfunction in certain spheres. For example, patients with unresolved castration fears or patients with latent homosexuality may, when threatened with heterosexual contacts, show a sharp anxiety reaction resulting in impotence or frigidity, as the case may be. With such patients there are usually many other concomitants of anxiety. Such cases of impotence are most resistive to treatment, and treatment should be intensive, by prolonged psychotherapy or psychoanalysis.

The student may also classify under this heading the *traumatic neuroses* described in books on analysis. This form of neurosis may be manifest by a blocking or decrease in the various intellectual functions, varying from confusion and misinterpretation of environmental reactions to actual periods of fainting and unconsciousness. These symptoms are defenses of the ego against the flooding of the consciousness with repressed material, stimulated or reenergized by environmental happenings. A traumatic neurosis may be manifest by the emotions—fear, irritability, or rage. In other patients the anxiety is manifest by sleeplessness or disordered sleep with anxiety or threatening dreams. Many other forms of neurotic reaction may be complications of the traumatic neuroses.

Dissociative Reaction 000–x02

The symptoms classified here are those which show disturbances in consciousness. These cases were formerly classified as hysterical amnesias, fugues, etc. They are characterized by periods of complete unconsciousness or by varying states of confusion. They are probably more nearly related to the traumatic neuroses and severe anxiety reactions than the hysterias. The psychodynamics of this group has not been worked out carefully, and it is doubted that it consists of a single group. Many of the groups are probably traumatic neuroses with the complication of an anxiety reaction, in which the ego protects itself by a complete dissociation from its true identity, by a partial dissociation in running away, or by periods of confusion. Particular patients are those who in a situation of chronic stress, such as prolonged marital or financial troubles, disappear and are later found wandering aimlessly and confused in some other area. The student should carefully distinguish between these patients and the malingerer who runs away from stress and claims amnesia. A person with a true dissociative reaction will be unaware of his former identity, and if he recovers it spontaneously, will be unaware of the events that took place during the episode. These can be reproduced during periods of hypnosis or by the use of Pentothal or Sodium Amytal interview techniques.

An example is a patient who was brought to the hospital with a history of having had several attacks of amnesia. Usually the patient would arrive home from work or from visiting friends without being aware of how she arrived there or of the time intervening since her last recollection. The time was typically a period from 1 to 3 hours. Admission was precipitated by awakening one morning in a strange hotel room with no recollection of how she got there or where she was. Checking with the manager of the hotel revealed that she had come by bus the night before and had checked into her room by herself. The hotel desk clerk had been a little concerned because he thought she probably was ill since she got off the bus in a small town without luggage. The patient's last recollection was that at 6:00 P.M. the evening before she was tired and lay down on the bed in her own room at home. Therapy under hypnosis revealed that the first episode had been a very short one and occurred when the patient was at home in her room and had received notice that her husband, who was overseas, was divorcing her in order to marry a girl in that country. She states she recalled walking around in her room stating, "you are single and you don't like it." The next thing she remembered she was walking down the street not far from her home but with a complete change of clothing on and with no idea of where she was going. Other episodes were longer and were very frightening to her. The patient was able to discuss the loss of her husband which was a blow and also her tremendous need for love and affection. Her mother, a dynamic, self-sufficient person whom the patient was fond of, had little time for affection or attention to the girl. The mother treated the patient as if she were still a child. The patient was anxious to have a home of her own. It also developed that the last episode had been preceded by a rather stormy discussion with her mother in which the mother advised her to rearrange her life and advised her to get out more with people of her own age and give up her circle of older and more intellectual friends. The patient's father died a few years before her marriage, and the patient had been very close to him. The patient stated that in her desire to establish a home and because of her great love for her husband, she had almost given up her own personality in an attempt to devote herself entirely to being a good wife to her husband. She was able to see that the

242242

nature of her amnesia had been an attempt to run away from the overwhelming sense of loss of her husband's love and her own identity, because she had incorporated many of his qualities during the marital period. This identification seemed to be an attempt to gain some of the features of her greatly esteemed father. The episodes subsided rapidly; the patient gained at least a superficial insight from the therapy and returned to her responsible position. She subsequently married another and more stable person and has continued to get along without further recurrence of her illness.

Treatment. It is often necessary to use some type of adjuvant therapy such as drug injections or hypnosis to initiate the therapy of these patients. After the therapy is underway, psychotherapy of an analytically oriented type or psychoanalysis is indicated, depending on the availability of analytic therapy and whether the patient's personality and ego assets warrant the considerable expenditure of time, energy, and money involved in an analysis. Many patients will make a superficial type of adjustment without extensive therapy if the external situation precipitating the episodes has been severe and can be avoided by environmental manipulation or reeducation of the patient.

Conversion Reaction 000-x03

In terms of the evolution of a neurosis, the conversion reaction should be discussed after the phobic reactions and one would predict that future editions of the American Psychiatric Association Classification Manual will make this transition.

In order to avoid confusing the student, however, we will follow the general outline of the classification in writing this book. As the student will see, the psychopathology of the conversion reaction is somewhat more complicated than that of the phobias. Hysteria has long interested psychiatrists, and many theories have been offered concerning its cause. Charcot concluded that hysteria was a degenerative state largely due to inheritance. Bernheim and Babinski were convinced that hysteria was a result of suggestion. Binet felt that the mechanisms of hysteria depended on a condition of double consciousness, practically two independent states separated by amnesic periods. Janet described hysteria as "a mental disease belonging to the large group of the diseases due to weakness through cerebral exhaustion."

Freud and Breuer laid the groundwork for the modern concept of hysteria when they published the case of "Anna O." in 1895. They believed that hysteria was due to psychic trauma, painful ideas usually associated with sexual conflict which in a particular individual are unacceptable to the conscious mind's code of ethics. These ideas are not given an emotional outlet but are relegated or repressed into the unconscious portion of the mind and thus become a buried source of conflict. Such repression often takes place during childhood. Later this unconscious material seeks expression either through a building up of tensions from emotional conflict or a weakening of the ego due to external events. The symptoms result as the person's solution to the fact that the ego can no longer keep this material repressed and must relieve the id pressures within the unconscious.

Fenichel states that the development of conversion has two prerequisites, the erogeneity of the body which makes it possible for any organ to express sexual excitement, and the psychologic turning from reality to fantasy or a replacement of real sexual objects by fantasy representatives of infantile objects.

Thus, in the introversion of hysteria patients regress from a disappointing reality to the magical thinking of daydreams. Freud states:

(1) The hysteric symptom is a memory symbol of a certain efficacious (traumatic) impression and experience. (2) The hysteric symptom is the compensation by conversion for the associate return of the traumatic experience. (3) The hysteric symptoms like all other psychic formations are the expression of a wishful realization. (4) The hysteric symptom is the realization of an unconscious fantasy serving as a wish fulfillment. (5) The hysteric symptoms serve as a sexual gratification and represent a part of the sexual life of the individual corresponding to one of the components of the sexual impulse. (6) The hysteric symptom in a fashion corresponds to the return of the sexual gratification, which was real in infantile life but has been repressed since then. (7) The hysteric symptom results as a compromise between two opposing affects or impulse excitements, one of which tries to bring to a realization a partial impulse or a component of the sexual constitution while the other tries to repress the same. (8) The hysteric symptom may undertake the representation of diverse and conscious nonsexual incitements which cannot lack sexual significance.

Expressed another way, it may be stated that conversion reactions are due to psychologic situations with which the developing child is confronted, but because the situation is unacceptable to his concept of morals and ethics, the material is repressed. This material becomes unconscious, and the energy associated with it seeks expression. During long periods it may be kept repressed, but if external circumstances further exacerbate these energies, or if the ego becomes preoccupied and distracted with other things and no longer capable of keeping the material from consciousness, further defenses are necessary. In persons with the proper sexual symbolization in some part of the body and with the proper development of the capacity for magical or fantasy thinking, the result is a conversion of this energy into hysteric symptoms which are socially acceptable to the person. By development of the symptoms, the patient obtains the symbolic gratification of the original wish and at the same time avoids the necessity for facing the fact that such desires are among his own thinking and concepts. With the development of the symptoms and the symbolic gratification of his original desire the patient obtains relief from the tensions produced by his denial of the original drive, and thus he becomes comfortable. Hysteric patients are often placid, calm, and satisfied with their illness. They "enjoy ill health."

Conversion hysteria takes many forms but is usually manifest by some disturbance in motility, sensation, or the special senses. Patients may have hysteric convulsions, tics, paralyses, anesthesias, paresthesias, blindness, aphonia, or deafness.

The symptoms are gross in character involving complete annihilation of the function. The mechanism is the same in each case, but the psychopathologic content varies. Each symptom shares characteristics in common irrespective of the body system involved. One of the most important symptoms is the patient's attitude toward his illness. The patient does not seem generally concerned or distressed about his health; in fact, he often seems to enjoy the illness and to find satisfaction in discussing it. Hysteric patients will subject themselves to any amount of examination or surgical manipulation in order to make their illness a more important and prominent part of their lives. This particular indifferent attitude toward the illness has been dubbed *la belle indifférence* by French writers. Most hysteric symptoms are unphysiologic in nature. Hysteric paralyses and anesthesias tend to involve body segments according to functional division rather than according to the facts of anatomy and physiology. For example, anesthesias usually involve the hand, the arm, or an entire side of the body, stopping at a sharp line of demarcation, usually the junction of one of the joints of the body, or at exactly the midline of the body. In such hemianesthesias it is common to find vibratory sense absent on one side of the skull but present on the other, with the line of demarcation being in the midline. Patients with hysteric blindness have normal pupillary reactions and frequently blink in the bright light. Light stimuli will also alter the EEG pattern in the same manner as it does in the person with normal vision.

Another feature of hysteria is the "secondary gain." These are the small profits patients gain from their symptoms, the extra care and attention from their family by virtue of the symptoms, which excuse the patients from unsavory aspects of their work and win simple bonuses in pleasure. The unconscious mechanisms and factors served by the illness are referred to as the "primary gain."

The choice of the organ to be afflicted in hysteria has been the subject of much discussion. It is generally believed that the organ which is chosen will be the one which has been the object of the unconscious sexual fantasies. Thus the particular segment of the body selected for special erotic significance depends upon the patient's previous experience.

An older theory still held by some is that the organ or system chosen will be one which for constitutional reasons is an area or zone of minor resistance. This perhaps colors its choice in some cases, but we feel that the organ which is the most satisfactory symbol to solve the frustrating situation will be chosen by the patient to express his neurosis.

Hysterias are most often seen among more primitive folk and in time of stress such as a military situation. An example of a rather simple type of hysteria is an 18-year-old girl from the piney woods of Texas. She was the ninth child of a poor sharecropper. She did not learn well in school, was not so attractive as her sister, and had not been accepted by the other children in the community. As a child she had some type of "spasms" which, according to the family, had been diagnosed as epilepsy. The convulsions started in infancy and persisted to the age of 7 years with fairly frequent attacks, and then subsided spontaneously. She had no further seizures until she was 14 years of age, except for an occasional fainting spell. She may have had another grand mal attack at age 14. The patient discovered that she received a great deal of attention from her family when she had these spells and was excused from working in the fields, which she did not like to do. When other members of the family or other events were the center of attention, the patient would call to her mother that she was going to have an epileptic spell and would then swoon and fall on the bed or a chair. Partially from the patient's direction and partially through the parents' experimentation it was found that if two members of the family massaged the patient's thighs on the inner aspects, and a third member massaged her breasts, she would revive from the spells more quickly. During the hospital stay the family was permitted to give her a treatment for one of these spells after which it subsided. During subsequent spells they were asked not to do so and were quite surprised when the patient recovered spontaneously after 10 minutes of shaking. It was observed that during the spells the patient would respond consciously to questions, and if she became interested in the conversation the spells would stop. The secondary gain in this case is obvious. The spells themselves represented coital movement, and it is undoubtedly true that the patient received a great deal of erotic stimulation from the treatments administered by the family. The dynamics in this case were not worked out. We can say that a rather inadequate person from a poor environment discovered that idiopathic epilepsy brought certain advantages within her own social group. She extended these seizures into the functional field and had convulsions on order. This type of hysteric reaction is difficult to distinguish from true simulation, and the psychopathology is probably very superficial. Some cases are much more complicated. We might add, parenthetically, that this patient had an abnormal EEG but she was not placed on treatment because the organic seizures were so infrequent it was thought unnecessary.

One of us treated in great detail a member of a religious order, following a long period of conflict because her erotic fantasies, being in conflict with her devout religious beliefs and dedication, prompted symptoms that led to a series of surgical operations. Following this, she began to develop swellings in one foot and leg, which the hospital staff suspected were due to the patient placing ligatures around her leg. This was not shown to be true. Prolonged and intensive psychotherapy revealed the deep-seated nature of the conflicts in this patient, her rejection of them, and her expression of these sexual strivings in the abdominal complaints and finally in swellings of the leg. The symptoms subsided with psychotherapy, but there remained a residual gait disturbance due to partial fixation of the joint and shortening of the tendo achillis in the affected extremity.

Treatment. Superficial, simple forms like that manifested in the country girl should be handled by supportive psychotherapy and reassurance. Occasionally Pentothal Sodium or Amytal analysis and synthesis are helpful. Some of these patients respond to direct suggestion, but the response is symptomatic and not deep. Intensive psychotherapy or psychoanalytic therapy, if available, is the preferred treatment for the severe conversion reaction, particularly if it occurs in the more complicated forms in people of higher intellectual capacity and ability.

Phobic Reactions 000-x04

These reactions are also called the *anxiety hysterias*. In these cases the fear or anxiety concerning an external object is the symbolic representation of the original feared object. A classic example is the case of little Hans, reported by Freud as a phobia in a 5-year-old boy.

We have previously stated that all the neuroses are manifestations of symptom formation and the particular neurosis will depend upon the psychogenic constellation. It will be obvious to the student that different people may resort to different ways of solving their neurotic problem. In the phobic reaction one has the situation of original trauma, such as castration anxiety (perhaps further influenced by fixations at one of the pregenital levels), repressed. Situations in the environment which place the ego under stress may make it difficult for the individual to keep this material repressed. Stimuli from the surrounding environment such as sexual temptations, castration threats symbolically expressed by authoritarian figures, or similar environmental situations may result in an increased energy of the repressed material. In order to preserve the ego and protect consciousness from flooding with anxiety, the individual finds a substitute outlet for the objectionable impulse. This usually permits a partial discharge of the repressed energy but the substitute object is often one which may be avoided. This offers a certain measure of relief, as the patient's anxiety attacks occur only when confronted with the symbolic object or situation. By avoiding these situations, he succeeds in relieving himself of considerable tension.

A person may develop a phobia about objects for which he unconsciously wishes. In other cases the object or situation that the patient fears colors the phobia. For example, patients with castration anxiety may fix their anxiety on a fear of knives or other sharp objects. In more complex cases the connection is not so clear, and the fear situation less directly represents the original fear-producing situation and may be looked upon as a symbol. Thus, little Hans, as reported by Freud, was afraid of horses instead of his father. The fear of falling from high places in a case seen by one of your authors represents a basic fear of being punished for homicidal wishes directed toward someone in the environment. Patients with unacceptable sexual fantasies which produce anxiety may develop phobias of crowds, and by avoiding crowds they avoid the extra stimulation of their erotic fantasies. At the same time they fix their anxiety on the symbolic object, the crowd, so that when alone they may have peace. These patients should be treated by intensive analytically oriented psychotherapy or psychoanalysis, if available. They usually form a transference easily and are excellent analytic candidates, providing they are of suitable age and intellectual and ego capacity.

These phobic reactions are among the early psychoneurotic reactions seen in children and are ordinarily considered the most primitive form of neurotic reaction. Perhaps everybody develops an anxiety hysteria to a certain degree. Children's fears of the dark, fears of imaginary "goblins," and similar fixations of the diffuse anxieties seen in children as they attempt to master the world are examples of immature and incompletely formed phobic reactions which serve the same purpose for the ego as the full-blown phobic reaction in the adult. That is, the reactions relieve the ego of a considerable flooding with anxiety and free energy for other purposes.

Obsessive Compulsive Reaction 000–x05

These reactions are sometimes referred to as *the psychasthenias*. Symptomatically they are of two types, the obsessive reactions and the compulsive reactions. The obsessive reactions are characterized by recurring ideas which the patient recognizes as being absurd but which continue to recur and annoy him nonetheless. The compulsive reactions are similar, except that here the patient has recurring impulses to carry out certain motor acts. The patient recognizes these acts as being absurd and unnecessary, and yet if he fails to carry them out, he feels anxious and uncomfortable. Most patients have a mixture of both obsessive and compulsive symptoms. These symptoms frequently occur in combination with phobias mentioned above, and older books often classify them as the obsessive compulsive phobic reactions, but this is improper as the psychogenic mechanism differs.

These obsessive compulsive symptoms usually occur in individuals of a certain type, thought to represent a definite constitutional pattern, although some authors doubt this. The patients are usually rigid, meticulous, orderly individuals with superior intellectual capacity. They always conform well to the religious and moral code of their group and are usually recognized as being dependable and conscientious. Frequently they are insecure and unsure of themselves, but they keep these traits well hidden from their families and friends. It is common in these patients to find that they are superstitious and often perplexed by great doubts and indecision. To make definite, clear-cut decisions is hard for persons of the so-called obsessive compulsive character. The essential psychopathology is, as is usual, an ego-protective device; the patient uses his ideas or his compulsive acts as a substitute for some unconscious urge which to him is unacceptable. The original pathologic material may be completely or incompletely repressed, but the patient makes a complete withdrawal of the emotion or affect from the original material. This is an ego-protective device known as isolation. It differs from hysteria, in which the pathologic material is completely repressed and the affect is displayed or converted into some other type of idea or activity which is more acceptable. Thus, the obsessive compulsive patient may be thought of as a person who lacks the power to force the original conflict material completely out of consciousness. His obsessive compulsive activity is a substitution and is a symbolic method of carrying out the original impulse, and at the same time it may be a form of expiation for the guilt feeling connected with the original idea. In contrast to the hysteric patient, he is unusually uncomfortable, has much anxiety, and is eager for relief from his illness. In the isolation phenomenon mentioned above the patient separates the appropriate emotion of guilt from the original act.

Obsessive compulsive symptoms are basically the patient's solution to frustrations and guilt feelings concerning the genital strivings encountered in the oedipal situation. We believe that the patient develops guilt feelings with some anxiety in this situation and regresses to an earlier stage of emotional development.

Obsessive states are distinguished from hysteria by the fact that the regression is to the anal sadistic phase of sexual development. Regression to this phase may be conditioned by unusual gratifications or unusual frustrations brought about by the mother or nursemaid by placing great attention on the bowel functions, or by the excessive use of cathartics, enemas, suppositories, etc. In other cases these tendencies may be produced when the anal phase of instinctual development is associated with an unusually strong sense of security and the love and affection of the parents. In the process of regression to the anal sadistic phase, the patient further protects himself by isolation of the emotions from the original feared object and invests the obsessive symptoms with an unusual amount of emotional energy, and thus makes them suitable objects for the relief of his tension.

In these patients the passivity feelings, which are a reaction formation to tremendous hostility, make them amiable, and they often have many friends but are thought of as the "lone wolf" or "cold" type of person. Their hostility is expressed in indirect and subtle ways.

Treatment. Some patients respond spectacularly to superficial explanatory psychotherapy of the supportive type. Most of them, however, require prolonged intensive and extensive psychoanalytic therapy. A few respond to intensive psychoanalytically oriented psychotherapy but in most cases only psychoanalysis will suffice. Difficulties in the transference situation, principally motivated by the patient's passivity, his tremendous fear of assult, and his subtle aggressions, prolong and complicate therapy. Because these people are usually of superior intellectual capacity and because their ego is often greatly handicapped by the obsessive symptoms, they are worth treating even though the treatment is long.

Depressive Reaction 000–x06

Reactive depressions are officially described under the neuroses although they are primarily conditions in which the symptomatology is expressed in the affective sphere. As in the psychotic depressions, the patient suffering from neurotic depression feels a loss of the necessary ego supplies, which in effect is a loss of self-esteem and a failure to obtain the necessary love and affection or "narcissistic supply" from the environment. The patient, being unable to fulfill these needs, begins to feel inferior. These patients are often obsequious and ingratiating, and demonstrate their misery before people around them. Those in the reactive stage of depression may often accuse those around them of having brought about this misery and thus force them to give the affection and attention the patients want. We believe that neurotic depressions are rooted in failure at the oedipal level. The repression and conflict use so much of the energy available the patient has little left to invest on the external world for enjoyment and interest.

By his very depressive symptoms the patient succeeds in dominating the world around him, as mentioned earlier in *Oedipus at Colonus*. The mechanism is hostility toward persons around one with resultant guilt feelings from the superego. The patient turns these hostility feelings on himself. This inward turning (introjection) is usually due to deprivation of affection from the world around him due to the loss of a person with whom he identified and for whom he felt mixed love and hostility. Objects symbolizing elements of loved persons may, if lost, precipitate a reactive depression. For example, a business failure with loss of status with family and friends may precipitate the depression.

Thus, introjection is not only a hostile act which destroys the object by its introjection, it is also an act which gains the object and seeks to achieve the wished-for ego supply. The situation is most apt to occur where the object of the ambivalent feelings has not represented love on an adult level but rather was used to supply infantile or narcissistic types of affection, and the patient must have some fixations at the oral level as the introjection is symbolized on an oral level.

The principal difference between the neurotic depression and the psychotic depression described in an earlier chapter is in the depth of the regression.

The actual cause of the injuries and fixations at the infantile narcissistic level, and the conditions which set the scene for a later depression, may vary. These vicissitudes in libidinous development may be abandonment and loneliness caused by the death or loss of the parents, or may result from the usual and unavoidable frustrations and disappointments such as the birth of siblings, penis envy, or the oedipal conflict.

It is assumed that persons who develop the predisposition to depressions on these bases have some type of organic or constitutional predisposition for the development of depressive reactions. In later life when environmental circumstances occur which trigger this original predisposition, a depression develops. For example, a daughter who has had mixed feelings of hostility and love toward her mother may develop a depressive reaction at the time of the mother's death. This is particularly true if the mother has been cold and rejecting and has contributed to the daughter's being an individual who is continually in need of affection.

Treatment. The treatment of choice in these depressions is intensive psychotherapy or psychoanalysis. If the depression is severe, it borders on a psychotic reaction, and one may give some thought to the judicious use of shock therapy followed by psychotherapy. In most instances, shock therapy is much less effective in the neurotic depressions than in the psychotic depression and in the involutional psychosis. Drugs often aid in treating these patients (see the treatment section).

PART THREE

Disorders of Psychogenic Origin or without Clearly Defined Physical Cause or Structural Change in the Brain: Personality Disorders

CHAPTER **19**

Personality Pattern and Trait Disturbances 000–x40, 000–x50

In this section are grouped the heterogeneous collection of disturbances which we do not classify as mentally ill or neurotic in the ordinary sense of the word, because the patients live their entire lives according to this general pattern of behavior. If a personality disorder is a neurosis or mental illness it is manifest by the lifelong behavior pattern rather than by any circumscribed series of symptoms. The individuals do not usually consider themselves ill or different from their fellows. The official Classification Manual of the American Psychiatric Association claims that their divisions are based on the dynamics of personality development. This is true only to a degree, as personality dynamics, at least of the psychoanalytic sort, would propose a different grouping of personality disorders or character types.

Another way of viewing these patients is to consider them as persons who show the type of lifelong patterns of reaction that make them ready for or susceptible to psychoses but who never become psychotic. Actually it would appear that by lifelong partial regression they avoid periodic total regressions into a psychotic state.

These are purely symptomatic descriptions and the dynamics of the disorder is not too well understood. The personality disturbances are usually described as pattern disturbances, trait disturbances, and sociopathic disturbances. These are descriptive terms that actually have no meaning in terms of cause, but they will be followed here to keep the student from confusion in using the classification manual in hospitals and clinics.

Personality Pattern Disturbance 000–x40

These disturbances are grouped together because they include cardinal personality types which are not altered by treatment. It is often thought
252

that these individuals have differentiating constitutional features. These persons under stress may develop a psychosis of the type indicated by the basic personality pattern.

INADEQUATE PERSONALITY 000–x41

In this classification are the individuals often seen in welfare offices, on relief roles, in prison, and occupying the lower levels of the social and economic strata. Some, by virtue of inheritances from their families or support from stable marital partners, may adjust at a higher social plane, but they never function effectively. These are the sorry, out-of-luck people. They are epitomized by some of the characters of William Faulkner and Erskine Caldwell. They lack the energy, the perseverance, and the ability to plan and execute anything successfully except the very simplest acts. Their lack of physical and emotional stamina and general ineptness make them an ongoing social problem. This type is apt to be confused with simple schizophrenia or borderline mental retardation. The psychopathology is either a faulty development of the ego or an ego so beset by internal tensions and pressure that all the energy is used up in repression. It is probably the former rather than the latter because these cases do not seem to improve under presently known methods of treatment.

SCHIZOID PERSONALITY 000–x42

These are the lonesome, artistic persons who manage to stay to themselves. They are usually fairly quiet; their hostility is suppressed or worked out surreptitiously so that they do not ordinarily show even normal aggressive feelings. They are the "Caspar Milquetoasts" and the "Walter Mitteys" of the world who work through their hostility and realize their ambitions principally through autistic thinking. They are often fearful, are emotionally detached, and avoid competitive situations. One sees these individuals involved in aimless and endless artistic pursuits. They are the authors who are always writing a book never published, the scientists who are always conducting experiments never completed. Some of them are shut in and become hermit-like recluses. Frequently they are eccentric. They are apt to be confused with simple schizophrenic patients, and the borderline is sometimes difficult to draw. These people are the prototype of the persons that the lay public thinks of as becoming schizophrenic, but by no means do all persons suffering from schizophrenic psychosis have this type of prepsychotic personality. When this type of person does develop a full-blown psychosis, however, he is usually not amenable to treatment. We believe that the psychopathology here is due to deficiencies in the ego, with the ego unable to permit emotional drives or make attachments to external objects. Many feel that these people have a strong constitutional organic element in their make-up, and that these are the ones that lead to the so-called "process" or organic type of schizophrenia.

CYCLOTHYMIC PERSONALITY 000–x43

These are the supersalesmen of the world, extrovertive, outgoing persons who adjust to life situations by aggression, friendliness, and mild expansivity. They seem to be trying to form emotional ties of a positive sort to everything and everyone in their environment; but withdrawal of emotion or opposition to their drive results in outbursts of irritability and rage. They may have short periods of sadness or dejection following defeat, but they usually bounce back rapidly. Persons with this type of habitual personality reaction may show intermittent manic or depressive attacks or alternating types of psychotic reactions. These are the persons who adjust well to contemporary America, providing their traits are not so highly specialized as to make them a nuisance. Some individuals of this basic trait accomplish much in the way of salesmanship, organization, and promotion of enterprises. Difficulties, when encountered, are usually through overcommitments and overexpansion in a marital or sexual way, in the excessive use of alcohol in pursuing friendly contacts, or in business judgment distorted by the persistent mood of euphoria.

THE PARANOID PERSONALITY 000–x44

These people are usually somewhat like the schizoid personality but are less withdrawn, and are more rigid and better organized. They often have a great deal of energy and enter into external contacts in competitive activities. Through it all, however, they remain aloof, suspicious, and hostile. They keep the world at an emotional arm's length by biting sarcasm in a verbal sort of aggression and hostility. These persons, under great stress, may develop a full-blown paranoid psychosis. The psychopathology is the same as that mentioned for the paranoid reactions in an earlier chapter, but these people manage to keep their paranoid ideas at the level of suspiciousness, jealousies, and generally difficult natures.

Personality Trait Disturbance 000–x50

In this category are placed those persons who, because of immaturity or faulty development of the ego, are unable to maintain a stable, independent personality function in the face of environmental stress. The principal difference between the cases classified here and those under the various forms of neuroses lies in the relative absence of the symptoms typical of the neuroses, with the presence of the immature malfunctioning personality as the principal symptom.

Emotionally Unstable Personality 000–x51

These are people who panic under stress, make rapid attempts to get away, start panics at fires, and get excited in the face of environmental mishaps such as accidents or family tragedies. They have very poorly controlled hostility, guilt reactions, and anxiety. They are often blustering and become involved in various fights and arguments. Temper tantrums are frequent. A lay person's concept of "hysterical attacks" are those of a person who is properly categorized under this classification. Many persons classified here were formerly classified under the emotionally unstable type of "psychopath."

Passive-Aggressive Personality 000–x52

These are of three ordinary types:

First is the passive dependent type. These individuals are as described, passive and dependent. They are the childish, helpless adults who act like children. Many are the clingers in the clinics, those who are dependent on welfare, and the persons who cling to their parents; the indecisive and ineffectual belong in this category. This type is sometimes confused with the inadequate personality, the principal difference being the passivity and the tremendous dependence present.

Second is the passive aggressive type. This individual differs from the above only in that he shows more childish aggression, manifest by stubbornness, pouting, and a subtle type of hostility, which blocks plans and endeavors at constructive activity. Persons of this type may agree to go along with some plan of action for their rehabilitation but their very way of cooperating makes it impossible for them to have a successful result. This is a rather common type of reaction in our culture.

Third is the aggressive type. These people react to minor frustrations with outbursts of temper, temper tantrums, and may even show destructive behavior. These are the throwers of instruments and articles of furniture, the persons who bear pathologic grudges and spread gossip in an attempt to tear down other people's constructive activities. They are closely related to the emotionally unstable and to the antisocial.

Compulsive Personality 000–x53

These are the so-called compulsive characters who do not have signs of a full-blown compulsive neurosis. They are the rigid, organized, meticulous persons with a tremendous capacity to work. They cannot relax.

Many of them live a very useful and constructive life but make people around them uncomfortable because of their driving rigidity. The psychopathology here is not unlike that of a compulsive neurosis, but the ego has not yet resorted to displacement of the affect onto obsessive thoughts or compulsive activities though the ego still handles the drives by a rigid organization of behavior patterns and repression.

CHAPTER 20

Sociopathic Personality Disturbances 000–x60

Individuals in this category show their neurotic symptoms in terms of an inability to conform to society and the demands which their culture makes upon them. Some of them show personal difficulties and maladjustment. Most of them believe they are getting along fine, and it is society that is not adapted to them. Many patients formerly classified as "constitutional psychopaths" belong in this category. With careful study and attempts at detailed therapy of patients correctly described in this category, the development of the causal factors may result in their being placed in one of the neurotic reactions or in one of the other forms of personality disturbance.

Antisocial Reaction 000–x61

These individuals are characterized by their emotional immaturity, lack of sense of responsibility, poor judgment, lack of appreciation of the consequences of acts, pronounced ability to rationalize behavior, and inability to postpone satisfactions. Most of the so-called constitutional psychopaths and psychopathic personality cases in the old classifications belong in this category. Patients properly categorized here show a general impulsiveness and inability to postpone gratifying their wishes and desires, marked lack of consideration for the accepted moral standards of the group in which they live, undependability, and unreliability. Other symptoms are an inability to form mature judgments, an inability to profit by past experience, an apparent lack of appreciation and understanding of the consequences of their acts, and a tendency to accept immediate pleasures without considering the long-term consequences to themselves or to the persons about them. Most of these patients have a

257

certain childlike confidence in the willingness of the people around them to rescue them from the consequences of the difficulties which their behavior produces. These symptoms of misbehavior have ordinarily been manifested for many years starting in early childhood.

The behavior of these patients may vary from amiable lying to criminal activity. There are patients showing some of the above symptoms who have neurotic reactions and who should be so classified. To be in this category, the antisocial behavior of the patient should be the principal manifestation of the disorder. The present concept of the dynamics of this disorder comes from the analysis of patients suffering from some one of the manifestations of this group. One of the puzzling symptoms is the patient's statement that he knows he should not carry out certain acts but that he is unable to refrain from doing so. This compulsive-like behavior makes some authorities believe that such patients are not responsible for their acts. Many of these patients will tell you that they carry out the action even though they are quite certain it will result in trouble, but at the moment they do not seem to care. The compulsive patient has an urge to carry out some act he does not like to do, does not want to do, and which he regards as unpleasant or silly, but does it to relieve his anxiety. In contrast, the "psychopath" does something that he feels he wants to do just because of the pleasure of it although he may recognize that it will get him into trouble. Thus a compulsive patient will come to the physician complaining that he is forced to carry out unpleasant or silly acts which make him suffer in terms of his own self-esteem and self-respect; but he must do them to keep himself comfortable. The patient with an antisocial reaction, on the other hand, will complain that the things he wants to do and likes to do and the things that give him pleasure get him into trouble.

The fact that patients in this category do the things they consciously want to do seems to generate aggression in legal authorities and in many physicians, and makes them classify these people as criminals or undesirable persons, instead of as sick people.

The impulsive and compelling character of these symptoms can be explained in several ways. Basically the personal moral code or superego of these people is poorly developed. This is usually due to the fact that in infancy and childhood, when the patient was developing this facet of his personality, the environment offered unsatisfactory sources of love, security, and guidance. This might be due to a broken home, parents who reject him, or other environmental reactions which produced severe trauma when the child was in the early stages of his libidinal development. This results in mixed feelings or ambivalence to the love objects in his environment. The impulsive behavior mentioned above is further evidence of this type of ambivalence. The child wants to do something he feels he must do because it gives him pleasure, and at the same time he rejects the idea because it is wrong. He also feels some justification for doing it and believes he can get away with it without punishment. Persons who belong in this group are often extremely personable and ingratiating individuals and are usually able to gain the confidence, love, and affection of their victims. Having reassured themselves that they can gain love, they then fear they cannot hold it and turn upon the love object, victimizing it in any one of the several spheres of behavior.

This mechanism describes certain persons who are always dissatisfied with what they have and who are supposedly "hypersexed." The symptoms are manifestations of a difficulty in forming attachments of a stable sort and the person attempts to find satisfaction by continually moving from one love object to another. This particular constellation occurs in several of the personality disorders.

Faulty or pathologic formation of the superego, which is the basic difficulty in the antisocial reactions, is felt to play a basic role in all the sociopathic disturbances. The student will recall that the formation of a stable superego is dependent on several things. It is necessary for the child to have firm but dependable objects of love in his environment. These usually are the parents. The shifting of parents through a broken home, remarriage, parents who are too unstable or too cruel to function as a dependable source of love, or parents who behave in such a manner that the child cannot form proper standards of behavior through identification, may result in poor superego formation. If the parent fails to inspire love and affection in the child at about the fourth or fifth year, when the superego takes on definitive forms, the child will not react properly to the oedipal situation. The guilt feelings aroused by his changes in attitude toward his parents will not be great enough to arouse sufficient anxiety to stabilize the superego and enable the child to build one strong enough to influence his behavior in the future. If the child's first well-objectified hostility manifested in the oedipal situation is not toward a person loved enough to produce guilt feelings and strong anxieties, the pattern will be set for carrying out the gratification of the instinctual impulses without sufficiently strong guilt feelings or sufficiently strong fears of the consequences to cause a patient to inhibit or modify his behavior.

This characterizes the behavior of the patient usually described as "a psychopath." These people appear to superficial observation to be anxiety free. They seem to carry out acts with no sense of guilt and to be completely free from remorse or other concern about the possible consequences of their activities. A deeper study fails to confirm this belief.

The restlessness, dissatisfaction, and continually moving from one love object to another in themselves offer a clue to the basic unhappiness and basic extent of anxiety carried by these patients. It is as though they were on the move to keep the anxiety and guilt feelings from having a chance to catch up and overcome them. This running away from the superego has been referred to by Reich, Fenichel, and others.

Dyssocial Reaction 000–x62

Persons categorized here differ from those with the so-called antisocial reactions in that they show more of a passive disregard or lack of concept of decent moral codes than an aggressive reaction to moral codes, characterized by the above group. In this category go those patients formerly classified as psychopathic personalities with asocial and amoral trends. The pathology in these patients is the same as in the above except that here there is more emphasis on the lack of adequate guidance or pattern for laying down adequate concepts of behavior. This class of persons seems to have a tremendous need for an instant gratification of needs and will grant them impulsively. Not being trained to postpone gratification, these people tend to grant desires impulsively and immediately and without thought for the result or consequences. A person having a wish or desire carries it through promptly without thinking how he is going to feel about it. The remorse and guilt feelings come later and are often not strong. It is believed that this form of avoiding the control of the superego results from lack of dependable love at the oral phase of libido development. Often the parents in cases of this sort are persons who have been immature and inconsistent in their emotional attitudes toward the children, showering them with love and affection at periods and at other periods rejecting them, neglecting them, or being indifferent, harsh, or cruel.

The patients in this group, in order to work out some of their inner tensions and anxieties, often go to elaborate details to justify their behavior. We see certain cults such as the nudists, certain bohemian groups, sexual clubs, and other groups which serve as a false superego upon which these persons can focus most of their energy. Many of these people have been raised in such surroundings, and their parents participated in the "slum life" with little in the way of moral or ethical teaching. This false front, as it were, permits them to carry out their impulses and decreases their secondary feelings of remorse. In fact, within their culture, secondary feelings of remorse are inappropriate and not expected. Thus, while the whole group is rejected by the world at large, individuals within their group find acceptance for their unusual behavior.

In both the antisocial and dyssocial groups, occasional patients commit suicide from impulsive feelings of remorse, hopelessness, or feeling that nothing can be done. Suicidal or self-destructive trends are seen in some of their behavior. Often their impulsive acts result in a great deal of punishment or imprisonment. Females in this category will often perform sexual acts without any attempt at protection against illegitimate pregnancy. Males and females both perform sex acts promiscuously without protection against disease. Sometimes they engage in criminal activity of an aggressive sort with no attempt to conceal their identity. The way the crimes are committed makes one believe that they were courting punishment. Gamblers will sometimes carry on their activity when they know the game is fixed and that they have little or no chance of winning. In all the above cases, success under these adverse circumstances would give them a greater instinctual kick, but, on the other hand, the element of hazard must be present, and the possibility of punishment must play a role in the pleasures brought about by the action.

Sexual Deviation 000–x63

Sexual deviation categorized here exists in those whose deviant behavior is not a symptom of a psychosis or obsessional neurosis. It is believed by most people that the deviant behavior is psychogenically determined and that it is a manifestation of a neurosis. Where it is the only or principal manifestation of the neurosis, these people are properly classified here. Not all forms of deviation can be described in a book of this length, but we will discuss the general prototype for the student's guidance.

Unusual forms of gratification of the sexual impulses have been recorded since ancient times. Their acceptance by the general population varies with different civilizations. At the time of the preparation of this edition there is a great deal of public interest in the problem of deviation. It is for that reason that this discussion will be extensive. To present all the views and knowledge and all the theories on the subject would be a work longer than this volume. We will attempt to state what the authors believe are the most reliable facts and theories concerning these anomalies of behavior.

Our views are analytically oriented because we believe Freud's discovery and investigation of the vicissitudes of infantile sexuality provide the basis for understanding these problems. It is true that certain deviates of the homosexual type show biologic characterizations both on superficial inspection and careful chemical testing of the ketosteroids. It is also true that patients with these anomalies represent an extremely small proportion of the problem of deviation and the presence of the anomalies does not always mean that the person practices sexual deviations, although he may give every external appearance of being a deviate. We do not at this writing have any conclusive evidence that greater or less quantities of sex hormones of any particular variety will influence a person's ideas and impulses in so far as satisfactory sexual objects are concerned.

Patients with sexual deviations are persons who have failed to develop beyond the infantile level of sexuality due to arrested development or who have regressed to infantile forms of sexual expression. This regression is due to frustrations or disappointment in some phase of sexual development. Fenichel states: "The simple formula presents itself: persons who react to sexual frustration with a regression to infantile sexuality are perverts; persons who react with other defenses or who employ other defenses after the regression are neurotics." Persons who show regressive tendencies in this sphere, like persons showing other forms of regression, retain a certain amount of the adult sexual function. Thus, in perversions, the person may achieve the stimulation through some unusual act such as watching nude people, watching fires, certain types of cutaneous sensation, or certain types of oral stimulation, but the final satisfaction usually results in a genital orgasm, thus showing some clinging to adult types of sexual expression. We believe that the factors which prevent genital stimulation from becoming the primary goal in this sexual activity are the same factors which produce other neurotic manifestations. The factor most active in the production of disturbances in genital primacy is castration anxiety and the attendant fears and guilt feelings that go with it. This may be brought about in children raised in environments that are extremely rigid, where there is a particularly cruel or inconsistent form of punishment, and where the child reacts to fears and guilt by identifying himself with the parent of the opposite sex instead of the parent of the same sex and thus hopes to escape detection and punishment.

It is felt that the choice of perversion is due to a process of fixation brought about by experiences which gave unusual satisfactions and feelings of security and which occurred at some time before the castration anxiety reached its peak. Thus, being confronted with anxiety produced by the castration complex, the child returns or regresses to the situation which in earlier childhood gave him great security and reassurance. The fact that the breast usually gives such reassuring comfort and that situations in later life do not may explain the fact that the oral perversions are the most common.

Detailed elaboration of the various forms of deviation would have little place in this book. For the student or practitioner who is particularly interested in this phase of the problem there are many works that one might refer to. Perhaps the most authentic one is the chapter on Perversion and Impulse Neuroses in Fenichel, *The Psychoanalytic Theory of Neurosis.* There are other popular and semipopular books which discuss the problems of deviation but often with too much emphasis on the symptomatic description of the patient's behavior and insufficient emphasis on the origin of the behavior. Kinsey's two books discuss the prevalence of deviant sex practices in the population based on a questionnaire. Some authorities regard these statistics as factual, and others feel that they are a result of a certain type of selection in terms of the questionnaire. The fact that perversions are reasonably common in the patients of a psychiatrist is not a new phenomenon. We have no figures better than Kinsey's as to their occurrence in the general population.

At the time of this writing, there is a great hue and cry over the incidence of perversions in the population. Federal government security regulations severely penalize anyone under suspicion of or treatment for perversions who is a member of the armed forces or an employee of several other governmental agencies.

To consider a person a criminal because of deviated sex tendencies is denying what is known to medicine and is penalizing the patient for choosing a particular type of neurosis as opposed to other types. It should be pointed out, however, that persons practicing deviations in this culture are susceptible to blackmail and therefore are probably not the most suitable persons to work in sensitive positions, particularly if the national safety is involved. It should be pointed out also, however, that not many generations ago patients with mental illness were regarded as criminals and punished, or viewed as witches and burned. In fairly recent times patients with neuroses or other forms of mental illness were regarded as malingerers, goldbrickers, and general no-goods. We feel that another generation will accept the sex deviate as a sick person. This does not imply that persons with sex deviations may not indulge in criminal activities. Those who resort to criminal functions which interfere with the health, liberty, or well-being of other citizens in an effort to gratify their sexual impulses must be confined because they interfere with other persons' rights, not because they seek sexual pleasures in ways other than those generally accepted.

Some patients suffer from latent homosexuality, that is, they fail to develop adult sexuality, but at the same time reject and repress their homosexual urges. These so-called "latent homosexuals" use various methods or means of working out their problems. One of the common ones is to remain a chronic, irritable, paranoid bachelor. At times a dancer or other artist may use his talents for sublimating unrecognized homosexual trends. The unsuccessful mama's boys and the alcoholic who goes to bed with his bottle may represent forms of latent homosexuality.

The recognition and management of these forms are definitely problems for the expert. The knowledge that such reactions exist and may explain some of the behavior of their patients is of interest, but the management should not be attempted by the student or nonpsychiatric physician.

Gambling in some persons is a form of sexual perversion. Gambling is sometimes looked upon as a result of guilt feelings centering about masturbation. It is felt that the excitement of gambling represents a form of sexual excitement, and the fact that individuals can win against large odds represents approval of the environment and of "fate" and thus offers a certain amount of protection against castration anxiety. There is also in gambling a strong aggressive trend for power, usually based on the failure to achieve satisfaction of the aggressive tendencies as a child, with anxiety and the desire to achieve this power by winning at gambling. This latter type of gambler usually attempts to carry on his gambling in professional places against experts because winning over them is associated with fewer feelings of guilt and a greater sense of power. The fact that he will lose a great proportion of the time also results in a certain amount of punishment to allay the remaining guilt feelings.

The form of deviated sex expression chosen by the patient will vary with his psychosexual development. The typical one, the so-called "homosexual" who practices fellatio, will characteristically be a person who has had either unusual gratification or unusual frustration at the primary or oral level of libidinous development. The patient thus is partially fixed in his libidinous development at this area. His attempts to form identifications with persons of the same sex and to have libidinous strivings toward persons of the opposite sex at the oedipal period will determine whether he becomes a homosexual or whether he develops into an adult with oral characteristics. If, in the case of a male child, the father is a passive, dependent person and the mother an aggressive type, the identification with the male becomes confusing, the female is often looked upon as castrating, and confused identity may result in regressions from genital sexuality to a latent type of homosexual trend. Such a person, in development, has difficulty in attaching himself to passive, feminine women. He is attracted either to mannish women or feminine men and seeks gratification in homosexual activity or some socially acceptable sublimation or reaction formation to this type of activity. The most common reaction formation is that of the big muscle man or the hostile, irritable paranoid character.

CHAPTER **21**

Sociopathic Personality Disturbances:
Alcoholism 000–x641

The term "alcoholic" has never been exactly defined. The term as used here does not include the alcoholic psychoses. A person may be considered alcoholic when he becomes dependent upon the toxic effects of the drug to carry out his work or meet his social obligations or when he is unable to indulge or forego the pleasure of alcohol, depending upon the propriety of the occasion. The alcoholism subcommittee of the Committee on Mental Health of the World Health Organization defines alcoholism: "Alcoholics are those excessive drinkers whose dependence upon alcohol has attained such a degree that it shows a noticeable mental disturbance or interference with their bodily and mental health, their interpersonal relations, and their smooth social and economic function; or who show the prodromal signs of such developments that they, therefore, require treatment."

Alcoholism is responsible for approximately 10 per cent of the admissions to mental hospitals. It appears as a complication in a substantial number of mental patients and a substantial number of psychoneurotic patients and is one of the great problems in industry in terms of absenteeism, illness, and inefficient performance. Some of our current highway accident rate may be attributed to alcoholism or at least excessive drinking prior to driving. Many persons consider alcohol as a stimulant. Actually, even in moderate doses, alcohol lessens motor activity, diminishes physical strength, lowers the fatigue point, interferes with clarity of ideation, impairs capacity for judgment in mental work, and interferes with the sharpness of memory. Alcoholism remains one of the greatest

265

sociologic and economic problems confronting the United States today. It is a problem that requires a combined medical and sociologic approach.

Etiology. Many interesting and verbally facile explanations have been given for why people drink excessively. The statements that they drink as an escape, that they use alcohol as a crutch, or that they use alcohol to protect themselves from the barbs of their environment are interesting but offer no fundamental understanding of the deep nature of the problem. In some patients the alcoholism is merely another symptom of a psychologic disorder such as mental illness, psychoneurosis, or response to an acute situational reaction. With a large number of other patients, and these are the majority of the problem drinkers, the alcoholism itself is the only symptom of pathology.

Roger Williams believes, as a result of prolonged animal experimentation and collaborative tests on humans, that alcoholism may have a genetotrophic basis.

We cannot say that we have fully demonstrated in a scientific manner the efficiency of nutritional treatment and that there is no room for doubt or questioning. We can say that, in view of the animal experiments which are clear cut, the inescapable logic of the genetotrophic concept and the striking results obtained with many of the alcoholics who have taken the treatment, we are convinced of its essential soundness and efficacy.

Other workers feel that alcoholism in its problem stage is an addiction and is due to a combination of physical factors as yet not understood and psychologic factors with obsessive qualities similar to those seen in other addicts. Most writers are not dogmatic about whether the so-called "physical factors" are constitutional or whether they result from earlier heavy use of alcohol in the preaddictive stage. The public's attitude toward alcoholics is not unlike the family's toward the "cute" child. In the initial stages, alcoholics are usually accepted and may be considered amusing. As they become more boisterous and become a source of annoyance and embarrassment, the public begins to ignore them or reject them. The alcoholic, like a child, is confused by the public's rejection of him for activity which has previously been condoned. The fact that the public accepts drinking and associates it with good fellowship, family reunion, or fraternity reunion contributes to the alcoholic's considering himself a reasonable person, until such times as the addiction is so far developed that he has lost control. At this time, the rejection by the public makes him feel hurt and abused, and he begins to conceal his drinking.

At this time, we may say that the causes of many cases of alcoholism are unknown. One should, therefore, temporarily consider alcoholism as a symptom of psychologic, physical, and social pathology. In the course of time, because of individual and perhaps environmental factors, the person develops a dependence on alcohol which makes it impossible for him to control his drinking except for short periods and in specific conditions.

Classification. There has been no satisfactory classification of alcoholics. The following is presented as useful in helping the student distinguish between the various types of alcoholics because of prognostic differences.

1. Social Drinkers. Under this group is the ordinary person who may drink festively and on appropriate occasions but in amounts suited to his capacity and never when it is inappropriate. These are sometimes called the normal drinkers. To be included in this group the person must in no way depend upon the toxic effect of the alcohol. Many persons who consider themselves social drinkers probably border upon the situational group, but they must be able to indulge in or forego the pleasure of the alcohol, depending on the propriety of the occasions.

2. Reactive Alcoholism. Within this group falls that heterogeneous assortment who drink in relation to or as an escape from some environmental situation. Persons drinking in relation to vocational, marital, economic, and physical difficulties not related to deep-seated personality problems may be properly included here. To be included here, the episode should be short, in relation only to the traumatic situation, and not continued or recurrent. Some patients who may apparently belong under this category actually are in the early stages of addictive drinking.

3. Symptomatic Alcoholism. A certain number of patients with psychotic reactions, psychoneuroses, or other causes of prolonged and chronic tension may drink as a part of their symptomatology. In these cases the alcoholism is merely one complicating symptom but not the basic pathology. Treatment directed toward the basic pathology with alleviation takes care of the alcoholism.

4. Alcoholism Simplex, Essential Alcoholism, Compulsive Drinking, and Addictive Alcoholism. There are a large number of synonyms for this group. This is a large catch-all in which most problem drinkers belong. The World Health Organization classification divides this alcoholic group into habitual symptomatic excessive drinkers and addictive drinkers (or alcoholic addicts). The World Health Organization organizes groups 2 and 3 of this classification into irregular symptomatic excessive drinkers. Most people who believe that alcoholism is a specific disease, of psychologic or of combined psychosocial, physical, and nutritional origin, confine this concept to the so-called "alcohol addicts." Physicians using this disease concept (which has been largely stimulated by the teachings of E. M. Jellinek, a member of the World Health Organization's Committee on Alcoholism) agree that the nonaddictive alcoholic is a sick person but they believe that the alcohol addict is a special case because of the loss of control which occurs in him and because he becomes dependent on the drug for his continued existence. Jellinek states:

> The loss of control is a diseased condition per se which results from a process that superimposes itself upon these abnormal psychologic conditions of which excessive drinking is a symptom. The fact that many excessive drinkers drink as much or more than the addict for thirty or forty years without developing loss of control, indicates that in the group of alcohol addicts, a superimposed process must occur. Whether this superimposed process is of a psychopathological nature or whether some physical pathology is involved cannot be stated as yet with any degree of assurance, the claims of various investigators notwithstanding. Nor is it possible to go beyond conjecture concerning the question whether the loss of control originates in a predisposing factor (psychological or physical) or whether it is a factor acquired in the course of prolonged excessive drinking.

The history of alcoholism is coextensive with the history of the human race. A drug of almost universal use which persists through the ages, surviving legislative and other efforts to eradicate it, must supply some tremendous need in the human animal. Perhaps it is the alcohol rosily blurring the hard, unpleasant outlines of reality which, if taken in sufficient quantity, effaces reality altogether. It is fantasy in a bottle. It is readily obtainable, produces its effect quickly, and in our culture its devotees escape social stigma for a long time. However, its pharmacologic effect may be supplying unknown needs of the tissue (Williams). It also produces psychologic regressive behavior. At a cocktail party, one sees portly middle-aged dowagers and gentlemen even older, with some of the infirmities of their years, have a half-dozen drinks and then begin to reenact, although not convincingly, occurrences from that remote day when respectively they were beautiful debutantes and gallant young bucks.

The alcoholic goes through certain phases in the development of his addiction. We propose to follow the outline of Jellenek because it clearly designates the symptomatic route followed by these patients.

The Prealcoholic Symptomatic Phase. All alcoholics probably begin as social drinkers. At this phase it may be difficult to distinguish a prospective addict from the nonaddict or normal drinker. World Health Organization statistics indicate that in no country do more than 5 or 6 per cent of the users of alcoholic beverages become alcoholic addicts. A candidate for addiction in this phase will probably take a drink more because he needs it than because the social proprieties prescribe it. He begins to look forward to the drink for relief, and in this phase he probably will be considered by himself and by his friends as a reactive alcoholic. He often will not become intoxicated but uses the drug to relieve his symptoms. He may drink only occasionally, but gradually his dependence on the relief brought by the alcohol of tensions and burdens seems to increase almost daily. He still has a drink only when he needs it, but the need seems to recur more often and with less real pressure from the environment. It will also be noted that he drinks more than his colleagues and is the type of person who will have a couple of "quick ones" before going out to drink with his friends.

The Prodromal Phase. In this stage, our above-mentioned heavy-drinking friend begins to have blackouts. These will be short periods of amnesia in which the patient will find that he is home in bed in the morning but cannot recall how he got there, who drove his car, or other events of the evening before. Checking with his friends will reveal that he carried on nicely during the evening, and drove his car home without accident. After reconstructing some of the details, a few minor events may focus hazily, but most of the time is lost. In advanced stages of intoxication a nonaddictive alcoholic may have these momentary lapses and blackouts, but they are uncommon. Recurring blackouts without extreme intoxication are prodromal signs. About this time the patient begins to show true signs of addiction, handling the alcohol as though it were something he had to have. At this time many patients begin to have some feeling that their drinking is different from their colleagues'.

Surreptitious drinking is a common symptom, and extra drinks are sneaked before going to a party, on the way, or in the kitchen while the others chat in the parlor. Alcohol becomes a preoccupation in that the patient plans his day's activities to ensure the inclusion of an adequate amount of alcohol. He also becomes a gulper at this time, throwing down drinks in a hurry in order to have a head start for the more socially acceptable type of drinking with his friends. This type of surreptitious behavior, plus the patient's awareness that the situation is getting out of hand, often produce guilt feelings about his drinking, and he begins to avoid talking about drinking. In this stage of the drinking an important change is made. The person who originally used alcohol as a social crutch now has begun to conceal his drinking because he recognizes it as a difference between him and others and as a type of drinking that will isolate him from his fellows. Fortunately, a good many alcoholics never proceed beyond this stage.

Other alcoholics, after periods of months or years of this type of drinking, proceed to what Jellinek calls the "crucial phase." This is the loss of control. One drink sets up a demand for the alcoholic to drink more and more until the alcohol brings oblivion or gastrointestinal rebellion. This may be touched off by a social drink or by the feeling that a drink is needed in response to some recognized or unconscious pressure. This loss of control is directly related to the alcohol itself. Patients may take the pledge, go on the wagon, or have prolonged periods of abstinence as the result of some type of drug treatment and have no difficulty maintaining their state of sobriety. However, one drink taken under stress, or as a test, or as an acquiescence to pressure of old friends to "take just one," sets up the obsessive craving, and the desire to have an unlimited supply until oblivion sets in. It is this type of loss of control that has led the Alcoholics Anonymous group to coin the phrase, "One drink is too many and a thousand are not enough."

Jellinek and many others have pointed out that the alcoholic repeatedly feels the need to test himself by taking the one drink. Most alcoholics recognize the fact that they are not cured of their alcoholism because they cannot drink in a socially acceptable or so-called "normal" manner. Some, after short or longer periods of abstinence, feel that they now have the situation under control and that their will power has been sufficiently bolstered by their treatment so that they can have "just one drink" or "take a drink or let it alone." In the authors' experience this inevitably leads to another drinking bout.

In this period the alibi of the alcoholic begins to develop, the so-called "alcoholic's lament." This is a series of rationalizations to explain each episode of drinking. Prolonged drinking bouts will result in loss of status at home and on the job. Frequently homes break up. Often the patients are demoted or discharged from the job, and one sees a gradual deterioration in them. They now begin to consort with people on a lower social plane where they are accepted, but this new group of friends finally pushes them further down in the social scale because they become a problem in each social circle. As financial pressures grow, patients begin to drink "canned heat," radiator alcohol, Jamaica ginger, and other things that may result in serious physical pathology. At this stage one sees periods of aggression and hostility mixed with periods of self-pity and depression. Some commit suicide at this stage. These patients usually show a marked decrease in their attention to nutrition, and at this stage the prolonged avitaminosis may produce pronounced liver pathology or any one of the alcoholic psychoses, and there is a beginning intellectual deterioration due to the excessive drinking.

These patients have now reached the chronic phase, as Jellinek calls it, in which there are prolonged periods of alcoholism that may last for weeks or months and, in some cases, perhaps for years. The mental deterioration is marked in these cases, but oddly enough with prolonged treatment many regain a surprising amount of their previous intellectual capacity. Others continue to deteriorate and die during a bout of delirium tremens, commit suicide, or are found dead of exposure, or of "acute alcoholism," which is better described as excessive alcoholism.

Jellinek summarizes the situation well:

By and large these reactions to excessive drinking—which have quite a neurotic appearance—give the impression of an alcoholic personality, although they are secondary behavior superimposed over a large variety of personality types which have a few traits in common and particularly low capacity for coping with tensions. There does not emerge, however, any specific personality trait or physical characteristic which inevitably would lead to excessive symptomatic drinking. Apart from the psychological and possible physical liabilities, there must be a constellation of social and economic factors which facilitate the development of addictive and non-addictive alcoholism in a susceptible terrain.

Treatment. This will be discussed in detail in the treatment section. It consists of a combined physical, sociologic, pharmacologic, and psychiatric approach. It must be adapted to the stage of progression of the alcoholism and the individual case.

CHAPTER 22

Sociopathic Personality Disturbances: Drug Addiction 000–x642

Morphinism

This classification includes addictions to opium or any of its natural derivatives or to the synthetics of like action. The medical and sociologic importance of this particular toxic reaction has been studied at length by officers of the United States Public Health Service. In recent years a wave of addiction among people in their late teens and early twenties has refocused attention on the problem. It seems to have become a serious social problem in New York City, and active measures to stamp it out are becoming successful. One hopes that it will be confined to specific areas and not allowed to spread and become generalized among adolescents. Gerard and Kornetsky made a study of the narcotic addicts among the adolescent group at the USPHS hospital in Lexington, Ky. These were all genuine addicts. They were mostly from the Negro and Puerto Rican populations of New York City and Chicago. They came from a variety of social backgrounds. Most were reared by families that were comfortable economically with middle-class education and occupation status. Most of the families contained elements of the type which psychiatric experience suggests might produce difficulties in adjustment. The youngsters all showed psychopathology. Some were either incipient or borderline schizophrenic patients. Some showed marked personality disorders, principally the antisocial type, although others were better classified as inadequate. They showed marked difficulty in entering into any type of close or prolonged friendly relationship with either their colleagues or with the personnel of the hospital. History revealed they had the same difficulty with their families. The authors believe that the addict,

272

by concentration on the difficulties of obtaining his drug, can avoid aware-ness of the real sources of discomfort and can use the need for it as an excuse to act out hostile feelings and impulses. These individuals live in a subculture in which deceit, manipulation, and suspicion are appropriate, acceptable behavior. The children said that the drug reduced their mental symptoms in many instances. Thus, as in the adult addict, the fact that these children use morphine or heroin to solve certain serious problems in adjustment may be looked upon as sociopsychopathologic.

The same authors made a further study of the same Puerto Rican and Negro patients at the Lexington Narcotics Hospital and compared it with a group in one of the New York State hospitals. They found again that the youth living in urban areas where illicit drug use is prevalent does not become addicted independently of psychiatric pathology. They postulate that the pathologic individual used as a control avoided addiction because he had not encountered situations which caused him stress or caused him to seek novel adaptation patterns.

At this time there is no doubt that the majority of addict patients use morphine or one of the opium alkaloids to aid them to adjust to some diffi-cult life situation. In some cases the situation is one that produces pain due to somatic disease or pain of psychologic origin. Others use the prepa-ration to overcome feelings of inadequacy and inferiority. Apparently among the teen-age set in certain social and cultural groups it gives a certain amount of status. Morphinism must thus be called a symptom and not a disease entity in itself; the etiology is to be found in the individual's own personality pattern and in the difficulty he has in adjusting to the world about him. In an effort to base a classification on these etiologic factors, Kolb and Parran grouped them as:

1. Normal individuals accidentally addicted, or medical addiction
2. Unstable persons, potential psychotic persons, and behavior prob-lems
3. Persons suffering from psychoneuroses
4. Persons with sociopathic disturbances
5. Inebriates where alcoholism accompanies or alternates with mor-phinism
6. The psychotic group

Symptoms. Patients taking morphine or one of its derivatives rarely become psychotic in the ordinary psychiatric sense. Toxic reactions due to morphine usually show progressive irritability, slow intellectual deteriora-tion, and a steady decline in moral habits. Whether this decline in moral habits is due to society's attitude toward the addiction or the result of the drug itself is by no means clear. It is obvious that even wealthy addicts need to resort to crime, prostitution, or other social deviations to obtain the drug. Hallucinations and delusions from the opium alkaloids are rare indeed except for opium dreams or pseudohallucinations that patients may induce by taking the drugs. In this country, drugs are rarely taken with the intent of producing these pseudohallucinations. Narcotics are usually used to induce a state of comfort, euphoria, or well-being that is far short of the so-called "pipe dreams" common in the Orient. Almost all patients show a progressive increase in the quantity of drugs taken as the years pass, but there is substantial individual variation between cases.

A typical example is a young white woman who was seen in the advanced stages of addiction. Her history revealed that she came from an excellent family but as a result of marital trouble began to drink. Her hangovers were treated with morphine and she rapidly began to develop an addiction. She complained of abdominal pains when morphine was not forthcoming from her physician, and her performance was so realistic that she was repeatedly subjected to unnecessary emergency surgery. During the accumulation of these surgical operations various organs were removed which left some pathology within the abdominal cavity. The patient went through a series of marriages and showed a progressive decline in her financial, moral, and social status. She was kept from complete poverty and degradation by the fact that her family, of substantial means, would repeatedly bail her out. She finally succumbed from what was thought to be an accidental overdose of morphine taken during a prolonged drinking bout in a small hotel.

A somewhat different case is that of a 63-year-old woman who had been taking morphine since age 18. She had supported herself in her early days as a performer with a small theatrical troupe. The morphine was allegedly started because of chronic asthma. She subsequently married happily, but to support her habit took a tremendous amount of the family's resources. However, throughout the years her dose rarely got above 15 mg of morphine per day. Whenever the local narcotic agents cut off her supply by arresting peddlers, she would enter the hospital to be "cured." After a few weeks in the hospital she would announce that she was cured and leave. After a time we began to realize that somehow she had received word that her supply was again available to her. This patient maintained a reasonable social position, with borderline economic difficulty, and never came into conflict with the law except when the Federal agents would clean out the narcotic peddlers and cut off her source of supply.

Treatment. Medical professionals have poor results in the treatment of persons addicted to morphine, and most workers give pessimistic prognosis for permanent relief of the condition. The United States Public Health Service has special hospitals in Lexington, Ky., and Fort Worth, Tex., for the treatment and study of these problems.

In spite of much information developed through the years, the therapeutic results of the treatment of morphine addiction still remain unsatisfactory in the confirmed addict.

The early treatment of adults and juveniles in the first stages of addiction may offer more hope. At this time one cannot say because statistical studies and reports are still in a preliminary phase and leave something to be desired.

For years we have spoken of controlling the production of the drug so that only the amounts necessary for the medical profession will be available at any place in the world market. Even this utopian device, which with present activities in Communist China has no possibility of being realized, has weakness, because an impressive percentage of addicts have been brought to their first acquaintance with the drug through its injudicious prescription by members of the medical profession. It is also true that a few unscrupulous physicians each year are apprehended selling morphine to chronic addicts under one pretext or another. While the Narcotic Bureau is alert in tracking down and punishing these physicians, they usually receive only a short sentence, and after a period in prison often are found again preying upon the unsuspecting public. The preventive problem here remains a legal and sociomoral one which deserves support from the medical profession.

Further details of the treatment of morphinism and its withdrawal will be discussed in the treatment section.

Prognosis. Chronically addicted patients seldom become entirely free of the habit.

Many patients relapse in a few days, but some will stay off for many months or years. For these patients treatment is certainly worthwhile because they manage to carry on during the interval between lapses and usually show less physical and moral deterioration than is seen in the chronic habitué.

A word seems necessary concerning some of the newer synthetic narcotic preparations. Many of them, particularly Demerol, methadone hydrochloride, and others, were brought on the market with the hope that they would be nonaddicting. Patients seem to become dependent upon these preparations just as they do upon morphine. It has been our impression, however, that withdrawal symptoms from these drugs are less severe than from morphine or Dilaudid, but the patient's psychologic dependence appears to develop almost as rapidly to these preparations as to morphine. This only means that the physician and student should observe the same precautions in prescribing these drugs for the relief of pain as has been used for morphine.

Cocaine Addiction

The general features of cocaine addiction are about the same as in morphine. Like morphine, it induces a state of well-being, and is used by many patients to overcome their sense of inadequacy or to cope with some environmental situation. The lethargy and relaxation seen in morphine addiction are not observed in cocaine addiction; in fact these patients seem to become stimulated, euphoric, and sometimes hyperactive. Cocaine is used to bolster the patient's ego when he has serious environmental stress. The incidence of cocaine addiction is not known, but is less in this country than is addiction to morphine and its derivatives. In our experience most persons addicted to cocaine have been prostitutes, physicians, or druggists—all marchers under the staff of Aesculapius! Popular gossip states that many criminals use this drug, but in our experience this is not true.

Cocaine is often taken by sniffing it into the nose, but some patients take it hypodermically. Many addicts use cocaine as others use alcohol, going on sprees with cocaine and then staying off it for several days. As with alcoholics, as time goes on the interval off the drug becomes shorter, and sprees become longer with increasing quantities of the drugs taken. The patients describe the sensation from the drug as, first, dizziness and then sometimes a mild headache. Hilarity and euphoria follow, and among many patients a marked push of speech and motor activity as well. The euphoria and increase in motor activity and speech probably explain its relative popularity with physicians, prostitutes, and others who must put on a good front before the public even if they are fatigued and bored. With prolonged use the patient generally becomes paranoid, suspicious, depressed, and at times develops an interesting combination of somatic hallucinations and delusions. These commonly take the form of cocaine "bugs," or a feeling that bugs and worms are crawling under the patient's skin. This type of hallucination is rather common among cocaine addicts but is not restricted to them because we have seen it in patients taking both alcohol and bromides. Withdrawal treatment of cocaine is identical to that of morphine which will be presented in the section on treatment.

As an interesting sidenote it might be mentioned that Sigmund Freud, prior to the discovery of psychoanalysis, did much of the neuropharmacologic work on cocaine, and he himself took the drug over a period of time before breaking himself of the habit.

In Ernest Jones' book Freud's own description of his experience with this drug is presented.

Marihuana Addiction (Cannabis Sativa)

This drug commonly called marihuana (marijuana) is referred to in slang as "hay," "griefoil," "Aunt Mary," "reefer," and many other titles. The plant grows wild in many areas of the continental United States, and in most sections of the country it apparently is readily available on the market. Most patients buy it, but some grow it and harvest the leaves which are dried and then smoked much as tobacco is used. The drug is commonly rolled into cigarettes. The incidence of the use of this drug is not known. In recent years it has excited a great deal of public interest, and its use is thought to be very widespread. We have seen one report that states that 1 person out of every 4 or 5 in the South uses this drug. This statistic seems without foundation in fact, but it is true that the drug is widely used among certain of the borderline economic and social groups. It is also assumed that its use is common among jazz orchestra players, theatrical people, and in the Mexican population. The fact that a popular band leader has been convicted of using the drug, and a famous movie actor accused of using it, lends credence to these beliefs but no proof.

In our experience persons take marihuana as a substitute for alcohol. It is usually taken to induce a sense of euphoria, often by a group of people on a spree or in a party mood. It is not infrequent for a number of people to sit down together and to pass the cigarettes from one person to another until all are feeling high. There is some indication that its use is associated with criminal activity. We do not feel that criminal activity results from the use of the drug itself, but rather that the person with criminal potentials who becomes high on the drug is more apt to commit crimes because the moral controls which he does have are momentarily lulled into unwariness. The appreciation of the consequences of this person's crime and concern about these consequences are inhibited by the toxic effect of the drug. The drug itself cannot give the patient criminal ideas.

There is also a popular belief that the use of marihuana leads to sexual excesses and sexual orgies of one type or another. Sensational publications in this country have done much to formulate this belief. Patients with a desire to carry out sexual excesses are more apt to do so if the inhibitions they possess are removed by the use of this drug or any other, but there is no drug known which will give the patient the idea of commiting a sexual crime or of participating in sexual excesses. These sexual urges come from within the person and may be carried out because the drug decreases inhibition. At present among some teen-agers—the so-called "cat" groups—the use of marihuana seems to impart a certain status. This again is a broad sociopsychiatric problem, and the drug is merely used because of the sense of status and well-being that it gives. It does not produce the social situation from which its use grows.

Symptoms. Intoxication with marihuana produces about the same symptoms as cocaine. Users become anxious and fearful at first. Then they become euphoric with a push of speech. Some patients at this time become irritable, this being an individual variation. Most of the patients describe a peculiar disturbance in the time sensation. Many of them feel that time passes slowly, and all distances appear far off. This disturbance of the time and space relationship is what supposedly makes marihuana attractive to jazz band performers; some of these persons feel that they can play faster while under the influence of the drug because of its apparent lengthening out of time. I know of no pharmacologic or experimental results to verify this, however, and one suspects that the ability to play more rapidly is subjective rather than objective. At times the patients have hallucinatory experiences. Many of them report great sexual stimulation, but as mentioned above, this is probably a removal of inhibitions. After 2 or 3 hours of being on a "jag" many of the patients go to sleep. There is one very interesting difference between marihuana and morphine or cocaine: marihuana produces no hangover, and patients do not as a rule build up a tolerance to the drug.

Treatment of marihuana addiction is essentially the same as that for morphine and cocaine except that the drug may be withdrawn abruptly without any danger to the patient in a physiologic sense. Marihuana has no therapeutic value, and control of this addiction would appear to be the obliteration of this class of vegetation from the world. Because it grows freely and wildly in so many areas of the world this becomes a formidable task.

Pathology. These patients rarely die. When killed in accidents their brain may be expected to show that characteristic of any toxic reaction, namely, brain edema. Their psychopathology is that of inadequate persons seeking something to give them a status and moral support.

A classic example is that of a 25-year-old single young man brought to one of us by his father. The father reported that the patient imagined people were trying to kill him, that he could see his girl friend with her throat cut, and could smell gas coming from his mattress. He also felt that he had been castrated. The patient stated that he was being tricked, that automobiles on the street jumped at him, and that somebody was giving him electric shocks as he walked down the street. Background revealed that the patient was a temperamental, unstable, fearful, and imaginative child who made few friends and had a poor school record. At the age of 13 his right testicle was accidentally injured. Shortly after this he began to drink whiskey and beer and to run around with the wrong class of youngsters, apparently attempting to compensate for his feelings of inferiority exaggerated by the above injury. During this time he would frequently get into fights and was usually beaten, further adding to his sense of inferiority. He began to take marihuana following a series of family quarrels over his behavior. At the time of admission to the hospital the patient was extremely apprehensive, hallucinating, and fearful. He was lewd and confused. Spontaneous activity was almost entirely in reaction to his hallucinations. On withdrawal treatment in the hospital, his symptoms very rapidly cleared up, and within a week of admission he was entirely free of the psychiatric symptoms. Attempts to go further into the psychogenic background were resisted by the patient and his father, and he was removed from the hospital 19 days after admission. This case is a rather typical example of marihuana intoxication, illustrating the instability present in most of these individuals and the fact that patients use marihuana to obtain a lift and bolster their ego. Many patients use it in place of a party beverage and often will state that they can get the same kick from a 50-cent "stick" of marihuana that they can from a pint of whiskey. Some point out the advantage that it does not produce a hangover.

Prognosis. Little is known about this. The use of marihuana is so bound up with socioeconomic factors that studies on its use and the follow-up of patients removed from it are almost nonexistent.

Barbital Intoxication

Drugs of the barbituric acid series are the most popular sedative used by the medical profession, and the use of barbituric acid derivatives in various forms is an ever-increasing problem. Most of the medications are used by persons who are either having some emotional crisis which induces nervousness, tension, anxiety, and disturbance in the sleep pattern or are suffering from one of the chronic neurotic disorders and use the drug for its quieting effect and to produce sleep.

The medical profession has been guilty of promoting the widespread use and abuse of these preparations. In many states the drug may be bought in any of its forms over the drug counter in a manner similar to that of any patent medicine or cosmetic. Other states, realizing the seriousness of the problem, have laws making it mandatory that druggists have a physician's prescription for the use of the preparation. Even in these states, the medical profession prescribes the drug at times in an indiscriminate and injudicious manner, and in some drug stores the barbiturates can be bought without prescription. The use of the drug is found in all ages, all sexes, and all racial groups. Some patients take the drug constantly for years; others take it in large doses over short periods and then refrain from its use. No really accurate statistics are available as to the incidence of its use, and we have no information as to how many patients become habitual users. Any person working for any time in a large public or private clinic must, however, be impressed by the number of patients who come back each year asking for a refill of the preparation, and many of the patients even describe the particular drug of the barbituric acid series they desire. We now believe that persons build up a definite physiologic dependence on the drug. The physiologic dependence does not seem to be so great as in the case of morphine, but there is no doubt that continuous use builds up the individual's tolerance, and some people take relatively large doses of the drug each day. Abrupt withdrawal can produce physiologic crises, especially convulsions.

Symptoms. The symptoms of barbital intoxication are rather simple. The patients experience a feeling of relaxation, lethargy, and general well-being. Most patients respond to the use of the drug by becoming sleepy, and many of them use it exclusively to induce the oblivion of sleep.

Withholding the drug often results in sleeplessness, increase in anxiety, and much motor tension. In some individuals abrupt withdrawal of the drug after long use will result in convulsive phenomena. Some persons believe that these people are latent convulsive patients, and others believe that the effect is purely the withdrawal of the pharmacologic inhibitory effect upon the central nervous system. Further investigation of these factors is indicated. The authors have seen patients who have been on this medication for many years who reveal no evidence of any type of intellectual or central nervous system degeneration or deterioration. Other patients become rather dull, lethargic, and irritable. In some individuals chronic paranoid tendencies seem to develop. Many of them undergo intellectual deterioration, become ineffective and inefficient in their business and social relationships, and in general resemble the picture sometimes seen in chronic alcoholic deterioration. This extreme picture is rare and occurs only after prolonged, excessive use.

We have seen one case of Korsakoff's reaction of a typical type in an elderly graduate nurse who had been ingesting 2 to 4 gm of one of the barbituric acid series daily for many years. It is interesting that this patient ate irregularly, and her food intake contained few of the vitamin-carrying foods.

Some of these patients enter the clinic with symptoms resembling organic deterioration and are originally felt to be suffering from some type of organic brain disease such as brain tumor or paresis. An occasional patient will show acute hallucinatory symptoms with the barbital, but in our experience this is the exception rather than the rule. When present, the delirious picture offers little to distinguish it from that due to any other toxic preparation.

Pathology. Patients who die following barbital intoxication usually show a "wet brain" and nothing more. There are reports in the literature showing certain specific types of chronic encephalitis-like symptoms supposedly due to chronic barbital ingestion. These studies should be further explored, but in general the central nervous system changes from barbital are thought to be reversible.

The psychopathology of these patients is somewhat akin to that of the other drug users but is much more complex. Like all sedative preparations this is used by patients as a crutch to tide them over real or fancied emotional crises. It has been our experience that the common users of the drug are chronic psychoneurotic patients; some are just inadequate. A few criminals and teen-agers take it as a form of jag, and it seems to give them a certain status in their groups. In most instances, however, the patients have gone to a series of physicians in clinics for relief of somatic symptoms. Many of them have been subjected to much unwise surgery and medical manipulation. In many instances a patient has been introduced to the use of the drug by his physician or by some interested person in the neighborhood who had first become acquainted with the drug through a physician or nurse. It is true that some physicians take the preparation themselves, and it is not uncommon to find people taking this drug more or less routinely to ensure sleep on a pullman train, in an airplane, or after a night of alcoholic excess. Such unwise and unwarranted use of the drug is probably only a reflection of the medical profession's general belief that the drug is relatively harmless. These beliefs are maintained in spite of much evidence to the contrary.

In the seventh edition of this book we noted that at that time the public was becoming somewhat aroused over the problems arising from abuse of the use of barbituric acid derivatives, and that such magazines as *The Reader's Digest* published articles concerning the seriousness of the problem. The theater, motion pictures, and television have used it as a theme also. Unfortunately this publicizing seems to have done nothing to reduce the incidence of barbital use. A few states passed laws regulating it, and Federal legislation was filed to control it, but public demand and consumption go on unabated. It is even becoming more popular among the fringe group economically and socially, and, as previously mentioned, in some quarters has substituted for marihuana in producing jags, creating a sort of status among the "cats." It should be remembered that persons who are normal and stable rarely become habituated to the use of the drug. Usually it is used to allay sensations of anxiety or tension. As a temporary crutch for patients who are fearful about being subjected to surgery or some other critical situation, the drug has its rational use. To prescribe it to alleviate chronic anxiety and complaints of psychoneurotic patients, however, is to give symptomatic treatment for a condition which had better be treated from an etiologic point of view.

Treatment. Treatment is gradual withdrawal of the drug, institution of eliminative therapy, and investigation of the psychologic and social factors which induced its use. Treatment will be discussed in more detail in a later chapter, but it is essentially the same as that for any drug withdrawal.

The Amphetamines

In recent years the amphetamines in various forms have been widely used in medicine. They are effective drugs in treating narcolepsy, as adjuncts to treatment of mild depressions, to aid in diets for obesity, and to provide stimulation in emergency situations. This latter use has led to their abuse by some truck drivers, students, and others who may want to postpone sleep or combat fatigue. As an emergency measure this is an effective use of the preparations. Continued use without rest, however, leads to false feelings of well-being without concomitant efficiency in physical or mental functioning. Some habitués build up a high tolerance to the drug.

Among the unstable, the use of these components to produce a sense of well-being is reputedly widespread. Stories of using it for sprees or parties, in the manner of marihuana, make the rounds among the "cats," the hobo jungle, and in some correctional institutions. One suspects that the effects are largely produced by suggestion in unstable persons.

The management is the same as for the barbiturates—control of the drug and sociopsychiatric programs aimed at the cause of the habituation.

Bromide Intoxication

The principles outlined under Barbital Intoxication apply equally well to bromides. In earlier editions of this book much space was devoted to the discussion of bromide intoxication because it was very common in the population. At present, drugs of the bromide series are not so popular as in the past, but are still prescribed by some physicians. They are also present in certain proprietary preparations, and the physician should be cautious concerning the possibility of bromide intoxication in any patient showing evidence of organic or toxic mental symptoms. In many states laws limiting the use of barbitals have forced patients on self-medication to the use of bromides. In our experience, however, this has not resulted in any great increase in the use of the bromide preparations, probably because the barbitals are still readily available in spite of legal prohibitions.

Symptoms. Bromide intoxication causes hyper somnolence punctuated by episodes of acute hallucinatory reaction. We have seen several cases referred because of brain tumor or other organic reaction which on examination proved to be bromide intoxications. Once suspected, the diagnosis is easily confirmed because simple tests of the blood serum for evidence of bromide will show a level of 300 mg per 100 ml of blood. Symptoms besides lethargy are those of hallucinations and delusion in a rather lethargic type of delirium. While bromide levels above 150 mg per 100 ml are ordinarily regarded as capable of producing delirium, a higher level than this is usually required. Methods of the detection of the levels were described by Otto Wuth.

Remarks made on the psychopathology of barbital intoxications also apply to the subject of bromide intoxication. It is usually taken as a form of ego support to blunt the onslaughts of the world and make the place more bearable for the patient.

Treatment. The treatment is elimination, which may be hastened by sodium chloride ingestion after the blood serum bromide level falls to about 200 mg. If the blood bromide level is 300 mg or more, sodium chloride should be withheld until it falls to about 200 mg per 100 ml. In our experience the administration of sodium chloride temporarily increases the blood concentration by hastening the liberation of bromide from the tissues, while elimination by the kidneys proceeds at the original rate. We have also consistently found that bromide intoxication is most likely to occur in cases which have concomitant cardiorenal or arteriosclerotic disease, which slow the elimination of the drug.

Almost any drug which man ingests can produce a delirious reaction. The ones mentioned are those commonly encountered in clinical practice. The patients will react to some of the antibiotic drugs, cortisone, and ACTH with the production of toxic symptoms. Alertness to the possibility of these conditions will result in the proper diagnosis and the withdrawal of the drug and will produce a prompt resolution of the symptoms.

CHAPTER **23**

Miscellaneous Symptoms

Special Symptom Reactions 000–x70

This is a catchall classification for those patients who show some particular symptom as the predominant form of their psychopathology. The habit or symptoms should be described.

LEARNING DISTURBANCE 000–x71

The problems in learning may be due to retardation and, if so, the patients should be classified in the section on mental deficiency or child psychiatry. The problems may be due to psychogenic factors and, if so, the patients should be classified in that section also. We should include here only those patients insufficiently studied for proper categorization.

SPEECH DISTURBANCE 000–x72

Most youngsters who have a disturbance in speech such as stammering, stuttering, lisping, etc., will be properly classified under child psychiatry. One may classify here the occasional case in which no suitable child psychiatric diagnosis can be discovered. On occasion one will see an adult who has developed a speech disturbance in adult life as the result of a neurotic or hysteric reaction. When the etiology is known this person should be appropriately classified. In this group will be included only those patients in whom no other pathology is found or where there is not sufficient pathology to warrant their classification elsewhere.

ENURESIS 000–x73

This will be discussed under the child psychiatric disorders and is appropriately classified there. Here would go only those occasional adults and childhood cases for which no other pathology is found. Occasionally an adult who probably belongs in the inadequate personality group would be found who has never been trained by his family nor forced by his environment to develop adequate sphincter control when asleep. Thus, if no other pathology or cause can be found, these patients may be classified here. This classification will be of principal use to the military authorities who had some problem with this, particularly during periods of mobilization of large numbers of troops.

Somnambulism 000–x74

Sleepwalking which may occur in children or adults is almost always a manifestation of anxiety. Where underlying pathology may be described or discovered, these individuals should be appropriately classified, with somnambulism as a subcategory. Here may be put those persons who become a problem in the mass mobilization of troops or persons with whom there is not sufficient time or information available for better classification.

Transient Situational Personality Disorders

This is a diagnostic category which is most useful in situations of the mass handling of patients, where a patient will not be completely understood. In situations of stress and panic, many people will react poorly. Under better conditions a more prolonged study of the individual would result in his classification elsewhere. This classification is included for the transient disorders, arising from response to acute situations, in which there is no apparent underlying personality disturbance. In cases of no apparent personality disturbance the classification here almost always stems from insufficient information and study. In the mass handling of people this may be unavoidable. These people should, therefore, be classified here to avoid connotations of more serious pathology when it has not been conclusively demonstrated.

Transient Situational Personality Disturbance 000–x80

This category is for the upset people seen in the emergency room or screaming and panicky at fires, auto accidents, or more widespread civil unrest. They usually respond to superficial reassurance, placebos, or short periods of rest with sedation when neither time nor interest permit a more conclusive diagnosis. This category should be recognized for the convenience of the physician and record librarian who wish to categorize these patients somewhere but have not sufficient information for accurate diagnoses.

GROSS STRESS REACTION 000–x81

These reactions differ from the above group only in that the stress here is greater and persons of a more nearly normal or stable personality pattern may show momentary behavior and psychologic disturbances to these situations. This category should be used only for persons who have shown these reactions under conditions of great fatigue or generalized fires, earthquakes, or other civil or military disasters. They should be designated as either Combat or Civilian Catastrophe.

ADULT SITUATIONAL REACTIONS 000–x82

Patients will be classified here who in a difficult or new situation show abnormal reactions, manifest by fainting, anxiety, alcoholism, poor morale, or running away. Most of these patients on study are found to have one of the more serious underlying disorders, but in many cases opportunities for a more accurate diagnostic study will not be available.

ADJUSTMENT REACTION OF LATE LIFE 000–x86

In our discussion of the chronic brain syndromes due to aging, we pointed out that some individuals show transient reactions which may be physiologic, situational, or psychologic reactions to environmental stress. Those who show transitory reactions and may not be truly diagnosed as psychotic and those who may be called simple senile would be properly classified here for diagnostic purposes. Because the borderline between the senile disorders and this group is not clear, the student will have to use his own best judgment as to which category the patient should be in. In general, if the predominance of the difficulty seems to be due to the confusion and memory changes incident to the organic process, they should be classified under the respective chronic brain syndrome. If the disorder seems to be predominantly one of those due to environmental pressures on the weakened ego from the aging process it should be classified here.

CHAPTER **24**

*Child Psychiatry and Mental Health Practice**

Adjustment Reactions of Infancy and Childhood 000–x83, 000–x84

CHILD PSYCHIATRY AS A SPECIALTY IN MEDICINE

Child psychiatry and mental health practice are new subspecialities of medicine and public health which are evolving very rapidly. They comprise an organized and concrete set of professional practices which are based on the modern, dynamic theory of the psychology and physiology of growth and development as well as the theory of culture, social systems, and interpersonal relations. The development of child psychiatry and mental health practice has had its source in the refreshing new approach to human behavior provided by Adolf Meyer and Sigmund Freud. The psychobiologic approach pointed the way to exploring the early life of the patient. Psychoanalytic theory not only has given a structural model for describing the mental apparatus and mental process but has also given us a theory of emotional growth and development which provides the foundation for present-day child psychiatry and mental health practice in America.

The child-guidance clinic as a medical institution is an American contribution to medical practice. William Healy, a consultant neurologist in Chicago, began working directly with the Juvenile Court in Chicago in 1909, with the idea of approaching behavior problems of juvenile offenders as medical problems worthy of scientific study and understanding. Healy early became interested in the work of Freud and introduced the dynamic viewpoint which is basic to the child psychiatry and mental health practice of today.

In 1917, Healy with Augusta Bronner began the Judge Baker Guidance

---

* By WARREN T. VAUGHAN, JR., M.D. Director, Division of Mental Hygiene, Massachusetts Department of Mental Health; Assistant Professor of Mental Health, Harvard School of Public Health.

Center in Boston. The concept of the community child-guidance center
was furthered in 1922 by the Commonwealth Fund in many large cities.
The child-guidance clinic, early interested in juvenile delinquency, found
itself soon working most closely with nonmedical community agencies,
schools, social agencies, and child-care agencies.

Child psychiatry within the framework of the medical school and teaching hospital has developed more slowly. The Yale Clinic of Child Development began in 1911, under the direction of Arnold Gesell. In 1930, a full-
time psychiatric consultation service began in the pediatric department of
Johns Hopkins Hospital and University, Baltimore, under the director-
ship of Leo Kanner. On the whole, however, it is only since World War II
that child psychiatry and pediatrics have developed effective and productive working relationships on a country-wide basis. Kanner has described
the difficulties which impeded the development of sound and reasonable
working relationships between child psychiatry and pediatrics during the
1920s and 1930s.

The scientific study of children is a development associated with the
rise of humanitarianism in the late nineteenth and the twentieth century.
William Healy states that in his neurologic clinic prior to the opening of
the Juvenile Psychopathic Institute in 1909, " . . . it seemed that the
handling of these young people largely by punitive measures, whether in
the home, school, or court, was so far removed from common sense application of scientific knowledge to the treatment of human beings that it
savored of the dark ages of man's dealing with his fellow men. And on
occasion I publicly said as much." The humanitarianism which shines
through in this quotation led the physician to join forces with other persons concerned with human behavior, child development, and child
welfare.

Over a period of some years there evolved the "child-guidance team,"
composed of the psychiatrist, the psychiatric social worker, and the clinical psychologist. Ethel Ginsberg described the development of the clinic
team as follows, quoting notes from a round-table discussion held in 1947:

In the beginning, the team approach was simple, naïve and quite specific. The
psychiatrist saw the child, the social worker saw the parent, the clinical psychologist tested the child; all three participated in the evaluation conference and
subsequently the psychiatrist treated the child, and the social worker manipulated the environment.

Later the social worker began to work with parents and derive satisfactions
on the job. Then the clinical psychologist began to do re-education work—
remedial, speech, and reading. It was recognized that speech and reading handi-

caps were associated with emotional problems and, since this work was already in his hands, the clinical psychologist continued to treat the child.

The psychiatrist took on adults; the social worker took on children and age was no longer the dividing line. Then the clinical psychologist took on parents.

Ginsberg divides child-guidance functions into six categories:

1. Therapy
2. Diagnosis
3. Research
4. Training
5. Consultation
6. Community relations

Each profession participates in all six functions with the basic responsibilities divided as follows:

1. Therapy—psychiatrist
2. Research—clinical psychologist
3. Community relations—social worker

Helen Witmer has traced the development of early community services and the team participation of the psychiatric social worker to the influence of Adolf Meyer. She states, "The origin of all these ideas is clearly traceable to Meyer's insistence upon obtaining more knowledge about the lives of patients."

Clinical psychology dates its origins from the work of Lightner Witmer at the Psychological Clinic of the University of Pennsylvania in 1896. In 1905, the Binet-Simon test was first published and Goddard began a psychologic laboratory study of mentally retarded children at the Vineland Training School. Following the publication of the Stanford revision of the Binet test in 1916, psychometrics and clinical psychology began to be widely used.

Developments in the field of psychodynamic theory, of extreme importance to child psychiatry, include not only the concept of infantile sexuality but also, of equal importance, the development of ego psychology in the 1920s and 1930s. The following statements are of particular relevance to child psychiatry:

1. That anxiety is a "danger signal," and has ego origins, rather than origins from a simple damming up of repressed instinctual energy (libido).

2. That the central governing part of the total mental apparatus (ego) develops its basic orientation to the self and to the outside world, and regulates strivings for instinctual gratification (pleasure principle) through, first, the perception and recognition of what modes of expression

and behavior are available and sanctioned (reality principle) and, second, by the use of various defense mechanisms.

3. That the development of the ego itself, growing out of an undifferentiated narcissistic self, driven by instinctual urges that need satisfaction, is dependent upon the human environment around the growing self for its healthy growth and development.

The development of ego boundaries, reality testing, self-perception, the use of various modes of defense, and other matters of theoretical interest to psychoanalysis and psychiatry found immediate practical application in the field of child psychiatry.

The development of psychiatric theory is continuing. Of current great interest to child psychiatry is the question of constitutional and other factors which may limit or potentiate the use of various modes of adaptation through ego development and the use of specific defense mechanisms in the growing organism as it may be exposed to various types of environmental stress. The work of Spitz, Fries, Sontag, and Kris should be consulted for further information and orientation concerning the problem of constitutional emotional growth and development and psychopathology.

The relationships between physiology, emotions, and personality development are extraordinarily clearly manifest in children, especially infants, who express emotional needs through direct somatic behavior with little use of symbolism, displacement, or reaction formation. Erickson in his volume *Childhood and Society* describes two little children and their manner of handling libido and aggression through somatic channels. In this extremely rewarding book, the reader lives with Erickson as he observes and understands the children as they use the mouth, the special sense organs, the eliminative organs, the skeletal musculature, and locomotion to express feelings and deep strivings. Current psychiatric literature is full of articles on psychosomatic illness in childhood. Child psychiatry may soon make major contributions to preventive medicine as it unravels the neurohormonal and other relationships between constitution, personality, organ function, and the human environment.

The psychotherapy of children today stems from the basic theoretical understanding and technical approaches developed by Anna Freud. Margaret Gerard has written a very lucid summary of the most pertinent elements in the technique of child analysis developed by Anna Freud. She says:

It is well known that a child attempts to master the anxiety produced by a traumatic experience with repeated reproduction of the scene in play. Anna Freud used such knowledge in her evaluation of the reasons for the child's choice of any one play activity. . . . Through the adroitness of her skill, Anna Freud obtained further richness of information from the child concerning his conscious and unconscious conflicts by the use of verbal and written fantasy, dreams, and drawings. She also made use of information from the parents' report of past history . . . and she kept herself aware of current happenings in the child's life through various methods of contact with the parents. With information gleaned from these various sources, she and the child cooperated in fitting together the bits into a complete pattern of symptoms and causes. In this way, interpretation did not consist merely in the therapist telling the child what was occurring . . . but in a joint understanding similar to that reached in an analysis of an adult. . . . She made herself a desirable ally of the child by working for him, sympathizing with his difficulties, communicating helpful knowledge and interceding with the parents to the advantage of the child when desirable. Thus she created a confidential relationship within the framework of which the child dared to expose his secret thoughts and feelings and from which he drew courage to grasp the relation of these feelings to the production of his difficulties. . . . She recognized the weakness of the child's ego relative to that of the adult; she understood his negative attitudes towards the therapist as due mainly to the fear of seduction produced by the relatively free situation of treatment, and only in part to a negative transference reaction. She early dealt with these negative attitudes by an explanation of his fears and with reassurance of a protective role by setting a few rules to prevent the license of impulsive activity. She encouraged the use of substitute activity and objects to strengthen the ego in socially acceptable expressions. By these means she temporarily became the ego ideal which the child used as a model for experimentation in new methods of expression and thus she instituted a pattern of constructive sublimation of the energy which was previously used in the service of the symptom. This latter technical device represented a part of the therapy which she considered educative and which constituted yet a further difference from standard analytic technique used with adults. It was based on knowledge of the fact that the child's character is in a developmental continuum and that it is dependent upon wise adult guidance for the development of adequate, socially acceptable superego concepts and ego mechanisms of energy expression. Although not a part of standard psychoanalytic therapy, this type of education is used by many analysts in the therapy of immature adults who thus gain maturity more rapidly and adequately than when left to their own experimentation.

Finally, Anna Freud did not neglect the environmental responsibility for the production of the child's neurosis, nor the danger to further healthy development inherent in traumatic experiences to which the child might be exposed if the environment remained unchanged. To protect the child's future, she aided the parents by education concerning the needs of the child.

The various modes of direct psychotherapy with children which have been experimented with and which occupied the attention of most child-guidance clinics during the thirties and forties represent variations of this basic approach described so well by Gerard.

David Levy experimented extensively with various modes of therapy. Special modes of therapy for children with gross ego defects, such as in delinquent children, have been developed in individual and group settings originally by Aichorn and since in the United States by various workers. The literature is replete with descriptive accounts of the psychiatric treatment of specific psychiatric disorders of children. The *American Journal of Orthopsychiatry* has devoted many round-table discussions to the problems of direct therapy of the child as well as the development of the team approach in working with the parents, school, and other agencies and groups concerned with the growth and development of the child.

It was soon recognized by child psychiatrists that often neither direct treatment of the child nor direct interpretation of the child's difficulty with instructions for modification of parental attitudes or the child's environment were sufficient to alter the abnormal course of development of the child. The child had to be viewed as a member of a dynamic set of social relationships, his "emotionally relevant human environment" (Lindemann). The psychiatric social worker began to develop techniques of social casework in order to work with the families as the psychiatrist worked directly with the child. Psychiatrists began to be concerned with the culture context—the sets of values of the parents, their modes of behavior, as well as the neighborhood, the school, and the community at large, which may sustain or sanction certain social and other environmental factors which are of direct relevance to the mental health of not only the child in treatment but also of other children in the community. Social scientists have become extremely interested in the relationship between mental health, psychiatric disorders, child growth and development, and sociocultural factors. By 1946 the stage was well set for mental health to become a formal part of *public health*, which was accomplished through the passage of the National Mental Health Act. Thus was born the era of mental health practice in which we find ourselves today.

The aims of child psychiatry have always centered about the public health concepts of prevention and health promotion. The early child-guidance-clinic movement aimed at the prevention of psychosis and the prevention of juvenile delinquency.

Helen Witmer wrote of these early experiences and pointed out that after child-guidance clinics developed their basic theory and professional practices, the notion of prevention had to be abandoned, because in reality the clinics were dealing with already full-blown serious psychiatric disorders. The concept of promotion of mental health was vague, as indeed, in many ways, it still remains. A scientific basis for the introduction of public health thinking into child psychiatry and mental health was strongly advocated by some public health leaders in the 1930s, most forcibly by Freeman at John Hopkins, where a mental health division was established in the Johns Hopkins School of Public Health and School of Hygiene. The public health sciences of epidemiology and biostatistics were brought to bear on the general problem of psychiatric disorders in communities. Under the leadership of Lemkau, surveys were conducted in the Eastern Health District, Baltimore. In the early 1940s the Rockefeller Foundation supported epidemiologic studies in rural settings by Roth and Luton, which were interrupted by the war.

The application of public health thinking to mental health has revealed many important theoretical and methodologic problems and has opened up many new areas for research. The science of epidemiology, concerned with mass phenomena of disease and the ecologic relationships between the human host, the environment, and the agents of disease, is now being employed in many significant research studies. In 1950, the Milbank Memorial Fund devoted a meeting to this new and vigorous approach to mental health.

Child psychiatry has contributed greatly to the development of modern mental health theory. It views a psychiatric disorder as more than an internal derangement of psychophysiologic mechanisms, but as intimately related to the emotionally relevant human environment in a dynamic fashion. The knowledge of interpersonal relationships can now be related to the knowledge of the emotional needs of the human being through his various life stages. Thus, we can now frame the problem as a public health problem. The study of interpersonal relations in various institutional settings and within various cultures and the application of efforts to change pathogenic relationships can indeed be thought of as an integral part of the public health field of environmental sanitation. We can speak of "sanitation of the human environment."

After World War II the trend toward a public health approach took firm hold, in large measure as a result of the effective application of the epidemiologic approach in army psychiatry. Today interdisciplinary research, combining the knowledge and skills of clinical psychiatry, the laboratory sciences, public health, and the social sciences, is tackling basic problems. There is a body of sound fact and theory which can enable us to develop mental health practice within the public health context and finally to combine our efforts in child psychiatry within the larger framework of public health. This embraces the development of a mental health practice which sees itself as:

1. Promoting the general mental health
2. Preventing specific psychiatric disorders
3. Effectively developing facilities for the early diagnosis and prompt treatment of children with psychiatric disorders
4. Rehabilitating and providing special education for children with special mental or emotional handicaps

EMOTIONAL GROWTH AND DEVELOPMENT OF CHILDREN*

We have knowledge of growth and development which gives us important information concerning the emotional and physical needs of children at different ages. We learn from the field of interpersonal relations how these emotional needs may or may not be met during various critical stages of growth and development.

In order to relate emotional needs and interpersonal relations during various stages of growth and development, we shall consider five stages: those of infancy, early childhood, preschool years, grade school years, and adolescence.

Obviously the characteristics of a given child at any time depend upon his life experiences during preceding stages. In almost every child one can find conflicts from earlier stages manifesting themselves in various complex fashions. There are healthy (successful) and unhealthy (unsuccessful) modes of resolution of childhood emotional conflicts. The mental health concept associated with the development of emotional conflicts is that of the crisis, implying *loss*, the rupture of emotionally important human relationships, or the *deficiency* or lack of necessary ingredients in emotionally important relationships. Nutritional deficiencies have been carefully studied and catalogued in public health; we still know relatively little about the incidence and prevalence of deficiencies in emotional need. We know that interpersonal conflicts are commonplace in most families in some degree or another, with concurrent emotional stress. We know that family solidarity enables most frustrations to become positive learning experiences for children when the frustrations are handled by mature parents who have "emotional reserve."

The most important models for identification are obviously the parents. Mature parents who are capable of giving love and understanding, support, and protection to their children represent the best assurance the child may have that he will enjoy good mental health. There is always a

---

* Some of the material in this section first appeared in "Mental Health and the Handicapped," a chapter in *Special Education for the Exceptional*. Frampton, M. E., and Gall, E. D., Editors. Porter Sargent, Boston, 1955.

large reservoir of children in need of psychiatric care who have either had a serious loss of a key figure in their life, or whose parents have themselves limitations of personality, health, or motivation, which act in a pathogenic fashion upon the child.

Infancy (Oral Stage). The child's first knowledge of the world is through contact with its mouth and skin and in relation to the feeding process. Frustration and discomfort are relieved through feeding and through the very important interpersonal processes surrounding feeding, such as being held close, being rocked, being snug and warm. These basic human needs must be met adequately in the first year. Basic attitudes are set in children at this time, attitudes toward the world being a friendly, loving, accepting place or being a frustrating, hostile, and potentially harmful place.

Interpersonal Relations. The important human relationship of infancy is, of course, the mother-child relationship. The dependency of the infant is remarkable. He cannot be left; he cries to attract his mother. He responds to warmth and bodily contact with her. The differentiation between self and not-self occurs in the first 6 months in relationship with the mother. The maturation of the central nervous system, with myelinization and development of the visual motor apparatus, goes hand in hand with this process. The child begins to recognize its mother as it distinguishes between itself and the outside world. It begins to laugh and smile in relation to mother's mood and facial expression. Children brought up without a mother figure are profoundly retarded in their development. The child at the end of the first year may not understand that its mother will return when she is out of sight. He begins to cry when left. The intuitive, sensitive mother will maintain contact with the child through talking or singing when she is out of its sight. The infant only slowly develops a time sense and a concept of the future. It takes some time for the infant to know that mother will return and that he will be fed and cared for. The first game played with infants is peek-a-boo, which helps the infant solve this basic emotional problem of loss. There is tension release with laughter when the missing face returns. Tensions and directed aggression often are expressed directly by biting, especially after teeth arrive.

Psychodynamics and Psychopathology. The importance of an intact relationship with a responsive, mature mother or mother substitute has attracted the attention of many clinicians and researchers in recent years. Experiences in infancy are viewed as extremely important for the development of the basic reaction patterns of the child to later stressful life situations. Cross-cultural and epidemiologic studies of maternal care are being conducted in order to develop more scientific knowledge and validation of the crucial importance of the maternal environment to mental health. New insights into the nature of infancy have soundly influenced a swing away from patterns of early rigid feeding, bowel training, etc., during this first year, which were so prevalent in pediatric care of the 1920s and 1930s. Issues of conformity, of socialization, of frustration, and the introduction of systems of reward and punishment all must wait until the basic emotional needs of the infant have been met. Oral fixation, oral frustration, and oral aggression in many complex, elaborated, and distorted forms are well-recognized in adult psychiatry. Psychosomatic ills, psychopathic personalities, paranoid states, schizophrenia, as well as various other types of neurotic illnesses and personality disorders have been attributed in part to initial trauma in the oral phase of development.

It is difficult to think of a "psychology of infancy" separated from physiology. Margaret Fries, Spitz, Sontag, and others have made careful behavioral observations of children and have noted such basic phenomena as activity patterns, energy levels, frequency of body movement, and fetal movements. These observations are biophysiologic.

The Gesell developmental scale is related to maturation of the central nervous system. The criteria for the early months are based on developing motor skills, changing reflex patterns, and emotionality. The criteria soon, however, include what may be considered psychologic factors, involving motivations, choice of play objects, play patterns, and patterns of interpersonal relations.

Spitz has written concerning the psychiatric disorders of infancy, focusing on the mother-child relationship. He divides "psychotoxic" diseases of infancy into two groups: those associated with the wrong kind of mother-child relations, and those associated with an insufficient amount of mother-child relations. He relates psychiatric disorders of infancy to pathogenic factors in mother-child relations as shown in the following classification:

1. Coma of the newborn—overt primal rejection by mother
2. Three-month colic—primarily anxious, overpermissive mother
3. Infantile neurodermatitis—hostility of mother in the garb of anxiety
4. Hypermotility (rocking)—oscillation between pampering and hostility by mother
5. Fecal play—cyclic moodswings in mother
6. Aggressive hyperthymic—hostility, consciously compensated by mother

Spitz discusses in detail each of these disease entities. In relation to 3-month colic, he mentions other factors besides the maternal anxiety, such as hypertonicity in the infant with a build-up of tension in the child and release through the oral route. He discusses the role of the pacifier in relieving 3-month colic in infants. With regard to infantile neurodermatitis, he identifies an anxiety-ridden mother who avoids touching her baby because of her hostility toward the child. This interferes with identification processes, inasmuch as tactile experiences, both superficial and deep, are extremely important in maintaining and developing the healthy mother-child relationship. The "aggressive hyperthymic" child is related to a mother who consciously compensates for hostile feelings toward the child by "subacid, syrupy sweetness." These infants become retarded in their social development and in early childhood are themselves particularly hostile and aggressive.

The children who are deprived of mother-child relationships suffer from "anaclitic depression." This state is manifest clinically by increased demandingness and weepiness, the loss of weight, and the arrest of developmental progress, with the child by the third month refusing contact with people and assuming a prone position in the crib with averted face. This position, Spitz says, is pathognomonic. Spitz states, "if within three to five months a mother or an adequate mother substitute is provided, the condition improves with surprising rapidity." Infants abandoned after World War II have been studied by Roudinesco and others who have demonstrated that after months of careful treatment in a psychiatrically oriented nursery setting some of these children can begin to form human relationships.

Total maternal deprivation has been described by Spitz in 91 children in foundling homes outside the United States who were with their mothers for the first 3 or 4 months, and then separated. The developmental progress was progressively delayed, with the children becoming completely passive and supine, with an empty face, defective eye coordination, and an imbecilic expression. The children might not be sitting, standing, walking or talking even by the age of 4. Thirty-seven per cent of such children died from malnutrition and infection at the end of 2 years. Pediatricians have described this clinical state under the term *marasmus*.

Valuable films by Margaret Fries, Spitz, and Roudinesco are available describing these distressing states in some detail.

Mental Health Practice and Infancy. Concepts of mental health practice merge with those of treatment as we consider the disorders of infancy. Symptoms can only be understood in terms of the mother-child relationship. Treatment, as in all psychiatry, depends upon the alliance of the therapist with the ego of the patient. In this instance, the ego belongs to the mother. Caplan described the development of mental health screening programs in the well-baby clinic setting, the development of a typology of mother-child relationships; he suggests ways in which the public health setting can be used to help mothers with emotional and functional aspects of child rearing. There are many current research projects striving to get basic information about the emotional needs of infants and the mother-child relationship. Mental health education programs bring to physicians, parents, child-care agencies, and others, basic information about the infant's emotional needs. Anna Freud and Burlingham discuss the problems of child rearing in institutional settings and suggest ways of structuring group living for infants and toddlers which will ensure a healthy ego development.

Mental health and the first year of life are deeply related, for basic strengths and faults in ego development, the ability to withstand later frustration, and the ability to channel energy—both aggressive and libidinous—into constructive, sublimated paths are seemingly largely determined at this early age.

Early Childhood (Anal Stage). The child's first move from the world of infancy into that of childhood occurs when he begins to walk. He is acquiring new skills daily and learning rapidly about the world around him. He is exploring and testing with respect to what he can do with this world. He is testing his ability to shape his environment and to control it. He begins to want to feed himself and is taught methods of feeding. He is also exposed to toilet training and during these years should develop control over anal and bladder sphincters.

The child is learning to use language. Language is used to communicate not only ideas but also feelings. Disturbances in interpersonal relations in the home or difficulty within the child in handling aggressive impulses may block language development.

In early childhood there are many issues which are loaded with tension for parent and child, issues involving socialization and control. Systems of reward and punishment are used. Concepts of right and wrong, good and bad, become part of the child's life. Some activities are praiseworthy; others are blameworthy. In early childhood we find the earliest formations of superego development. Most children know when they have been naughty. The child is testing his wings, his power. He gives up pure pleasure-seeking with some reluctance. Aggressive-destructive impulses are expressed, and mastery over them comes only through positive identification and through the continued love and affection from the parents. The secure child gains pleasure from learning to be a successful member of his family group.

Play becomes an important medium through which the child expresses his feelings and discharges his tensions. Blocks are piled up and knocked down. Water is splashed about. Mud, dirt, and, more lately, finger paints are smeared indiscriminately on self and elsewhere.

Learning to adjust to siblings becomes important. The little child disturbs older children. New babies later disturb the little child.

Childhood illnesses at this period have their important emotional aspect, especially in relation to the severity of the illness and the manner in which it is handled by parents and others.

Interpersonal Relations. The father-child relationship now joins the mother-child relationship as of great importance to the child. The father traditionally plays the more active role in discipline and limit-setting. However, today, flexible partnership arrangement, with a sharing of roles by the mother and father, is considered desirable by many authorities on family life. All agree, though, that this demands more of parents in the way of patience, understanding, and mutual confidence.

The child can now control the frequency of interactions in his family setting. He moves for himself; he can come into the parents' bedroom in the morning; when he finishes his nap, he can get out of bed himself. Mother no longer has control of the frequency and amount of interaction she has with the child. This becomes of special importance when another baby is born into the family.

The behavior of the child and how to mold it are topics of importance between parents, grandparents, in-laws, and neighbors. Considerable anxiety and guilt may be present in parents concerning their actions and feelings, related to frustrating experiences with the child. Parents begin to react to their own childhood experiences as they deal with the many issues of control which highlight early childhood.

Psychodynamics. From an interaction point of view, the important milestone is gaining the ability to walk erect, to move away from and to the mother, and to enjoy freedom. From the point of view of psychologic growth and development, the important event is weaning, giving up the sucking at the bottle or breast, and the shift of the pleasure zone from the mouth to the anus and urethra.

Pearson and English write:

Observations of children between the ages of one year and two or two and a half give interesting results. Children at this age are very preoccupied with the *act of excretion.* They are proud when they produce a big bowel movement, they try to watch themselves urinating or moving their bowels and to watch others, children, adults and animals doing the same thing. They talk unabashedly about their toilet activities to adults or to children. They show much pleasure in being *able to control* their excretions—i.e., in excreting when and where they like, regardless of whether the place or act may be offensive to anyone else. They show a particular interest in the *product*. They do not mind looking at, touching, handling, smelling or tasting urine or feces, whether their own or someone else's.

These writers continue with reference to training and character formation:

Incorporated parental commands form the nucleus of the new part of the personality—the superego—which stands guard over the acts by which the ego would give free rein to the desires of the id, just as the mother did over the child's desire for uncontrolled pleasure in excretory activities. Like the mother, the superego controls the ego by the use of such concepts as must, ought, ought not, must not. In later life, this nucleus develops into an internal conscience with its codes of morality, ideals, cleanliness, etc. . . . Training affects the child's pleasure in the product of excretion, the act of excretion and the desire to be an uncontrolled person.

Pleasure in the product is handled in socialization and training through the psychologic defense mechanisms of displacement and sublimation.

Aggressive-destructive instincts, in conflict with authority and demands from the parents, become fused with the libidinal drives related to elimination. We find the child taking pleasure in destruction and cruelty. This is the anal sadistic position of psychosexual development. Obviously, the child is now experiencing conflict, feelings of love and hate for the same object. The behavior of these children has often been characterized by the term *negativism*.

The manner of resolution of the intense conflicts depends greatly upon emotional attitudes of the parents towards bowel and bladder training, socialization, control, cleanliness, and acceptance of the anger of these little children. Parental attitudes determine, to a great extent, character formation and the course of symptom formation for the child in later years and in adult life. There are many choices for the displacement of anal instincts. Some of the more common routes are discussed below under childhood psychiatric illnesses. We do not have careful clinical and epidemiologic studies of problems of this age, such as we have for infancy. There are tremendous cultural factors which determine how the socialization and training process of children will be conducted. The personality structure of the parents, the composition of the household, the age and sex of siblings, and many other variables begin to make a complicated problem for the researcher. Data considering mental health aspects of the father-child relationship at this age are lacking.

Nevertheless, mental hygiene principles for early childhood are developing and being applied by family agencies, parent educators, pediatricians, and family physicians. On the whole, they include the following:

1. That the basic love and care of the parents for the child, his health and well-being continue, as in infancy, to be the *sine qua non* of mental health.

2. That the parents understand the nature of the child's growth strivings; that he be allowed to explore, to try new things, and that parental anxiety and anger be handled through other means than acting out with the child as the direct target.

3. That the training process be seen as a slow one, with its eventual successful outcome based on the child's own basic desire to be a successful and loved grown-up member of the family group.

4. That the child, himself, needs controls and understanding restraint in order to be assured that he will not be allowed to destroy or in turn be destroyed.

Most mental health work for early childhood is done in the well-child conference and the physician's office. There is a trend toward more use of child psychiatry and child-guidance clinics by parents with problems of children at this age.

The Preschool Child (Genital Stage). From 4 to 6 years of age impressive events unfold themselves in the emotional growth and development of children. During the preschool years the child begins to be concerned with the basic mysteries of life, begins to ask "why." He begins to be more aware of differences between father and mother, begins to realize that there are two types of people in the world, men and women, boys and girls. The child's unconscious mental life is consumed with the emotional problems embraced under the term Oedipus complex.

Freud early postulated that, in the deep emotional life of children at this age, they fall in love with the parent of the opposite sex and have, in consequence, desires to replace the parent of the same sex and be rid of that parent. Of course, we do not see the Oedipus complex displayed in any pure form, for, as stated above, these "wishes" are emotional strivings deeply buried in the unconscious. This is as it should be. However, we see that the results of this matter in many ways. A most striking form which demonstrates itself is seen in childhood anxieties, nightmares, and phobias. These reactions come from the child's fear or retaliation against its strong, aggressive wishes. We find that some children are very concerned with the meaning of death; afraid themselves of dying, afraid of punishment in the hereafter, afraid of the dark, and afraid of going to bed. These problems, growing out of this phase of life, may be present during school years, adolescence, and adulthood.

The positive strivings in the Oedipus complex are manifested in other patterns of behavior. Children want to be big, want to do grown-up things; want to dress in grown-up clothes. They want to win, they want to be Superman, they listen to stories of heroes doing great things and making good win over evil. Children in their fantasy life and in their play act out scenes over and over, day after day, which represent the power strivings of the Oedipus complex.

Girls at this age are aware of sex differences and frequently wonder why they do not have the genital organ of the boy, or of their father. They may not have so much fear of being harmed as boys, but they feel that they have already been harmed, been deprived, and they blame mother. They turn to father, at first only concerned with their own body, to have him restitute the missing organ. Gradually, the little girl realizes that she can have a baby and the unconscious strivings are for the father to put the baby in her. Compensations are readily found by healthy girls for the fact of being a girl. Some go in the direction of enhanced femininity, interest in dresses, clothes, hairdos, dancing. Others go in the direction of tomboyishness and rivalry with boys in boys' activities. This may represent a denial of the whole problem of being a girl. Preschool girls begin to play mother, using the doll house and dolls to act out their anticipated special role.

How is this great emotional storm resolved? It is resolved through the powerful mental mechanisms of identification and repression, with the aid of an increasingly developed sense of reality. The small boy, in essence, gradually "wakes up to reality." He says to himself, "I'm just a little boy, I cannot replace Father, but what I can do is grow up to be like Father." The child takes into himself the set of values and standards of the parents. He begins to have a conscience, experience more grown-up feelings of personal responsibility and guilt. When the child has completed the resolution of the Oedipus complex, he is ready for school, for he is psychologically motivated to grow up, to learn, to strive to be a success. However, children come into the first grade only more or less finished with the Oedipus complex and pregenital conflicts. They take with them to school the "unfinished emotional business of early childhood" (Dawes).

Interpersonal Relations. During the genital phase there is considerable intensification of emotion in the relationship between the child and the parent. The child's strivings for the father's or the mother's job represents more than the tensions of preceding years, when the child was simply "naughty." Now the parent may feel the need to "put the child in his place." The parent may feel somewhat personally threatened by the child at times of tension and be, therefore, all the more cross with him.

Kindergartens provide a community setting where these tyros can try their wings in the company of their peers. Some 4- and 5-year-olds, completely involved in their own fantasy world, do not participate with other children in the kindergarten. Other children will be primarily involved in creative work, using clay, crayons, and other media. This is especially true of girls who seem to be much more creative than boys at this age and during the early school years. There are some well-adjusted and aggressive children who play together in active games with destructive aims, such as building forts and then knocking them over. Occasionally in a kindergarten one will see a small group of boys and girls actually playing house, acting out through identifications with their parents and other models, playing at being grown up.

Psychodynamics and Psychopathology. The basic elements of the Oedipus complex have been roughly sketched above. Through identifications, displacements, reaction formations, and other mental mechanisms the basic personality structure is being fixed as the child uses his pregenitally set basic attitudes and ways of coping with the world to solve the Oedipus dilemma. Children with oral frustrations and those who have great difficulty in handling their aggressive drives will find it more difficult to handle the intense oedipal conflicts. Personality traits such as activity and passivity also influence the mode of resolution of the Oedipus complex.

The so-called "partial instincts," through which libido may be discharged and pleasure obtained, include the sadomasochistic instincts and the scoptophilic-exhibitionistic instincts. The manner in which these partial instincts are utilized to the service of the pleasure principle is important to the character development of the child. Successful sublimation of these partial instincts is an essential component of good mental health. The degree of difficulty the parents themselves have with masculinity-femininity, active-passive trends, and sadomasochism, influences the success of identifications by the children of both sexes.

Mental health principles which suggest themselves at this age center around issues of learning. The child who asks "why" about the nature of the world, about sex, and about life and death should be given simple, straightforward, truthful answers. Anxiety has to be countered by reassurance. The parent's task is not only to set limits, control anxiety, and strengthen the sense of reality in the child. Love and patience with children of this age are essential. Children may be particularly anxious about unusual procedures, illness, hospitalization, surgery. They are especially susceptible to anxieties and fantasy distortions of reality, so such problems must be handled with great care and understanding. In some instances it seems better to avoid or delay medical and dental procedures. At this age children's emotional disturbances can usually be detected by trained workers in the public or private kindergarten setting. Mental health programs with case finding, parent-consultation services, and child-diagnostic services are particularly effective in work with children of this age.

The Grade School Years (Latency Stage). During these years psychosexual drives lie dormant, the energy derived therefrom pouring into the development of new skills and the acquisition of new knowledge. In early latency the emphasis is on personal development and self-awareness, while in later latency the emphasis is on group participation and the control of basic instinctual drives, especially aggression. Organized social groups, such as the Cub Scouts and Brownies, and organized sports with the concept of team play, enter the lives of children around age 8. Left to their own devices, children at this age organize their own neighborhood clubs. The grade school child is busy continuing the growing-up process set in motion by the resolution of the Oedipus complex. He is busy learning more about the world; he is busy mastering new skills. He is concerned with himself, his own and others' views of himself. He becomes judgmental and critical of himself. His place in the social group is important to him. He has much practice in school conforming to the standards of behavior set by authority figures. He meets many people outside his family circle.

Interpersonal Relations. Grade school children spend a good part of the time in school where they are "on their own" and where both the school and their parents hold certain expectations with regard to what their behavior and academic achievement will be. The child's place in the group, his status, depends on many factors. Most important seem to be his performance skill at specific tasks and his basic human relations, both of which he has developed during his preschool years. Relationships with adults are reflections of the emotional life children have in relation to their parents. The teacher as a parent substitute is particularly important in early latency. The relationships of children to the teacher run the gamut from overdependency and passive compliance through complete indifference. In the latter most of the energy is poured into learning and peer group relations, and to hostile, demanding attitudes toward the teacher with a daily testing of classroom rules and the teacher's patience and endurance. Sibling rivalry may become particularly difficult for both boys and girls during these years. In play life, in school work and school activities, and at home, the children are continually reliving earlier difficult situations, striving for new ways of handling anxiety.

Psychodynamics. The unfinished emotional business of early childhood is worked at throughout latency and into adolescence and adulthood. Regression as a mechanism for handling intense emotional conflicts is stressed as a feature of early latency by Bertha Bornstein. She says:

The ego is a mediator between the inner and outer world, adopts at an early point defensive measures against painful stimuli from within and without. Under the influence of reality, the ego is enabled gradually to tolerate greater amounts of tension. The open pursuit of the child's gratifications is hindered by the parent's opposition. The growing functions of intellect and judgment assist the child further to postpone gratifications and to block impulses from direct discharge.

She continues:

The ego, still buffeted by the surging impulses, is threatened by the new super-ego which is not only harsh and rigid but still a foreign body. This first phase of latency is complicated because of the intermingling of two different sets of defenses; the defense against genital and the defense against pregenital impulses. As a defense against genital impulses a temporary regression to pregenitality is adopted by the ego. . . . Increased ambivalence is a regular feature of early latency, even if the child is not in the process of developing an obsessive neurosis. The ambivalence is expressed in the child's behavior by an alternation between obedience and rebellion; and rebellion is usually followed by self-reproach.

Dr. Bornstein says that children in early latency are quite conscious of emotional distress and readily accept help from an outside source. In later latency the situation is different:

The ego is exposed to less severe conflicts, a virtue of the fact that, on the one hand, the sexual demands have become less exerting and, on the other, the super-ego is less rigid. The ego now can devote itself to a greater extent to coping with reality. The average eight-year-old is ready to be influenced by the children around him and by adults other than his parents. . . . His belief in the omnipotence of his parents subsides. Coinciding with the partial degradation of parents, there is a parallel change in the attitude of the superego towards the ego.

The family romance is a normal fantasy of late latency, when children may dream of themselves as really coming from another family with greater prestige and more power than their own.

Adolescence. Each child meets the crisis of maturing, with its accompanying physical body changes and emotional reactions, in his own unique way, dependent upon his emotional growth and development during the years preceding. Emotionally healthy children are striving for emotional and physical maturation. They anticipate the "coming of age" and feel proud. Physical appearance is important. Physical achievement becomes extremely important to teen-age boys and girls alike. Throughout the teen-age years and into adult life growing boys and girls, men and women, are concerned about their body, their appearance, and their accomplishments.

The increased instinctual energy accompanying physical and glandular development poses real problems for teen-agers. Genital sexuality becomes a reality. The energy of teen-agers is unbounded. The problem is to channelize it into satisfying and constructive activities. Sexual maturation is accompanied by worry, feelings of inferiority, anxiety, and guilt.

Conflicts with parental authority and the questioning of the parents' way of life, mores, and standards are normal in adolescence. Teen-agers want to make their own decisions and take responsibility for themselves. However, they are often not ready for this. Regression and progression in development occur in cycles. Excitement and thrill-seeking through new experiences are natural. Trouble lies ahead when the child does not have sound home relationships to help him make sound judgments. The early teen-ager is very much concerned with himself as a person, but may care little for parental standards in relation to dress and cleanliness. Parents are helped by extrafamilial community institutions such as school, church, or scouting, where boys and girls are closely involved with other adults who take authority and who are at the same time personally interested in teen-agers.

In the early teens, peer life is characterized by attachment to one's own sex. This is especially seen in junior high, where boys have their own groups, as do the girls. Dating begins at various ages, becoming a normal social institution in the high school. Children begin dating with various degrees of anxiety and heightening of concern over the self. Social scientists view dating as a peculiar American custom in which the main issues are narcissistic in their orientation. The emphasis is on personal achievement and how one is regarded by others. Mature concern with the partner comes only later in true courtship and marriage but may even be lacking then.

During adolescence boys and girls are seriously preparing for their place in the adult world and are concerned about their own capabilities and their future. School failure is a serious problem among teen-agers. Teenage children need the most skilled guidance, vocational and medical, to help them face and plan for their future. Children run through the various phases of adolescence at their own pace. Some mature early, some much later.

Interpersonal Relations. The teen-ager responds to the dignity, respect, and understanding which characterize mature adult relationships. He uses interpersonal relations to develop his perception of himself. Some teen-agers are more peer-group oriented than adults. There are a certain few who are social isolates but who have meaningful relationships and special skills and interests such as studies, science, art, or music. Some may be well adjusted. However, in the main, the peer-group life of the teen-agers, from the gang formation of early adolescence to the dating of later years, is intimately related to healthy emotional growth and development. The development of social skills and satisfying self-respect is achieved not only through peer-group activities, but also through the availability of helpful adults in the form of parents and others.

The relationship of teen-agers to the grown-up world revolves around authority and authority conflicts. Teen-agers express the problem by using the word "fair." Teen-agers are delighted to have limits clearly set by authority, for they have anxiety and uncertainty with respect to whether they can themselves successfully set limits to their behavior. The fact that authority conflicts exist does not mean that parents and other adults should not exercise authority and set standards for group and individual behavior.

Mental health agencies are being called upon more and more to help with problems of adolescence. Special adolescent clinics providing comprehensive medical care for adolescents, with physical, psychologic, and academic diagnostic facilities, have been developed in recent years.

Psychodynamics. The psychodynamics of adolescence revolve around the problem of handling the intensified sexual energies through extremely active ego and superego mechanisms. Cultural taboos keep this process very secret. Adolescent masturbation is a central problem. It serves to discharge sexual tensions, but at the same time represents an acting out of various instinctual urges. The sadomasochistic and scoptophilic-exhibitionistic set of instincts likewise demand expression. The problem is to arrive at solutions which are compatible with the demands of the strict superego, solutions which are satisfying and yet do not produce overwhelming anxiety or guilt. We know that many adolescents have impossible tasks to perform in their emotional maturation due to the fact that they do not move into adolescence with adequate ego and superego structures. Symptom formation and acting out are commonplace. The problem is one of disengaging the sexual object from the parents and other family figures to extrafamilial objects, leaving behind the childhood situation. Unresolved oedipal fixations may create an intolerable situation for the child during adolescence.

The child is transferring object relations from the home to the community. At the same time the child is concerned with his self-image. Object choices usually have a marked narcissistic component to them. In every adolescent community one can see in the daily life of the children youngsters who are handling their basic conflicts well, and those who are in trouble. Sadistic-destructive behavior, intense power strivings, sexual inversion, heterosexual acting out, depressions, inability to work, exhibitionism, and masturbation anxiety and guilt—all are present to one degree or another.

PSYCHOPATHOLOGY IN CHILD PSYCHIATRY

It is impossible to do more than indicate what kinds of psychiatric disturbances occur in children and what kinds of problems are currently being treated by child psychiatrists in hospital and community clinics and in private practice.

When satisfactory defense mechanisms for handling overwhelming tensions in the individual do not develop, pathways for the expression and resolution of conflicts will ensue which have a crippling, unhealthy aspect to them. Freud developed the basic theory of emotional illness and its relationship to personality development in his volume *The Problem of Anxiety*, in which he discusses the relationships between anxiety, symptom formation, and inhibitions.

In child psychiatry we are primarily concerned with inhibitions, acting out, and symptom formation.

Pearson and English divide psychologic problems of children as follows:

A. Anxiety states
   1. Acute diurnal anxiety attacks
   2. Nocturnal anxiety attacks (nightmares)
   3. Chronic anxiety states and phobias
B. Psychogenic disturbances of physiological function
   1. Disorders of visceral function
      a. Disorders of the function of the upper gastrointestinal tract (oral zone)
      b. Disorders of the functions of the lower gastrointestinal tract (anal zone)
      c. Disorders of the functions of the urinary tract
   2. Disorders of motor function
C. Disturbances of adaptation
   1. Aggressive reaction
   2. Inhibitions of social behavior
      a. Intellectual
      b. Social
   3. Sexual perversions

Anxiety attacks and phobias are related to intense libidinal or aggressive drives inside the person, when the fact of the drive with its aim and object is repressed. Childhood phobias and nightmares are commonplace. Frequently children who are afraid to go to school have real fears that something may happen to the parent or sibling at home toward whom there is an intense repressed aggressive destructive feeling.

The treatment of anxiety states ranges from simple manipulative procedures such as leaving a bedroom light on at night, reassurance, and education concerning the absence of dangers in the real world, to a sympathetic understanding and interest on the part of parent or physician and psychotherapy in the child-guidance setting. Shyness as a sign of chronic anxiety and other character problems involving inhibition may be seen in children in the early school years. These children respond well to child-psychiatric treatment. Anxieties and phobias in adolescence most frequently revolve around sexual concerns. Psychotherapy with adolescents is a complex matter. Sometimes, but not often, a sex-education interview with the doctor may relieve the distressing symptoms of the moment, but such an approach is usually not sufficient to untangle the underlying emotional conflicts.

Disorders of orality in children consist of a reactivation or prolongation of thumb-sucking and nail-biting, a disturbance of food intake such as anorexia, dysphagia (refusal to eat), stomach upsets, nausea, or vomiting. These symptoms have a meaning which can only be understood in the context of the child's emotional problems and his relationships at home. Anorexia, dysphagia, nausea, and vomiting—all may have a symbolic meaning and consequent value to the child's emotional economy. Symptom formation represents a compromise. Symptoms are usually overdetermined. For instance, anorexia, nausea, and vomiting in a latency-age child may simultaneously stand for fear of being harmed by the mother, guilt over the interest in feces (displacement upward), anger at the parents, or pregnancy fantasies. Thumb-sucking and nail-biting, as neurotic traits, serve many youngsters as helpful tension outlets, substituting for anxieties, direct expressions of anger and resentment, and conflicting genital masturbatory urges. The current trend is for the act itself to be accepted by the parent as necessary for the child at the moment thereby supporting and accepting the child himself, but with primary attention given to the basic causes of the persistence of the habit.

Speech disturbances, in particular stammering, as well as certain psychosomatic disorders, such as asthma and childhood tics, are described by Fenichel as "pregenital conversions." The symptoms in these conditions symbolize a conflict between antagonistic tendencies, but the tendencies are those around oral and anal issues rather than genital issues. Successful treatment of psychogenic asthma, stuttering, and tics can be achieved in the child-guidance and child-psychiatric clinics over a number of years. Work with the parents is extremely important, although difficult. Constipation and soiling in children are usually accompanied by an obsessive compulsive character structure with intense anal sadistic and masochistic trends underlying. Psychotherapy with these children, where inhibition, fear, and guilt prevent free expression, is based on the idea of providing a situation where the child can find other outlets through play and verbalization for the direct expression and eventual sublimation of his aggressive energies. Again, work with the parents in the child-guidance setting is extremely important. Children with such disturbances in latency usually have parents who themselves have fixations at a pregenital level of development and are overreacting to the child's handling of his early childhood emotional drives. If insight, understanding, and emotional growth are possible in the parent, then the child can move ahead more freely in his emotional growth and development.

Enuresis is another common childhood symptom with many meanings for the child in his emotional economy. Some children are enuretic from birth, while others begin suddenly after having been dry for several years. Unnecessary and traumatic diagnostic and surgical procedures should be avoided with these children prior to a psychiatric study. Enuresis represents a regressive clinging to infancy; it is also used by children to express anger and resentment; and it is further used to show weakness, thereby denying strength. Many enuretic children have passive, ineffectual types of personality structure. Treatment of the enuresis itself may be directed toward helping the parents with their attitude toward the symptoms and the child, and toward developing a more reasonable routine for the child at home. Treatment has to be directed toward the underlying principal causes. This may be easily accomplished or may be extremely difficult. Some writers report enuresis stopping after several clinical interviews and even immediately after an intake interview in a clinic when the child is never seen, while enuresis associated with severe personality disturbances may persist into adulthood.

Disorders of motor function, involuntary movements, head banging, nervousness, tics, and breath holding require intensive psychiatric treatment.

Children with disturbances of social adaptation are conspicuous in every school system and fill the waiting lists of child-guidance clinics. The differential diagnosis of these children is extremely important, for if a dynamic understanding of the underlying causes of the aggression is not at hand, treatment is impossible. Recent writers have emphasized the importance of mild cerebral damage from birth injuries, infections, or prematurity.

Chronic aggressive destructive behavior ordinarily has extremely important emotional components. Children with mild degrees of brain damage can be helped by psychotherapy. Adjuvant drug therapy is helpful in many cases. Unrecognized by most parents and educators is the fact that anxiety is usually underlying the aggressive antisocial behavior. This is especially true of disturbed children in the primary grades. Needless to say, children so disturbed fall into the predelinquent or delinquent category, with antisocial acts involving aggression. Lying, stealing, disobedience, malicious destruction, fire setting, sexual aggressions, and truancy represent various modes of symptom expression. The treatment of these conditions is extremely difficult and represents a major health and social problem in the American culture today. Many of the children with gross social maladaptation come from homes where there is a lack of parental love, care, supervision, or control, or the presence of extreme parental ambivalence. This makes cooperation with treatment programs extremely difficult. Clinics join with other agencies concerned with human relations in treating these youngsters. These include the school, the juvenile court, the child-protective agencies, the recreation agencies, and the church. Clinical work by itself may not suffice. Consultation work in the field is often an essential adjuvant in these cases.

The child with inhibitions in social development, the shy, withdrawn child, and the child who cannot produce and cannot learn needs psychiatric study. Psychologic causes for disturbances of the learning function have interested child psychiatrists for many years. In order to learn a child must have full use of his abilities and desire to look and see, to reach out and take, and to incorporate within himself. Ambivalences and conflicts in these functions, involving curiosity and aggression, pleasure and achievement, may block the learning process.

Forbidden sexual experiences in childhood are common. Children explore and are seduced. The problem for the medical practitioner is one of assessment of the severity of the underlying disturbance in the child, to reassure the parent when possible and establish a healthy protective attitude toward the child and the parent, with follow-up and psychiatric referral if indicated.

Mixed sexual identifications in children present a real problem of some magnitude. These adjustments, resulting from abnormal resolutions of the Oedipus complex and other factors, should be recognized by early adolescence. The parental figures themselves must be worked with. Homosexual activities may represent a flight from heterosexuality. Children with basic problems of sexual identification often have deep fears of destruction by one or the other parent. The child psychiatrist cannot plan to remake the personality structure, but can be of tremendous help in reducing anxiety, improving motivation and the self-image, or releasing inhibitions. The therapist as a model for identification becomes of importance, especially during the teen-age years.

Obsessive compulsive neuroses, anxiety neurosis, and depressions are frequently seen in young children, though not in so clear a form as in adults, inasmuch as the symptoms are expressed in behavior and organ dysfunction more than as inner feelings. These cases need psychiatric treatment but often are treated in the office of the general practitioner, the pediatrician, or by school guidance workers.

A final paragraph must be devoted to the subject of children with structural defects in ego development. Much attention has been paid in recent years to children who have been variously diagnosed as having childhood schizophrenia, infantile autism, atypical development, or mental deficiency. Beata Rank describes the outstanding clinical symptoms as "withdrawal from people, retreat into a world of fantasy, mutism or the use of language for autistic purposes, bizarre posturing, seemingly meaningless sterotype gestures, impassivity or violent outburst of anxiety and rage, identification with inanimate objects or animals, excessively inhibited or excessively uninhibited expression of impulses." Traits common to all these children are a lack of contact with reality, little or no communication with others, and a lack of integration and uniformity of ego development. These severe disturbances are as yet not fully understood. Some writers consider them to be predominantly constitutional—hereditary in origin—while others are more impressed with the characteristics of the early human environment. Obviously, a combination of factors go into the development of this extremely serious state. The importance here is in the presentation of a differential diagnosis when a child is slow in language development, in social development, in learning, and in the handling of aggression and frustration.

Treatment has been on the whole not very encouraging, although many clinicians are experimenting with therapeutic nursery school environments and with the mother and the father in psychiatric treatment as well as the child.

Community Mental Health Practice

Running through this chapter are the themes of emotional growth and development, the mastery of instinctual drives at the various stages of growth and development with the integration and use of energies for ego development, and the eventual mastery of the inner world of feelings and the outer world of people and things. The human environment feeds and sustains the growing child during growing up and also points the way to maturity through teaching and through identification. Mental health crises are found at every stage of growth and development—birth, weaning, going to school, and adolescence.

The mental health approach is to build community programs around these naturally occurring crises and special programs for children who are handicapped or who sustain unusual life crises, such as death of parents, severe illness, hospitalization, or crippling. The human environment at home and in the community must be mobilized hand in hand with clinical facilities.

In the school situation, children beginning school differ greatly in their readiness for the learning process and for mixing with persons outside their own families. Mental health teaches that the behavior and achievement of children in school are related with their limits of constitutional endowment to:

1. Interpersonal relations and emotionally relevant experiences in the child's early preschool life
2. Current emotional crises in the child's family and neighborhood life
3. Unique personal meanings of the school experience to the child

The performance of the child in both the social and academic spheres is symptomatic of his mental health and can be understood only in terms of the emotional growth and development of the individual child, studied longitudinally in the context of his emotionally relevant human environment.

Mental health practice involves work with both emotional-need-meeting agencies (school, church, home, physician, and recreation agencies) and crisis-oriented agencies (school, courts, physician, and child-care agencies). Through the integration of these into a public health–oriented mental health service, some dent may be eventually made on the incidence and prevalence of psychiatric disorders.

Preventive medicine, child psychiatry, and pediatrics are coming together within this public health–oriented approach. There is a great need for basic research, using public health and social science techniques. There is a tremendous shortage of trained personnel in mental health work and almost no facilities in the country for training in community mental health practice. There is, however, a sound body of fact and theory available from the field of child psychiatry, social psychiatry, anthropology, pediatrics, and education which can form the basis for sound mental health programs.

SECTION III

The Treatments

In this section the therapies will be presented. Some of these therapies are used in more than one type of mental reaction. This section will present only the general principles in management because each type of psychiatric reaction and each individual patient within each reaction must be treated appropriately to his own needs. Common combinations and variations of these general forms of treatment will be discussed, but the student must look to his personal teachers for individual guidance in particular cases as he accumulates experience.

CHAPTER **25**

Psychotherapy

Psychotherapy is a general term for the treatment of the patient by mental manipulation. The term is used very loosely in psychiatry and may be used to name anything that in any way influences a patient's activities or behavior. In this chapter we shall confine its use to intentional acts on the part of a physician involving the exchange of emotions, thoughts, and information. By this the physician seeks to guide a patient's thoughts, emotions, and behavior so that he is relieved of his symptoms and, if possible, of the illness causing the symptoms.

Psychotherapy may be used as individual and group treatment in almost any type of psychiatric disorder. In a neurosis it seeks to find chiefly the conscious causes of the patient's difficulties and remove the causes where they are consciously or environmentally motivated. In more intensive psychotherapy unconscious material may be developed which must be handled by interpretations, linking it with current emotional and intellectual behavior. If this is not possible, the physician attempts through psychotherapy to build up the patient's ego strength and resistance and improve his methods of sublimation to the point where he adjusts well, even though the basic conflicts may remain unresolved.

Psychotherapy may also be used in combination with various drug therapies and with shock therapies in patients suffering from the major psychotic reactions. The goal of psychotherapy in the psychoses is the same as in the neuroses but is used in combinations with other measures in order that the patient may be able to cooperate with the treatment and comprehend what goes on.

In organic patients—patients with other types of handicaps—and in some patients suffering from chronic illness, supportive psychotherapy may be used to help the patient adapt to his handicaps. It is of particular value in persons with mental retardation or various types of neurologic handicaps, or in patients of advanced years as they adapt to their new role in life as senior citizens.

The mechanism of psychotherapy, that is, how informed talking to a person can help him, as opposed to idle gossip, has been studied, but many of the processes at work in psychotherapy and analysis are still not clearly understood. Max Gitelson shows three ways in which psychotherapy may work:

The first involves a "cure" by repression in which a patient forms a good relationship with the psychiatrist and talks freely with him but encounters topics which are too sensitive to the central problem. These patients have the ego strength to muster up their good will and resistance and, as a result, the symptoms disappear. The patient is further "cured" by elaborating his neurosis, increasing his ego strength through the relationship with the therapist, and improving his repression, thus getting symptomatic relief.

The second concerns the patient exemplified by a man having difficulty with his boss. He discusses it with the therapist, discovers similar attitudes toward his father and toward his boss; then he understands the antagonisms toward the boss and, as a result of this new knowledge or insight, adjusts to his work situation and a relief of symptoms comes through insight.

The third involves the patient who does not get along well in his environment; this is an example of how supportive psychotherapy is of value. This type of patient does not develop deep insight but becomes dependent upon the person of the psychiatrist by leaning on the psychiatrist's ego, which Gitelson calls a "sustaining transference figure." By receiving support and guidance from him, the patient gets along well for short periods. This type of patient remains dependent upon the therapist and must continue to see him periodically in order to remain free of symptoms.

It will be noted that in none of these patients has the basic conflict or the neurotic core of the patient been unraveled; but conscious material in the first two cases has been developed which enables the patient to adapt to his symptoms. Psychotherapy always involves an intellectual and emotional interchange between the physician and the patient. The skill of the physician will depend upon the understanding of his own mental processes, of the patient's mental processes, and of the emotional and intellectual situations initiated by the interaction between them.

One of the simplest forms of psychotherapy is the informed, yet personal interest a physician takes in his patient, and the quiet confidence that the patient feels in the physician he has selected. A preliminary interview is most important and has been defined by Thomas Rennie:

A psychiatric interview is not the same as a social conversation. It is a process especially designed to permit the patient to express anxieties and uncertainties fully and without reservation to the physician who will not interfere or hamper the spontaneity by injecting his own personality or his convictions into the situation. In essence, it is sensitive, objective, understanding, noninterfering listening.

In the usual psychotherapy the patient will confine himself, during initial interviews at least, to conscious material. Then the patient begins to feel secure in the relationship with his physician or becomes more confident that the physician will help him. The patient now begins to develop feelings which are called *transference*. In analysis the transferent situations and manipulation are at the core of the treatment. In psychotherapy, however, the transference is on a more superficial level and is more controlled. The patient usually looks upon the therapist as an authoritative, dependable figure, admired and, in a general way, beloved. The therapist, in the mind of the patient, is a person who understands and who has accepted him and wants to help him. In general psychotherapy there is an attempt to keep the transference at about this level. At times the patient may develop antagonisms toward the therapist which are related to the negative transference seen in analysis, but an attempt is made to keep this at a minimum level and antagonisms are discussed on a conscious level with explanations to the patient. The depth of understanding which the physician brings to the situation and the skill with which he manipulates these emotional forces for the patient's benefit determine the outcome of the psychotherapy. In some cases reassurance and education of the patient may be all that is required. For example, a mother who is worried that she is not bringing up her child properly because of his seemingly odd behavior may receive tremendous benefit from talking to a pediatrician or a physician who explains that the puzzling behavior is seen in normal children. This may reassure the mother. Some mothers get confidence by reading Spock's book.

Another example of education being an effective psychotherapeutic force would be with the person who has normal sexual impulses but whose education and information in the field have been faulty and who looks upon these things as sinful. Reassurance with emotional support can usually alleviate this situation if it is truly based on lack of information.

In more severe cases, parents' conflicts with their children, poor adjustment in marriage, or poor adaptation to fellow workers may be the result of conscious incompatibility which has its roots in unconscious forces which make the patient's attitude toward the situation an immature or otherwise unhealthy one. Even in these cases emotional support and confidence in the physician's judgment, as part of a moderate positive transference to the physician, and the blowing off steam or ventilation, brought about by telling the physician all about it, often relieve the conscious processes so that the patient can cope with his own basic attitudes.

Talking with the patient in psychotherapy sometimes aids the production of the conflict material. One of the methods of encouraging talk is to borrow from the psychoanalytic method the free association process. In this technique the patient sits or lies in a relaxed manner in the presence of the physician and allows his thoughts to wander with little conscious direction. He verbalizes his thoughts as they appear, making no attempt to edit or organize them. This may be used as a form of ventilation. When significant semiconscious or unconscious material appears, this is discussed on a conscious basis with the patient in psychotherapy. In effect the material is explained to him. The amount and nature of the discussion will depend on the skill and training of the physician and the needs of the patient in terms of his illness. In other patients it may be necessary to aid the flow of material by using hypnotic trances for the interviews. In such cases it is sometimes desirable to discuss the material while in the hypnotic trance and to create certain posthypnotic suggestions in terms of behavior or symptoms. In other cases, intravenous drugs, such as Amytal or Pentothal, are used to elicit information. With other patients the entire interview, both eliciting information and explaining it, may be carried on under the influence of drugs. Some physicians favor the use of inhalation drugs, such as carbon dioxide, either as a treatment or to conduct psychotherapy after the patient has had carbon dioxide hyperventilation.

Many, or any, of the above methods may be applied in conferences with the patient in order to detect and, if possible, remove the cause of certain conscious symptoms. Patients who require more drastic revision of their unconscious processes and major renovations of their ego and superego structure will require psychoanalysis. This will be discussed subsequently.

Another important factor in psychotherapy is the manipulation of the patient's environment. This may be done by interviews with members of the patient's family, his boss, or fellow workers. These interviews may be done by the physician or, in most instances, by a skilled social worker who collaborates with the physician in the care of the patient. At times the clergyman can be of tremendous help in counseling the patient and offering religious guidance.

Variations for Different Disorders

The above general principles are applicable to many forms of illness. Individual variations will be necessary, however. For example, psychotherapy with children will usually involve participating in some type of play, such as drawing, telling stories, constructing things, or other activities with which the child may relate.

Disturbed schizophrenic patients may require prolonged therapeutic sessions in which the therapist sits on the ward or in the room with the patient and gives particular attention to both verbal and nonverbal communications, gestures, facial expression, and posturing. This requires tremendous patience and skill but is helpful.

It has been our experience that psychotherapeutic sessions with depressive patients should be shorter but more frequent. These patients probably profit more from two 15- to 20-minute therapeutic sessions per day than from a single one of from 40 to 50 minutes. This is not always practical to work out in a schedule, but in hospitalized patients it is worthwhile.

In organic and delirious patients the therapy must be of a simple, reassuring type and it must be repetitious, preferably, more than one session per day, where time and opportunity afford.

Combinations

Psychotherapy may be used in combination with almost any other type of treatment directed toward mental disorder. Its usefulness in any of the mental disorders is probably limited only by the time available to the physician for the patient.

Patients in psychoanalysis should not be undergoing simultaneous psychotherapy with another therapist. This sounds like a redundant piece of advice, but patients in analysis who begin to show resistance may run back to their referring physician or the referring psychiatrist for reassurance, sympathy, or other forms of ego support. This should not be done unless it is first discussed with the analyst, because the patient may manipulate the therapist into being a bolster to his resistance, thus prolonging treatment and making more difficult his ultimate recovery.

With patients receiving electroshock therapy, psychotherapy must be simple, short, and composed of direct expressions of reassurance or directions as needed. Memory defects that accompany prolonged shock therapy make other types of psychotherapy futile.

Cameron uses selected recordings from previous interviews for "psychic driving" in some patients in intensive psychotherapy. He describes the technique as offering a possible new psychotherapeutic method, and reports experiments with its use.

Complications

Psychotherapy not skillfully handled may result in a welling up of further anxiety in the patient and this may result in the patient's running away from psychotherapy and resorting to further surgery or medical treatment. It may result in the patient's treating his anxiety with overdoses of drugs, particularly alcohol. A few cases regress further and become psychotic, and an occasional one will commit suicide. The fact that there are complications possible in psychotherapy should not deter one from attempting psychotherapy, but it should be on a level of which the patient is capable and should be accompanied by supervision and frequent discussions, at least in the initial phases, with a trained therapist. Psychotherapy cannot be learned from a book and only experience with treating patients under the guidance and direction of a trained supervising therapist will teach this valuable technique.

CHAPTER 26

Group Psychotherapy

Group psychotherapy has the same general aims as psychotherapy with the dynamics being different. It is carried on by the therapist with a group of patients and many of the therapeutic influences are not therapist to patient, but patient to patient. Group therapy has been used widely in mental hospitals, in outpatient clinics, and in some correctional institutions. In the past decade it has become increasingly popular because it offers hope for extending a form of therapy to many patients not heretofore accessible to the all-too-few trained psychiatrists, psychologists, and other workers. Some patients not cooperative to individual therapy, do well in groups.

In some hospitals, groups are conducted by attendants, nurses, social workers, ministers, occupational and recreational therapists, and psychiatrists. In most hospitals the groups are supervised by a psychiatrist. In some the group therapists themselves are carried in group therapy by the supervising psychiatrist. The goals of these groups vary with the experience, training, and fortitude of the group leader. In some instances the groups are very large, comprising almost the entire population of a ward, with as many as 40 or 50 patients; in others, they may be very small with as few as 7 or 8 patients. In some the therapy takes the form of gripe sessions; in others, it takes the form of explanation and elicitation of symptoms and adjustment problems. In a few it takes the form of patient government in which the patients' behavior and symptoms are subjected to discussion and criticism by fellow patients. These patient groups often assume a large part of the responsibility for self-discipline. Properly supervised, this is a constructive experience and does not become a kangaroo court.

It should be remembered, however, that the goal of group or individual

323

psychotherapy is to help the patient solve his conflicts and difficulties by giving himself insight into his own motivation and actions, particularly as they influence his activities with others. In group therapy, there are many opportunities for new interpersonal relations and influence, and innumerable opportunities for testing these with a free, and often critical, discussion of results. Frank describes the aims of group psychotherapy as

. . . to strengthen the patient's self-respect so that he gains the courage to seek better ways of dealing with his conflicts. Second, to help the patient maintain a level of tension or distress sufficient to keep him working towards better solutions but not so great as to force him back into his maladapted pattern. . . . Third, the aim of all forms of psychotherapy is to supply some guides or models to the patient as he struggles to modify his attitudes in an atmosphere which encourages him to experiment, provides him with accurate information as to how well he is doing, and minimizes the penalties for failing.

Individuals even in groups operated by relatively untrained persons develop cohesiveness or a sense of membership within the group. This familiarity with one another leads to deep discussions of behavior, reasons therefor, and better methods of reacting in the same situation.

An example is a group being conducted by an attendant who was also the manager of that hospital's league baseball team. In the session witnessed, one of the patients was berating the group leader for not removing the third baseman in the game played the night before, after he made his second of four errors. Two of the patients in the group attributed the loss of the game to these errors and felt that the group leader had erred in failing to take the patient out. The group leader explained that the patient who was referred to, also a member of the group, lacked self-confidence and had feelings of guilt and that the group leader thought it would be bad for him to be taken out. This led to a discussion as to whether it would have been bad for the third baseman to have been removed. Although no final solution was reached, they discussed such subjects as the patient's necessity to learn to face reality which sometimes means being taken out of the game and his learning that a single failure in a single game did not necessarily mean that his whole life would be spoiled. The other patients also pointed out to the complaining one that he tended to be too aggressive, too interfering, and too thoughtless of feelings of others. Reasons for this were discussed, and it was pointed out that it was probably his own desire to be liked and to be helpful that made him so disliked and difficult. While the participants in the group and the group leader were not aware of the dynamics of these things, either theoretically or in the particular cases involved, at least they all developed insight and desensitization concerning such events in the daily life of the two participants. A repeated recounting of these experiences within the security and understanding of the group helped these patients to adapt much better to feelings which arose in themselves and in others and to have less difficulty in controlling them. In groups conducted by a trained therapist, it is possible to explore further the actual causes that produce such behavior, with even greater improvement in the adaptive capacity of the patients.

Group therapy is as difficult as individual psychotherapy, and the student interested in it should place himself under the guidance of a skilled group therapist. There are also excellent reference works available.

Moreno developed an interesting type of group therapy called *psychodrama*. In this the patient and the group leader take various roles, and then they exchange parts. This quickly leads to group participation by both the actors and the audience made up of the other members of the group. Many insights and the principles of adaptive living can be learned by properly operated psychodrama. Again, this must be done by persons skilled in the technique. It can be learned only by participation in the technique under the direction of a skilled psychodrama therapist.

Social studies in our hospitals show that participation in group discussions and group therapy not only improves the patients and their attitudes but brings about needed changes in the attitudes of attendants, psychologists, social workers, physicians, and even in the administration. This is more apt to be true with hospitalized patients in group therapy than with those in the clinic.

Frank pointed out certain advantages of group therapy over individual therapy, some of which we have mentioned above.

With respect to their effects on patients, two potential advantages of group over individual therapy have been stressed. First, groups offer a wide range of therapeutic tasks which can be tailored to the needs of different types of patients. Secondly, through fostering a sense of belongingness they strengthen patients' feelings of freedom and of responsibility for themselves and others. These inevitably lead to improved communication throughout the social structure of the hospital. Thus, from the standpoint of the hospital, therapy groups are both expressions of the democratically oriented therapeutic community and necessary means towards this end.

Group therapy with disturbed patients may need to be started in terms of group activities—bands or athletic events such as volleyball, baseball, or swimming events. More retarded and slower patients may be helped by group singing, dances, or participation in plays such as psychodrama. It is often necessary to entice these patients into activities by having slightly more active patients participating in group games or singing in the patients' environment.

Combination

Group therapy may be used for patients who are getting infrequent sessions of individual therapy. It is the practice, where possible, especially in follow-up clinics, to use individual therapy sessions once each week or two weeks and have patients attend group meetings more often. Patients attending groups once or twice a week may have an individual therapeutic session once a month. This needs to be tailored to the individual patient and will be most helpful for patients with many tensions and anxieties.

Complications

The complications of group therapy are essentially the same as those of individual therapy. In some patients the threat of the group is too great. This is particularly true of those patients with latent homosexual trends or with feelings of hostility. They cannot accept other patients moving in on them emotionally and they have to take the group in very small doses. If pushed too rapidly, they may regress into panic-like reactions and run away, resort to drugs, or commit suicide.

Occupational Therapy

Occupational therapy is an ancient adjunct to the care of patients. This is particularly so in mental hospitals, but in recent years its use has spread to day hospitals, outpatient departments, and wards of hospitals giving continued care to orthopedic, tuberculous, and cardiac patients. It is one of the best vehicles for group therapy and has an advantage in that trained therapists know how to exploit advantages gained in group therapy situations. The work of the shop offers a large variety of combinations. Creative patients may do art work or modeling. Patients who have the desire or need to smear and decorate may also participate in art work which may vary from painting walls or boxes to murals or individual paintings if they have the talent and the desire. Other creative activities are expressed in wooden objects, metalwork, pottery, or weaving. Destructive urges may be worked out in shaping heavier bits of metal or wood, in working in yard projects or demolition projects, or in digging or moving rocks. Skilled occupational therapists discuss with the student or physician the needs of his patient and suggest appropriate projects after interviewing the patient and learning his desires and potentialities. The skilled occupational therapist also uses the mechanism of working with the patient on these projects in helping him work through some of the deeper conflict material. The physician should collaborate with the occupational therapist, stressing goals for the therapist and spheres of activity for the occupational therapist.

Occupational therapy should not be looked upon as recreation. The shop is not a place to put the patient during the day when nothing else goes on. The student should recognize that the purpose of the occupational therapy department is therapy and not the production of beautiful or usable objects. Certain attractive productions will inevitably result, but these should be produced only by patients where the production of an attractive, useful article is the goal of the therapy and serves a use in the treatment of the patient. Patients can project conflict material into the occupational therapy projects; they can objectify it, understand it, and work out ways of handling this material in relation to their fellow workers, first, in the medium of the material and the interrelationship with the therapist, and then, in relationship with the other persons in their occupational therapy class.

Recreational Therapy

Recreational therapy offers many of the advantages of occupational therapy, although it is somewhat less flexible and not nearly so highly developed as the latter. However, the recreational therapist, particularly in collaboration with the occupational therapist, can do a great deal through group activities for patients. Here, music, singing, dancing, athletic events and gym classes offer a vehicle or medium for the patient to express his conflicts, work out his inner tensions, and discover new ways of adapting his drives and needs to his fellow participants in the class and to the therapist. We believe that the recreational therapist should be a person skilled in psychodynamics rather than a person possessing only those skills taught in the usual physical education courses.

Music Therapy

In recent years there has been an increasing interest in the use of music as a means for patients to work out their conflicts and to find new ways of expression. In most institutions music is a part of the recreational program. Music therapy as such is still in the investigative phase, but there is little doubt that music will often be the first means of communicating with withdrawn and retarded patients. As part of an over-all group-activity program it has much to commend it. Perhaps further investigation and research by people with more research skills and less need to prove the correctness of their opinions will make this a less crude tool than it now is.

Bibliotherapy

This is a term of nonspecific meaning in therapy which is sometimes used to describe assigned reading for patients. This material is then discussed individually with the therapist. This reading is designed to give the patient further knowledge concerning the workings of human emotions or to give him knowledge concerning certain specific activities in the interpersonal field. Most places that use it, however, have the participation in the form of group discussions in which a book is reviewed by one patient and then discussed by the group with interpretations and guidance from a group therapist. This has some advantages and sometimes is a way of initiating a regular group on the ward, particularly among better-preserved or neurotic patients. It is probably more adaptable to outpatient therapy and to the so-called "open wards" of a mental hospital than it is to the disturbed or locked wards. Like music therapy, this form of therapy in individual cases has great usefulness but as a generally describable technique needs further development.

Movies as a Form of Therapy

Certain teaching films are used as initial stimuli for group discussions. Most mental health departments and some hospitals have film libraries available in which films suitable for use to precipitate patient discussion are available. These should always be accompanied by explanations and by the participation of the therapist who is familiar with the movie and can guide the discussion in the interpretation of the film. Discussion often becomes spontaneous like that of any other group therapy session. Like a book review, this use of movies helps launch a group and quickly weld it into a workable unit. This is especially true with outpatient groups, with lay groups who are not strictly patients but who are there for mental health promotion and educational purposes, and on the open or neurotic wards of mental hospitals.

CHAPTER 27

Psychoanalysis (as a Therapeutic Discipline)

Psychoanalysis is not a technique for the general physician or for the student or resident. It is a technique reserved for those persons who have had training in psychiatry, who have had training in a certified analytic institute, and who are either students doing control analytic work under the supervision of a training analyst or who have completed the course of training as approved by the American Psychoanalytic Association.

It is essential that persons who wish to become psychoanalysts have a therapeutic psychoanalysis, followed by a training analysis. It is desirable for other psychiatric residents to have a therapeutic or personal analysis in order that they may better understand the workings of the human mind and better see their own conflicts, prejudices, and biases. Persons preparing themselves for careers in psychology or social service work and some going into psychiatric nursing also avail themselves of a personal analysis as part of their training. This is desirable when the analytic talent and funds are available.

Psychoanalysis is a therapeutic discipline of specific techniques which has as its goal a reliving of the significant and insignificant events in the development of the libido, the ego, and the superego functions. It has its greatest usefulness in the field of research in the psychodynamics of human behavior.

Where analytic talents are available, analysis is particularly useful in the obsessive compulsive neuroses, in the phobic or anxiety hysterias, and in the anxiety neuroses. In recent years we have also come to believe that analysis can be of great help in treating the schizophrenic patient, particularly in the early phases of his illness, and in treating depressed patients, either those mildly depressed or the more severely depressed ones, between attacks. It has proved to be a tremendous weapon in psychosomatic research and is of great value in treating properly selected psychosomatic disturbances. Research in the treatment of sexual deviations and criminal offenders offers hope that more will be learned about the pathology of crime. We now understand most of the sexual deviations. The modifications of analytic technique to bring about consistent therapeutic results is still a matter of study. At present certain cases respond favorably to prolonged and patient analysis.

Contraindication

Analysis should not be used when patients are overtly psychotic without modifications of the technique. These are less drastic than once thought, and further researches may indicate that the necessary variations in technique are less marked than was once believed.

The principal contraindication to analysis is a person whose reality situation is so difficult that the additional ego burden brought about by analysis might be more than he could bear and might precipitate a severe psychotic break. Again, with increasing skill and further knowledge of analytic techniques, the contraindications become fewer. It is, of course, unwise to attempt to carry out analysis in a person of advanced years or a person of limited ego or intellectual potential—not that an analysis would not benefit the individual, but it is a waste of the very limited number of analytic hours available in terms of the large number desired for therapy, research, and training.

Mechanism

The exact mechanism of analytic cure is not known but is an object of research. Gitelson says:

One of the as yet unsolved problems of psychoanalysis is concerned with the essential nature of psychoanalytic cure. It is not insight; it is not the recall of infantile neuroses; it is not cartharsis or abreaction; it is not the relationship to the analyst. Still, it is all of these in some synthesis which has not yet been possible to formulate explicitly. Somehow, in successful analysis, the patient matures in his total personality. Somehow a developmental process, which has been halted or sidetracked, resumes its course. It is as though the person reexperiencing his past in the transference, finds in the new conditions a second chance and redevelops while he is reliving.

In analysis emotions originally experienced are transferred to and relived in feelings for the analyst and vary substantially during the period of the analysis. With the study of these reactions as they are relived in feelings for the person of the analyst and an interpretation of their meaning and significance, the patient gains insight. This mental reliving and understanding of former experiences from an adult point of view, and their resolution in the person of the analyst, somehow brings about a basic change in the ego structure and a relief of the presenting symptoms. Analysis is a long, unpleasant, and arduous task. Great technical skill and training on the part of the analyst are necessary if the result is to be constructive rather than disastrous for the patient. It is not a field for amateurs.

Technique

The basic technique is that of free association. In most instances the treatment sessions are 50 minutes in length and are held five times weekly. Some analytic institutes experiment with 40- or 45-minute sessions held two or three times per week. However, such modifications seem to complicate rather than simplify the picture, although individual exceptions may be made.

Not only are patients asked to produce free associations but they are encouraged to bring to the analytic session dreams that develop during the course of treatment, as they offer clues to unconscious processes. Association to these dreams and analysis of them aids in resolving resistances. This method of dream analysis is quite different from interpreting dreams from a dreambook, and there are no valid generalizations concerning the significance of a particular dream, although some dreams seem to have a fairly consistent meaning from one patient to another.

The analytic technique as usually described, that is, the use of free association with the patient on a couch in 50-minute sessions five times a week, may be varied, particularly in the treatment of certain psychotic disorders.

It has been shown that work with schizophrenic patients sometimes demands a more informal setting for the analytic session. In fact, in some cases the analyst may join the patient sitting on the floor in a seclusion room during the initial interviews. As a technique and treatment develop, however, the patient may usually be brought to the physician's office for the continuation of therapy. In the analysis of children, play techniques and various other projective techniques are used along with the patter and chatter that goes on with the interpretation and the direct experiencing of the acting out between the analyst and the patient. Persons hated or feared are created and destroyed in effigy—in dolls or in illustrations. Conflicts are illustrated by words, fables, stories, or art work. Except in these two situations, the analytic therapy varies little whether the patient is a candidate for analytic training who is receiving a didactic and training analysis or whether he is a patient suffering from a neurosis or psychosomatic disturbance.

Combinations

Patients with certain psychosomatic disorders, such as coronary disease, psychosomatic diabetes, or psychosomatic allergic conditions, may be treated by their regular physician at the same time they are under analysis. This complicates the analysis but probably does not make treatment impossible, provided the other physician understands something of the analytic process and does not play too strongly into the patient's resistances. Institutionalized patients, in a hospital or prison, are also subjected to certain administrative routines which may either complicate or aid the analytic process. In recent years some persons have attempted to use a form of administrative psychotherapy in collaboration with the analysis as part of the over-all management of these patients. This seems to offer substantial benefits to some patients but it is still a matter of research. There is hope that the new drugs, particularly chlorpromazine and reserpine, given to psychotic patients may make more of them amenable to regular psychoanalytic techniques during the period of their psychosis.

Complications

With some patients, analysis lowers resistances of the ego and floods the consciousness with anxieties or awareness of certain conflict patterns that are unbearable. The usual result in such a case is to break off analysis and to run away from it as a form of resistance. Others, finding their resistances weakened, may commit suicide, and a rare patient regresses further into a full-blown psychosis.

There are certain misconceptions about psychoanalysis. Perhaps the most common is that psychoanalysis is all about sex and deals only with sexual conflicts. Another common misconception is that psychoanalysis condones sexual promiscuity. These are unfortunate misunderstandings arising out of early studies that involved, principally, sexual pathology. They are also due to a misunderstanding of the word *libido* and the meaning of sex drive as used in the broad sense in analytic literature. These misconceptions are further strengthened by the fact that a good many psychiatric symptoms are due to sexual conflict. This is not strange when the student considers that the world in which we live provides generously for opportunities for food and shelter and even gives social prestige to the individual who by aggression accumulates wealth and power. At the same time this same society places very strict rules on expression of the sexual drives. These rules are necessary because we are a monogamous people and because, owing to our educational and economic system, we postpone marriage until well after sexual maturity. Our religion sanctions sexual outlets only in marriage.

Another common false belief is that psychoanalysis is opposed to religion. This too is a misunderstanding. Psychoanalysts, being human, are of all races, colors, and religious creeds. Freud himself was of Jewish extraction and a free thinker. Among present-day analysts in the United States there are atheists, devout Catholics, Protestants, and Jews. The fact that some analytic papers discuss religious beliefs and their significance for certain patients has no more relevance to the acceptance or rejection of religion as a basic creed than the fact that a baseball bat may be a sexual symbol in the analysis of some patients (which bears no relevance to the fact that Ted Williams can make a home run with a bat or that a bartender may use one to allay his own anxieties on a boisterous Saturday night).

History of Psychoanalysis

Psychoanalysis was originated by Sigmud Freud, a Viennese. He was originally a research man interested much in neurology and neuroanatomy, and did some of the original research work on cocaine. He became interested in mental mechanisms after studying under Charcot who at that time used hypnotism in treating patients. Following this, Freud treated a hysteric patient, now famous in medical annals as *An Analysis of a Case of Hysteria,* but more familiarly referred to as "The Case of Anna O." Freud and his collaborator Joseph Breuer published an account of this and some other cases in 1893. Their concepts at first were met with disbelief and Breuer deserted the movement when Freud reported his observations on the manifestations of infantile sexuality.

After a turbulent beginning, the teaching of Freud and the development of psychoanalytic psychology have had a most significant influence on human thought. As in other new sciences, psychoanalytic theory has been modified from time to time as further observation and experience indicated changes in factual detail. The science continues to grow and expand. This has been true in other fields with growth and expansion, and the earlier pupils of Freud developed independent modifications of their own, most of which have gradually become accepted and incorporated in the over-all psychoanalytic theory.

In some instances, however, the theoretical concepts developed by the pupils differed in important fundamentals from the basic teachings of Freud, and new schools of thought were thus formed. Most notable among these new schools were those organized by Jung and Adler. While there are still a few proponents of these two schools of thought among psychiatrists, the majority of current analysts are Freudian.

Freudian teachings have spread into all phases of psychiatric teaching and into many of the social sciences. Even some of the so-called "non-analytic psychiatrists" embrace and use many Freudian concepts in their daily therapy with patients. Persons in the social sciences, particularly anthropology and sociology, have in many instances submitted Freudian tenets to careful testing. In most cases their study verified Freud's observations although there are exceptions. The influence of cultural forces on the personal development of the instincts is still incompletely understood and is the subject of much careful research. The day may come when impulses and emotions in human behavior are understood in terms of chemical and physiologic processes. It is theoretically possible that some day thought, emotion, love, and hate may be influenced by drugs or pills. At present, however, the analytic theories and facts as formulated by Freud are the most workable approach for handling the behavior aberrations of normal and sick human beings.

CHAPTER 28

Environmental Manipulation (Cultural Therapy, Social-pressure Therapy)

This chapter is separate from the group therapy chapter because it is believed that the methods to be described here are less well understood than the factors in the group process and because there are fundamental differences. In group therapy, while there is a group leader, the pressures on the patient are the direct interactions between him and the leader or between him and other members of the group.

In modern life, both inside and outside the hospital, there are certain social pressures. Outside the hospital they are known as government regulations, company policy, or shop rules, and in the hospital are known as administrative regulations. Here, the patient is reacting not to another individual or a group of individuals but to a depersonalized system which is enforced or carried out by other persons with whom he reacts. Much needs to be known about this particular form of influence and what effect it has on people. Stanton and Schwartz, Greenblatt, York, and Brown, and many others have discussed this. Many of the social studies in the hospitals are beginning to bring new information, and some of the social studies in industry and in the community in general throw further light on the subject. We are perhaps presumptuous in including these subjects with therapy in this edition because there is still not enough known to make this an easily described, prescribed, or administered therapy. Some things we do know, however.

Patients in a hospital do better if their attendants think they are administering treatment to the patients and the patients think they are receiving treatment. This "therapeutic attitude" has a definite, positive

335

effect on the patient whether the actual medium employed has any real pharmacologic or physical effect.

For example, one of us observed a spectacular improvement in a group of hospital patients who were administered a particular drug which was physiologically almost inert, but the physician, the attendants, and the patients all thought of it as therapy directed toward clearing up excreta carelessness, disrobing, and disturbed behavior, and it worked! Other patients in wards for the irritable and paranoid responded well to being assigned a responsibility for their own management in patient government with permissive supervision by the attendants and physician. The assessment of the value of some of the new drugs to be described in later chapters is rendered difficult by the fact that even an intrinsically worthless drug is known to be effective if administered to the patient in the right spirit! It affects both the morale of the patients and their attendants and has profound therapeutic effects.

Improving the morale and sense of status of the employees, particularly the nurses and attendants, does much to cut down disturbed activities on the part of the patient. We suspect, but know less about the fact, that cutting down on the disturbance among the patients does much for the élan and morale of the attendants, thus further improving the situation by lessening absenteeism and "sick-book time."

At present we think this type of treatment is useful in all kinds of group management of patients in a hospital. It is particularly useful among the continued-care patients, especially among the disturbed, dirty, and deteriorated. We suspect that much of the untidiness and deterioration of these patients is due to the environment in which we place them rather than to the illness from which they suffer. A great deal of further experiment and research are necessary in the management of these cases. It seems desirable to create a small village in which some of these patients could live, making their own rules, with the least restrictive type of city management carried on by the nurses and physicians. This is a project for the future, however, and not a proper subject for this text.

CHAPTER 29

Drug Therapy

At the time of this writing many new drugs that favorably influence psychiatric patients are being placed on the market. One hesitates to place in such a permanent reference source as a textbook any material on the use of drugs. The student will be given what seems to be the best knowledge available at this time but is urged to consult current literature for the latest innovations in the type of drugs and for information that may be available on complications due to prolonged use. We will discuss some of the promising ones at this time because their advent in the psychiatric picture has sharply changed the whole complexion of the staffing and operation of some of our larger hospitals.

Chlorpromazine

Chlorpromazine is the generic name for 10-(3-dimethylaminopropyl)-2-chlorphenothiazine hydrochloride. It is a synthetic compound first developed in Europe and its obvious therapeutic effect on patients with nausea and apprehension from the condition producing the nausea quickly led to its use in psychiatric disorders. Discussion here will concern only its use in psychiatric disorders.

Chlorpromazine is of great value with all types of psychiatric patients showing marked motor disturbance. It seems particularly effective in those cases whose disturbance is in response to hallucinatory and delusional activity. It has almost the same effect as a lobotomy and has the advantage of being reversible. Patients who suffer from hallucinations and delusions begin to react less to them and ignore them, and finally the hallucinations disappear. It has great usefulness in many forms of schizophrenia and in manic-depressive illness. Its effectiveness in depression is less clear cut but seems to be of value in depression showing a great deal

337

of anxiety and agitation. This is more commonly seen in the involutional than in the depressed phase of the manic-depressive patient. The drug is also of use with disturbed children, both those with psychoses manifest by overactivity and destructiveness, and in the so-called "organically driven" children. Chlorpromazine is of great value during the withdrawal symptoms of narcotic addiction and during the tremulous state of alcoholism, particularly when patients suffer from delirium tremens or a bad case of the alcoholic "shakes" with nausea.

Patients with organic disorder, particularly disturbed and agitated senile patients, do well on chlorpromazine and become much more tractable. It is our belief that many of these patients could be kept home if the drug were prescribed early enough.

In none of these cases is the drug believed to cure the illness; it rather controls the behavior so that psychotherapy or other methods of treatment can be made much more effective.

Chlorpromazine is also being used in large quantities in outpatient clinics and in private offices for the treatment of anxious, tense patients. Whether this use of the drug makes it easier for the patients to benefit from psychotherapy or whether the relief of the anxiety makes them ignore deeper treatment is a matter about which we have little information at the moment since most of its use is uncontrolled in terms of the collection of statistics. The reports of physicians using it are, for the most part, enthusiastic, with here and there a sharp contrary opinion. However, it is not altogether clear whether the use of this drug with outpatients has any advantage over phenobarbital, other than the fact that it is new and different.

At the moment one can say that the drug is of great value in the treatment of psychotic patients, particularly the disturbed ones, for almost any of the reaction types, and it has probable value in the treatment of anxious, tense neurotic patients. There is urgent need for more careful research in the latter group.

Contraindications. In a small percentage of cases the drug produces an obstructive type of jaundice. For this reason it should not be used in patients with cirrhosis of the liver or other evidence of liver disease. We feel it is of little use in the retarded, withdrawn, underactive patients. Some authors believe it complicates these symptoms. Because the drug is a potent one and tends to produce complications in some patients, it should be used only under close medical supervision.

Mechanism of Action. Exact mechanism of the action of chlorpromazine is not known in so far as it brings about improvement in the mental state. The drug acts on the midbrain and in its action apparently cuts down on the patient's autonomic and general emotional response to the symptoms of his illness. This relieving of the patient's symptoms apparently makes him more tractable and makes him able to communicate with the other patients and with the personnel on the ward. It seems that by controlling the midbrain impulses it relieves the cortex, perhaps keeps the ego from using all its energy combating the anxiety, thus leaving more energy available for adaptation and forming contacts with persons of significance in the environment. More work needs to be done in this area.

Techniques. Chlorpromazine comes in two forms: preparations for intramuscular injection and a preparation for oral administration. Intramuscular injection should be confined to those patients who are so disturbed and uncooperative that oral medication is impossible. In most cases, after approximately 24 to 48 hours on intramuscular injection—sometimes after only one injection—the patient is cooperative enough to take the drug by mouth. Authors vary substantially in the amount of the drug given; most agree that the patient should be started on approximately 150 mg per day given in three or four doses. The initial intramuscular dose is usually 50 mg and is repeated each 6 to 8 hours. If after 24 hours the patient is still not responding to the drug, the intramuscular dose may be increased to 75 or 100 mg every 6 to 8 hours. The oral doses are usually started at 25 or 50 mg (usually the latter), also at 6- to 8-hour intervals. The dosage is usually increased if the patient fails to respond in 3 to 8 days. Most physicians now run the dose up more rapidly than before, and it is generally believed that the dose should be pushed until some symptomatic relief is obtained. Daily doses of 500 to 1,000 mg are not unusual and Kinross Wright reported doses of over 4,000 mg in 24 hours. In our experience the average patient who responds favorably to the drug will do so on a daily dose not exceeding about 600 to 1,000 mg in 24 hours, although some go as high as 1,500 mg.

In our opinion, the use of chlorpromazine should be combined with an active ward program and, as the patient begins to show signs of improvement, psychotherapy, either on an individual or group basis, should be available. In crowded wards where this is impossible, other types of group activities such as occupational therapy, singing, team work, and other forms of rehabilitation must be instituted if the full value of the drug is to be exploited. Also, we believe that patients who are to have this medication who are on a disturbed and wet ward should be moved from that ward since continuing their care in such surroundings cannot conceivably do them any good. It has also become increasingly practical to place patients who are to have chlorpromazine into one section of the hospital so that the whole section is under treatment at one time and all of them may be exposed to the same group activities and other rehabilitation measures. This group-medication approach is not fully worked out but probably offers the best opportunity for the effective use of this particular drug in poorly staffed hospitals.

Obviously in smaller hospitals or in treating patients in a more individualized way, both the dose of drug and the management of the patient on the drug will show substantial individual variation. In large hospitals with masses of patients, some modifications will be necessary, and the above-mentioned group approach is probably the most desirable one.

Combinations. In our experience chlorpromazine alone is often very effective. In a limited number of patients, particularly very agitated, involutional patients and in some overactive, disturbed schizophrenic patients, chlorpromazine combined with electric shock therapy is much more effective than either modality used alone. In our opinion all patients on chlorpromazine should have psychotherapy, either of the individual or group type. Recreational therapy and other group activities are also desirable for these patients at times other than their therapeutic sessions. One of us has also attempted to combine chlorpromazine with some of the other drugs but has found little to be gained from this, and in some cases it seemed that the results were less satisfactory than with chlorpromazine or with one of the other drugs alone.

Complications. As with all potent drugs there are complications to chlorpromazine. The only serious one is an occasional case of agranulocytosis. It is our practice to have patients who are on chlorpromazine have a weekly blood count, at least during the initial phases. If they show no sensitivity to the drug, later the blood-count examination may be dropped to once or twice a month. In our opinion patients should have frequent checks of the blood count as long as they are on the drug. Not all authorities agree with this. It has been our experience that if the beginning shift in the white count is noted and the drug is stopped, the patient inevitably recovers spontaneously. There have been deaths from agranulocytosis with this drug.

One of the more spectacular complications is the development of jaundice. This jaundice is of an obstructive type and in our experience rapidly subsides when the drug is withdrawn. Some persons have been placed again on the drug and apparently tolerate it without recurrence of the jaundice. It has been our practice, however, in most cases to shift to one of the other drugs when this complication develops.

Some patients are reported to develop photosensitization, and in these cases the drug should be withdrawn. If the patients are again treated with it, they should be kept out of the sun. The cases reported occurred principally in the South and during the summer.

An occasional case will develop a parkinson-like syndrome from this drug. It is more common with one of the other new drugs but does occur with chlorpromazine. This complication seems to occur when patients are on a higher dosage. All these complications are so rare that one need not fear using the drug, but should use it with adequate medical supervision.

Reserpine

Reserpine is a crystalline alkaloid of the *Rauwolfia serpina* root. This drug was first developed for lowering blood pressure in hypertension but was found to have a tranquilizing effect on psychiatric and neurotic patients. This has led to a great spread in its use in psychiatric disorders. This drug in parenteral and oral solutions is used in approximately the same types of patients as chlorpromazine. Parallel experience with the two drugs indicates that sometimes one works better than the other in a given patient. Reserpine is of great value to many patients. It is useful in patients who show disturbed behavior from any one of the functional or organic psychiatric disorders and is of value in patients with anxiety and tension states.

Contraindications. Reserpine may be safely used for all patients except those with hypotension. Since it has a depressing effect on the blood pressure, marked hypotensive effects from use of the drug should be carefully controlled, and if they are too severe reserpine should be discontinued. Since this drug tends to produce parkinson-like symptoms in many patients who take it, reserpine probably should not be used in those patients already showing evidence of parkinsonism on the basis of post-encephalitic or arteriosclerotic changes. There has been no work on this, and perhaps subsequent editions will modify this statement.

Mechanism of Action. Reserpine apparently works on the midbrain. Some studies demonstrate that it inhibits the action of serotonin in the brain (see Chapter 3). The psychologic response is not fully understood. Apparently there is a loss of hostile and aggressive behavior as a defense. A few patients show emotional lability. Some patients are reported to be more disorganized in an emotional sense and produce a groping, immature type of emotional contact with persons around them.

It would appear that in this preparation, as with chlorpromazine, the patient's reliance on his psychotic symptoms or his uncooperative behavior as a mechanism of defense is reduced by this drug, and apparently the drug allays some of the push of anxiety by its midbrain effect. This relief of the patient's ego makes it possible to use more of his energy in functions that promote constructive contacts with persons around him.

Much further study needs to be done in this area as the psychologic concomitants of the physiologic effects of these drugs are not well known; but we believe that to exploit fully the use of these drugs, such concomitants should be studied in great detail.

Technique. Most persons use 2.5 mg of reserpine intramuscularly or intravenously, the latter method reserved for those patients showing marked disturbance in behavior. Patients not reacting to this dosage are then boosted to approximately 5 mg daily. Patients who can cooperate in taking the drug by mouth are started on about 1.5 to 2 mg per day with the dose increased to 4 to 8 mg per day, depending on the over-all physiologic and psychologic effects of the drug on the patient. As with chlorpromazine, further experience tends to bring increasing dosage and the student is advised to consult the current literature as to the advised doses of these drugs.

More cooperative patients placed on reserpine should be informed that in the initial stages the drug sometimes produces a certain feeling of depression and of fullness in the nose, much like coryza or an attack of hay fever. While this goes unnoted in most of the disturbed psychotic patients, psychoneurotic patients and more cooperative persons complain about this discomfort and sometimes do not desire to continue with the drug. In acutely disturbed schizophrenic or manic patients, an initial intramuscular or intravenous dose may produce quieting of the symptoms. The change from a difficult nursing problem to a cooperating patient is produced in a matter of 2 to 3 hours.

Variations. Reserpine is given in small doses, 0.5 to 1 mg once to three times per day, and is prescribed for some psychoneurotic patients on an outpatient basis. It has also been reportedly used in certain obsessive patients and others showing much anxiety and tension in response to environmental events. There are a few as yet unauthenticated reports that some of these latter groups of patients when placed on reserpine developed depressive feelings. The drug should not be used without close medical supervision. The claimed advantages of this drug over phenobarbital for use in outpatients are still unsupported by research. There can be no doubt at this time that it is a useful drug for hospitalized patients, particularly those suffering with psychotic disorders that produce major behavior disturbances or major hallucinatory and delusional content with anxiety and suffering.

Combinations. There are reports of the combination of reserpine with electric shock therapy. However, more recent reports indicate that this may be hazardous, and one cannot recommend it at this writing. It is possible that further experience will show that these fatal results have been coincidental. The student should consult the current literature concerning the advisability of this particular combination. We have in some cases used this drug in combination with chlorpromazine but are not prepared to say that the combination of the two offers any advantage over the use of either alone.

Complications. Many of the patients placed on reserpine complain of feelings of discomfort, fullness or stuffiness in the head, and other symptoms not unlike those of an acute attack of hay fever or the onset of a cold. This does not necessitate withdrawal of the drug. A few patients will develop a skin rash, and the drug should be withdrawn temporarily when this happens. A limited number of patients develop signs of parkinsonism. This is probably an indication that the drug has reached the therapeutic level, and reduction in dosage usually results in prompt clearing up of the symptom. The only drastic effect of this drug is that in some patients it produces a sharp hypotension with a resulting potential for the development of thrombosis. It is probably advisable to withdraw this drug in patients on whom it has a marked hypotensive effect. Unauthenticated reports state that in some patients with neuroses, depressive symptoms result from exhibition of the drug. It is probable that further experience will show that this actually was misdiagnosed; that the patient was in the early phases of depression and that the disease progressed in spite of the drug rather than developed because of it. All patients on reserpine should receive psychotherapy and the benefits of ward activity. It is not believed that this drug exercises its full potentialities alone but rather that the use of the drug makes patients more susceptible and amenable to other forms of psychiatric and rehabilitation routines.

Meratran

This is a trade name for α-(2-piperidyl) benzhydrochloride. Meratran has been used much less widely than chlorpromazine and reserpine. It was first used as treatment for narcolepsy. It has also been reported of use in depressive patients and apparently works as a central nervous system stimulant. The usual dose is 2.5 mg two or three times a day. Some patients cannot take this much and in others the dose must be increased. In some depressed patients as much as 15 mg per day has been used. At least one author states that it combats sluggishness and lethargy which are seen in patients on chlorpromazine and reserpine. In our experience the cerebral stimulants have inhibited the effectiveness of chlorpromazine, but further experience may show that some combination of these drugs is valuable.

Frenquel

This is a trade name for α-(4-piperidyl) benzhydrol hydrochloride, a drug closely related to Meratran.

It has been reported by Fabing that it blocks the psychoses produced by lysergic acid (LSD-25). It has been reported to produce desirable changes in behavior in chronically disturbed hospitalized psychotic patients. Experience with Frenquel and Meratran is limited at this time. The student is advised to consult the current literature to see what its later development may be. As of this writing, it would appear that these two drugs have particular value in depressive patients of the milder sort. The drugs seem to be freer of complications but less effective than chlorpromazine and reserpine in disturbed and delusional patients. There are some reports on the value of the drug in disturbed psychotic patients, but we need further research to fully evaluate its usefulness.

Barbituric Acid Derivatives

These drugs come under the general heading of sedative drugs but are of great use in psychiatric disorders. The most common use of these drugs is to produce sleep or to allay tension and anxiety in an acute period of stress. Care in the use of these drugs is required because many patients develop habituation to them. However, for patients who have an acute period of stress or need a crutch for a few days to modify their sleep pattern, they are safer, simpler, and cheaper than some of the more potent compounds mentioned above. The drugs have a different action in that they cut down cortical function rather than act on the autonomic system and therefore they have usefulness in a different group of disorders. Theoretically they should be used to cut down a patient's reaction to environmental or personal situational states that are conscious in origin, temporary in nature, and modifiable. An exception to this is the use of phenobarbital as one of the forms of therapy for grand mal epilepsy. It still remains one of the basic drugs in the treatment of this disorder.

Pentothal Sodium or Amytal Sodium may be used in psychotherapy to aid patients in association or in the discussion of basic problems with the physician where anxieties, blockings, or more conscious inhibitions prevent this. In older editions of this text we also relied heavily on the barbiturate acid series for the production of sleep treatment. With the advent of the modern drugs we doubt the feasibility of using sleep treatment in modern psychiatric practice. For that reason it will not be included in this edition of the text. A modification of sleep treatment with Pentothal Sodium is of great value in the treatment of tetanus but the proper place for the discussion of this is a textbook of neurology or internal medicine. The use of intravenous Amytal or Pentothal Sodium is recommended to induce sleep quickly, safely, and for a period of several hours, for patients under acute environmental stress whose anxiety is mounting to panic-like proportion. This use may be most valuable in military and civilian disasters.

CHAPTER 30

Shock Therapies (Electroconvulsive, Insulin, Convulsive)

Electroconvulsive Treatment (Electric Shock Treatment)

This form of shock therapy is commonly administered by stimulation of the cortex with an electrical apparatus with electrodes which fit on the skull. The goal of the stimulation is to produce sufficient motor area excitation to produce a grand mal seizure. Prior to the development of electric apparatus the same results were produced by the intravenous injection of Metrazol.

Indication. The principal indication for ECT (electroconvulsive treatment) is in psychotic depressions of such severity that suicide or physical depletion is a hazard. It is also very helpful in agitated depressions in which the patient becomes suicidal or so agitated that there is danger that he will develop physical exhaustion from overactivity and lack of nutrition. Electroshock therapy was formerly used in treating disturbed and overactive patients in both the schizophrenic and the manic reactions but it is now believed that the newer drugs, particularly chlorpromazine or reserpine, are preferable for this purpose. Some cases respond well to a combination of chlorpromazine and ECT.

Contraindication. Electroshock therapy may be used for almost any patient in which it is indicated by the patient's clinical condition. Patients with marked skeletal decalcification or with unhealed fractures should not have electroshock therapy. It was formerly believed that cardiac pathology, tuberculosis, and other chronic disorders contraindicated shock therapy, but with proper supervision by the internist most patients with these can be treated if the motor agitation and anxiety complicate the organic picture sufficiently to justify the extra hazard.

346

We do not know why ECT works. Apparently somehow, a combination of physiologic and psychologic reaction to the convulsive treatment produces profound changes in the ego's defense system. Whether these changes are primarily chemical, physiologic, or psychologic is by no means clear. One leans to the physiologic theories, but this is based on rationalization and not facts. The treatment does work in severe depressions and in the involutional reactions. It also helps some patients suffering from schizophrenia.

Technique. The technique is simple but should be adapted to the individual case. There are several acceptable devices on the market for administering electric shock treatment. Most psychiatric centers have physicians using treatment of this type daily. Basically the technique consists of applying skull electrodes of various types, generally over the motor area, usually 3 to 5 cm in diameter. The electrodes are ordinarily applied with some type of electrode jelly, always ensuring that they are applied snugly to the scalp. With some types of apparatus some physicians recommend stimulation of one side of the head only, but most use a bilateral technique. Resistance may be measured to make sure contact is adequate. The strength of the stimulus is then adjusted according to a predetermined figure calculated by estimating the voltage, amperage, and duration of the stimulus required to produce a convulsion. There will be substantial variations in what is required in an individual patient, and the current must be adjusted for each case.

There are many types of machines on the market. In some apparatus ("shock box") the amperage is variable, and in others the voltage is variable; in some, both may be varied. Most of the machines are unidirectional in current but the form of the wave of current varies from one machine to another. Each manufacturer claims certain advantages for his particular type of apparatus. Some persons working with shock treatment feel that the Glissando technique produces less postshock confusion than others, but this type of treatment is also less comfortable for the patient because he feels a shock unless anesthetized. With the standard electric shock, no electric current is felt by the patient. After receiving basic instructions in the use of the apparatus, the physician is advised to select the one best suited to him and his practice, or to use more than one type of machine for various cases if his practice and use of shock therapy are large.

The basic technique used varies among physicians, but often the patient is placed in the hyperextended position, usually with a small pillow or roll under the dorsal spine. The patient responds to the shock with short clonic, tonic, and longer clonic phases of the convulsion, followed by a period of apnea. The patient then begins to breathe deeply and regularly although the respiratory response following electric treatment is not quite so prompt as when Metrazol is used. Many physicians use variations in the technique to adapt the patient to the treatment. These variations are of two types: (1) to reduce the initial anxiety of the patient to the treatment and to reduce any consciousness of pain or discomfort during the treatment; and (2) to modify the convulsion so that incidence of fractures and dislocations that may occur with unmodified convulsions may be decreased. Allaying the patient's anxiety and possible discomfort may involve preshock medication, usually one of the quick-acting barbitals. Some centers use some type of group recreational activity to divert the patient's attention.

Perhaps the commonest modification and certainly the most effective is intravenous Pentothal Sodium, or some variation, just before the patient goes into the shock room. This is administered to the point of sleep or light anesthesia. The patient, at the time of awakening, has had a shock treatment and the postshock nausea that may occur in some cases will have passed. If this modification is to be used, it is safest to have it administered by a person trained in anesthesiology. At any rate, the physician using it should work with persons experienced in the use of the intravenous anesthetic until he is thoroughly adept in its use.

Modifications to cut down the number of postshock complications started with the use of curare in the form of Intocostrin. There are now available on the market a large number of synthetics which may be used to decrease the severity of the muscular reaction. Most effective is Anectine. This drug is almost always used in conjunction with Pentothal Sodium, and is given to the point of respiratory paralysis, respiration being maintained by means of anesthetic machine and tracheal intubation. The attendance of a skilled anesthetist or physician trained in the use of intratracheal resuscitation is essential before this technique is used. Some centers use this routinely; most confine it to those patients showing enough skeletal decalcification to make the possibility of fracture during the convulsion great enough to warrant this use. This technique is ideal for the severe case. It is our opinion that it is not necessary to use such complete modification of the seizure in all patients. Some of the other synthetic preparations with curare-like action are reasonably safe and may be administered intravenously to the point that the patient develops a ptosis or inability to raise his head. At this moment shock should be given. The patient will have a definite seizure and the incidence of fractures will be negligible. Very few of these patients require resuscitation but resuscitation apparatus should be available. Physicians should not attempt the use of shock therapy until they have been thoroughly trained in the use of the type they choose.

Frequency of Treatment. Standard treatment by electric shock therapy is three times per week for the ordinary acute depression. Very disturbed and agitated patients may be given daily or twice-daily treatments for four or five times and then treated three times per week. It is also customary to decrease the frequency of treatment as the patient improves. Most depressive patients will respond in ten to twenty treatments; some in much less. Schizophrenic patients and very severe involutional patients may require more, but ordinarily not more than forty are required. Some schizophrenic patients who are chronically disturbed and overactive may be carried on electric shock once every 10 days to 2 weeks, some as infrequently as once per month, with good results.

It is our belief that these same patients may be handled with chlorpromazine or reserpine on a continuing basis. The treatment with these drugs, potent as they are, is safer than with shock treatment. In spite of its drastic nature, electric shock treatment is relatively safe, and, when properly administered and properly controlled, shows a mortality rate of less than 1 per cent.

The principle complication is a compression fracture of the body of the thoracic vertebra and occasionally a fracture of the femur or the head of the humerus. Proper modification of the treatment and proper technique during administration can reduce these complications.

Many patients develop marked confusion and forgetfulness after they have had several treatments. These organic signs are often concomitant with the beginning improvement in the patient's psychiatric syndrome, but if they become too severe, the frequency of treatment should be decreased or treatment discontinued for a short time. It is our policy to advise the patient and his family that such memory disturbances may be expected during the treatment and that they are usually transitory and reversible as treatment is discontinued. Electric shock therapy may be combined with insulin coma therapy to advantage in certain schizophrenic disorders.

METRAZOL THERAPY

Metrazol has the same indications as electroconvulsive treatment. It was the first form of convulsive treatment used. The technique here is the same as for electroconvulsive treatment except that 3 to 4 ml of a freshly prepared 10% aqueous solution of Metrazol is injected by vein as rapidly as possible using 12-gage needle and large syringe. The convulsion follows very rapidly after the injection so that in these cases the mouth gag is placed in the patient's mouth prior to the intravenous injection. We prefer electric shock to Metrazol treatment because the Metrazol produces a sensory aura which is fear-producing. Patients describe the aura as "lightning flashes," or "streaks of fire before the eyes," and occasionally an auditory aura of loud noises or explosions is experienced. These sensations frighten the patients, and make the treatment less effective. The aura can be avoided by the use of intravenous Pentothal Sodium prior to treatment.

PRESHOCK WORK-UP

In our opinion the patient should have a complete physical and laboratory examination before treatment. This should include an electrocardiogram as well as routine blood studies. Patients should be very carefully examined to rule out the evidence of any type of intracranial pathology, especially neoplasm, since convulsions in such patients may result in fatality. Patients with a history of automobile accidents or patients who have participated in contact sports during their childhood or adolescence should have x-rays of the spine. A surprising number of people will show evidence of old incomplete compression fractures that they did not know existed. If the patient develops a backache during treatment, check x-rays may reveal this, and it may be erroneously assumed to be due to the treatment.

Patients showing cardiac pathology or metabolic pathology such as hypertension, urinary retention, diabetes, or infectious diseases such as tuberculosis or arthritis should have a medical consultation. A decision to use shock therapy in such cases would be based on whether the mental symptoms were causing complications to recovery from the physical disorder. If the patient is recovering from the physical disorder in spite of the mental illness, we postpone the shock treatment until physical recovery is completed.

Pregnancy sometimes presents a complication to treatment, but in our experience the pregnancy, up to the sixth or seventh month, does not present a contraindication to shock therapy. Needless to say, an obstetrician should be consulted and should participate in the management of the patient between shock periods. Shock therapy in a pregnant woman should be used only if the patient is suicidal or very agitated so as to be presenting a hazard to her own life as well as that of the fetus. Since we recommend shock therapy only in such cases anyway, this problem will not often arise. With physicians using shock for milder cases, it would be best to postpone the shock treatment pending delivery of the infant.

Insulin Coma (or Hypoglycemic Shock)

Insulin coma has been a very satisfactory form of treatment of the schizophrenic disorders. Insulin subshock with intravenous drip of glucose and thiamine has been used in the treatment of delirium tremens, and subshock alone in the treatment of anxiety neuroses and mild depressions. The use of hypoglycemic coma is usually confined to the treatment of the schizophrenic disorders.

Insulin shock has been used on many patients and over a long period so that data are available on the follow-up result of schizophrenia. Bond and his coworkers report that on 780 patients treated between 1936 and 1951, 63.3 per cent originally improved had a relapse, 44 per cent of their relapses occurring within 30 days of the termination of treatment and 78 per cent within 1 year of treatment. A second insulin course brought about an improvement or a remission in 52 per cent of those who relapsed. Of the patients followed within the first 5 years of treatment, 85 per cent showed a capacity for improvement, 67 per cent having responded to insulin and 18 per cent to additional hospital therapy following failure of insulin. Only 15 per cent remained continuously psychotic during the first 5 follow-up years. The authors state, "It is clear that insulin coma treatment is an effective agent in altering the immediate outlook in schizophrenia. The long-term picture is not so bright. On the basis of the high relapse rate it is evident that insulin coma therapy does not produce permanent resistance to schizophrenia even though in a few of our cases it appears to have done so." They point out that insulin may only bring the patient to a prepsychotic level, but prolonged and intensive psychotherapy is necessary in order to have the patient achieve "a correction of the internal factors that predispose these persons to regress to psychosis." They emphasize that insulin has the advantage of making patients more accessible to psychotherapy and does not interfere with it. Insulin coma therefore accomplishes somewhat the same thing chlorpromazine and reserpine accomplish. Whether these newer drugs, which are simpler and cheaper to use, will replace insulin coma therapy cannot be determined at this time. It is our belief that they will, because an unlimited number of patients can be placed on the drug depending on the availability of therapeutic personnel to deal with the patient during his period of accessibility.

Because the future status of insulin is still uncertain at this time, we shall repeat in this edition the description of the techniques for its use. In our experience this method should not be used until mastered in some hospital using this type of treatment. There are reports in the literature advising the use of this treatment in the home. We believe this is unwise.

Insulin coma therapy is arduous, and dangerous in unskilled hands. It is not suited to office or home administration and should be given only in well-equipped modern hospitals. It should be administered by a central insulin service or department within the hospital where all the personnel are trained in managing these cases. The patient should have a complete physical check including laboratory procedures, such as electrocardiogram, chest x-ray, and complete blood-chemistry studies. Persons showing evidence of metabolic disturbance, pulmonary infection, or myocardial damage should be rejected for this form of therapy. In addition to the careful routine history and mental-status examination, the Rorschach test, association test, motor test, and certain of the thinking-disorder tests are indicated in order to check on improvement. Administration of the shock in trained hands is not complicated.

1. Treatments are administered daily, except for one rest day each week. On this day insulin, 15 units, is given.

2. On the evening before treatment, patients are given a light supper at 5:30 P.M. and no food until after the shock period the following day.

3. "Old" or ordinary insulin is given, with an initial intramuscular dose of 15 units. The dose is increased 10 to 20 units per day until the patient reaches a stage of somnolence, profuse perspiration, or muscular twitching. The dose is then increased 5 to 10 units daily until a deep-shock phase is reached. Protamine zinc and similar insulins are unsatisfactory for these treatments.

4. In the deep-shock phase the daily dosage remains constant until the clinical course of the shock indicates an increase or decrease in the dose. The depth of the shock bears little relation to the dose of insulin in the series of cases; patients show varying degrees of sensitivity to the medication. Some will go into shock on 1,000 units; others on 25. In any individual case the depth of shock is roughly proportional to the initial dose but the total dose varies. Ordinarily, after the patient is well in shock, the dose can be progressively reduced until sometimes amazingly small doses are sufficient to maintain the patient in coma. The depth of shock can be judged and controlled only by the clinical findings.

The stages of the shock are as follows:

1. The preshock phase: the patient is somnolent; can be aroused. In the later stages of this phase, the patient may show sweating or mild myoclonic twitchings. In the early phases of this stage patients tend to arouse spontaneously after 30 to 60 minutes of somnolence. They may be rather confused. Termination is made by permitting the patient to drink a sugar solution until he ingests approximately 2 gm of sugar/unit of insulin dose. Some patients take this in orange juice, some centers administer fudge,

and some use other types of sweetened drinks. This phase is also referred
to as insulin "subshock" and is the type used to stimulate appetites in
neurotic and mildly depressed patients and is used to treat alcoholics and
drug addicts with withdrawal symptoms. In our opinion this use of insulin
was useful, but the newer drugs work better.

2. The shock phase: the majority of patients show *wet shock*. Perspiration is profuse, the pulse is rapid and thready, the temperature drops, the
heart sounds are mushy, the blood pressure is 80–90/60–70. The skin is
pale, wet, and cold. Respirations are deep and stertorous. There is usually
profuse salivation with drooling; the patient should be restrained in a sitting position or on his side to prevent aspiration of the saliva. In this stage
the patients are in a deep coma. The tendon reflexes are hyperactive; ankle
and patellar clonus is present; corneal reflexes are abolished and the cough
reflex is usually absent. Pathologic toe and thumb signs are elicited. After
approximately 1 to 2 hours, perspiration decreases and the skin becomes
dry. The usual time of termination is after approximately 1 hour of shock.
The patient is given 2 gm of sugar per unit of insulin dose, as a 50% sugar
solution; this is administered by means of a stomach tube inserted through
the nose. In some centers patients receive 50 ml of 50% glucose intravenously. When they arouse, they drink the remainder of the preparation.
Some patients fail to perspire and are said to be in *dry shock*. The signs
are essentially the same as those listed above, except that the perspiration
and salivation are less marked. In dry shock many persons show myoclonic
twitchings, and an occasional patient will have a tonic-clonic convulsion.
In our practice we terminate the shock session after a convulsion but very
often the patient terminates it himself by the seizure. In our opinion this
is not a contraindication to continuing shock therapy. We believe that the
shock phase is essential for therapeutic results in schizophrenia.

Combinations. In all cases psychotherapy should be available for the
patient in the between-shock portion of the day. This should be individual
where possible, but at least in groups, and the patient should be encouraged to participate in group, recreational, and occupational therapy sessions. Patients who are very disturbed and agitated are sometimes given
electric shock therapy two or three times a week. It is our policy to administer the electric convulsion after the administration of intravenous
glucose to terminate the insulin shock.

Complications. Complications are infrequent in properly conducted
departments. Convulsions may occur in any insulin reaction at any time.
They are usually self-limited, and the shock may be terminated by the
usual method after they subside. If the convulsions persist, the treatment
should be terminated by intravenous glucose in 50% solution. Cardiac or

respiratory collapse may occur but this is infrequent. The administration of 50% glucose intravenously, epinephrine 3 to 6 minims intravenously, and oxygen inhalations usually restore these functions in short order.

The most serious complication is prolonged or persistent coma. If the patient fails to respond within 30 minutes after the gastric gavage, he should receive intravenous glucose in 50% solution. If this fails to bring about a prompt reaction, that is, within 2 to 3 minutes, it is our practice to introduce, by venoclysis, 1,000 ml of 10% glucose in Ringer's solution. If the patient shows any tendency to hyperpyrexia, 1,000 ml of whole blood as a transfusion is also administered. In our opinion the prompt use of whole blood by transfusion will usually promptly terminate prolonged coma. The adrenal cortical hormones also have a profound effect on reversing the trend in prolonged insulin coma. The physician should recognize that prolonged coma can result in death, and the more rapidly the whole blood and the adrenal cortical hormones are exhibited, the more rapidly may one expect recovery and the lower will be the mortality rate. Complications such as aspiration pneumonia and pulmonary edema are avoided by careful nursing care during the shock phase.

Duration of Treatment. The treatment is usually continued from 30 to 60 shocks, depending on the clinical course of the patient.

Carbon Dioxide (CO_2) Treatment

Carbon dioxide inhalation to the point of unconsciousness has been used as a type of shock therapy. It was recommended by Meduna. It has also been used in modification by others as a form of abreaction treatment. There is a great difference of opinion about the effectiveness of this treatment, and psychiatrists fall into two groups: those who are enthusiastic about it and those who reject it completely.

A brief discussion will be presented here and the student can draw his own conclusions. We have had little success with it. Meduna reports that it is of benefit in the treatment of character neuroses, including alcoholism, overt passive homosexuality, chronic inferiority feelings, neurotic depression, anxiety neuroses, phobias, irritability and tension symptoms, stuttering, female frigidity, and obscure skin reactions of the psychosomatic types. The mechanism of the treatment is not known. Meduna believes it is an organic approach to the problem of the psychoneuroses, but states, "It is extremely difficult to construct a harmonious picture of the above-mentioned changes that could be correlated either with the fact of psychoneurosis or the clinical improvement produced by CO_2." He concludes that a psychoneurotic patient's brain is hyperirritable and does not balance the energy demands with the oxidative processes or that there is a disturbance in the distribution of the oxidative process. He also believes that there is a disturbance in the interaction of the pituitary, adrenal, and thyroid glands, and perhaps others. He feels that somehow CO_2 rectifies these disturbances.

Miscellaneous

Many other preparations have been used to produce shock or shocklike states in mentally disturbed patients. Examples of these preparations are malononitrile and lysergic acid which produce a toxic psychosis; controlled nitrogen inhalations which produce unconsciousness and convulsions; picrotoxin which produces convulsions; and many other compounds devised by the ingenuity of man. None of these seems to possess any particular advantages over the more standard shock treatments. The student interested in them is referred to the library where literature is available.

CHAPTER 31

Miscellaneous Treatments

Surgical Treatment

Prefrontal lobotomy, leukotomy, transorbital leukotomy, topectomy, cauterization of the thalamic nuclei, damage induced by ultrasonic waves, and variations of these surgical assaults on the brain have been advocated for chronic schizophrenic patients and certain other chronic psychiatric disorders. These treatments offer some hope for paranoid or assaultive patients who fail to respond to other forms of treatment after prolonged and intensive therapy. We believe that these operations should be looked upon much as an amputation is looked upon in surgery. At times they make the patient's life more tolerable; may make him happier in an institution or perhaps even enable him to return to the environment in a limited capacity. They always leave crippling defects which may or may not incapacitate the patient, depending on the severity of the operation and the complexity of the environment to which he must return.

In our opinion surgery is indicated only as a last resort in certain patients with involutional reactions who fail to recover. Some authorities recommend it for use in patients with an obsessive compulsive neurosis of an incapacitating degree who do not respond to psychotherapy of the psychoanalytic sort. We do not recommend this treatment in such patients. The basic operation was developed by Moniz, a Portuguese neurosurgeon. Its use was further expanded in this country, principally under the stimulation of Walter Freeman.

Mechanism of Action. Theoretically speaking, as was pointed out by Solomon and his coworkers, leukotomy reduces the function of cells and circuits in the frontal lobes, thus decreasing impulse energy and temporal delay. This means that the patient will perhaps lose drive. He will be less

356

affected by past experience and more conscious of immediate stimuli and he will be less able to elaborate experiences and to sustain them. In a neurosis or a psychosis where the symptoms are increased by any of these three factors, a lobotomy may be expected to bring about improvement.

In a detailed study of patients, it was found that hostility decreased after a lobotomy and that in patients given the bimedial cingulate operation, the release of tensions or anxiety permitted greater spontaneity. The patients showed an upward shift in emotional capacity and a marked reduction in belligerency and impulsiveness. They improved in their community or social adjustment. Psychoanalytic observation of some of these patients by Zetzel indicated that the long-term results of the lobotomy could be accounted for in terms of a quantitative defect; that is, in the dynamic restriction of the ego boundaries. All this boils down to the fact that the patients' psychologic function is simpler. Their behavior is more determined by stimuli from their immediate environment and their experience is less individualized. They seem to function more freely because tension is not diverted by anxiety-induced interruptions.

Technique. The techniques of surgery vary, as indicated in the introductory paragraph. The surgery should be done by skillful neurologic surgeons. Only transorbital lobotomies are performed by other than a neurosurgeon. We do not recommend these blind operations.

In general the operation that produces the least damage to the brain and still produces results would be the one most desirable. At the moment the fulguration of certain thalamic nuclei and the bicingulate sectioning seem to be the preferred operations.

We believe it is extremely important that these patients be integrated into an extensive psychotherapeutic and environmental rehabilitation program after the operation. One suspects that these patients who will live with limited capacity following the operation can adapt if sufficient time and effort are spent on rehabilitation and psychotherapeutic efforts. It is illogical to expect a patient who could not adjust to a given environment with an intact brain to do better in that same environment with a brain that has been damaged. Little will have been accomplished if the patient who formerly responded to an unsatisfactory environment with belligerence and anxiety, after being deprived of this form of defense by a lobotomy, regresses into a vegetable sitting in a corner.

Combinations. Some patients who respond incompletely to lobotomy subsequently do fairly well on chlorpromazine, and some patients get along well if given an additional shock treatment. In our opinion they must all have modified psychotherapy, probably of the group sort, and a well-organized rehabilitation program after operation.

Lobotomy is sometimes used in combination with sedatives for patients with chronic, incurable, painful conditions such as cancer. We believe this is silly, except for research purposes. Patients with chronic progressive disorders, such as cancer, can be adequately relieved with narcotic drugs, and there is no sound reason why they should be subjected to further mutilation. The fact that they may become addicted to morphine in the chronic progressive and incurable stage of cancer is inconsequential.

Complications. The principal complications are postoperative and most often involve a hemorrhage into the brain. Rarely is there postoperative infection. Some patients have convulsions as a late complication. Since one is dealing with drastic procedures in chronic incurable patients, these complications seem to be of little significance and should not deter one from the use of the operation, if the operation itself is indicated.

Hydrotherapy and Physical Therapy

In past generations hydrotherapy was one of the principal forms of treatment available to the psychiatrist managing very disturbed or anxious psychiatric patients. It was also used to stimulate retarded, withdrawn individuals. With the perfection of other methods of treatment, hydrotherapy is becoming of less use, and many modern psychiatric hospitals are built without special hydrotherapeutic equipment.

Because some physicians continue to find it useful in a few cases, we will discuss certain general features, and the interested student is referred to some excellent books on the subject which are available at any good medical library.

Continuous Tub or Prolonged Bath. This is a device modified from an ordinary bathtub in which water, thermostatically controlled to the body temperature, flows over the patient. In times past, to quiet patients in disturbed and overactive states, they were left in these tubs for hours on end. Many patients drop off to sleep in the tub. Patients with acute anxiety often feel greatly relaxed and refreshed after an hour or two in one of these tubs. Treatments are usually given for such patients, 1 hour twice daily. Attention to the skin is necessary since patients sometimes develop a skin rash, but any commercially available hand lotion from the hospital pharmacy or ladies' cosmetic counter will do much to control this if used routinely. Olive oil and lanolin are also helpful but messy. Patients with delirium tremens from alcohol or patients showing restlessness, agitation, and tremors from other types of drug intoxication often respond well to hydrotherapy.

A few patients developed circulatory collapse in the tub and it required a skilled technician to administer treatment. Because the treatments were usually at least 1 to 2 hours in length, a limited number of patients could receive this treatment in a 24-hour period even where large areas of floor space and as many as 8 to 12 tubs in a unit were available.

The treatment also had the disadvantage that some of the attendants and nurses used these tubs for a modified form of restraint unless the policing of the area was very strict. Some physicians still find continuous tubs useful in detoxification, in acute anxiety states, and in disturbed and overactive patients. We have largely replaced the use of continuous tubs with medications and with a combination of chlorpromazine and shock therapy in very agitated patients.

Showers. The principal form of shower used in the old hydrotherapy suites were needlepoint showers and the Scotch douche. The needlepoint shower consisted of a series of shower heads running from about 6 feet in the air to floor level, and sufficient numbers around the circle to hit all parts of the patient's body simultaneously. The pressure through these heads was controlled as was the temperature. They were usually started with warm water gradually changed to cold with increasing pressure. It was a sort of water massage which anxious patients found relaxing and which some retarded, withdrawn patients found quite stimulating.

The Scotch douche is two fire hoses with controlled pressures mounted on a stand. Patients are sprayed with alternate hot and cold water of gradually increasing pressure; this is also a form of water massage which anxious, tense patients find very relaxing. In our opinion these treatments still have some place in the management of neurotic patients, alcoholic patients, and certain other patients on drug or shock therapy. We doubt that the therapeutic value is worth the cost of the equipment and the floor space allotted to them. We believe that approximately the same thing can be accomplished by ordinary, well-equipped shower stalls in which the patient is encouraged to spend a little more than the usual time taking his daily shower and with the water turned on at a rather high pressure.

Packs. Dry packs and cold wet packs were formerly given the patients. Many patients spent hours in these packs because the staff had the idea that they produced relaxation and sleep. They did with certain patients, but packs were more often used as a form of restraint. We believe packs should be regarded as restraint and used only as such. Many patients left in a pack too long developed a hyperpyrexia and expired.

In a modern hospital equipped with seclusion rooms, and with the availability of chlorpromazine, reserpine, and shock therapy, the pack has no place. In Massachusetts hospitals packs are reported to the central department as restraint. They are practically never used.

Massage, Whirlpool Baths, and Therapeutic Exercises. These methods in the hands of a skilled physical therapist can be invaluable in caring for bed patients and patients with various types of neurologic disturbances, particularly those with paralyses or limitations of motion due to joint pathology. Much can be done to mobilize these patients, and this has a profound beneficial effect, not only on their physical motility and potentialities for rehabilitation but also on their psychology. We believe physical medicine is an integral part of the rehabilitation program for patients. The techniques for psychiatric patients differ little from those in general use.

Therapeutic Use of Restraint and Seclusion

The present trend, and a very good one, in psychiatry is permissiveness, the use of open wards, a sharp decrease in the use of seclusion rooms, and in many hospitals no use of restraint. This in general is good. The careful physician, however, should bear in mind that some patients derive tremendous temporary benefit from some periods of seclusion. An occasional patient asks for, and should be allowed, some type of restraint. This will often be a restraint in motility, such as a locked door on the ward or transfer for short periods to a locked section. It should be used only on individual prescription and only after the physician has the patient in individual therapy and understands that dynamically freedom at this particular stage of the treatment is a threat to the patient which may be too great and interfere with treatment. In such cases there is every reason for the psychiatrist to prescribe either restraint or seclusion. He is, however, obligated to explain to the other personnel on the ward why it is being used in this particular case and what may be expected from it. In most instances such treatment is transitory in nature but may be very helpful. It should not be used as a rationalization for security measures or to assuage the anxiety of the doctor or nurse who fears the patients may try to escape.

CHAPTER **32**

Treatment of the Toxic Reactions (Including Delirium, Alcoholism, and the Addictions)

Treatment of the Delirium Proper

A toxic state may produce a confused, apprehensive, delirious patient. One of the first considerations in the treatment of any delirious reaction is the discovery of the cause and elimination of it whenever possible. In the exogenous reactions this consists simply in the detection of the toxic agent and elimination of the patient's ingestion of the drug. In the endogenous reaction the elimination varies with the illness and may be medical, surgical, or a combination thereof, depending upon the reagent to which the patient is reacting. In all toxic states certain general principles are applicable and should be used from the moment the case is diagnosed as having a toxic delirium. These treatments are: (1) to support the patient and protect him during the stage of confusion, and (2) to eliminate the cause, or source, of the toxic disturbance.

Technique

General medical measures directed toward support of the cardiorespiratory functions are of paramount importance. These consist of ensuring adequate fluid intake, electrolyte balance, and food and vitamin ingestion. Nasal feedings by means of the stomach tube or intravenous administration of glucose and plasma are used as indicated. Respiratory embarrassment or circulatory failure is best combated by means of an oxygen tent or an oxygen room, but lacking these facilities, the administration of oxygen by nasal catheter or mask is helpful. Repeated explanation and reassurance are necessary in order to get delirious patients to tolerate and remain in the oxygen tent or to retain the nasal catheter. The brain edema is combated in several ways; simplest and most commonly used is the intravenous administration of a hypertonic glucose solution, which provides a temporary decrease in intracranial pressure and some nourishment and combats acidosis. Concentrated plasma has also been recommended. This probably results in a more prolonged decrease in brain volume. Spinal drainage helps in some instances. Whole blood is very helpful when available. Whole blood and concentrated plasma do more to remove fluid from the brain, where it causes damage, than any other combination of measures we have tried.

Most patients show less confusion and fewer hallucinatory experiences in the morning and during the bright daylight. Toward evening, as the ward darkens and the shadows begin to fall, the delirious phenomena become more pronounced. Placing the patient in a room kept brightly lighted helps considerably. In many instances the presence of some member of the family is a constant source of reassurance and comfort to the patient. The selection of the person is important because in some instances the patient has paranoid projections centering around some or all the members of his family, and then the relative may produce anxiety rather than relieve it.

In examining the patient and in carrying out nursing and treatment procedures, each step should be carefully explained to the patient, since this will often prevent him from becoming apprehensive due to misinterpretation of what is intended. Such precautions are particularly necessary to soften such indignities as enema administration, rectal temperatures, or taking blood specimens. The patient should not be left alone, even for a few moments, in corridors or outside x-ray rooms, heart stations, or laboratories. In these circumstances the confusion and passing of traffic will often become panic-producing and at times lead to violent outbursts of combativeness in escape attempts. Saline cartharsis and colonic irrigations tend to aid in elimination of the toxic substances. One of the best sedative and toxic eliminative measures is the prolonged neutral tub where available. These are of particular value in the exogenous states but may be used judiciously in those endogenous reactions where there is no contraindication from the disease itself.

Sedation should be used sparingly, if at all, during the day, and should be reserved for the night when the patient becomes more disturbed, or when it is customary for him to rest. Sedatives should be given in large doses and the use of quick-acting hypnotics, such as paraldehyde, are preferable to the more slowly eliminated drugs such as the barbituric acid derivatives. Drugs of the opium alkaloid series should be avoided unless needed for alleviation of pain.

Where it is possible, delirious patients should be kept in a room to themselves because ward noises, activities, and conversations of other patients and their treatment tend to aggravate the hallucinatory experience and give rise to many related phenomena.

It is desirable to have the windows in the room fixed so that they cannot be raised sufficiently for the patient to get out. Many patients who are thought to have committed suicide in general hospitals by jumping from windows had not intended suicide at all, but were attempting to escape from their imagined persecutors. The presence of a special nurse or attendant whom the patient trusts, or some trusted member of the family, does much to avoid these complications. For some patients, particularly those where the delirious episode is due to alcohol, treatment with intravenous glucose containing insulin sufficient to produce a mild insulin reaction and containing large amounts of the vitamin B complex will often clear up the delirium in a period of a few hours. There is also some reason to believe that the intramuscular administration of chlorpromazine or reserpine helps clear up delirious states and makes the patient comfortable and clear rather than apprehensive, jittery, irritable, and hallucinating.

Treatment of Alcoholism

The treatment of early alcoholism in those alcoholics showing excessive drinking as their only symptom can be most successfully done in an outpatient department. This may be the alcoholic clinic in a general hospital or one operated by a private or governmental agency. Many alcoholics are successfully treated by their private psychiatrist. Psychotherapy is thought to be an integral part of the outpatient management of an alcoholic, and the degree and depth of psychotherapy will vary with the skills of the physician and the individual needs of the patient. Some require superficial psychotherapy of a general supporting type. This type can be given by a skilled general physician who has taken the trouble to learn the rudiments of supportive psychotherapy. As discussed in an earlier chapter, supportive psychotherapy in the alcoholic will center around education, building up his self-confidence and self-respect, helping him alleviate his guilt feeling, and instructing him in a mode of life which will enable him to get along without the support of the alcohol. Sometimes the social worker or the physician can help him alleviate conditions at home or at work which will greatly improve things. Patients at this level should all have careful physical examinations with thorough attention to their nutritional requirements. Williams, Trulson, Fleming, and Stare report substantial improvement in a series of alcoholics by the management of their nutrition. It is also necessary to recognize that some alcoholics when managed as outpatients, although dry, go through symptoms which are similar to those after an alcoholic bender. These have been reported by Flaherty, McGuire, and Gatsky. They believe that this results in some of the relapses seen in the outpatient management of alcoholics. Alcoholics at this stage should have more detailed psychotherapy by skilled therapists if such are available.

There is a group among the alcoholics who suffer from definite neuroses or beginning psychoses in which the alcoholism is a symptom, and careful examination reveals the underlying neurotic or psychotic state. These patients must be handled preferably by detailed psychoanalytic or dynamically oriented therapy, but this can usually be given in an outpatient setting. Many alcoholic clinics maintain a psychiatrist on their staff to work in consultation with the other personnel of the clinic and to treat patients. It is our belief that the alcoholic clinic, where possible, should be under the direction of a psychiatrist who is skilled in the handling of alcoholic patients. With proper outpatient management, a limited number of alcoholics will require hospital care.

When these patients are brought into the hospital, it should be for the purpose of detoxification. It has been our experience that relatively short periods, 10 to 30 days, in a private or public psychiatric hospital with ample treatment facilities, is the most satisfactory way to manage these patients. Where available, the psychiatric ward or the medical service of a general hospital may also be used. As mentioned under Deliria, the use of chlorpromazine or reserpine intramuscularly or intravenously and the use of the adrenocortical hormones, particularly ACTH, will often do much to hasten the detoxification of these patients. In the ordinary alcoholic all that will be required on admission to the hospital is prompt removal of the alcohol, sedation with reserpine or chlorpromazine, replacement of fluids with glucose solution containing vitamins, and small doses of insulin. If the patient is unable to sleep after reserpine or chlorpromazine, paraldehyde, 8 to 15 cc by mouth, in some type of vehicle, will often reduce the "jitters." In our opinion barbital should be used sparingly, if at all, in alcoholic patients, because they tend to become habituated, and nothing is accomplished if an alcoholic is changed to a barbital addict.

Some institutions use hydrotherapy, such as the Scotch douche mentioned above and the prolonged neutral bath. These are useful, if available, but certainly not necessary.

Mild insulin shock, along with intravenous glucose, will usually be sufficient to stimulate the patient's appetite. Careful attention to diet, using high-potency multivitamin preparations, plus a high-protein high-caloric diet will usually straighten out this difficulty. Some patients who have been drinking for a long time show evidence of peripheral neuritis, as evidenced by paresthesias and some loss of muscle tone, particularly over the peripheral portions of the extremities. These usually respond fairly promptly to medication with vitamins.

While in the hospital the patient should be placed on active psychotherapy, which should be of the dynamic, analytically oriented type, and, in selected cases, psychoanalytic therapy. Recreation therapy should be also available. These therapies should be continued through the outpatient department or the physician's private office after the patient has been discharged.

The patient should also continue on the high-vitamin, high-protein intake, although the total caloric content may be cut down to keep the patient from gaining excessive weight.

In our opinion the psychologic therapy of an alcoholic presents special problems that must be recognized for both the outpatient and hospital treatment. The patient should agree to cooperate with certain rules, agreements, or conditions of treatment:

1. He must understand that he is having difficulty controlling his drinking and that he needs help. He must have a desire to be helped. The patient who is coerced into this agreement by his wife or boss will usually not be successful.

2. The patient must agree to try to remain abstinent from alcohol during the treatment.

3. He must be frank in all dealings with the therapist and truthful about lapses from his agreement not to drink.

4. The patient must agree to notify the therapist promptly if he relapses from his treatment, so that further supportive treatment can be given promptly and not after the patient returns remorseful from a prolonged binge.

Psychotherapy—Supportive Type

The therapist must be unemotional, not censoring and objecting. The patient has already been watched, praised, blamed, rewarded, and threatened by friends. He must consider the therapist a dependable person interested in him, not someone who will become emotionally upset at either the success or failure of the treatment. The patient should be treated like an intelligent adult and the therapist should act like one. The therapy should concern the patient's general life problems and not devote itself entirely to the subject of alcoholism. The goal should be the production of greater ego strength or the development of more emotional maturity. The therapist should try to increase the patient's resilience, or bounce, so that he will not need alcohol to protect himself from the bombardments of the world.

The principle in therapy is that the patient should be asked to make his own decisions and not seek advice from the therapist. The therapist will discuss the pros and cons of pending decisions with the patient, pointing out blind spots the patient may have, but the final decision must rest with the patient.

The patient must come to a true understanding of what motivates him to get well. He may be filled with remorse, but often the patient and therapist will learn that he is getting well for himself and that rationalizations that he is getting well for his wife and children are not usually valid.

Some patients who are seriously neurotic or who have tremendous potentials for future contributions to the world may be subjected to psychoanalysis. Analysis of these patients in selected cases can be successful. Depending on the nature of the patient's alcoholism and what leads him to drink, one can expect greater or lesser degrees of success. Some reports in the literature are very pessimistic; but one feels that the authors are unduly pessimistic considering the severity of the cases they attempted to treat. It is our impression that a combination of support in the outpatient department, the use of drugs, inducing a conditioned reflex, and the use of disulfram (Antabuse), plus ample diet and vitamins, results in effective rehabilitation of a large number of alcoholics. True, a substantial proportion will go off on an occasional "bat," but they usually lose less than 30 days from their job and will then have another prolonged period in which they work effectively as worthwhile citizens. It is no more reasonable to abandon an alcoholic because he occasionally needs further treatment than it would be to abandon diabetic patients because they must take insulin the rest of their lives.

There have been many types of treatment and "cures" advocated for alcoholism. In modern times the most common ones are the so-called "conditioned reflex" treatment and disulfram.

The conditioned reflex treatment, principally promulgated by Voegtlin and LeMere, is a process of inducing emesis in patients by the injection of Emetine Hydrochloride, which the patient thinks is an injection of a vitamin preparation. When the patient begins to show moderate sweating or other vasomotor signs of nausea, he is given a large drink of liquor in a setting of ceremony with other items of positive suggestion. The resulting emesis is usually interpreted by the patient as having been induced by the whiskey. This is repeated according to a well-set routine, and in the course of time the patient begins to show signs of nausea when he sees or smells alcoholic beverages. In some hands spectacular results are attained, particularly if this treatment is combined with adequate supportive psychotherapy. Our experience with this form of treatment has been limited.

In our experience a more useful drug is disulfram (Antabuse). Patients taking this drug have no symptoms, but if they ingest alcohol, even in small doses, they get violent vasomotor reactions, palpitations, and often emesis. Patients are unable to handle any large quantity of alcohol while under the influence of this medication. While taking the drug, they become afraid to drink. It must be used under carefully controlled clinical conditions. In the first place, the patient should be carefully examined to make sure he does not have any severe cardiovascular illnesses. If he has, the drug should not be used. Patients are then placed on the drug, 0.5 gm three times a day for 2 to 3 days. It is then reduced to 0.5 gm twice daily, and on the fifth day to 0.5 gm daily. The patient can then be maintained on 0.5 to 0.75 gm/day. On the fifth and eighth day of administration of the drug, the patient is given a test with some alcoholic beverage, preferably whiskey, in order that he may understand the effect alcohol may have upon him. Having experienced the vasomotor phenomena that accompany alcohol combined with this drug, the patient is then kept on the medication and recognizes that he must stay off alcohol. The defect in this form of treatment is that the patient and his family must agree to his continued ingestion of the drug. It is necessary to warn the family that patients who want to take a drink in a few days may avoid taking the medication by placing the tablet under their tongue and later expectorating it. Some patients go to the bathroom and induce emesis in order to get rid of the preparation before it can be absorbed.

Antabuse can be looked upon as a deterrent to the occasional impulsive relapse so common in alcoholic patients. It is useful to them when they meet former drinking cronies or attend some social function where well-meaning friends attempt to force a drink upon them. Patients who wish to relapse usually manage to run out of the preparation or elude their family for a few days, and then they can resume drinking. Paraldehyde may not be used when patients are taking this drug since it produces the same reaction as alcohol. In our opinion the patient must be under close medical supervision when taking these drugs, particularly with checks on blood count and liver function. We believe it is useful only for those patients during the initial stages of their rehabilitation, when impulsive relapses may occur. Patients who are well settled into psychotherapy and have a good transference to their therapist usually will not require further disulfram.

In our opinion rehabilitation of the severe alcoholic is greatly facilitated if he joins the group known as Alcoholics Anonymous. This is a nation-wide organization, with individuals in many communities who are responsible for its management and operation. The founders of the group and the principal workers are all individuals who have been alcoholics and who have brought their drinking under temporary or permanent control through this group. A large and heterogenous group of this sort will vary in its efficiency from community to community, but the general picture is one of efficient and conscientious focus upon one of the major sociologic features of the rehabilitation of the alcoholic patient.

Only advanced alcoholic patients are approached by members of AA—patients who feel that they are no longer able to handle their problem because of the advanced stage of physical, psychologic, and moral degradation which they have reached as a result of their habit. Thus, it is useful only for those patients whose alcoholism is so advanced that they have to come into the hospital, and only for the more seriously addicted of this group. The ordinary patient handled in the outpatient department, without recourse to hospital care, is not a satisfactory candidate for Alcoholics Anonymous. Contact between the group and the patient is usually made through the authorities in the jail or the hospital where the patient may have gone for detoxification. Members of this group can visit the patient and try to indoctrinate him with the basic tenet of the group. This is briefly: As an alcoholic he is unable to manage his own life and he needs help in managing his day-to-day activities. This consists, first, of associating with recovered alcoholics in the group and, second, of appealing to the deity for daily guidance and care. This particular approach combines the association with former alcoholics and the acknowledgement of dependence upon a deity of a moralistic type to supply needs of the ordinary chronic alcoholic patient. It provides socialization with individuals who understand his problem and who will not urge him to take a drink for "old times' sake." It also gives him an interest or goal in life, which is to help other individuals who are in the same circumstance as he formerly found himself. Alcoholics Anonymous has a profound influence and offers a constructive form of motivation for the alcoholic patient. The appeal to religion is often effective and helpful in those alcoholics who have a strong urge for dependency and who have never been able to find a socially acceptable person upon whom they can continue to be emotionally dependent during their adult life. It is, in effect, assuming a parent-child relationship, with the deity in the role of the parent. (It is interesting, of course, that the deity, according to our present conception, is an all-forgiving, ever-loving individual who is strict in his rules but tolerant and forgiving toward the child who repents and asks forgiveness after transgression.)

There is nothing in the activities of the Alcoholics Anonymous group that conflicts with attempts to manage these patients from an orthodox medical and psychiatric point of view. Patients in analytic or intensive psychotherapy may continue to be affiliated with this group. We believe the group should be encouraged and that those who work with alcoholic patients should cooperate with AA.

It is our opinion that the intensive application of what we now know of outpatient management of these cases, through the use of supportive psychotherapy and dynamically and intensively administered psychotherapy for those with neurotic concomitants, and the application of vitamin and diet management, general rehabilitation therapy, plus support in the community through various social agencies, including Alcoholics Anonymous, will result in much better therapeutic results than we now have. Since this is a serious social and economic problem, such applications are worthwhile.

Narcotic Addiction

Patients become addicted to opium alkaloids, or the synthetic substitutes, and cocaine. In our opinion these patients must be placed in a psychiatric institution or preferably in one of the Federal hospitals at Fort Worth, Texas, or Lexington, Ky., during the period of withdrawal of the drug. This should then be followed by intensive rehabilitation measures much like those used with the alcoholic patient. Patients are usually removed from the drug either abruptly or rapidly, depending on the patient's past dosage and his general physical condition. Abrupt withdrawal is suitable for the healthy person only mildly addicted. In the ordinary private physician's practice, patients suitable for this form of withdrawal make up about 80 per cent of the cases. Such patients are rarely taking more than 45 to 50 mg of morphine a day, which is usually given by an ethical physician for pain but which they find themselves increasingly dependent upon.

Rapid Withdrawal. Patients on larger doses of morphine or patients showing evidence of physical debilitation must be taken off the drug a little less abruptly. Patients are stabilized on a dose of the drug, depending on the amount they have taken. In our opinion, however, rarely is it necessary to give patients more than 40 to 60 mg of the drug in any 24-hour period, irrespective of what story the patients tell you about the dose. The patients are usually inaccurate. Often they will intentionally give you a story of an increased amount since they feel that they will then come off the drug with less discomfort because you will give them more during the withdrawal period. Others have been taking drugs diluted by the peddler so that actually their dose is much smaller than they think. In our opinion patients should be given 3 or 4 mg to see whether this relieves the withdrawal symptoms. If it does not, patients will then be placed on a dose of about 40 mg per day and are kept on this stabilizing dose for 2 to 3 days while the preliminary examinations of a physical nature are made. This dose is then reduced by ⅕ each day so that by the tenth hospital day patients are off the drug.

Whether one uses rapid or abrupt withdrawal, the patients will need a certain amount of support during the withdrawal period. Most of them will complain of withdrawal symptoms. Motor collapse, diarrhea, sweating, or abdominal cramps are the common signs. Many patients will greatly exaggerate these symptoms, but the physician will have to judge for himself in terms of the physiologic concomitants that should be present. It has been our experience that patients tend to exaggerate the withdrawal symptoms. Recent reports indicate that intramuscular chlorpromazine or reserpine, in doses similar to those used in other psychiatric patients, will often greatly relieve the withdrawal symptoms. The patient becomes quiet, cooperative, and is able to eat, and even sleep. Some patients require extra sedation in the form of paraldehyde or barbital to induce sleep, but these drugs should be used with caution as the patient tends to become addicted to them. In most cases, getting the patient off the drug and on a diet high in protein and vitamins is not a difficult task. The real problem is during the rehabilitation and follow-up of the patient. Steps outlined for the rehabilitation of alcoholics apply equally well to patients addicted to narcotics. The latter are more difficult to manage, and one has a higher percentage of failures with them, but one should continue to exert every possible means of getting these patients attached to one of the therapists in the clinic in order that they may be floated along with at least supportive psychotherapy, if not more intensive psychotherapy, during the rehabilitation period.

Addiction to Sedative Drugs

Many patients become addicted to barbital and some to bromides. Patients taking one of the barbituric acid series in large doses should be removed gradually from the drug over a period of 10 to 14 days in much the manner described for the rapid withdrawal of morphine. Patients removed more rapidly are prone to have tremendous difficulty in sleeping, develop motor restlessness, and in some instances they have severe convulsions. It has been our practice in treating patients who take large doses of the barbitals to start them on Dilantin, 15 to 20 mg three times a day as an anticonvulsion medication. The rehabilitation of these patients, after withdrawal, is the same as outlined in detail for the alcoholic and the drug addict and consists essentially of psychotherapy and general environmental supportive measures.

CHAPTER 33

Treatment of Chronic Brain Syndromes

The treatment of chronic brain syndromes is always of two types: (1) treating the underlying organic disorder, trying to improve the basic cause of the trouble, and (2) using support psychotherapy and environmental support, aiding the patient in adapting to his reduced brain function as the result of the disease. In this particular section we shall confine our discussion to the treatment of the underlying organic defects.

Treatment in Neurosyphilis

Treatment of parenchymatous syphilis of the brain requires more intensive and prolonged therapy than other forms of syphilis. The reasons for this are assumed to be due to the fact that the blood–cerebrospinal-fluid barrier is relatively difficult for penicillin and the arsenical drugs to penetrate. Whatever the reason, treatment must be prolonged and intensive as compared to the other forms of syphilis. Sufficient time has elapsed and sufficient cases have been treated with penicillin that we can now say that penicillin is the best treatment for parenchymatous syphilis of the nervous system. In our opinion it should be instituted promptly on making a definite diagnosis of general paresis. In our hands the optimum treatment has been one of the aqueous solutions of penicillin given as 300,000 units twice daily for a total dose of 10 to 12 million units. Patients who still show active symptoms and signs of active infection in the nervous system as manifest by increased cell count and increased protein at the conclusion of this course may be continued on further treatment. Some authors recommend a course of fever therapy if this situation takes place. It has been our experience that neither of these need to be done promptly. Some patients will continue to improve as much as 4 to 6 weeks after the

371

penicillin treatment has been discontinued. If at the conclusion of that period, however, symptoms are still fulminating, or if in the interval the symptoms seem to progress, we are prone to give a second course of penicillin. Fever therapy, in one of its forms, is now used only in those patients proving penicillin-resistant. In our opinion this is rare. Some patients who have considerable vascular involvement may show evidence of a Herxheimer reaction when placed on heavy doses of penicillin. It has been our practice to continue to give penicillin therapy, irrespective of this, and most cases promptly clear up. It does not seem to affect the ultimate prognosis.

Patients treated for paresis with penicillin therapy should have follow-up therapy including complete blood, spinal fluid, neurologic, and mental examinations at least every 6 months for at least 5 years. In our experience, few of these cases relapse. In fact, penicillin treatment of early syphilis is so effective that the only ones developing paresis are those who, due to their nomadism, alcoholism, or some other form of neglect, fail to get treatment in the early phases of syphilis.

We no longer use tryparsamide in treating syphilis of the nervous system.

Fever Therapy

Some authors feel that penicillin-resistant cases or those not responding promptly to penicillin should be treated with fever therapy. There are two forms of fever therapy: artificial fever therapy and malaria therapy.

Artificial Fever Therapy. This is a technique of increasing the patient's body temperature to therapeutic levels by means of mechanical or physical modalities. It could be done with a hot bath and a blanket. The system ordinarily used is one of three types: a heated and humidified cabinet, manufactured under the name of Hypertherm, an infrared cabinet, which is an insulated heater in which the patient lies, or a short-wave apparatus, usually called an inductotherm, which is basically a short-wave diathermy machine set up to heat the whole body.

If one of these types is used, the nurse who operates it and the physician who supervises her should have taken special instructions in the operation of the particular machine. Fever therapy is safe in skilled hands but hazardous in the hands of the neophyte.

Before fever therapy is given, the patient should have a complete physical checkup, including blood chemistry, urine, electrocardiographic study, and x-ray of heart and lungs. Patients are prepared by the omitting of breakfast and the giving of an enema, exactly as they would be for surgery. After being placed in the cabinet, the skin is usually rubbed with some type of oil, cold cream, or lanolin. The temperature is usually elevated to the desired level, which is 105.8°F rectally, in about 1 hour. Patients in poor condition may be treated for shorter intervals or at lower temperatures, but we believe that any temperature much below 104° is not of much use in syphilis of the nervous system. During the period of heating, patients are given fluids by mouth, containing salt, and it has been our practice also to give at least 2 liters of Ringer's solution intravenously. Temperature is either controlled through an automatic recording device with a thermometer in the rectum, or by the periodic checking of the rectal temperature. The temperature is usually maintained at 105.8° for a period of 3 hours, although some clinics use longer periods. The temperature is reduced by taking the patient from the cabinet and blowing air over him by fan. He is then given a bed bath. After resting in bed for approximately 3 hours, at which time he can take fluids and food ad lib., the patient is usually able to be up and around, although he will often feel a little fatigued. Some patients are able to go home if the family is prepared to care for them. Patients can ordinarily go home in an automobile and some are able to take public transportation. We feel it desirable, however, to keep the patient in the hospital if feasible.

A course of artificial fever is 35 to 40 hours of fever of 105.8°F. Complications are infrequent. An occasional patient will receive a superficial skin burn. The only serious complication is a heat stroke in which the temperature shoots up and seems uncontrollable. This is due to the poor management of fluid intake during the treatment and is usually quickly controlled by giving salt solution by vein and by massaging the skin with rubbing alcohol, which causes it to flush, and at the same time evaporating the alcohol by blowing air over the skin by fan. Occasionally, during the induction period, patients will develop tetany due to calcium deficiency which is relieved by the injection of calcium gluconate intravenously.

Malaria Therapy. Malaria therapy is another method of inducing fever treatment. This is an older form of treatment and formerly was used in large institutions where great numbers of patients required fever therapy. The number that could be inoculated with malaria depended only on the nursing care available. The patient was ordinarily inoculated with 2 to 6 ml of blood from a patient running tertian malaria from *Plasmodium vivax*. In the days when syphilis of the nervous system made up 10 per cent of our admissions, any large hospital always had patients running malaria, and it was simple enough to keep a strain going. With the advent of penicillin, and only an exceptional case requiring fever therapy, most institutions no longer maintain a malaria strain. There were workers who felt that malaria therapy was superior to fever therapy, although the scientific validity of these opinions was not better than that of the staff who felt that the "hot boxes" were better than the malaria. We prefer the fever cabinet because patients seem to gain physically instead of being debilitated by the malaria.

The technique of administering malaria therapy is as follows: The patient receives exactly the same physical work-up as for the artificial fever, and it is essentially the same as that before any major surgical procedure. He is then inoculated I.M. (intramuscularly) with 2 to 6 ml of blood from an infected patient. If the blood is fresh 2 to 3 ml may be given intravenously. The patient is placed on a high-caloric, high-vitamin diet with iron preparations given to combat anemia. When the patient has his initial chill he is placed in bed and covered with blankets and hot water bottles in order to get a maximum rise in temperature and to maintain it as long as possible. The patients cooperate during the period of the chill, but when the chill subsides and the temperature shoots up to 105 to 106°, they usually want to uncover. Great diplomacy is required on the part of the ward personnel to get patients to stay covered up. The temperature subsides in 3 to 5 hours, but it should be maintained for a maximum of 5 hours above 104° if possible. The goal is to run a series of chills until the patient has accumulated 50 hours of fever above 104°. In some patients the strain of malaria dies out before this goal is reached. An occasional patient will show a heat stroke as they do in the hot box; in this case the patient should be uncovered, given a hypertonic salt solution by vein, and be cooled by the fan while his skin is massaged with alcohol. An occasional patient will develop severe anemia on malaria therapy, and it may be necessary to terminate the treatment and treat him with transfusions. All patients develop a leukopenia, and it has been our practice to terminate the treatment if the white cell count drops below 2,000. Some authors say this is unnecessary. Very rarely a patient will develop signs of albuminuria, shown by a marked increase in albumin and casts in the urine and by an accumulation of N.P.N., urea, or creatinine in the blood. In these cases the treatment should be terminated. Patients running fever with malaria may have convulsions, probably indicating some type of meningeal involvement, but this is not an indication for terminating the course of malaria fever therapy. It has been our policy to maintain such patients on phenobarbital or Dilantin, similar to the plan used in convulsive disorders. Between malaria paroxysms, which in a well-regulated tertian course will be every other day, the patient is encouraged to participate in group activities on the ward and to continue a high-caloric, high-vitamin intake to cut down as much as possible the debilitation produced by the malaria itself.

Management of the Senile Disorders

We believe that the senile disorders should be managed on an outpatient and preventive basis so far as possible. There has been much interest recently in prolonging physical vigor through the adequate supervision of exercise and food intake. This, plus sociologic measures directed toward making the patient feel that he has a useful role in the world, will do much to prevent the incidence of senile deterioration. One seldom sees a senile patient coming to the hospital when he still has 2 to 3 years of unfinished work ahead of him. In modern society old folks tend to be shunted aside because of small, crowded apartments, retirement laws that necessitate dropping out of productive activity at age 65, and a general orientation of our society to the youthful and the untried as opposed to the old and the tested.

Many of these patients who show symptoms can be handled by proper medical, psychiatric, and social-service supervision in a geriatric clinic. A few will be committed to the mental hospital. Of these patients, at least one-third will prove to be suffering from an involutional psychosis of either depressed or paranoid type, or from symptoms secondary to metabolic disturbances, cardiac decompensation, or dietary errors. These patients respond promptly to treatment, and most of them will be back in the community in 4 to 8 weeks. They should not be sent back into the community without adequate follow-up and supervision through one of the geriatric clinics. Some patients come to the hospital moribund and promptly die. Between these two groups is a smaller but still substantial number of patients suffering from typical senility who recover from their confusion and psychotic state with the removal of environmental stress. There is a residual of only about 15 or 20 per cent of the admissions to our hospitals in patients over age 60, if the therapeutic program is properly set up and operated. All the patients require support psychotherapy and environmental manipulation. These patients adapt particularly well to the group activities—singing, dancing, and other group recreational support. These patients love occupational therapy, religious services, movies, and book reviews. Some assume the responsibility of caring for other older people who are slightly more feeble than they are.

We believe that the usual pessimism associated with the diagnosis of senile deterioration is unwarranted. The proper combination of drugs, diet, rehabilitation, psychotherapy, and social supervision can do much for a large number of these patients.

There is one complication in the senile patients' rehabilitation. Some of them coming to the hospital get accustomed to the ward, like it there, find other old persons there that they become fond of, and do not want to leave. Because of this and because some of them have no place to go, one of us is setting up a plan whereby these people can live in chronic disease hospitals without being committed there. With this edition it is too early to say how successful this will be but we are optimistic.

Various drugs such as glutamic acid, nicotinic acid, and cytochrome C have been tried by us but prolonged experience with them has been disappointing.

Patients who develop psychotic symptoms should be protected from the consequences of their behavior. There is always the possibility of physical injury and of judgment defects which will dissipate their property or get them into legal difficulties. Patients sometimes cause explosions or fires due to the careless handling of gas appliances. Some of them commit suicide in their desperation and loneliness. An easily digested diet, warm clothing, and measures against constipation should be provided. Insomnia may be controlled by mild sedation or simple hypnotics. In some of the agitated ones, the newer drugs, such as chlorpromazine, work very well in reducing this agitation.

When institutional care seems inevitable for these cases, special institutions should be provided. The incarceration of these patients in hospitals designed to care for acute mental disturbances is to be deplored. Specially designed institutions to care for the aged and infirm are to be preferred and should provide special facilities for recreation, sunning, and other types of activity within the physical limits of the patient. There should be ample facilities for visiting in semiprivacy with members of the family and friends. Provisions should be made for the patient to have about him some of his personal possessions to which he ascribes sentimental value. This is one type of patient for whom the provision of facilities away from urban areas, rather than in the center of population, is to be preferred.

Treatment of the Arteriosclerotic Disorders

At present we know of no way of reversing the sclerotic process in the central nervous system or other parts of the body. We have found that many cases improve with measures directed toward supporting the general nutrition and general physiology of the body and with support psychotherapy. We have found that an adequate diet helps these patients clear up. Careful control of sedation is necessary. In our clinical experience nicotinic acid, approximately 400 mg a day, given in 100-mg doses and on an empty stomach, produces a flushing of the skin and the patients seem to feel better. Further laboratory experiment with this drug under controlled situations indicates that its effect is probably psychologic and not physiologic.

Some patients develop symptoms of depression and agitation with the sclerosis and these patients should be treated with electric shock therapy. In general, the measures used for the senile reactions are applicable to the arteriosclerotic psychotic patient. Where there is hypertension, reserpine not only helps control the agitation but also the blood pressure. Where tension is normal, chlorpromazine is probably to be preferred when patients show a good deal of agitation and paranoid projection. We believe that these patients should be handled in the same manner as the senile cases, with added measures directed toward the hypertension.

Psychosis with Convulsive Disorders

Treatment of these disorders may be divided into two principal groups comprising: measures toward controlling the convulsions, and general hygienic and supportive measures. The hygiene measures indicated are those of support psychotherapy and more dynamic psychotherapy where there are neurotic complications. (General measures of rehabilitation are discussed in other sections of this book.) Routine anticonvulsive medications described in the textbooks of neurology will be briefly reviewed here.

DRUGS

Historically speaking, bromide in various forms is the oldest and one of the most widely used forms of the treatment of epilepsy. In recent years the bromides have fallen into disrepute because they have a lower anticonvulsion activity, and because many physicians are afraid of bromide intoxication. However, if other means fail, they may be tried.

Phenobarbital. This is still the most widely used and most popular drug in treatment of the convulsive disorders. The dose varies according to the patient's age and may run from as small as 30 mg in an infant to as much as 0.6 gm in a large adult; it should be controlled according to the patient's need. It is very effective in both grand mal and petit mal but seems less effective in the psychomotor equivalents and in the epileptic psychoses. Phenobarbital has the advantage of being simple to use, almost free of complications if taken in the prescribed dosage, and cheap.

Dilantin (Diphenylhydantoin Sodium). Dilantin was developed a number of years ago by Merritt and Putnam. In spite of the fact that many new drugs have since come on the market, Dilantin is still the best general-purpose anticonvulsion drug that we have. It has no sedative effect, and the patient thus escapes the sleepy, dopey feeling sometimes induced by phenobarbital and the bromides. A few patients develop skin rashes, vertigo, and headache from Dilantin, but most patients take it without difficulty. In an occasional case there will also be an overgrowth of the gums which is disfiguring but not serious. Most patients may take from 20 mg to 0.3 gm of the drug without difficulty. In our experience this drug is very valuable, particularly when combined with phenobarbital, in controlling grand mal seizures. It is in our experience the most effective drug in treating the so-called convulsive equivalent states. It is less effective in the petit mal disorders.

Tridione and Paradione. These two preparations are effective in petit mal epilepsy. Paradione is a modification of Tridione, and it has a less toxic effect on the vision and has produced a suppression of the white count in fewer instances. Patients on either of these drugs will often complain of photophobia, particularly in bright light, and complain of a visual smokiness or frostiness obscuring external objects. Wearing sunglasses relieves these symptoms and there is no permanent impairment of vision. Visual symptoms recede promptly when patients are taken off the drug.

Patients sometimes develop agranulocytosis on Tridione or Paradione, and we feel that all patients on either of these preparations should have at least bimonthly white blood counts. The drugs are given in doses of 0.3 gm, three to five times per day. In our experience they are the most effective drugs in controlling petit mal epilepsy and are used in those cases which do not respond to phenobarbital.

Mesantoin. This drug was introduced for the control of psychomotor equivalent states. In our experience it is very much like Dilantin but less effective. Some patients become drowsy and lethargic on the drug. In some this effect is so pronounced that it is impossible to continue the use of Mesantoin. An occasional patient will complain of marked constipation, and it is sometimes necessary to give the drug with small doses of Prostigmine to pep up the bowel tone.

Glutamic Acid. Glutamic acid has been recommended by some in the treatment of petit mal epilepsy. It increases the cerebral oxygen utilization and is probably physiologically a sound preparation to use. Clinical experience with it has been disappointing as an anticonvulsion medication. The first disadvantage is that the dose is 12 gm per day, and the drug comes in large 0.5-gm tablets. It is sometimes difficult to persuade patients to take this many tablets in a day. We prefer the use of Paradione or Tridione.

In the last few years there has been a rash of new drugs for the treatment of epilepsy. A few of these are Propazone, Dimedione, Malidione, Phenurone, Gemonil, Mysoline, Hibicon, Diamox, and Milontin. These are all synthetic drugs developed to treat convulsive patients not being controlled by the ordinary standard medications. Our experience with some of these preparations is extensive and some of the others have not been tried at all by us.

Many patients with petit mal attacks respond very well to Benzedrine or Dexedrine Sulfate. These usually have no effect on grand mal epileptics but are somewhat helpful in some of the petit mal cases. Where they work, they are preferred to the Tridione-Paradione group for the simple reason that they do not have toxic effects on the hematopoietic system. Reports in the literature for each of the newer drugs are both favorable and unfavorable. In the authors' experience these drugs are useful in some cases and should be tried when patients do not respond to phenobarbital, Dilantin, Tridione or Paradione, or Dexedrine or Benzedrine. Literature is available on all these drugs from the drug houses manufacturing them and in most medical libraries.

DIET

At one time a ketogenic diet was recommended for epilepsy, particularly for children, but the anticonvulsant medications are so effective and the ketogenic diet so unpleasant that we do not recommend it. Lenox and Cobb summarized the desirable dietary measures: "Anything that keeps a patient dehydrated, acidaemic and oxygenated, favorably influences the seizures. Constipation must be combated."

It is our practice to ask the patient to limit the fluid intake within reason and to avoid drinking alcohol or large quantities of beer and soda water. We usually ask the patient to take a full general diet and to add generous portions of carbohydrates between meals and before retiring. We believe that preservation of a satisfactory blood sugar level can decrease the frequency of seizures. This type of dietary management is extremely popular, particularly among children and overweight adults.

GENERAL HYGIENIC MEASURES

Anything that improves the patient's basic physical tone and general health will decrease the incidence and frequency of seizures. The reverse is also true. Many of our patients who are easily controlled on drugs have "spells" only when they become ill, emotionally upset, hungry, over-fatigued, or when constipated.

We recommend that patients take exercise, preferably of the nonviolent type, such as walking, golf, bicycling, or horseback riding; the latter, only after the seizures have been controlled. We recommend that they indulge in these exercises by gradually increasing stages. We recommend that they refrain from piloting aircraft or going for long swims in deep water. When they swim in pools, we recommend that they have a companion with them. We recommend that they carry on an active, normal social life with any recreation or occupation they see fit, other than those mentioned above.

It is important to give these patients the proper philosophy toward their illness. This is usually done in terms of explaining a seizure to them and illustrating it with the use of electroencephalographic tracings. It is pointed out to the patient that the electrical activity in his cortex is abnormal when he is off medication, but when he is on the proper dose the cortical activity is not distinguishable from that of an ordinary person. The use of the medication is explained to him as a substitution medication and the analogy of diabetic patients using insulin or myopic patients using glasses is drawn. Patients are encouraged to think of themselves as lacking something in terms of the control mechanism in the electrical activity of the cortex rather than having some type of disease or mental disorder. This type of view appeals to most patients, and they are able to adjust to their condition with less concern and feeling of shame.

Every effort should be made to overcome the convulsive patient's tendency to withdraw from social contacts because he fears he will have a seizure in public and because he finds in the public mind much misunderstanding and fear of his illness.

CHAPTER 34

Treatment of Affective Disorders

The treatment of these disorders must be highly individualized if one is to avoid either neglecting patients or overtreating them. A few general principles which apply to other forms of psychiatric reaction will be discussed.

Patients with mild depressive symptoms, the so-called neurotic and reactive depressions, and patients with the mild hypomanic state can be treated satisfactorily as office or clinic patients. The treatment of choice in these cases is psychotherapy, either dynamic psychotherapy or psychoanalysis, depending on the patient's ego potentials, his financial situation, the role he has in the community, and the availability of analytic treatment.

All these patients need as a minimum is mild support psychotherapy, Desoxyn, or one of the other amphetamines, and sedation for sleep. When patients are treated in either hospitals or clinics, special attention is necessary to make sure that they do not develop more severe symptoms which may result in lack of attention to nutrition, loss of sleep, and, in the case of the manic patient, uncontrolled behavior. The social service department is useful in checking with the family, interpreting the patient's illness to the family, and following his general behavior in the community.

Hospitalization becomes necessary when patients with poorly controlled behavior begin to have severe difficulties with sleep, eat improperly, or have suicide preoccupations associated with mounting anxiety or tension. In our experience open ward facilities are usually adequate. Commitment is rarely necessary. Patients with severe agitated depressions or patients in extreme manic states may have to be committed temporarily to keep them under control. In the hospital of one of the authors no patients with

381

affective disorders are accepted except on a self-committed basis and little difficulty is encountered in persuading these self-committed patients to stay, particularly if the cooperation of the family is elicited and if the treatment is instituted promptly without prolonged delay or ambivalence about the treatment to be used. We find it helpful with these patients to have a member of the family come to the hospital with them and stay with them. Hospitalized patients should be confined, or locked in, only if their behavior becomes unmanageable, if they become dangerous to themselves, or if they are creating too much nuisance in so far as the public is concerned. Patients should be observed for evidence of mounting tension or preoccupations that warn of impending suicide.

Psychotherapy in the emotional state requires some modification of the general principles outlined in the chapter on psychotherapy. In a manic-depressive patient the initial phase of psychotherapy is best in short interviews. In our experience 20 to 30 minutes a day, or in hospitalized patients 15 to 20 minutes twice a day in the initial stage, is preferable to an hour two or three times a week. We believe these patients do not tolerate prolonged discussions or producing too much material in too short a time in the initial phases. Too much material or too much mulling over their problems in the initial phase may result in increasing anxiety and an increase in activity, each signaling an increase in the severity of the illness or a breakdown of the ego. In the initial stage our psychotherapy is usually of a very short, reassuring type, best described as support psychotherapy. We usually explain to the patient the nature of his illness, the good prognosis, and the steps necessary in the management. Then we elicit the underlying or precipitating factors and attempt to tie these factors to an earlier experience which has conditioned the patient to this type of illness.

In patients with mild symptoms their cooperation is usually excellent, since they come voluntarily and want relief. Patients in advanced manic or depressive states usually have received one of the more drastic therapies such as electroshock or the newer drugs, chlorpromazine or reserpine, by the time this stage of treatment is reached, so that they become cooperative to deeper probing in psychotherapy.

If patients are to receive psychotherapy, and we think they all should, and if they are also to receive shock therapy, the convulsions must be spaced and supervised closely so that the memory defects do not become so severe as to make psychotherapy futile. Certain shock methods seem to involve memory less severely than others. Patients in the hospital require special attention in addition to the above psychotherapeutic procedures.

Protection of the Patient

There are many symptoms and situations that expose the patient to danger. Suicide is an ever-present risk at any stage of a depression, particularly when the patient begins to improve. The best protection is watchful, tactful, and efficient nursing service. In the initial stages of treatment the patient needs protection against large numbers of visitors. Relatives and friends often argue with the manic patient and make attempts to cheer the depressed patient. Members of the immediate family, however, after understanding the patient's needs, may be very helpful and may be stimulating to depressed and retarded cases. Some patients need protection from each other. The depressed patient should never be left to the mercy of the manic, and other patients must be safeguarded from the annoying, bellicose, and often aggressive attention of acute manic patients. The motor drive of severe mania may lead to bruises, abrasions, and lacerations. Here, the prolonged bath was formerly used. Most clinics now use chlorpromazine or reserpine to control this phase of the behavior in a matter of hours rather than weeks. Erotic tendencies may lead the untreated manic patient into disgraceful behavior, or eroticism plus a spirit of mischief may dictate the insertion of foreign matter into the body orifices. Depressed patients driven by delusion into suicidal attempts may multilate themselves, swallow foreign bodies, or attempt to commit suicide with instruments obtained on the ward. Patients with advanced symptoms of mania or depression need attention to the general hygiene of the body. Attention must be given to the teeth, bowels, bathing, the care of the nails and hair. Patients in an acute psychotic state, particularly those with somatic delusions, must be carefully supervised because some of these patients will in the course of time develop somatic illness, such as appendicitis, gallbladder disease, or other acute medical or surgical conditions, which may be masked by the familiar complaints of the patient. It should be recalled that a psychosis gives no immunity to any medical or surgical condition, and these patients will often ignore physical symptoms or blend them with the delusions, with which the ward personnel will be familiar. Usually differences in the patient's behavior, and signs such as vomiting, diarrhea, and increased pulse rate or temperature, should tip the nurses, attendants, and ward physicians that something is amiss.

Nutrition

Attention to adequate food intake is important, particularly during the obvious manic attacks or the deep depressions with stupor.

In times past, the state of nutrition in these patients would become so grave that it would be necessary to feed them with gastric gavage by means of a stomach tube. Earlier editions of this book contained a formula for highly nutritious compounds that could be given by nasal tube. Any well-equipped dietician can compound such a preparation for the physician if necessary.

Actually the advent of shock therapy and the new drugs makes patients' symptoms evolve so rapidly that patients are usually cooperative enough to assure adequate food intake by ordinary methods, and the resident of today fortunately has little opportunity to develop the dexterity in handling stomach tubes for resistant patients which some of his older colleagues developed.

General Supportive Measures (Rest, Exercise, and Physiotherapy)

During the acute stages of these illnesses, both the manic and the depressive state, there is a marked sleep disturbance. Hypnotic drugs are often needed, but their use should be limited and should be carefully controlled. In the older editions of this book we recommended massage, hydrotherapy, packs, and neutral tubs for inducing sleep. In their time these treatments were invaluable, since the sleep problem, like the feeding problem, had to be struggled with for many weeks. With modern treatment, however, these methods of management are largely superfluous because the patient usually begins to sleep within a week of the institution of shock therapy, and sometimes within days when treated with chlorpromazine or reserpine. For this reason it is much simpler and safer for the patient to use one of the quick-acting hypnotics such as one of the barbituric acid series or paraldehyde. We prescribe a schedule of daily activities made up of periods of recreation, constructive work in the occupational therapy shop when the patient is cooperative enough, and group activities such as athletics, singing, swimming (where a pool is available), and workouts in the therapeutic gymnasium. We prescribe a short rest period after the noon meal, although this is sometimes difficult to enforce with overactive manic patients. It may be necessary to substitute volley ball for the patients and let the nurses rest.

Drug Therapy

The principal drug therapy in the manic patient or in patients with agitated depression is the use of reserpine or chlorpromazine, which have been described in a separate chapter. Other medications are of help to these patients as a support to the main line of treatment. They are particularly useful with mild depressive patients. It is our practice to start these patients on one of the amphetamines: Desoxyn, Dexedrine, or Benzedrine, or some other corresponding preparation. These preparations vary somewhat in their potency. We usually use a dose of 0.5 to 1 mg of Desoxyn or Dexedrine or 2.5 to 5 mg of Benzedrine twice daily. The method of using these drugs is of extreme importance in their effectiveness. Inasmuch as depressive patients feel worst on awakening, the patients are instructed to place one of the tablets and a glass of water by their bed and immediately upon awakening in the morning they are to take the tablet before getting out of bed. This usually results in partially allaying the tremendous depression, inertia, and hopelessness that trouble these patients when they first get up. The second tablet is taken with lunch and helps tide the patients over the midday letdown. If the patients have symptoms of anxiety, tension, and agitation, we combine one of the rapidly acting barbitals in a 0.1-gm dose with the amphetamine preparation. Most drug houses now prepare a combination tablet or capsule under various trade names. We find these preparations helpful to patients with mild depressions, particularly those in the outpatient department. In severely depressed states we have found the preparations to be of little or no benefit even though used in large doses.

Sedative and hypnotic drugs have a place in the treatment of depressive reactions and in manic patients during the acute phase of their illness. They are used to combat sleep disturbance from which all these patients suffer. They are usually unnecessary with patients who are aggressively and promptly treated by modern methods and are prescribed for only a few days or 2 to 3 weeks at the most.

We believe the sedatives and hypnotics are of no value in reducing the agitation of patients; they merely make patients more confused and ataxic. In agitated patients, reserpine or chlorpromazine are the drugs of choice. If these are not to be used, the agitation should be treated with electric shock or, if the physician chooses to be stubborn about modern treatment methods, with the prolonged neutral bath.

In combating the sleep disturbance it is important that appropriate drugs be used to fit the patient's particular sleep pattern. Keeping a graph and plotting the patient's periods of sleeping and awakening during the night for 3 to 4 days will usually suffice to establish a definite rhythm of sleep. Patients with a great deal of content disturbance and preoccupation will usually experience difficulty in falling asleep. This is particularly true of very agitated depression and manic patients. Once asleep, some of these patients sleep very well. In such cases a quick-acting barbital or paraldehyde is the drug of choice. Other patients with anxiety and tension, but less content disturbance, particularly in the depressive phase, fall asleep very rapidly but tend to awaken between 1:00 or 2:00 in the morning and toss restlessly the remainder of the night. For patients of this sort we believe that drugs with a more prolonged action are of greater benefit. In our experience, USP barbital is the most desirable drug. Billings has recommended the use of one of the rapidly acting barbitals placed in a "time bomb" capsule which is constructed to dissolve in the patient's stomach just prior to the calculated time of wakefulness. The drug companies now compound capsules containing barbitals in small bead or shotlike capsulettes inside the large capsules. The coatings on these little capsules dissolve at various periods of time, and there is a prolonged gradual effect from the drug. Proper selection of these fine preparations is of great help in managing sleep disturbances of the early-morning-awakening variety, and the drugs should be selected with the idea of reaching the peak of action at about the time the patient usually awakens.

Various endocrine products have been advocated in the treatment of depressions. The reported results vary greatly. Most people now feel, however, that endocrine preparations are indicated for gynecologic reasons only. If there are marked vasomotor reactions or medical gynecologic indications for the preparations, the presence or absence of a mental illness is no contraindication to their use. One should not anticipate that the gynecologic treatment will have any other than a psychologic effect on the course of these illnesses. Its benefit or harm will depend upon the patient's reaction to the gynecologic disturbance. Since these patients should be having psychotherapy, the physician will be able to judge in individual cases whether or not the patient will benefit from the use of endocrines to control vasomotor phenomena or other disturbances within the scope of the pharmacologic action of the sex hormones. In our experience they are rarely of use with these patients.

Nursing Care and Ward Management

The effectiveness of therapy always depends much upon the skill of the ward staff in managing the patient during his daily routine. Special treatments in terms of psychotherapy, shock therapy, or other treatments administered by the physician take up at most a small portion of the patient's time. The rest of the time he is in the charge of attendants and nurses on the ward, and they largely determine the type of world in which he lives. Special psychiatric training of the nurse and attendant is indispensable, and most hospital physicians will have to train their own staff. Only through the intelligent cooperation of the medical and nursing staff can optimum results be obtained.

In the manic phases the entire nursing procedure should be planned in such a manner as to offer the maximum protection to the patient and a minimum of stimuli. This is very difficult because the patients react aggressively against restriction, and it is therefore necessary to keep the patient constructively occupied and amused in a nonstimulating environment. In acute phases of disorder the patients are often kept in a private room where they are allowed to have books, magazines, and occupational therapy suited to their interests and their disturbed mental condition. We make an effort to have the same nurse, O.T. instructors, and attendants care for these patients from day to day. We discourage visitors for this particular group of patients. By removing the patient's audience and minimizing his chances for conflict with the environment, by providing diverting but nonstimulating entertainment, the patient tends to be less overactive and has fewer outbursts of aggression. In our experience this greatly minimizes his anxiety, shortens the course of his illness, and improves his response to the more specific therapies. As the patient improves, environmental stimuli and responsibilities are slowly increased.

In the depressed phase special nursing techniques are also indicated. The patient must be carefully protected against attempts at self-mutilation and self-destruction. These will seldom occur if he is accompanied by someone throughout the 24-hour period. He should be kept in a ward which is bright and attractive, with frequent changes of pictures, flowers, and clothing. Shifting him from one room to another often helps. Tactful efforts should be made to interest patients in occupational therapy—outdoor exercise, movies, reading, etc. The skill and tact of the nurses and attendants in approaching these subjects are very important when the patients are negativistic or feel hopeless and tend to reject any attempts to divert them from their endless melancholic ruminations.

Use of the Social Worker

After the acute phase of the illness subsides the social worker who will manage this patient and his family after discharge should make contact with the case. While the patient is under therapy the social worker's visits should be almost entirely on a superficial, get-acquainted basis. The patient will at this time be forming emotional attachments to his physician and with certain members of the ward staff, and the social worker should not compete for or interfere in this beginning establishment of relationship. In this stage, however, the social worker should be forming firm bonds with significant members of the patient's family and, where indicated, with his employer. A great deal of the patient's success and adjustment after he leaves the hospital will depend upon the social worker's skill in preparing the setting for his discharge. As the patient begins to improve and one can project a time of discharge, the skillful physician, nurses, and occupational therapists will transfer or broaden the patient's emotional drive to include the social worker. Toward the end of his treatment, the social worker should play an increasingly significant part in the patient's management, and this is usually best accomplished by having her enter the picture when the patient begins to participate in excursions into the community for recreational purposes, to purchase clothing, to see about his job, etc. Too often hospitals lack sufficient social service personnel to bring about this gradual transition of dependence from the ward personnel to the social worker, but one can always hope that the student will be working in an area sufficiently staffed with these valuable people. By the time the patient is ready for discharge his treatment should be largely under the management of the social worker and the ward physician. If he is to be transferred to another physician in the outpatient department, this transition also should be made during the patient's last days in the hospital. As the patient's acute affective symptoms subside, the psychotherapeutic procedure also shifts from superficial support and the reassuring type of reaction given during the acute stages of the illness to dynamically oriented psychotherapy or to the beginning phases of psychoanalysis if such is to be used.

Fortunately these days many patients come to us early in their reactions and may be treated entirely in the office or clinic. In this mild stage dynamically oriented psychotherapy can always be started by a skillful physician. Selected cases may be placed in analysis, although the analysis of affective cases requires great skill to prevent a further deepening of the depressive reaction or a flowering of the mania.

The details of the use of psychotherapy, the special drugs, shock therapy, and occupational therapy have been presented in other sections of this book. The general principles of rehabilitation are also presented elsewhere and this factual material should be blended with the outline of over-all management of these cases presented here.

Involutional Psychoses

Treatment of these disorders shares so many things in common with the affective disorders that it will be presented here.

PREVENTIVE TREATMENT

Every man and woman should be prepared psychologically for the involutional period. In our culture the myths that people must have nervous trouble, that their usefulness comes to an end with the involutional period, and that they lose sexual attractiveness or sexual ability should be combated by the medical profession. Women particularly must be made to understand that the involutional period is a normal physiologic state, just as adolescence was, and that the unpleasant physiologic sensations which accompany it are neither permanent, severe, nor do they call for changes in their way of life. The only definite changes taking places that are significant to women are: no longer expecting the monthly menstrual period, and no longer worrying about birth control techniques in marital relations. The decreasing frequency of sexual contact on the part of the woman's husband is not due to her lack of attractiveness but to the fact that the husband is also aging. Vasomotor reactions due to the endocrine involution may be combated with estrogenic hormones if these symptoms are severe. In most instances we find that reassuring the patient concerning her physical and psychiatric status will make the use of endocrine therapy unnecessary.

In male patients additional steps are necessary. Many male patients, noting a decline in their sexual powers, refuse to integrate properly to the concept of aging and, in an attempt to prove that their virility is unimpaired, may become involved in disgraceful extramarital affairs, particularly with young and attractive women whose favors may be bought or who are seeking a father.

Management of the Acute Phase of the Illness

A few patients who develop an involutional reaction may be managed in the outpatient department or in a nursing home with special nursing care. It is usually better to hospitalize these patients in a psychiatric institution properly equipped for intensive treatment. The principles of management outlined for the depressive reaction apply almost in toto to this group of patients. Sometimes the presence of complicating physical disorders such as arteriosclerosis, hypertension, or diabetes complicates the picture. While the prognosis is not uniformly good as in the manic-depressive reaction, prompt, vigorous, and total treatment of these patients will often result in their recovery.

CHAPTER 35

Treatment of Schizophrenia

Prevention

The exact cause of schizophrenia is not known, therefore, we cannot certainly say that we know how to prevent this disorder. It is reasonable to believe, however, that general mental health principles, particularly during the period of childhood and early adult life, will do much to build up the ego strength and thus cut down the opportunity for the development of schizophrenia. We believe that the child should find the home a place of security, love, and affection. The home should be a source of guidance and support as he begins to broaden his social contacts with the external world. The physical, emotional, or social shortcomings of himself, of members of his family, or of his environment should be faced realistically by the child, and the parents and teachers should encourage him to understand these situations in terms of his emotional and intellectual development. The material presented in the first section of this book and in the chapter on child behavior and psychiatry is particularly appropriate in building strong egos in patients in an attempt to protect them against schizophrenia. The objective is to build up a strong ego, to strive for a balance between interest in self and the environment, and to encourage the formation of strong, dependable, emotional ties to significant people in life. Situations of stress and conflict should be detected early by the alert school nurse, the schoolteacher, or the family physician. Correcting these in infancy or childhood is often relatively simple. As the person develops with these imperfections in his ego, adjustment becomes more difficult and precarious.

Treatment of the Psychosis

The earlier the treatment of the schizophrenia, the better the chance of recovery. Psychiatrists should use any and all knowledge available in the treatment of these patients. In assessing a patient for therapy it is well to look at the total situation. Such questions should be asked as: What does the patient have to react with in terms of ego strength, intelligence, and physical resources? What is the situation he faces in terms of his family, job, occupation, educational opportunities, and social status in the community?

By considering these questions the physician can more intelligently plan the course of treatment for his patient. The management of schizophrenia is particularly difficult, and it is our belief that some physicians, nurses, and attendants do better with these patients than others. Fromm-Reichmann stated:

. . . his own security (the psychiatrist's) may be threatened by the content of the patient's anxiety, thus arousing problems which may possibly strike too close to home. Some psychiatrists may be frightened by the schizophrenic's ability to sense and seek out their weak points and to comment on them or play upon them without words. In any of these instances the psychiatrist may become too preoccupied with his own need for safety, security and prestige; hence, too defensive and argumentative to relate himself successfully to schizophrenic patients, or vice versa.

Whitehorn in a series of studies of schizophrenic patients treated with psychotherapy noted that the person of the therapist rather than the technique used seemed most important.

Frank, in discussing the reaction of different groups in terms of the physicians' technique, stated:

This leads me to wonder whether the particular technique used in the treatment of schizophrenics may not be largely irrelevant. Perhaps what really matters is the general attitude of the doctor. More important than the particular technique used appeared to be the attitude of the doctor. Groups did worse in which the doctor was inconsistent, vacillating, or in other ways failed to exert leadership. Those groups did best in which the doctor appeared as a perceptive, strong, accepting person who structured the situation clearly for the patients and supported them in their emotional turmoil.

This typifies one of the difficult situations in schizophrenia. As a schizophrenic patient begins to enter into therapeutic situations, he tentatively forms emotional ties to persons in the environment. If the people in the environment are capricious, inconsistent, or do not understand the schizophrenic patient and his needs, the patient withdraws and retires further into his psychosis. Some physicians, nurses, and attendants on the ward are more sensitive to the schizophrenic patient's needs, have a greater empathy with him, and respond better to his changing emotional needs.

We believe valuable information on the basic needs of some of these patients can be gained by familiarity with significant persons in the patient's family. Often one detects the parents or other significant people who failed the patient because of their own neurotic or other adjustment difficulties. Often by being aware of these facts the psychiatrist can, in the structure of the therapeutic situation, supply some things the patient failed to gain from his family. In some instances this may be permissiveness, in others it may be a bit more aggressive, but always it must be supportive and understanding.

Much more needs to be known about the actual psychotherapeutic management of schizophrenic patients. At present we know that some physicians do well with them, others do not. We also know that in hospitals certain nurses and attendants do very well with the schizophrenic groups, and others have nothing but conflict and turmoil with them.

Psychotherapy

We believe that every schizophrenic patient should have psychotherapy. In the earlier stages and in the developmental stages the patients may be managed on an outpatient or office basis, with psychotherapy carried on during the patient's visit. It is sometimes difficult for the psychiatrist to form a kind of transference with the schizophrenic patient. The physician should go slowly and not force the situation, psychologically speaking. Building up confidence, persuasion, suggestion—particularly indirect suggestion—and gradually establishing a transference situation with the patient is an essential first step. This implies some degree of accessibility on the part of the patient. If he is so delusional or so disturbed and overactive that this is impossible, the use of shock therapy, particularly insulin shock, or the use of chlorpromazine or reserpine often makes the patient accessible to psychotherapy.

Where possible, we believe that a patient should receive individual psychotherapy that is psychoanalytically oriented. Lacking this, well-structured group therapy also rooted in dynamic psychiatry is the second choice. For some patients it may offer advantages over individual psychotherapy. Patients who are hospitalized because of their illness will inevitably receive a form of group psychotherapy from the general ward management and environment, and the psychiatrist therefore must take pains to structure this for the patient's advantages. We believe the ward situation should provide an opportunity for the patient to form firm, dependable emotional ties to some person or persons. Ideally this would be the ward physician, but, failing this, some attendant would serve. Efforts should be made to keep the ward personnel stable so that the patient does not have to go through the difficult and painful process of repeatedly reestablishing emotional contacts.

The environment of the wards should offer opportunities for group participation. Often the first things will be going to the cafeteria, watching movies, participating in book reviews, dancing, or group singing. Sometimes athletic events, tea parties, or sewing circles, depending on the sex of the patient, will be the first type of group activity in which the patient may participate. There should be opportunities for the patient to be alone since groups are sometimes threatening to these patients and they must have short periods of solitude. Some patients may request seclusion, and this should be granted, although it is not necessary to lock the door.

These patients should be encouraged to participate in group therapy, and in some the first breakthrough in the psychotic ruminations and the first significant rise to reality come through the occupational therapy department when the patient becomes interested in some type of creative endeavor and begins to form ties and affiliations to the occupational therapist.

In some settings the physician will spend his time productively in lending support, advice, and guidance to the ward personnel, who will themselves form significant ties to the schizophrenic patients. This is particularly true where there are large groups of schizophrenic patients and a great shortage of medical personnel.

Early or mild cases of schizophrenia or patients in remission may be placed in orthodox psychoanalysis.

Rosen has recently been using what he calls a modified form of psychoanalysis in the treatment of schizophrenia. Studies indicate that he brings about marked improvement in some schizophrenic patients. It apparently is difficult for him to transmit or teach what he does to other people. In an earlier edition of this book we expressed doubt that other persons would be able to utilize the Rosen technique. At the time of this writing we can say that few people have done so, but Rosen has served as a stimulus to further exploration and experimentation with deeper psychotherapeutic methods with the schizophrenic patients.

Drug Therapies

Practically every compound in the pharmacopeia has been given to schizophrenic patients in attempts to modify their psychosis. Casperson and his group have used malononitrile. One of us used glutamic acid, cytochrome C, and antireticulocytic toxoid serum without benefit, although some patients show temporary responses to these treatments. Histamine therapy has been advocated for some patients. Others used nicotinic acid, ACTH, and various other compounds.

At present we may safely say that none of these drugs produces any prolonged or significant effect on the schizophrenic process.

Reserpine and chlorpromazine drastically modify the schizophrenic process, making uncooperative patients available for group or individual psychotherapy in many instances. Insulin shock and electric shock have also proved of great value. These have been discussed under those individual headings.

Total Push Therapy

This term was introduced by Myerson to describe a generalized therapeutic regime utilizing physiotherapy in its various forms, careful attention to diet, an active program of exercise and games, and ensuring that patients are attractively clothed and groomed. Cooperation in the plan is rewarded with extra privileges, and infraction of rules or lack of interest in the program results in removal of certain privileges. This is in effect an excellent program of nursing care with group participation. The total push program resulted in a lower incidence of chronic deteriorating processes, fewer disturbances on the ward, and an increased incidence of discharges.

The general attempt to use this system throughout the Massachusetts hospital system has resulted in an improved discharge rate for schizophrenic patients. We feel that further modification of this, with more enlightened involvement and manipulation of the group situation by the attendants and nurses, and more active participation in group therapy by the physician, psychologist, and social workers, should be encouraged. It has resulted, where applied throughout the country, in a still greater improvement rate in the schizophrenic group.

We believe that there is still much to be learned about the mass application of these techniques, and our colleagues from the social sciences have participated in studies for which we have great hope. We feel a physician would be shortsighted in attempting to utilize any one kind of treatment or theory in the management of a disastrous disorder like schizophrenia. We believe in combining everything that is now known about the biologic, sociologic, and psychoanalytic approach in the management of these patients. Each should be modified for the patient's particular need in the setting in which he finds himself—whether it is one that provides for individual care or one that means that the treatment must be applied in mass by relatively unskilled attendants. We must do the best with what we have, but what we have should be intelligently applied.

Rehabilitation

When these patients improve and get ready to leave the hospital, the integration of the social service worker and the outpatient staff, if different from the hospital staff, into the patient's therapeutic team must be carefully planned, as discussed under Depressions. We believe that many of the relapses of schizophrenic patients in returning to the hospital are due to poor follow-up management and poor planning. While we rationalize these on the basis of shortage of personnel, one often feels that we do not use available resources with due efficiency. Studies in the institutions operated by one of the authors are offering new light on the dynamics of the rehabilitation process; rehabilitation probably plays a larger role in the schizophrenic than in the manic-depressive psychoses, but the principles are essentially the same in each. The details will differ with each case.

CHAPTER 36

Treatment of Neuroses

Treatment of the psychosomatic disorders and those classified as psychoneuroses (psychophysiologic autonomic and visceral disorders and psychoneurotic disorders) principally involves psychotherapy, or psychoanalysis in selected cases. The psychotherapy may vary from simple support therapy administered by the family physician to detailed and dynamically oriented psychotherapy administered by the well-trained psychiatrist. A few patients may be treated by psychoanalysis if their ego strength and the over-all situation warrant it. Most of these patients can maintain and continue their occupation. A limited number need to be brought into the hospital. In our opinion they should always come on a voluntary basis, and many of them are better cared for in a part-time day hospital or night hospital setting than in one giving complete hospitalization.

In addition to the psychotherapy, certain patients gain some support from the judicious use of sedative drugs. At present there is some indication that chlorpromazine or reserpine may be of benefit as a crutch in some of the more severely incapacitated patients, but we have not had so much experience under controlled situations with the use of these drugs in neuroses as we have in the psychotic disturbances.

Tentative experiments in treatment of the neuroses with carbon dioxide inhalations, either as a modified form of a shock treatment or to bring about abreactions on the part of the patient, have been of little benefit in our experience.

Many neurotic patients are able to carry on in the external world and gain enough ego support from the therapeutic situation so that no other aid or assistance is needed. In a few cases the external situation is so complicated that it may be necessary for the psychiatrist to refer a spouse,

396

parent, or child to another therapist for management to help resolve the external situation. In a clinic setting a social worker or clinical psychologist, preferably the former, may be able to work with the significant people in the environment to bring about constructive changes in the situation. There are patients who are maladapted to their occupation and placing them in a rehabilitation program can sometimes mean the difference between success and failure of the treatment. Patients with religious conflicts should be referred to the clergyman of their faith, and the clergyman should be one who has insight and skills in counseling techniques involving psychiatric problems.

Some patients with a great deal of anxiety and tension get pleasure from massage or the use of showers or other hydrotherapeutic methods where these are available. These methods, however, should be looked upon as crutches and not treatments in themselves.

Patients coming to day hospitals or night hospitals or who are being institutionalized get great help from group activities. For the neurotic patients the group activities most helpful to them are either actual group therapy situations, psychodrama, or work with occupational therapists who are dynamically oriented. Recreational programs will help work off some anxieties and tensions but these again are symptomatic and do not bring about real changes in ego structure in most neurotic patients.

Handling the mild neurotic patient and the mild psychosomatic patient is the field of psychiatry in which the family physician plays the largest role. The sections on psychotherapy are written particularly for the management of these patients, and this material will not be repeated here.

Treatment of Personality Disorders

Personality disorders are, in general, adjustment failures owing to incompletely formed neurotic patterns; neurotic patterns manifest principally by adjustment problems in relation to the external world, particularly manifest by conduct disturbances of various sorts. Perhaps genetic or biologic factors which result in basically poor material leave the patient trying to compete in a tough world with inferior equipment and he develops many secondary adjustment and neurotic problems.

These problems are sociologic problems in which psychiatry shares with the other social sciences the responsibility for the understanding and care of these persons. It appears that the best way to manage these disorders is to prevent them!

Theoretically if every child could have an appropriate set of ancestors, good health, and loving, dependable, stable, and understanding parents, and be born into a world offering satisfaction of his impulses on a basis acceptable to him and to his fellow man, there would be no need for the development of this type of disorder.

Since we do not live in a Utopia and since we do not have any immediate prospects of creating one, the prevention of these difficulties will probably have limited applications.

Most parents probably do as well as they can by their children within the limits of their understanding. Their own resources, personal and economic, often leave much to be desired in terms of the responsibility for raising children. Under the stimulation of the Parent-Teachers Association, mental health societies, and the various mental hygiene clinics, much education has been done through child-study groups. Whether these have contributed anything toward preventing future generations of personality disorders, neuroses, or psychoses, only time will tell. Statistics in this area are notably infrequent and undependable. Too often people attempting to teach these principles do not communicate with their audience too well, and the mothers and teachers only partially hear what is said, and interpret what is heard in terms of their own education, background, and comprehension of the language used. One sometimes suspects that the modern mother perhaps does less well by her child because she is attempting to do what she thinks she heard some authority or pseudoexpert say to her about rearing her child rather than following what may be sound, natural impulses. At least the possibility of prevention offers enough hope to continue further research on techniques and methods. We refer the student to the section on child psychiatry which describes the theories used by one of the authors' in the hopes that we may be preventing future generations of personality disorder and neuroses.

It is our opinion that the institutionalization of people suffering from personality disorder does little or nothing for them. It may be necessary to protect the world from the acting out of these persons, but it should not be rationalized on the basis that it is helping the individual. We believe that those patients brought for therapy should be placed in a combination of psychotherapy which may vary from support therapy to psychoanalysis, depending on the availability of therapy and the over-all potentials of the person.

Any kind of psychotherapy for these patients is difficult. Experiments with group therapy, analytically and nonanalytically oriented, have offered interesting results in some controlled studies, and we are hopeful that further developments of techniques may prove this an effective method for handling certain of these disorders. It is our opinion that these patients should all be placed in some type of rehabilitation program if their personality disorders result in occupational and family conflicts.

Various types of surgical treatment on the brain have been recommended in these patients but we do not recommend them. The techniques are essentially those described in the section on psychosurgery in this text.

The new drugs, chlorpromazine and reserpine, have been tried on these patients as have all other new forms of treatment. In patients showing aggression, overactive behavior, and hostility, these drugs undoubtedly prove of help since they cut down these forms of behavior in psychotic patients and presumably do so in patients suffering from personality disorders. We doubt that they have any long-term effect on these patients, but the drugs may be useful in making those institutionalized or imprisoned more amenable to psychotherapeutic and rehabilitation techniques. If experience should show that maintenance of some of these patients on these drugs, more or less permanently, would solve their adjustment difficulties in the world, these drugs should certainly be given to them on an outpatient basis.

CHAPTER **37**

Rehabilitation

In recent years, particularly since World War II, a vast profession has grown up known as *rehabilitation*. Unfortunately, the concept has become so popular that the use of the word no longer has much specific meaning. In one context it may mean teaching a partially paralyzed person to feed himself or care for his own bowel functions. In another it may mean taking a person with permanent handicaps and placing him on a job at which he can support himself, constructively contributing to the economy and preserving his own self-respect. In still others it may mean taking a person who is adjusting reasonably well to an occupation but is discontented because of a lack of future, and equipping this person through education and increased skills to realize more fully his total potential as a productive person in the world.

The initial steps were made by Howard Rusk and his associates and were broadening the application of the principles of physical medicine. With the great success of these programs, however, it has become obvious to the workers in this new specialty that the psychologic factors in many of their patients with physical handicaps were often the deterrent to further progress. This has resulted in affiliating their teams with psychiatrists, psychiatric social workers, and clinical psychologists. These persons make valuable contributions to the rehabilitation team.

This textbook is not the appropriate place for a general discussion on rehabilitation. There is an abundant literature on this subject. We propose to discuss here the role of rehabilitation and the rehabilitation agencies in the care of psychiatric patients.

For our purposes we would use the term "rehabilitation" to describe those portions of treatment that have to do with placing a patient back in the community at a level of work compatible with his capacities and abilities, whether these are less than, the same as, or greater than the level of occupation before the psychiatric illness. In this rather broad definition

400

we would include the housewife who returns to the care of her family but with help in adjusting at a maximum level of her capacities.

As Millet has stated:

. . . the new rehabilitation team must include individuals specially qualified to assess the degree of disability, to formulate the steps necessary to its partial or complete cure, to evaluate the final result and to provide the maximum possible opportunity for the individual who has benefited from these services, to regain the position as a worker in the community to which his efforts and self-respect entitle him.

As one views the use of rehabilitation services in a psychiatric organization, it is possible to classify them in at least two different ways. Because they present different aspects of the problem, we propose to discuss them both ways and hope the student will not be confused.

In the first place it is possible to discuss the use of the rehabilitation services in the terms of the patient's job status: (1) patient unemployed; (2) patient employed but poorly adjusted to his job; (3) patient constructively employed but at a level lower than his potential.

The second way of surveying a rehabilitation program is to view it from the point of contact with the patient in the social institution: (1) rehabilitation services in an outpatient or private office practice; (2) rehabilitation in hospitalized patients; (3) rehabilitation in patients dismissed from the hospital to the follow-up clinic.

Patient without Job

A jobless patient coming to the attention of psychiatrists will usually be unemployed because of economic stress in the community, which makes competition more difficult than he can meet. This situation may stem from his lack of training, lack of skills, laziness, personality disorders which make it difficult for him to get along with his fellow workers or boss, inability to accept responsibility, excessive drinking, or absenteeism. The patient may be so physically deteriorated and weak from neurotic symptoms that he is unwilling to work; he may have been in a hospital for a long time and lost contacts with external institutions that offer possibilities of employment.

The need of a team approach is obvious. The psychiatrist makes a careful assessment of the patient's physical and mental condition, using consultants in psychology for aptitude testing and the measurement of mental capacity and medical specialists for the assessment of details of physical conditions if somatic pathology is discovered. An assessment should be made as to treatability of the psychiatric or somatic disorder and the appropriate therapy should be instituted where available. The social service department will develop the patient's work record, assay the environmental situation in which he lives, educate the persons in the situation to which he is to return, and ascertain the amount of support he can receive from the significant persons in his environment during the initial stages of his rehabilitation. The trained rehabilitation counselor in conference with the social worker, the psychologist, and the psychiatrist then make an over-all assay of their findings plus such other information as may occur to them to determine the employability of the patient in his community.

As a result of this team determination it will then be decided whether the patient should be referred for further therapy, should have further training, or should be employed at a less-than-optimum level during the period of his continued treatment or continued training or both. The assignment of roles in the future rehabilitation plan of the patient will be largely determined by the rehabilitation counselor and will vary with the detailed findings of a particular case.

The student will see that there is an infinite number of possibilities, but the maximum resources of a particular person can be used only if all these trained professions collaborate and if the matter of role status can be determined according to the patient's needs.

Patients Poorly Adjusted to Job

A general approach to this type of case is the same as above but with some differences in details. The social worker will not only contact the patient's family but also his foreman, perhaps his fellow workers, or his boss. The goal is to get their view of the patient's work ability and his employment record. The psychologist should not only test the patient's general aptitude but also, particularly, his aptitude for the work he is handling.

The psychiatrist's problem will be essentially the same in the two cases; a careful assessment of the patient's physical and mental capacities to adapt to life in general and to his job and family in particular. The skilled rehabilitation worker will be familiar with the requirements for the job the patient is employed in and will be able to decide whether the job is too difficult for the patient, whether it fits his capacities and does not cause his maladjustment, or whether it is so far below the patient's capacity that it is rendering him unhappy and disgruntled. After assessment of the over-all picture it may be necessary for the patient to have some type of medical or psychiatric treatment. It may be necessary to help him solve family problems which may be psychotherapeutically handled or may be handled by the social worker. It may be a problem of working out a better adaptation to his job which the rehabilitation counselor will probably handle himself, or it may be a matter of further training or transfer to another department which will be handled in conference with the patient's employer. Again, the role and status of each individual in the therapeutic rehabilitation team will vary with the particular needs of the particular patient.

Patients Working in Jobs below Their Potential

This field of rehabilitation has not been highly developed. With our expanding economy and with the tremendous need for highly skilled and technically trained persons, this area of persons working in jobs below their full potential probably holds the greatest hopes for the use of "rehabilitation techniques." Perhaps the phrase is a poor one for this area of activity. There are undoubtedly many persons working at jobs which are far below their potential capacity. We feel that if job foremen can be taught to detect these persons, and if they can be referred to a rehabilitation center for a careful evaluation of their health, aptitude, and social status, many of these patients would be worthwhile candidates for further training and education to upgrade their potential capacities. It is essential that these people be surveyed carefully because some persons, though they may have the physical and intellectual resources, do not have the emotional stability to handle jobs of greater responsibility than those in which they find themselves. However, careful assessment by the fully staffed rehabilitation center should be able to pick from the general mass of people large numbers of persons who could be trained to fill the many gaps in our professional and semiprofessional spheres.

Financing the education of these persons through part-time education while they work, or some type of privately or government-sponsored loan system to be repaid from the rewards of their increased occupational skills, should not prove too difficult to work out if people become convinced of the desirability of doing so. Perhaps closer collaboration between rehabilitation centers and the guidance, counseling groups in public school systems will be the first coarse screen for detecting those persons with greater potentials. Applying motivation to the individual for upward striving in the social economic scale must start in the secondary schools or perhaps even at the primary level as we learn more about testing for a skill.

Rehabilitation Viewed from Psychiatric Agency Contacted by the Patient

REHABILITATION AT OUTPATIENT LEVEL

Patients under treatment at an outpatient level will in many instances be gainfully employed, and it will be found that the occupation is a support and a help to therapy. Rehabilitation will not play a great role in this group of patients.

Many, however, will fit into one of the three categories discussed above and they should be referred to the rehabilitation center as they continue their therapy in the outpatient department. If the outpatient psychiatrist managing the case is not connected with the rehabilitation center he can at least work out a liaison with his counterpart in that center.

Job adjustment may play a major role in the difficulties of some patients seen in an outpatient department, and working through the rehabilitation center and the job-adjustment counselor may handle the entire matter, sparing the psychiatrist's time for cases requiring more intensive psychotherapy. Many patients seen in the clinic are persons who fit into the latter two categories. In a few instances we have seen good results when persons were stimulated to further educational opportunities offered through the rehabilitation counselor in order to upgrade their status.

Many patients seen in the outpatient department will recover sufficiently to require no particular adaptation to their job and present no problem. A good many patients, however, will need help in selecting a job that they can handle in terms of their neurotic residuals. A shy, retiring, masochistic person would do poorly in the sales department but might be ideal on the complaint desk. The adjustment counselor, by explaining these needs to the patient's employer and by seeking positions within the service of the employer, may do well to increase the efficiency of the employer's business and contribute much to the successful management of the patient.

PATIENTS IN THE HOSPITAL

Patients who have been in the hospital for a short time may be able to return to their job. In this case, if their recovery is complete, it may be necessary only to explain the nature of the patient's illness and the fact that he is ready to resume his old job at his old level of efficiency. This can be done by a social worker.

If on the other hand the patient returns to work incompletely cured or in a state of partial remission, it will be necessary for the team to assess the patient's employability. They must prognosticate accurately his future course, whether he may be expected to improve further, stay the same, or relapse, and to explain this to the employer. Then a work plan for the patient is made out, increasing his responsibility or decreasing it as the circumstances of the case may dictate. It is our belief that the rehabilitation services for patients who are to go out should be contacted as soon as it is finally determined approximately when the patient will be able to leave the hospital. In long-term patients it will be possible to give several weeks' notice. In shorter-term patients it may be necessary to have the organization set up so that these services can be carried out within 1 to 2 weeks when patients are ready to leave the hospital, and during their posthospital period. It is possible to find patients in all three of the job-status categories. There will be patients fully recovered, those with capacity for better jobs, and those with limited potentials for whom jobs must be found in which the handicap does not interfere with the efficient carrying out of the particular job assignment.

Another phase of rehabilitation concerns the patient who is still under active treatment in the hospital. This phase of the program has been developed fairly well in some places and not in others. We believe that the rehabilitation program may be made an integral part of the patient's treatment. Certainly with a patient whose disorder has a short course and a uniformly good outcome, such as acute depression, the social worker should start work with the family at the time the patient is admitted, preparing them for the patient's ultimate discharge. Contacts with the patient's employer should also be in terms of the patient's prompt return to employability and his old job. During his hospital stay the patient should be kept in contact with his fellow workers and be kept job oriented. If in the course of treatment it is found that it will be necessary for the patient to have a transfer of work, or if it seems desirable to train him for greater responsibilities, these steps also may be incorporated into the over-all management of the patient in the ward. It is desirable to have a rehabilitation director in the hospital who will devote full time to coordinating these services in the hospital with those in the community. It is possible in the recreational program, in the physical therapy program, and in the occupational therapy program to do something to improve the patient's skills and coordination in certain types of activities.

Some larger hospitals have experimented with employing their patients on a part-time basis while treatment is carried on by the therapist, rehabilitation workers, and social service department. These patients maintain themselves in employee quarters. This has been quite successful and not only trains the patient to take responsibility but prepares him to do a more effective job for his future boss.

Other institutions experiment with sheltered workshops, training programs, and collaborating with local universities and trade schools, with great promise in speeding up the rehabilitation and effective reemployment of patients.

PATIENTS IN THE FOLLOW-UP CLINIC OR POSTHOSPITAL PROGRAM

If the rehabilitation program in the hospital has been sufficiently well developed, the transition from this to an outpatient rehabilitation program, described above, will be a fairly simple one. Some large mental health agencies have separate clinics for patients who have been discharged from the hospital and for those who have not yet been in the hospital. This is done in terms of geographic location or volume of patients, but in either case the follow-up clinic should have the same firm liaison with the local rehabilitation agencies that is advocated for the outpatient departments. The persons in the hospital proper who are responsible for the rehabilitation service are the logical ones to work out these liaisons for the clinics if the clinics do not have a rehabilitation worker of their own.

The authors recognize that the role of rehabilitation is not yet fully exploited. It is our belief that much improvement in our therapeutic results and in the general efficiency of the economy can be brought about by further expansion of the rehabilitation programs and greater liaison between existing psychiatric, social, and rehabilitation agencies. Further research into providing incentives and motives both for the patients to be rehabilitated and for their prospective bosses is necessary. Tremendous progress has been made in the last 12 to 15 years, and each year opens up new vistas of hope.

BIBLIOGRAPHY

Adams, E. D., Chornesky, G., and Haycox, J.: Psychosomatic investigations of cerebral arteriosclerosis with psychosis. *Dis. Nerv. System* **16**:165, 1955.

Aichorn, A.: "Wayward Youth." The Viking Press, Inc., New York, 1935.

Aldrich, C. K.: "Psychiatry for the Family Physician." McGraw-Hill Book Company, Inc., New York, 1955.

Alexander, F.: Influence of psychologic factors upon gastrointestinal disturbances: Symposium; general problems, objectives, and preliminary results. *Psychoanalyt. Quart.* **3**:501, 1934.

Alexander, F.: Fundamental concepts of psychosomatic research: Psychogenesis, conversion, specificity. *Psychosom. Med.* **5**:400, 1943.

Alexander, F., et al.: "Psychoanalytic Therapy." The Ronald Press Company, New York, 1946.

Alexander, F. G.: Indications for psychoanalytic therapy. *Bull. New York Acad. Med.* **20**:319, 1944.

Alexander, L: Wernicke's disease: Identity of lesions produced experimentally by B₁ avitaminosis in pigeons with haemorrhagic polioencephalitis occurring in chronic alcoholism in man. *Am. J. Psychol.* **16**:61, 1940.

Alexander, L., Pijoan, M., Schube, P. G., and Moore, M.: Cevitamic acid content of blood plasma in alcoholic psychoses. *Arch. Neurol. & Psychiat.* **40**:57, 1938.

Allen, E. V., and Brown, G. E.: Neurosis of extremities following phlebitis. *M. Clin. North America* **15**:123, 1931.

Allen, F. H.: "Psychotherapy with Children." W. W. Norton & Company, Inc., New York, 1942.

Alpers, B. J.: Personality and emotional disorders associated with hypothalamic lesions. *Psychosom. Med.* **2**:286, 1940.

Alvarez, W.: "Nervous Indigestion." Paul B. Hoeber, Inc., New York, 1931.

Alzheimer, A.: Beiträge zur kenntnis der pathologischen Neuroglia und ihrer Beziehungen zu den Abbauvorgängen und Nervengeweibe. *Histol. u. histopath. Arbeiten, ü. d. Grosshirninde.* **3**:401, 1910.

American Psychiatric Association: Psychiatric Research Reports. 1. "Pharmacological Products Recently Introduced in the Treatment of Psychiatric Disorder." Washington, D. C., July, 1955.

Anastasi, A.: "Genetics and the Inheritance of Integrated Neurological and Psychiatric Patterns." Edited by D. Hooker and C. C. Hare. Vol. 33, chap. 5. The Williams & Wilkins Company, Baltimore, 1954.

Anderson, O, D., and Liddell, H. S.: Observations on experimental neurosis in sheep. *Arch. Neurol. & Psychiat.* **34**:330, 1935.

Anderson, O. D., and Parmenter, R.: A long-term study of the experimental neurosis in the sheep and dog. *Psychosom. Med.* 1941.

Anderson, O. D., Parmenter, R., and Liddell, H. S.: Some cardiovascular manifestations of the experimental neurosis in sheep. *Psychosom. Med.* **1**:93, 1939.

Anderson, R., and Watkins, H.: Occupational therapy for the mentally retarded. *Ment. Hosp.* **6**:26, 1955.

Appel, J. W.: Incidence of neuropsychiatric disorders in the U. S. Army in World War II. *Am. J. Psychiat.* **103**:196, 1946.

Appel, K. E., and Strecker, E. A.: "Practical Examination of Personality and Behavior Disorders of Adults and Children." The Macmillan Company, New York, 1936.

Arestad, F. H., and McGovern, M. A.: Hospital service in the United States. Twenty-ninth annual presentation of hospital data by the Council on Medical Education and Hospitals of the American Medical Association. *J.A.M.A.* **143**:25, 1950.

Arieti, S.: An interpretation of the divergent outcome of schizophrenia in identical twins. *Psychiatric Quart.* **18**:587, 1944.

Arieti, S.: "Interpretation of Schizophrenia." Basic Books, Inc., New York, 1955.

Armstrong, M. D., and Tyler, F. H.: Studies on phenylketonuria: I. Restricted phenylalanine intake on phenylketonuria. *J. Clin. Invest.* **34**:565, 1955.

Aronson, M. L.: A study of the Freudian theory of paranoia by means of the Rorschach test. *J. Projective Techniques* **16**:397, 1952.

Ashby, W.: An approach to the solution of mental dysfunction through brain enzyme studies. *Am. J. Psychiat.* **106**:491, 1950.

Ashby, W., and Weickhardt, G. D.: Study of carbonicanhydrase in the pallium in nineteen cases of paretic neuro-syphilis. *J. Nerv. & Ment. Dis.* **106**:107, 1947.

Ashby, W., and Weickhardt, G. D.: Study of carbonicanhydrase in thirty-seven brains with reference to symmetry of distribution. *J. Nerv. & Ment. Dis.* **106**:540, 1947.

Association for Research in Nervous and Mental Disease, Proceedings: "Acute Epidemic Encephalitis (Lethargic Encephalitis)." Paul B. Hoeber, Inc., New York, 1921.

Association for Research in Nervous and Mental Disease, Proceedings: Behavior Pattern of Foetal Infant and Child. In "Genetics and the Inheritance of Integrated Neurological and Psychiatric Patterns." Edited by D. Hooker and C. C. Hare. Vol. 33, chap. 9. The Williams & Wilkins Company, Baltimore, 1954.

Association for Research in Nervous and Mental Disease, Proceedings: The Inherited and Acquired Components of Behavior. In "Genetics and the Inheritance of Integrated Neurological and Psychiatric Patterns." Edited by D. Hooker and C. C. Hare. Vol. 33, chap. 5. The Williams & Wilkins Company, Baltimore, 1954.

Association for Research in Nervous and Mental Disease, Proceedings: "Manic-Depressive Psychosis," vol. 11. The Williams & Wilkins Company, Baltimore, 1931.

Association for Research in Nervous and Mental Disease, Proceedings: "Schizophrenia (Dementia Praecox)," vol. 5. Paul B. Hoeber, Inc., New York, 1928.

Astrachan, M.: Group psychotherapy with mentally retarded female adolescents and adults. *Am. J. Ment. Deficiency* 60:152, 1955.

Bair, H. V., and Herold, W.: Efficacy of chlorpromazine in hyperactive mentally retarded children. *A.M.A. Arch. Neurol. & Psychiat.* 74:363, 1955.

Barcroft, J.: "The Brain and Its Environment." Yale University Press, New Haven, Conn., 1938.

Barker, L. I.: Multiple neuritis with macrocytic anemia in an alcoholic addict. *J. Nerv. & Ment. Dis.* 92:1, 1940.

Barnacle, C. H., Ebaugh, F. G., and Ewalt, J. R.: Comparative study of combined artificial hyperpyrexia and tryparsamide versus therapeutic malaria. *J.A.M.A.* 107:1031, 1936.

Barrabee, P., and Von Mering, O.: Ethnic variations in mental stress in families with psychotic children. *Social Prob.* 1:48, 1953.

Beck, A. T.: "Psychoanalytic Psychiatry and Psychology." Edited by Robert P. Knight. International Universities Press, Inc., New York, 1954.

Beck, S. J.: "Introduction to the Rorschach Method." George Banta Publishing Company, Menasha, Wis., 1937.

Bell, A.: Colitis—pathogenically motivated. *J. Nerv. & Ment. Dis.* 77:587, 1933.

Bellak, L.: "Manic-Depressive Psychosis and Allied Conditions." Grune & Stratton, Inc., New York, 1952.

Bellak, L.: The multiple factors psychosomatic theory of schizophrenia. *Psychiatric Quart.* 23:738, 1949.

Benda, C. E.: Acromicria Congenita or the Mongoloid Deficiency. In "The Biology of Mental Health and Disease." Paul B. Hoeber, Inc., New York, 1952.

Benda, C. E.: "Developmental Disorders of Mentation and Cerebral Palsies." Grune & Stratton, Inc., New York, 1952.

Benda, C. E.: "Mongolism and Cretinism," ed. 2. Grune & Stratton, Inc., New York, 1949.

Benda, C. E.: Psychopathology of Childhood. In "Manual of Child Psychology." Edited by L. Carmichael. John Wiley & Sons, Inc., New York, 1954.

Benda, C. E.: Structural Cerebral Histopathology of Mental Deficiencies. In "The Proceedings of the First International Congress of Neuropathologists in Rome." Tipografia G. Donnini, Perugia, Italy, 1952.

Benda, C. E., and Farrell, M. J.: Psychopathology of Mental Deficiency in Children. In "Psychopathology of Childhood." Edited by P. H. Hoch and J. Zubin. Grune & Stratton, Inc., New York, 1955.

Benda, C. E., Farrell, M. J., and Chipman, C. E.: The inadequacy of present day concepts of mental deficiency and mental illness in child psychiatry. Am. J. Psychiat. 107:721, 1951.

Bender, L.: Psychopathic Behavior Disorders in Children. In "Handbook of Correctional Psychology." Edited by R. M. Lindner and R. V. Seliger. Philosophical Library, Inc., New York, 1947.

Bender, L.: "The Psychopathology of Children with Organic Brain Disease." Charles C Thomas, Publisher, Springfield, Ill., 1955.

Bender, L.: Childhood schizophrenia. Psychiatric Quart. 27:663, 1953.

Bender, L.: Twenty Years of Clinical Research on Schizophrenic Children with Special Reference to Those under Six Years of Age. In "Emotional Problems of Early Childhood." Edited by G. Caplan. Basic Books, Inc., New York, 1955.

Benjamin, J. D., and Ebaugh, F. G.: The diagnostic validity of the Rorschach test. Am. J. Psychiat. 94: 1163, 1938.

Bennett, A. E.: Convulsive (pentamethylenetetrazol) shock therapy in depressive disorders. Am. J. M. Sc. 196:420, 1938.

Bennett, A. E.: Metrazol convulsive shock therapy in affective psychoses. Am. J. M. Sc. 198:695, 1939.

Bennett, A. E.: Preventing traumatic complications in convulsive shock therapy by curare. J.A.M.A. 114:322, 1940.

Bergson, H.: "Creative Evolution." Henry Holt and Company, Inc., New York, 1911.

Berry, H. J.: Significance of maternal bereavement before age eight in psychiatric patients. Arch. Neurol. & Psychiat. 62:630, 1949.

Bettleheim, B.: "Love Is Not Enough." Free Press, Glencoe, Ill., 1950.

Bibb, J. L.: Nervous indigestion. *J. Tennessee M. A.* 25:276, 1932.

Bibrung, E.: Klinische Beitrage zur Paranoia-frage. *Internat. Ztschr. Psychoanal.* 14:508, 1928.

Bickel, H., Gerrard, J., and Hickmans, E. M.: Influence of phenylalanine intake on phenylketonuria. *Lancet* 2:812, 1953.

Bickel, H., Gerrard, J., and Hickmans, E. M.: The influence of phenylalanine intake on the chemistry and behavior of a phenylketonuric child. *Acta. paediat.* 43:64, 1954.

Biernoff, J.: Traumatic neuroses of industry. *Indust. Med.* 15:109, 1946.

Billig, O., and Sullivan, D. J.: Personality structure and prognosis of alcohol addiction: A Rorschach study. *Quart. J. Stud. Alcohol* 3:554, 1953.

Billings, E. G.: "A Handbook of Elementary Psychobiology and Psychiatry." The Macmillan Company, New York, 1939.

Bleuler, E.: "Dementia Praecox, or the Group of Schizophrenias." Translated by J. Zinkin. International Universities Press, Inc., New York, 1951.

Bleuler, E.: "Textbook of Psychiatry." Translated by A. A. Brill. The Macmillan Company, New York, 1924.

Bleuler, E.: "The Theory of Schizophrenic Negativism." Nervous & Mental Disease Publishing Company, New York, 1912.

Bliss, E. L., Midgeon, C. J., Branch, C. H. H., and Samuels, L. T.: Adrenocortical function in schizophrenia. *Am. J. Psychiat.* 112:358, 1955.

Bloom, N., Lynch, J. P., and Brick, H.: Mesantoin poison with aplastic anemia and recoverage. *J.A.M.A.* 138:498, 1948.

Boak, R. A., Carpenter, C. M., and Warren, S. L.: Studies on the physiological effects of fever temperatures: III. The thermal death time of *Treponema pallidum* in vitro with special reference to fever temperatures. *J. Exper. Med.* 56:741, 1932.

Boek, W. E., and Boek, J. K.: "Society and Health." G. P. Putnam's Sons, New York, 1956.

Bonafide, V. I.: Chlorpromazine (Thorazine) treatment of disturbed epileptic patients. *A.M.A. Arch. Neurol. & Psychiat.* 74:158, 1955.

Bond, D. D.: "The Love and Fear of Flying." International Universities Press, Inc., New York, 1952.

Bond, E. D.: Results of psychiatric treatments with a control series: a 25-year study. *Am. J. Psychiat.* 110:561, 1954.

Bornstein, B.: On Latency. In "Psychoanalytic Study of the Child," vol. 6. International Universities Press, Inc., New York, 1951.

Bower, W. H.: Chlorpromazine in psychiatric illness. *New England J. Med.* **251:** 689, 1954.

Bowlby, J.: "Maternal Care and Mental Health." World Health Organization, Palais des Nations, Geneva, Switzerland, 1952.

Bowman, K. M., Wortis, J., Fingert, H., and **Kogan, J.:** Results to date with pharmacological shock treatment of schizophrenia. *Am. J. Psychiat.* **95:**787, 1939.

Bowman, K. M., Goodhart, R., and **Jolliffe, N.:** Observations on the relation of vitamin B₁ in the etiology and treatment of Korsakoff psychosis. *J. Nerv. & Ment. Dis.* **90:**569, 1939.

Braceland, F. J.: Men in their fifties. *J. Omaha Mid-West Clin. Soc.* **15:**1, 1954.

Breuer, J., and **Freud, S.:** "Studies in Hysteria." Translated by A. A. Brill. The Williams & Wilkins Company, Baltimore, 1936.

Bridgman, P. W.: The task before us. *Proc. Am. Acad. Arts & Sc.* **83:**95, 1954.

Brill, H.: In "Chlorpromazine and Mental Health." Lea & Febiger, Philadelphia, 1955.

Brogden, W. J., and **Gantt, H. W.:** Intraneural conditioning. *Arch. Neurol. & Psychiat.* **48:**437, 1942.

Bromberg, W.: "Man above Humanity: A History of Psychotherapy." J. B. Lippincott Company, Philadelphia, 1954.

Bromberg, W.: Marihuana intoxication. *Am. J. Psychiat.* **91:**303, 1934.

Brooks, G. W.: In "Chlorpromazine and Mental Health." Lea & Febiger, Philadelphia, 1955.

Bruetsch, W. L.: Activation of the mesenchyme with therapeutic malaria. *J. Nerv. & Ment. Dis.* **76:**209, 1932.

Bruetsch, W. L.: Chronic rheumatic brain disease as a possible factor in the causation of some cases of dementia praecox. *Am. J. Psychiat.* **97:**276, 1940.

Bruetsch, W. L.: The histopathology of therapeutic (tertian) malaria. *Am. J. Psychiat.* **12:**19, 1932.

Bruetsch, W. L.: Penicillin or malaria therapy in the treatment of general paralysis? *Dis. Nerv. System* **10:**368, 1949.

Brussel, J. A., Grassi, J. R., and **Melniker, A.:** The Rorschach method and postconcussion syndrome. *Psychiatric Quart.* **16:**707, 1942.

Bunbury, D. E., and **Wagner, C. P.:** Incidence of bromide intoxication among psychotic patients. *J.A.M.A.* **95:**1725, 1930.

Burling, T., Lentz, E. M., and **Wilson, R. N.:** "The Give and Take in Hospitals: A Study of Human Organization." G. P. Putnam's Sons, New York, 1956.

Burr, C. W.: Heredity in epilepsy: A study of 1,449 cases. *Arch. Neurol. & Psychiat.* **7**:721, 1922.

Busse, E. W., Barnes, R. H., Silverman, A. J., Thaler, M., and Frost, L. L.: Studies of the processes of aging: X. The strengths and weaknesses of psychic functions in the aged. *Am. J. Psychiat.* **111**:896, 1955.

Cameron, D. E.: "Objective and Experimental Psychiatry," ed. 3. The Macmillan Company, New York, 1946.

Cameron, D. E.: Psychic driving. *Am. J. Psychiat.* **112**:503, 1956.

Caplan, G.: Mental hygiene work with expectant mothers: a group psychotherapeutic approach. *Ment. Hyg.* **35**:41, 1951.

Carlisle, C. L.: Depressions following apparent success. *Am. J. Psychiat.* **95**:729, 1938.

Carpenter, C. M.: Physiologic effects of fever therapy. *J. Lab. & Clin. Med.* **18**:981, 1933.

Carpenter, C. M., and Boak, R. A.: The effect of heat produced by an ultra-high frequency oscillator on experimental syphilis in rabbits. *Am. J. Syph.* **14**:346, 1930.

Carter, H. R.: Mesantoin—a new anti-convulsant in the management of epilepsy. *Rocky Mountain M. J.* **44**:614, 1947.

Cheney, C. O.: Body Development and Endocrine Glands. In "Guides for History Taking and Clinical Examination of Psychiatric Cases." State Hospital Press, Utica, N.Y., 1934.

"Chlorpromazine and Mental Health: A Symposium." Lea & Febiger, Philadelphia, 1955.

Claudé, H.: The paranoid psychoses. *Encéphale* **20**:137, 1925.

Cobb, S.: "Borderlands of Psychiatry." Harvard University Press, Cambridge, Mass., 1943.

Cobb, S.: "Foundations of Neuropsychiatry." Williams & Wilkins Company, Baltimore, 1952.

Cohen, I. M., and Archer, J. D.: Liver function and hepatic complications in patients receiving chlorpromazine. *J.A.M.A.* **159**:99, 1955.

Cohen, M. B., Baker, G., Cohen, R. A., Fromm-Reichmann, F., and Weigert, E. V.: An intensive study of twelve cases of manic-depressive psychosis. *Psychiatry* **17**:103, 1954.

Conner, L. A.: Psychic factor in cardiac disorders. *J.A.M.A.* **94**:447, 1930.

Corsini, R. J.: Historic background of group psychotherapy. *Internat. J. Group Psychotherapy* **8**:213, 1955.

Corwin, W., and Thompson, J. W.: Treatment of the total organism in schizophrenic patients. *Am. J. Psychiat.* **95**:1059, 1939.

Cowgill, G. R.: "The Vitamin B Requirement of Man." Yale University Press, New Haven, Conn., 1935.

Crohn, B. B.: Psychoneuroses affecting gastrointestinal tract. *Bull. New York Acad. Med.* **6**:155, 1930.

Cummings, J. N.: Chemical changes in the blood and the occurrence of uremia following head injury. *J. Neurol. & Psychiat.* **5**:40, 1942.

Curtis, A. C.: Modern treatment of syphilis. *Postgrad. Med.* **6**:22, 1949.

Curtis, A. C., Kruse, W. T., and Norton, D. H.: Neurosyphilis. Evaluation after Three Years of Treatment with Penicillin Alone and with the Combination of Penicillin and Malaria. In "Recent Advances in the Study of Venereal Diseases." National Institute of Health, U.S. Public Health Service, Washington, D.C., 1949.

Dana, C. L.: "The Modern and Technical Study of Heredity." Cornell University Medical Bulletin 14, No. 1, 1924.

Daneman, E. A., Chornesky, G., and Haycox, J.: Psychosomatic investigation of cerebral arteriosclerosis. *Dis. Nerv. System* **16**:165, 1955.

Daniels, G. E.: Neuroses associated with the gastro-intestinal tract. *Am. J. Psychiat.* **13**:529, 1934.

Dattner, B.: Penicillin Failures in Neurosyphilis. In "Recent Advances in the Study of Venereal Diseases." National Institute of Health, U.S. Public Health Service, Washington, D.C., 1949.

Davidoff, E., and Reifenstein, E.: The results of 18 months of Benzedrine sulphate therapy in psychiatry. *Am. J. Psychiat.* **95**:945, 1939.

Davidoff, E., and Whitaker, C. A.: Prepsychotic personality in alcoholic psychoses. *Psychiat. Quart.* **14**:103, 1940.

Davidson, D. T., Lombroso, C., and Markham, C. H.: Milontin in epilepsy. *New England J. Med.* **253**:173, 1955.

Davies, D. T., and Wilson, A. T. M.: Observations on the life history of chronic peptic ulcer. *Lancet* **2**:1353, 1937.

Davison, C.: Circumscribed cortical atrophy in the presenile psychoses—Pick's disease. *Am. J. Psychiat.* **84**:801, 1938.

DeJong, R. N.: Effect of Tridione in control of psychomotor attacks. *J.A.M.A.* **130**:565, 1946.

Denny-Brown, D., and Russell, W. R.: Experimental cerebral concussion. *Brain* **64**:93, 1941.

Doust, J. W. L.: Capillary system in patients with psychiatric disorders. *A.M.A. Arch. Neurol. & Psychiat.* **74**:137, 1955.

Doust, J. W. L.: Spectroscopic and photo-electric oximetry in schizophrenia and other psychiatric states. *J. Ment. Sc.* **98**:153, 1952.

Draper, G., and Touraine, G. A.: Man-environment unit and peptic ulcer. *Arch. Int. Med.* **49**:616, 1932.

Dunbar, H. F.: "Psychosomatic Diagnosis." Paul B. Hoeber, Inc., New York, 1949.

Dunlap, C. B.: Dementia praecox: Some preliminary observations on brains from carefully selected cases, and a consideration of certain sources of error. *Am. J. Psychiat.* **3**:403, 1924.

Dunlap, C. G.: Recent studies on spirochetes in general paresis. *Arch. Neurol. & Psychiat.* **8**:589, 1922.

Dynes, J. B.: Melancholia: involutional treatment with estrogens. *Arch. Neurol. & Psychiat.* **42**:248, 1939.

Eaton, J.: "Culture and Mental Disorders: A Comparative Study of the Hutterites and Other Populations." Free Press, Glencoe, Ill., 1955.

Ebaugh, F. G.: Neuropsychiatric sequelae of acute epidemic encephalitis in children. *Am. J. Dis. Child.* **25**:89, 1923.

Ebaugh, F. G.: Progress in teaching psychiatry. *Psychiatric Quart.* **4**:133, 1930.

Ebaugh, F. G.: Psychotherapy in the general practice of medicine. *J. Indiana M. A.* **28**:124, 1934.

Ebaugh, F. G.: Significance of psychoneurosis in general practice of medicine. *Nebraska M. J.* **16**:377, 1931.

Ebaugh, F. G., et al.: Comparison of 100 army psychiatrists and 100 enlisted men. *War. Med.* **4**:283, 1943.

Ebaugh, F. G., and Strecker, E. A.: Psychoses occurring during the puerperium. *Arch. Neurol. & Psychiat.* **15**:239, 1926.

Einstein, A.: "Out of My Later Years." Philosophical Library, Inc., New York, 1950.

Elliott, K. A. C., Page, I. H., and Quastel, J. H. (editors): "Neurochemistry, The Chemical Dynamics of Brain and Nerve." Charles C Thomas, Publisher, Springfield, Ill., 1955.

Elvidge, A. R., and Reed, G. E.: Biopsy studies of cerebral pathologic changes in schizophrenia and manic-depressive psychoses. *Arch. Neurol. & Psychiat.* **40**:227, 1938.

Erickson, E. H.: "Childhood and Society." W. W. Norton & Company, Inc., New York, 1950.

Everett, G. M., and **Richards, R. K.:** Comparative anticonvulsant action of 3,5,5-trimethyloxozolidine-2,4-dione (Tridione), Dilantin and phenobarbital. *J. Pharmacol. & Exper. Therap.* 81:402, 1944.

Ewalt, J. R.: Neurosyphilis. *Texas Rep. Biol. & Med.* 1:243, 1943.

Ewalt, J. R.: Organic behavior problems. *Texas Rep. Biol. & Med.* 3:247, 1945.

Ewalt, J. R.: Psychosomatic problems. *J.A.M.A.* 126:150, 1944.

Ewalt, J. R.: What is mental illness? *Texas Rep. Biol. & Med.* 9:292, 1951.

Ewalt, J. R., and **Bruce, E. I.:** Newer concepts of schizophrenia. *Texas Rep. Biol. & Med.* 6:97, 1948.

Ewalt, J. R., and **Ebaugh, F. G.:** Treatment of dementia paralytica. *J.A.M.A.* 116:2474, 1941.

Ewalt, J. R., Parsons, E. H., Warren, S. L., and **Osborne, S. L.:** "Fever Therapy Technique." Paul B. Hoeber, Inc., New York, 1939.

Ewalt, J. R., and **Ruskin, A.:** The E.E.G. in patients with heart disease. *Texas Rep. Biol. & Med.* 2:161, 1944.

Fabing, H. D., and **Hawkins, J. R.:** A year's experience with Frenquel in clinical and experimental schizophrenic psychoses. *Dis. Nerv. System* 16:329, 1955.

Farrell, M. J.: The adverse effects of early institutionalization of mentally subnormal children. *A.M.A. Am. J. Dis. Child.* 91:278, 1956.

Farrell, M. J.: "The Mentally Subnormal Child." World Health Organization, Palais des Nations, Geneva, Switzerland, 1954.

Faulkner, W. B., Jr.: X-ray evidence of emotional influence upon esophageal functions. *Am. J. Psychiat.* 98:227, 1941.

Federn, P.: "Ego Psychology and the Psychoses." Edited by Edoardo Weiss. Basic Books, Inc., New York, 1953.

Fenichel, O.: "The Psychoanalytic Theory of Neurosis," ed. 2. W. W. Norton & Company, Inc., New York, 1945.

Fetterman, J. L.: Neuropsychiatric aspects of industrial accidents. *Indust. Med.* 15:96, 1946.

Finiefs, L. A.: Results of treatment of 1,000 cases of schizophrenia. *J. Ment. Sc.* 94:575, 1948.

Flaherty, J. A.: Effect of chlorpromazine medication on children with severe emotional disturbance. *Delaware M. J.* 27:180, 1955.

Flaherty, J. A., McGuire, H. T., and **Gatski, R. L.:** Psychodynamics of the dry drunk. *Am. J. Psychiat.* 112:460, 1955.

Foelling, A.: Ueber Ausscheidung von Phenylbrenztraubensaure im Harn als Stoffwechselanomalie in Verbindung mit Imbecillitat. *Ztschr. physiol. Chem.* 227:169, 1934.

Ford, H., and Jameson, G. K.: Chlorpromazine in conjunction with other psychiatric therapy. *Dis. Nerv. System* 16:179, 1955.

Foster, M. W., Jr., and Gayle, R. F., Jr.: Dangers in combining reserpine with electroconvulsive treatment. *J.A.M.A.* 159:1520, 1955.

Fox, H. M., Gifford, S., et al.: "Metabolic and Psychologic Investigation of the Pituitary-Adrenal Responses to Stress." A report to the Ford Foundation from Harvard University Medical School. 1955.

Frank, J. D.: "Bibliography on Psychotherapy." International Universities Press, Inc., New York, 1952.

Frank, J. D.: "Group Therapy in the Mental Hospital." American Psychiatric Association, Washington, D. C., 1955.

Frank, J. D.: Group Therapy with Schizophrenics. In "Psychotherapy with Schizophrenics." Edited by E. B. Brody and F. C. Redlich. International Universities Press, Inc., New York, 1952.

Frazier, C. N.: Effect of elevation of body temperature on the course of experimental syphilis in the rabbit. *Arch. Dermat. & Syph.* 16:445, 1927.

Freed, H., and Peifer, C. A.: Treatment of hyperkinetic emotionally disturbed children with prolonged administration of chlorpromazine. In press.

Freeman, A. W.: Mental hygiene and the health department. *Am. J. Pub. Health* 28:241, 1938.

Freeman, W.: Deficiency of Catalytic Iron in the Brain in Schizophrenia. In "Schizophrenia." Williams & Wilkins Company, Baltimore, 1931.

Freeman, W., and Watts, J. W.: "Psychosurgery," ed. 2. Charles C Thomas, Publisher, Springfield, Ill., 1950.

Fremont-Smith, F.: The influence of emotion in precipitating convulsions. *Am. J. Psychiat.* 13:716, 1933.

Freud, A.: "The Ego and the Mechanisms of Defense." Translated by Cecil Baines. International Universities Press, Inc., New York, 1955.

Freud, A.: "The Psychoanalytical Treatment of Children." Imago Publishing Co., Ltd., London, England, 1946.

Freud, A., and Burlingham, D.: "Infants without Families." International Universities Press, Inc., New York, 1944.

Freud, S.: "Civilization and Its Discontents." Edited by Ernest Jones. Hogarth Press, Ltd., London, England, 1949.

Freud, S.: "Collected Papers." Edited by J. Strachey. Hogarth Press, Ltd., London, England, 1952.

Freud, S.: "The Ego and the Id." Translated by Joan Riviere. Hogarth Press, Ltd., London, England, 1952.

Freud, S.: "Gesammelte Schriften." *Leipzig. Internat. Psychoanal. Verlag* 11:362, 1928. (See S. Cobb: "Borderlands of Psychiatry.")

Freud, S.: "Interpretation of Dreams." Translated by A. A. Brill. The Macmillan Company, New York, 1913.

Freud, S.: "The Problem of Anxiety." W. W. Norton & Company, Inc., New York, 1936.

Freud, S.: "Sammlung kleiner Schriften zur Neurosenlehre, 1906–1909." Translated by A. A. Brill. Nervous & Mental Disease Publishing Company, New York, 1909.

Fries, M. E.: Psychosomatic relationships between mother and infant. *Psychosom. Med.* 6:159, 1944.

Friess, C., and **Nelson, M. J.:** Psychoneurotics—5 years later. *Am. J. M. Sc.* 203:539, 1942.

Fromm-Reichmann, F.: Some Aspects of Psychoanalytic Psychotherapy. In "Psychotherapy with Schizophrenics." Edited by E. B. Brody and F. C. Redlich. International Universities Press, Inc., New York, 1952.

Frostig, J. P.: Sakel's pharmacologic shock treatment for schizophrenia: tentative directions and system of recording. Translated by Joseph Wortis. *Arch. Neurol. & Psychiat.* 39:219, 1938.

Frostig, J. P., and **Spies, T. D.:** Initial nervous syndrome of pellagra and associated deficiency diseases. *Am. J. M. Sc.* 199:268, 1940.

Funfgeld, E.: Ueber anatomische Untersuchungen bei Dementia praecox mit besonderer Beruckisichtigung des Thalmus opticus. *Ztschr. ges. Neurol. u. Psychiat.* 95:411, 1925.

Funkenstein, D. H., and **Meade, L. W.:** Nor-epinephrine-like and epinephrine-like substances and the elevation of blood pressure during acute stress. *J. Nerv. & Ment. Dis.* 119:380, 1954.

Gammon, G. D., et al.: Penicillin in neurosyphilis. *J.A.M.A.* 128:653, 1945.

Gatski, R. L.: Chlorpromazine in the treatment of emotionally maladjusted children. *J.A.M.A.* 157:1298, 1955.

Gellhorn, E.: The action of hypoglycemia on the central nervous system and the problem of schizophrenia from the physiologic point of view. *J.A.M.A.* 110:1433, 1938.

Gellhorn, E.: "Autonomic Regulations: Their Significance for Physiology, Psychology, and Neuropsychiatry." Interscience Publishers, Inc., New York, 1943.

Gerard, D. L., and **Kornetsky, C.:** Adolescent opiate addiction: a case study. *Psychiatric Quart.* 28:367, 1954.

Gerard, D. L., and Kornetsky, C.: A social and psychiatric study of adolescent opiate addicts. *Psychiatric Quart.* 28:125, 1954.

Gerard, M. W.: Direct Treatment of the Child. In "Orthopsychiatry, 1923–1948. Retrospect and Prospect." American Orthopsychiatric Association, New York, 1948.

Gerard, R. W.: Biological roots of psychiatry. *Am. J. Psychiat.* 122:81, 1955.

Gesell, A., and Amatruda, C. S.: "Developmental Diagnosis: Normal and Abnormal Child Development," ed. 2. Paul B. Hoeber, Inc., New York, 1947.

Gesell, A., and Ilg, F. L.: "Infant and Child in the Culture of Today." Harper & Brothers, New York, 1943.

Gesell, A., and Thompson, H.: "The Psychology of Early Growth." The Macmillan Company, New York, 1938.

Gibbs, F. A., Gibbs, E. L., and Lennox, W. G.: Cerebral dysrhythmias of epilepsy: measures for their control. *Arch. Neurol. & Psychiat.* 39:298, 1938.

Ginsberg, S.: The Mental Health Movement and Its Theoretical Assumptions. In "Community Programs for Mental Health." Edited by R. Kotinsky and H. L. Witmer. Harvard University Press, Cambridge, Mass., 1955.

Ginsburg, E. L.: Psychiatric Social Worker. In "Orthopsychiatry, 1923–1948. Retrospect and Prospect." American Orthopsychiatric Association, New York, 1948.

Gitelson, M.: Psychoanalysis and dynamic psychiatry. *Arch. Neurol. & Psychiat.* 66:280, 1951.

Glover, E.: Lectures on technique and psychoanalysis. *Internat. J. Psycho-Analysis* 8:486, 1927.

Glud, E.: The treatment of alcoholic patients in Denmark with "Antabuse." *Quart. J. Stud. Alcohol.* 10:185, 1949.

Goitein, P. L., and Rubin, J.: Spastic colon and instinctual repression. *J. Crim. Psychopathol.* 4:217, 1942.

Goldberger, J.: Pellagra: causation and a method of prevention. A summary of some of the recent studies of the Public Health Service. *J.A.M.A.* 66:471, 1916.

Goldfarb, W.: Consequences of Psychologic Deprivation in Infancy. In "Psychopathology of Childhood." Edited by P. H. Hoch and J. Zubin. Grune & Stratton, Inc., New York, 1955.

Goldfarb, W., Bowman, K. M., and Wortis, J.: The effect of alcohol on cerebral metabolism. *Am. J. Psychiat.* 97:384, 1940.

Goldman, D.: Treatment of psychotic states with chlorpromazine. *J.A.M.A.* 157:1274, 1955.

Goldstein, H., and McFarland, R. A.: The biochemistry of epilepsy. *Am. J. Psychiat.* 96:771, 1940.

Goldstein, K.: "After-effects of Brain Injuries in War." Grune & Stratton, Inc., New York, 1942.

Goldstein, K.: "The Organism." American Book Company, New York, 1939.

Goodenough, F. L.: "Developmental Psychology," ed. 2. Appleton-Century-Crofts, Inc., New York, 1945.

Goodhart, R., and Jolliffe, N.: Effects of vitamin B (B₁) therapy on polyneuritis of alcohol addicts. *J.A.M.A.* 110:414, 1938.

Goodwin, O. P.: Traumatic neuroses without external evidence of brain injury. *M. Bull. Vet. Admin.* 7:821, 1931.

Gottlieb, J., Kline, N. S., Lahmon, W. T., Moll, A. E., Himwich, H. E., and Saslow, G.: Articles presented at research conference on chlorpromazine, reserpine, Meratran, and Frenquel. American Psychiatric Association, Washington, D. C., 1955.

Grace, W. J., Seton, P. H., Wolf, S., and Wolff, H. G.: A detailed study of lysozyme-bacteriolytic and mycolytic enzymes present in tears, hypersecretion, and gastric juice. *Am. J. M. Sc.* 217:241, 1949.

Greenacre, P.: "Notes on the Mechanisms of Depression in Affective Disorders." International Universities Press, Inc., New York, 1953.

Greenblatt, M.: The electroencephalogram in late post-traumatic cases. *Am. J. Psychiat.* 100:378, 1943.

Greenblatt, M., and Solomon, H. C.: "Frontal Lobes in Schizophrenia." Springer Publishing Co., Inc., New York, 1953.

Greenblatt, M., York, R., and Brown, E. L.: "From Custodial to Therapeutic Patient Care in Mental Hospitals." Russell Sage Foundation, New York, 1955.

Grinker, R. R.: "Neurology." Charles C Thomas, Publisher, Springfield, Ill., 1934.

Grinker, R. R.: Treatment of war neuroses. *J.A.M.A.* 126:142, 1944.

Grinker, R. R., and Spiegel, J.: "Men under Stress." Blakiston Division, McGraw-Hill Book Company, Inc., New York, 1945.

Guirdham, A.: "Disease and the Social System." W. W. Norton & Company, Inc., New York, 1942.

Gurdjian, E. S., Webster, J. E., and Stone, W. E.: Cerebral metabolism in experimental head injury. *War Med.* 6:173, 1944.

Guttmann, L., and Kirschbaum, W.: Das encephalographische Bild der progressiven Paralyse und seine klinische Bedeutung. *Ztschr. ges. Neurol. u. Psychiat.* 121:590, 1929.

Hall, G. W., and MacKay, R. P.: Post-traumatic neuroses. *J.A.M.A.* 102:510, 1934.

Halstead, W. C.: Brain injuries and the higher levels of consciousness. In "Trauma of the Central Nervous System." Williams & Wilkins Company, Baltimore, 1945.

Ham, G. C., Alexander, F., and Carmichael, H. T.: The psychosomatic theory of thyrotoxicosis. *Psychosom. Med.* 13:18, 1951.

Handy, L. M., Rosanoff, A. J., and Plesset, I. R.: The etiology of manic-depressive syndromes with special reference to their occurrence in twins. *Am. J. Psychiat.* 14:725, 1935.

Harris, M.: Insulin sensitivity of patients with mental disease. *Arch. Neurol. & Psychiat.* 48:761, 1942.

Harris, M. M., Horwitz, W., and Milch, E. A.: Regarding Sodium Amytal as a prognostic aid in insulin and Metrazol shock therapy of mental patients (dementia praecox). *Am. J. Psychiat.* 96:327, 1939.

Harris, T. H., and Ewalt, J. R.: Complications following the use of sodium diphenyl-hydantoinate therapy. *Oklahoma M. J.* 35:365, 1942.

Harris, T. H., and Otto, J. L.: Use of Mesantoin as an anti-convulsive drug. *Texas J. Med.* 43:328, 1947.

Harrowes, W. Mc.: The depressive reaction types. *J. Ment. Sc.* 79:17, 1933.

Healy, W., and Bronner, A. F.: The Child Guidance Clinic: Birth and Growth of an Idea. In "Orthopsychiatry, 1923–1948. Retrospect and Prospect." American Orthopsychiatric Association, New York, 1948.

Heath, R. G.: "Studies in Schizophrenia by the Tulane Department of Psychiatry and Neurology." Harvard University Press, Cambridge, Mass., 1954.

Hebb, D. O.: The mammal and his environment. *Am. J. Psychiat.* 111:826, 1955.

Heisenberg, W.: The theory of elementary particles. *Science* 122:1215, 1955.

Hemphill, R. E.: The significance of atrophy of the testis in schizophrenia. *J. Ment. Sc.* 90:696, 1944.

Hemphill, R. E., Reiss, M., and Taylor, A. L.: A study of the histology of the testis in schizophrenia and other mental disorders. *J. Ment. Sc.* 90:681, 1944.

Henderson, D. K., and Gillespie, R. D.: "A Textbook of Psychiatry for Students and Practitioners," ed. 6. Oxford University Press, New York, 1930.

Hendrick, I.: "Facts and Theories of Psychoanalysis." Alfred A. Knopf, Inc., New York, 1934.

Heppenstall, M. E., and Hill, D.: Electroencephalography in chronic post-traumatic syndromes. *Lancet* 1:261, 1943.

Hicks, S. P.: Some effects of ionizing radiation and metabolic inhibition on the developing mammalian nervous system. *J. Pediat.* **40**:489, 1952.

Himwich, H. E.: Prospects in psychopharmacology. *J. Nerv. & Ment. Dis.* **122**:4, 1955.

Hinsie, L. E., and Blalock, J. R.: "Electropyrexia in General Paralysis." New York State Hospitals Press, Utica, N. Y., 1934.

Hixon Symposium: "Cerebral Mechanisms in Behavior." Edited by L. A. Jeffress. John Wiley & Sons, Inc., New York, 1951.

Hobbs, G. E., Goddard, E. S., and Stevenson, J. A. F.: The diurnal cycle in blood eosinophils and body temperature. *Canad. M. A. J.* **70**:533, 1954.

Hoch, A.: Constitutional factors in the dementia praecox group. *Rev. Neurol. & Psychiat.* **8**:463, 1910.

Hoch, A.: The problem of toxic infectious psychoses. *New York J. Med.* **13**:86, 1913.

Hoch, A.: A study of some cases of delirium produced by drugs. *Rev. Neurol. & Psychiat.* **4**:83, 1906.

Hoch, P. A.: Aims and limitation of psychotherapy. *Am. J. Psychiat.* **112**:321, 1955.

Hoch, P. H.: Personality factors in alcoholic psychoses. *Psychiatric Quart.* **14**:338, 1940.

Hoffer, A., Osmond, H., and Smythies, J.: Schizophrenia: A new approach. II. Result of a year's research. *J. Ment. Sc.* **100**:29, 1954.

Hohman, L. B.: The abortive and recurrent depressive psychoses. *J. Nerv. & Ment. Dis.* **80**:273, 1938.

Hohman, L. B.: A review of 144 cases of affective disorders after seven years. *Am. J. Psychiat.* **94**:303, 1937.

Hollingshead, A. B., and Redlich, F. C.: Schizophrenia and social structure. *Am. J. Psychiat.* **110**:695, 1954.

Homburger, F., and Smithy, G.: Chlorpromazine in patients with nausea and vomiting due to advanced cancer. *New England J. Med.* **251**:820, 1954.

Horan, M.: Psychogenic aspect of dermatology. *Practitioner* **127**:675, 1931.

Hoskins, R. G., and Sleeper, F. H.: Basal metabolism in schizophrenia. *Arch. Neurol. & Psychiat.* **21**:887, 1929.

Hoskins, R. G., and Sleeper, F. H.: A case of hebephrenic dementia praecox with marked improvement under thyroid treatment. *Endocrinology* **13**:459, 1929.

Hoskins, R. G., and Sleeper, F. H.: Endocrine factors in dementia praecox. *New England J. Med.* **200**:361, 1929.

Hoskins, R. G., and **Sleeper, F. H.:** Endocrine studies in dementia praecox. *Endocrinology* 13:245, 1929.

Hotchkiss, G., Lida, C., Ogilby, A., and **Wiesenfeld, S.:** Mothers of young male single schizophrenic patients as visitors in a mental hospital. *J. Nerv. & Ment. Dis.* 121:452, 1955.

Hsia, D. Y.: Personal communication.

Huddleson, J. H.: Constitutional inferiority. *J.A.M.A.* 86:1960, 1926.

Hunt, R. C.: Relation between precipitating situation and outcome in manic-depressive psychoses. *Am. J. Psychiat.* 95:65, 1938.

Hunt, R. C., Feldman, H., and **Fiero, R.:** Spontaneous remissions in dementia praecox. *Psychiatric Quart.* 12:414, 1938.

Hurler, G.: Uber einen Typ multipler Abartungen, vorwiegend am Skelett-system. *Ztschr. Kinderh.* 24:220, 1919.

Hurst, A. F., and **Stewart, M. J.:** "Gastric and Duodenal Ulcer." Oxford University Press, New York, 1929.

Hyden, H.: "Protein Metabolism in the Nerve Cell under Different Functional Conditions." Edited by J. F. Danielli and R. Brown. The Macmillan Company, New York, 1947.

Hyden, H.: Protein metabolism in the nerve cells during growth and function. *Acta. physiol. scandinav.* 6:1, 1943.

Hyden, H., and **Hartelius, H.:** Stimulation of the nucleo-protein production in the nerve cells by malononitrile and its effect on psychic functions in mental disorders. *Acta psychiat. et neurol.* Suppl. 58, 1948.

Ingalls, T. H.: Causes and prevention of developmental defects. *J.A.M.A.* 161:1047, 1956.

Jacobsen, E.: Physiological conception and treatment of the common psychoneuroses. *Am. J. Psychiat.* 98:219, 1941.

Jameison, G.: Suicide and mental disease. *Arch. Neurol. & Psychiat.* 36:1, 1936.

Janet, P.: A case of psychasthenic delirium. *Am. J. Psychiat.* 1:319, 1922.

Janet, P.: "État mental des hystériques." Translated by C. R. Corson. Rueff et Cie., Paris, France, 1893.

Jasper, H. H., and **Nichols, I. C.:** Electrical signs of cortical function in epilepsy and allied disorders. *Am. J. Psychiat.* 17:835, 1937.

Jasper, H., and **Penfield, W.:** Electroencephalogram in post-traumatic epilepsy. *Am. J. Psychopath.* 100:365, 1943.

Jastak, J.: Rorschach performances of alcoholic patients. *Delaware M. J.* 12:120, 1940.

Jelliffe, S. E.: "The Technique of Psychoanalysis," ed. 2. Nervous & Mental Disease Publishing Company, New York, 1920.

Jellinek, E. M.: "The Phases of Alcoholism." World Health Organization, Palais des Nations, Geneva, Switzerland, 1952.

Joffe, P. N., and Jolliffe, N.: Gastric acidity in addicts with observations on relationships of B vitamins to achlorhydria. *Am. J. M. Sc.* **193**:501, 1937.

Johnson, C. E., Jr.: Management of neurosyphilis. *J. Nerv. & Ment. Dis.* **109**:451, 1949.

Johnson, C. S.: The Influence of Social Science on Psychiatry. In "Mid-century Psychiatry." Edited by R. R. Grinker. Charles C Thomas, Publisher, Springfield, Ill., 1953.

Jolliffe, N., and Colbert, C. N.: Etiology of polyneuritis in alcohol addicts. *J.A.M.A.* **107**:642, 1936.

Jolliffe, N., and Goodhart, R.: Beriberi in addicts. *J.A.M.A.* **111**:380, 1938.

Jones, E.: "Life and Work of Sigmund Freud." Basic Books, Inc., New York, 1953.

Josephy, H.: Zur histopathologie und therapie der dementia praecox. *Deutsche med. Wchnschr.* **34**:391, 1910.

Jung, C. G.: "The Psychology of Dementia Praecox." Translated by A. A. Brill. The Williams & Wilkins Company, Baltimore, 1936.

Kaadabirger, R., Andersen, P. E. R., and Jansen, J., Jr.: Amygdaloid nucleus in unanesthetized cats and their visual hallucinations. *Neurology* **4**:48, 1954.

Kaf, W., and Prick, J. J. G.: Pathogenesis and clinic of delirium tremens. *Schweiz. Arch. Neurol. u. Psychiat.* **45**:303, 1940.

Kahn, E.: "Psychopathic Personalities." Translated by H. Flanders Dunbar. Yale University Press, New Haven, Conn., 1931.

Kahn, E., and Thompson, L. J.: Concerning Pick's disease. *Am. J. Psychiat.* **13**:937, 1934.

Kalanowsky, L. B., and Hoch, P.: "Shock Treatments." Grune & Stratton, Inc., New York, 1946.

Kallmann, F. J.: Genetics in relation to mental disorders. *J. Ment. Sc.* **94**:250, 1948.

Kallmann, F. J.: Genetic theory of schizophrenia; analysis of 691 schizophrenic twin index families. *Am. J. Psychiat.* **103**:309, 1946.

Kanner, L.: Autistic disturbances of affective contact. *Nerv. Child* **2**:217, 1943.

Kanner, L.: "Child Psychiatry." Charles C Thomas, Publisher, Springfield, Ill., 1948.

Bibliography 425

Kanner, L.: Early infantile autism. *J. Pediat.* 25:217, 1944.

Kant, O.: The evaluation of prognostic criteria in schizophrenia. *J. Nerv. & Ment. Dis.* 100:598, 1944.

Kardiner, A.: The Roles of Deprivation and Stress in Health and Disease. In "Beyond the Germ Theory." Edited by I. Galdston. New York Health Education Council, 1954.

Kardinar, A., Linton, R., DuBois, C., and West, J.: "The Psychologic Frontiers of Society." Columbia University Press, New York, 1945.

Karpman, B.: Principles and aims of criminal psychopathology. *J. Crim. Psychopath.* 1:187, 1940.

Karpman, B.: A psychiatrist looks at constitution and environment and is puzzled. *M. Ann. District of Columbia* 14:141, 1945.

Kasanin, J., and Hanfmann, E.: An experimental study of concept formation in schizophrenia. *Am. J. Psychiat.* 95:35, 1938.

Kennard, M., and Nimes, L. J.: The effect on the electroencephalogram of lesions of the cerebral cortex and basal ganglia of *Macaca mulatla*. *J. Neurophysiol.* 5:335, 1942.

Kennedy, F., Frantz, A., and Hare, C. S.: "The Inter-relationship of Mind and Body." The Williams & Wilkins Company, Baltimore, 1939.

Kibbe, M. H.: Clinical and laboratory findings in two hundred head injuries. *Neurology* 5:336, 1955.

Kinross-Wright, V.: Chlorpromazine—a major advance in psychiatric treatment. *Postgrad. Med.* 16:297, 1954.

Kinross-Wright, V.: Chlorpromazine treatment of mental disorders. *Am. J. Psychiat.* 111:907, 1955.

Kirby, G. H.: Mental reaction types associated with organic brain disease. *State Hospital Quart.* 6:467, 1921.

Kisker, G. W.: Abstract and categorical behavior following therapeutic brain surgery. *Psychosom. Med.* 6:146, 1944.

Kitaboyashi, S.: *Mitt. med. Fak. kais Kyushu Univ.* 1924.

Kitzinger, H., Devere, A. G., Cartwright, R. W., and Shapiro, D.: A preliminary study of the effects of glutamic acid on catatonic schizophrenia. *Rorschach Research Exchange* 13:210, 1949.

Klauder, J. V., and Winkelmann, N. W.: Pellagra among alcoholic addicts. *J.A.M.A.* 90:364, 1928.

Klopfer, B., and Kelley, D. M.: "The Rorschach Technique." World Book Company, Yonkers, N.Y., 1942.

Knauer, A.: The psychoses occurring as a result of acute articular rheumatism. *Ztschr. ges. Neurol. u. Psychiat.* 21:491, 1916.

Knight, R. P.: "Psychoanalytic Psychiatry and Psychology." International Universities Press, Inc., New York, 1954.

Kolb, L. C.: An evaluation of lobotomy and its potentialities with future research in psychiatry and the basic sciences. *J. Nerv. & Ment. Dis.* 110:112, 1949.

Kooser, J. H., and Blankenhorn, M. A.: Nicotinic acid in treatment of pellagra. *J.A.M.A.* 112:2581, 1939.

Kraepelin, E.: "Psychiatrie: Ein Lehrbuch fur studierende und Aerzte von Dr. Emil Kraepelin," ed. 6. Johann Ambrosius Barth, Leipzig, Germany, 1899.

Kraepelin, E., and Plaut, F.: General paralysis in Negroes and Indians. *J.A.M.A.* 88:187, 1927.

Krusen, F. H.: The blood picture before and after fever therapy by physical means. *Am. J. M. Sc.* 193:462, 1937.

Krusen, F. H., and Elkins, E. C.: Fever therapy by physical means. *J.A.M.A.* 112:1689, 1939.

Kubie, L. S.: Manual of emergency treatment of acute war neuroses. *War Med.* 4:582, 1943.

Kugelmass, I. N.: "The Management of Mental Deficiency in Children." Grune & Stratton, Inc., New York, 1954.

Lampl de Groot, J.: On development of ego and super-ego. *Internat. J. Psycho-Analysis.* 28:7, 1947.

Lashley, K. S.: See Hixon Symposium.

Langfeldt, G.: Sympathetic system with special regard to dementia praecox. *Norsk. mag. Lægevidensk* 86:1, 1925.

Laughlin, H. P.: "The Neuroses in Clinical Practice." W. B. Saunders Company, Philadelphia, 1956.

LaVerne, A. A.: Rapid coma technique for carbon dioxide inhalation therapy. *Dis. Nerv. System* 14:141, 1953.

Lehmann, H. E.: Selective inhibition of affective drive by pharmacologic means. *Am. J. Psychiat.* 110:805, 1954.

Lemere, F.: Psychological factors in conditioned reflex treatment of alcoholism. *Quart. J. Stud. Alcohol.* 8:261, 1947.

Lemkau, P.: Why are we interested in mental health? *Ment. Hyg.* 39:553, 1955.

Lemkau, P., Tietze, C., and Cooper, M.: A survey of statistical studies on the prevalence and incidence of mental disorder in sample populations. *Pub. Health Rep.* 58:1909, 1943.

Lennox, W. G.: Petit mal epilepsies. *J.A.M.A.* **129**:1069, 1945.

Lennox, W. G., and Jolly, D. H.: Seizure Brain Waves and Intelligence Tests of Epileptic Twins. In "Genetics and the Inheritance of Integrated Neurological and Psychiatric Patterns." Edited by D. Hooker and C. C. Hare. Williams & Wilkins Company, Baltimore, 1954.

Lennox, W. G., and Gibbs, E. L.: Oxygen saturation of blood draining the brain and the limbs of patients with epilepsy. *Arch. Neurol. & Psychiat.* **36**:13, 1936.

Lester, D.: A study of prolonged coma following insulin shock. *Am. J. Psychiat.* **95**:1083, 1939.

Levine, A., Abramson, H. A., Kaufman, M. R., and Markham, S.: Lysergic acid and diphenylamine. *J. Psychol.* **40**:53, 1955.

Levine, M.: "Psychotherapy and Medical Practice." The Macmillan Company, New York, 1952.

Lewin, B.: "The Psychoanalysis of Elation." W. W. Norton & Company, Inc., New York, 1950.

Lewis, N. D. C.: "Constitutional Factors in Dementia Praecox." Nervous & Mental Disease Publishing Company, New York, 1923.

Lewis, N. D. C., and Pacella, B. L.: "Modern Trends in Child Psychiatry." International Universities Press, Inc., New York, 1945.

Lidz, T., and Lidz, R. W.: The family environment of schizophrenic patients. *Am. J. Psychiat.* **106**:332, 1949.

Limburg, C. C.: "The Need for Psychiatrists and Psychiatric Training Facilities." Paper read at American Psychiatric Association, Washington, D. C., 1948.

Lindemann, E., and Finesinger, J. E.: The effects of Adrenalin and Mecholyl in states of anxiety in psychoneurosis. *Am. J. Psychiat.* **95**:353, 1938.

Lindner, R. M.: "Rebel without Cause." Grune & Stratton, Inc., New York, 1944.

Lindquist, J. L., and LeRoy, G. U.: Pathogenesis of symptoms of cerebral concussion. *J.A.M.A.* **118**:1325, 1942.

Linton, R. (editor): "The Science of Man in the World Crisis." Columbia University Press, New York, 1945.

Livingston, S., and Boks, L.: The use of the dione drugs in the treatment of epilepsy in children. *New England J. Med.* **253**:138, 1955.

Lombard, J. P., Gilbert, J. G., and Donofrio, A. F.: The effects of glutamic acid upon the intelligence, social maturity and adjustment of a group of mentally retarded children. *Am. J. Ment. Deficiency* **60**:122, 1955.

Lounsberry, C. R.: Dermatological neurosis. *California Med.* **33**:44, 1931.

Lowenstein, R.: "Depression and Aggression: Drives, Affects, Behavior." International Universities Press, Inc., New York, 1953.

Ludwig, A. O.: The practical importance of modern concepts of psychosomatic relations. *New England J. Med.* 238:175, 1948.

Mackinnon, I. H., Hoch, P. A., Cammer, L., and Waelsch, H. W.: Use of malononitrile in the treatment of mental illness. *Am. J. Psychiat.* 105:639, 1949.

Malamud, W.: Alzheimer's disease; contribution to its etiology and classification. *Arch. Neurol. & Psychiat.* 21:805, 1929.

Malamud, W., and Rothchild, D.: The Barrier between the Blood and the Cerebrospinal Fluid. In "Distribution Ratio of Bromides in Schizophrenia." The Williams & Wilkins Company, Baltimore, 1931.

Malzberg, B.: A follow-up study of patients with dementia praecox treated with insulin in the New York Civil State Hospital. *Ment. Hyg.* 23:641, 1939.

Malzberg, B.: Outcome of insulin treatment in 1,000 patients with dementia praecox. *Psychiatric Quart.* 12:528, 1938.

Mann, J.: Some theoretic concepts of the group process. *Internat. J. Group Psychotherapy* 5:235, 1955.

Marcuse, H.: *Obersteiners Arb.*, vol. 26.

Margolin, S. G.: Psychoanalytic observation and physiologic observation on a case of gastric fistula in a human. *Psychoanalyt. Quart.* 20:349, 1951.

Margolin, S. G., and Kaufman, M. R.: What is psychosomatic medicine? *M. Clin. North America* 32:609, 1948.

Massachusetts Legislature: Chapter 514, Acts of 1954. Division of Public Documents, State House, Boston, Mass.

Masserman, J.: Psychobiologic dynamisms in behavior. *Psychiatry* 5:341, 1942.

Masserman, J. H.: The hypothalamus in psychiatry. *Am. J. Psychiat.* 98:633, 1942.

Masserman, J. H.: "Principles of Dynamic Psychiatry." W. B. Saunders Company, Philadelphia, 1946.

Mayfield, A. L.: Differential diagnosis of hyperthyroidism and neurosis. *Wisconsin M. J.* 33:181, 1934.

McFarland, R. A., and Goldstein, H.: Biochemistry of dementia praecox. *Am. J. Psychiat.* 94:509, 1938.

McFarland, R. A., and Goldstein, H.: The biochemistry of the manic-depressive psychosis. *Am. J. Psychiat.* 96:21, 1939.

McFarland, R. A., and Goldstein, H.: Biochemistry of the psychoneuroses. *Am. J. Psychiat.* 93:1073, 1937.

McDermott, N. T., and Cobb, S.: A psychiatric survey of bronchial asthma. *California Med.* 1:203, 1939.

Meadow, A., Greenblatt, M., and **Solomon, H. C.:** Looseness of association and impairment in abstraction in schizophrenia. *J. Nerv. & Ment. Dis.* 118:27, 1953.

Medical Service, Joint Armed Forces: "Statistical Classification and Basic Diagnostic Nomenclature." Washington, D.C., 1949.

Meduna, L. J.: "Carbon Dioxide Therapy." Charles C Thomas, Publisher, Springfield, Ill., 1950.

Meduna, L. J.: Common factors in shock therapies. *Dis. Nerv. System* 6:283, 1945.

Meduna, L. J.: Modification of carbon dioxide treatment using nitrous oxide. *Dis. Nerv. System* 14:102, 1953.

Meduna, L. J.: Physiological background of the CO_2 treatment of the neuroses. *Am. J. Psychiat.* 110:664, 1954.

Meduna, L. J.: Convulsion therapy of schizophrenia: Results of producing therapeutic epilepsy by intramuscular injections of Metrazol. *Psychiat. Neurol. Wchnschr.* 37:317, 1935.

Meduna, L. J.: Experiments on biologic control of outcome of schizophrenia by producing epileptic attacks with injections of camphor and Metrazol. *Ztschr. ges. Neurol. u. Psychiat.* 152:235, 1935.

Meduna, L. J.: Significance of epileptiform seizures in combined insulin and Metrazol therapy of schizophrenia. *Psychiat. Neurol. Wchnschr.* 39:331, 1937.

Menninger, K.: "Love against Hate." Harcourt, Brace and Company, Inc., New York, 1942.

Menninger, W. C.: "Psychiatry in a Troubled World." The Macmillan Company, New York, 1948.

Menninger, W. C., and **Leaf, M.:** "You and Psychiatry." Charles Scribner's Sons, New York, 1948.

Mental Health Act of Pennsylvania: Section 302, Article III, 1923.

Merritt, H. H., and **Putnam, T. J.:** The drug therapy of epilepsy. *J.A.M.A.* 114:1347, 1940.

Merritt, H. H., and **Putnam, T. J.:** A new series of anticonvulsant drugs tested by experiments on animals. *Arch. Neurol. & Psychiat.* 39:1003, 1938.

Merritt, H. H., and **Putnam, T. J.:** Sodium diphenylhydantoinate in the treatment of convulsive disorders. *J.A.M.A.* 111:1068, 1938.

Meyer, A.: The anatomical facts and clinical varieties of traumatic insanity. *Trans. Am. Medico-Psychol. A.* 10:106, 1903.

Meyer, A.: Constructive formulation of schizophrenia. *Am. J. Psychiat.* 1:355, 1922.

Meyer, A.: Differential diagnosis of general paresis. *Am. J. Insanity* 71:51, 1914.

Meyer, A.: Fundamental conceptions of dementia praecox. *Brit. M. J.* 2:757, 1906.

Meyer, A.: Modern Treatment of Nervous and Mental Diseases. In "The Modern Treatment of Nervous and Mental Diseases." Edited by W. A. White and S. E. Jelliffe. Lea & Febiger, Philadelphia, 1913.

Meyer, A.: The nature and conception of dementia praecox. *J. Abnorm. & Social Psychol.* 5:274, 1910.

Meyer, A.: Outline of Pathergasias (unpublished—cited by Muncie).

Meyer, A.: "The Commonsense Psychiatry of Dr. Adolf Meyer." Edited by Alfred Lief. Blakiston Division, McGraw-Hill Book Company, Inc., New York, 1948.

Meyers, R. C.: "Is the Public Ready to Fight Mental Illness?" Fisher Publication, New Jersey Department of Institutions and Agencies, 1955.

Michales, J. J., and Steinberg, A.: Persistent enuresis and juvenile delinquency. *Brit. J. Delinquency* 3:114, 1952.

Milbank Memorial Fund: "Epidemiology of Mental Disorders." New York, 1950.

Milbank Memorial Fund: "Inter-relations between Psychiatric Disorders and the Social Environment." New York, 1952.

Miller, M. I.: A psychological study of a case of eczema and a case of neurodermatitis. *Psychosom. Med.* 4:82, 1942.

Millet, J. A. P.: "Newer Concepts on Rehabilitation." Annual Report by the American Rehabilitation Committee, Inc., New York, 1951.

Milligan, W. L.: Treatment of psychoneuroses. Modified carbon dioxide abreaction. *Brit. M. J.* 1:1426, 1951.

Mitchell, E. H.: Chlorpromazine in the treatment of acute alcoholism. *Am. J. M. Sc.* 229:363, 1955.

Mittleman, B., Wolf, H. G., and Scharf, M. P.: Experimental studies on patients with gastritis, duodenitis, and peptic ulcer. *Psychosom. Med.* 4:5, 1942.

Moreno, J. L.: Group psychotherapy, theory and practice. Recommendations presented at the American Psychiatric Association's Philadelphia Conference on Group Methods, June 1932. *Internat. J. Group Psychotherapy* 3:142, 1932.

Moreno, J. L.: "Who Shall Survive? Foundations of Sociometry, Group Psychotherapy and Sociodrama." Beacon House, Inc., New York, 1953.

Mott, F. W., and y Suck, M. P.: Further pathological studies in dementia: pathological studies in dementia praecox. *New York J. Med.* 116:244, 1922.

Muncie, W.: "Psychobiology and Psychiatry." The C. V. Mosby Company, St. Louis, 1939.

Myers, H.: The male climacteric. *J.A.M.A.* 126:472, 1944.

Myerson, A.: Theory and principles of the "total push" method in the treatment of chronic schizophrenia. *Am. J. Psychiat.* **95**:1197, 1939.

National Committee for Mental Hygiene: "Statistical Manual for the Use of Hospitals for Mental Diseases." New York State Hospitals Press, Utica, N.Y., 1934.

National Institute of Mental Health: "Patients in Mental Institutions." Federal Security Agency, Public Health Service, Bethesda, Md., 1947.

National Research Council, Committee on Psychiatric Investigation: "Problem of Mental Disorder." McGraw-Hill Book Company, Inc., New York, 1934.

Neymann, C. A.: "Artificial Fever." Charles C Thomas, Publisher, Springfield, Ill., 1938.

Neymann, C. A., Heilbrunn, G., and Youmans, G. P.: Experiments in the treatment of dementia paralytica with penicillin. *J.A.M.A.* **128**:433, 1945.

Nichols, I. C., and Weigner, W. C.: Pick's disease. *Brain* **61**:237, 1938.

Noce, R. H., Williams, D. B., and Rapaport, W.: Reserpine (Serpasil) in the management of the mentally ill and mentally retarded. *J.A.M.A.* **156**:821, 1954.

Noyes, A.: "Modern Clinical Psychiatry." W. B. Saunders Company, Philadelphia, 1953.

Noyes, A. P.: "Text Book of Psychiatry." The Macmillan Company, New York, 1924.

Oberndorf, C. P.: Consideration of results with psychoanalytic therapy. *Am. J. Psychiat.* **99**:374, 1942.

Oberndorf, C. P.: The psychogenic factors in asthma. *New York J. Med.* **35**:41, 1935.

O'Leary, P., Brunsting, L. A., and Ockully, O.: Penicillin in neurosyphilis. *J.A.M.A.* **130**:698, 1946.

Pacella, B. L., Kopeloff, N., Barrera, S. E., and Kopeloff, L. M.: Experimental production of focal epilepsy. *Arch. Neurol. & Psychiat.* **52**:189, 1944.

Pavlov, I. P.: "Conditioned Reflexes and Psychiatry." Translated and edited by W. H. Gant. International Publishers Co., Inc., New York, 1941.

Pearson, G. H., and English, O. S.: "Common Neuroses of Children and Adults." W. W. Norton & Company, Inc., New York, 1937.

Penfield, W., and Jasper, H. H.: Highest level seizures. *A. Res. Nerv. & Ment. Dis., Proc.*, p. 252, 1947.

Penrose, L. S.: "Mental Defect." Rinehart & Company, Inc., New York, 1934.

Petersen, M. C., Bickford, R. G., Sem-Jacobsen, C. W., and Dodge, H. W., Jr.: Symposium on intracerebral electrography; depth electrogram in schizophrenic patients. *Proc. Staff Meet. Mayo Clin.* **28**:170, 1955.

Pincus, G., and Hoagland, H.: Adrenal cortical responses to stress in normal men and in those with personality disorders. *Am. J. Psychiat.* 106:641, 1950.

Pincus, G., Hoagland, H., Freeman, H., and Elmadjian, F.: Adrenal functions in mental disease. *Recent Progr. Hormone Res.* 4:291, 1949.

Polatin, P., Effron, A. S., and Robertiello, R. C.: Histamine therapy in psychiatric disorder. *Psychiatric Quart.* 27:254, 1953.

Polatin, P., Friedman, M. M., Harris, M. M., and Horwitz, W. A.: Vertebral fracture produced by Metrazol-induced convulsions. *J.A.M.A.* 112:1684, 1939.

Pollock, H. M.: Dementia praecox as a social problem. *State Hosp. Quart.* 3:370, 1918.

Pollock, H. M.: Frequency of dementia praecox in relation to sex, age, environment, nativity, and race. *Ment. Hyg.* 10:596, 1926.

Pollock, H. M.: Use and effect of alcohol in relation to alcoholic mental disease before, during, and after prohibition. *Ment. Hyg.* 24:112, 1940.

Pollock, H. M., and Furbush, E. M.: "Comparative Statistics of State Hospitals for Mental Diseases." New York State Hospitals Press, Utica, N.Y., 1922.

Pollock, H. M., Malzberg, B., and Fuller, R. G.: "Hereditary and Environmental Factors in the Causation of Manic-Depressive Psychoses and Dementia Praecox." New York State Hospitals Press, Utica, N.Y., 1939.

Pollock, M. P., and Pollock, M.: "New Hope for the Retarded." Porter Edward Sargent, Boston, 1953.

Powdermaker, F., and Frank, J. D.: "Group Psychotherapy: Studies in Methodology of Research and Therapy." Harvard University Press, Cambridge, Mass., 1953.

Pendergrass, E. P.: Encephalography: an explanation of a possible error in technique. *Am. J. Roentgenol.* 25:754, 1931.

Price, J. C., Waelsch, H., and Putnam, T. J.: dl-Glutamic acid hydrochloride in treatment of petit mal and psychomotor seizures. *J.A.M.A.* 122:1153, 1943.

Prue, P.: "Outline of Psychiatric Case Study." Paul B. Hoeber, Inc., New York, 1939.

Purves-Stewart, J.: Study of delirium and coma. *M. Press* 203:428, 1940.

Rank, B.: Intensive Study and Treatment of Preschool Children Who Show Marked Personality Deviations or "Atypical Development," and Their Parents. In "Emotional Problems of Early Childhood." Edited by Gerald Caplan. Basic Books, Inc., New York, 1955.

Redl, F., and Weinman, D.: "Children Who Hate." Free Press, Glencoe, Ill., 1951.

Redlich, F. C., Hollingshead, A. B., Roberts, B. H., Robinson, H. A., Freedman, L. Z., and Myers, J. K.: Social structure and psychiatric disorders. *Am. J. Psychiat.* 109:729, 1953.

Reese, H. H., and Vander Veer, A.: Protamine zinc insulin: its unsuitability for hypoglycemic shock therapy. *Arch. Neurol. & Psychiat.* 39:232, 1938.

Reich, W.: Der Triebhaste Charakter. *Internat. J. Psycho-Analysis*, vol. 5, 1925.

Reisman, D.: "Individualism Reconsidered." Doubleday & Company, Inc., New York, 1955.

Report of Special Commission to Investigate and Study Training Facilities Available for Mentally Retarded Children. December, 1953. Available at Documents Room, State House, Boston.

Rhein, J. H. W., and Ebaugh, F. G.: Affective disorders following acute epidemic encephalitis in children. *Am. J. Psychiat.* 3:791, 1924.

Richter, D., and Lee, M.: Serum choline esterase and anxiety. *J. Ment. Sc.* 88:428, 1942.

Riggs, A. F., and Terhune, W. B.: The psychoneuroses: a problem in re-education. *Am. J. Psychiat.* 4:407, 1925.

Rinaldi, F., Rudy, L. H., and Himwich, H. E.: The use of Frenquel in the treatment of disturbed patients with psychoses of long duration. *Am. J. Psychiat.* 112:343, 1955.

Ringelheim, D., and Polatsek, I.: Group therapy with a male defective group. *Am. J. Ment. Deficiency* 60:157, 1955.

Rinkel, M., Hyde, R. W., and Solomon, H. C.: Experimental psychiatry: III. A chemical concept of psychosis. *Dis. Nerv. System* 15:259, 1954.

Rinkel, M., Hyde, R., and Solomon, H. C.: Experimental psychiatry: IV. Hallucinogens: Tools in experimental psychiatry. *Dis. Nerv. System* 16:229, 1955.

Rinkel, M., Hyde, R. W., Solomon, H. C., and Hoagland, H.: Experimental psychiatry: II. Clinical and physio-chemical observations in experimental psychosis. *Am. J. Psychiat.* 111:881, 1955.

Rivers, A. B.: Clinical consideration of etiology of peptic ulcer. *Arch. Int. Med.* 53:97, 1934.

Roberts, J. A. F., Norman, R. M., and Griffiths, R.: Studies on a child population: I. Definition of the sample, method of ascertainment, and analysis of the results. *Ann. Eugenics* 6:319, 1936.

Rogers, C. R.: "The Clinical Treatment of the Problem Child." Houghton Mifflin Company, Boston, 1939.

Romano, J., and Ebaugh, F. G.: Prognosis in Schizophrenia. *Am. J. Psychiat.* 95:583, 1938.

Romano, J., Michael, M., Jr., and **Merritt, H. H.**: Alcoholic cerebellar degeneration. *Arch. Neurol. & Psychiat.* **44**:1230, 1940.

Rorschach, H.: "Psychodiagnostik," ed. 2. Hans Huber, Bern, Switzerland, 1921.

Rose, A. M., and **Stub, H. R.**: "Mental Health and Mental Disorder: A Sociological Approach." W. W. Norton & Company, Inc., New York, 1955.

Rosen, V. H., and **Gantt, W. H.**: Effect of Metrazol convulsions on conditioned reflexes in dogs. *Arch. Neurol. & Psychiat.* **50**:8, 1943.

Rosenbaum, M.: The cerebrospinal fluid in delirium tremens. *J.A.M.A.* **116**:2487, 1941.

Rosenbaum, M., Lewis, M., Piker, P., and **Goldman, D.**: Convulsive seizures in delirium tremens. *Arch. Neurol. & Psychiat.* **45**:486, 1941.

Rosenbaum, M., Piker, P., and **Lederer, H.**: Delirium tremens: a study of various methods of treatment. *Am. J. M. Sc.* **200**:677, 1940.

Ross, J. R., and **Malzberg, B.**: A review of the results of the pharmacological shock therapy and the Metrazol convulsive therapy in New York State. *Am. J. Psychiat.* **96**:297, 1939.

Ross, T. A.: "The Common Neuroses." Longmans, Green & Co., Inc., New York, 1923.

Roth, W., Jr., and **Luton, F. H.**: The mental health program in Tennessee: I. Description of the original study program. II. Statistical report of a psychiatric survey in a rural county. *Am. J. Psychiat.* **99**:662, 1943.

Rothchild, D.: Alzheimer's disease. *Am. J. Psychiat.* **14**:485, 1935.

Rothchild, D.: Pathologic changes in senile psychoses and their psychologic significance. *Am. J. Psychiat.* **14**:485, 1935.

Roudinescu, J.: Severe maternal deprivation in personality development in early childhood. *Understanding the Child* **21**:104, 1952.

Roundtree, L.: Mental and personality disorders in selective service registrants. *J.A.M.A.* **128**:1084, 1945.

Rowe, C. J., and **Daggett, D. R.**: Pre-psychotic personality traits in manic-depressive disease. *J. Nerv. & Ment. Dis.* **119**:412, 1954.

Rudolph, G. de M.: The treatment of depression with desoxyephedrine. *J. Ment Sc.* **95**:920, 1949.

Ruegamer, W. R., Bernstein, L., and **Benjamin, J. D.**: Growth food utilization, and thyroid activity in the albino rat as a function of extra handling. *Science* **120**:184 1954.

Rusk, H. A., and **Taylor, E. J.**: "New Hope for the Handicapped: The Rehabilitation of the Disabled from Bed to Job." Harper & Brothers, New York, 1946.

Russell, L. B.: X-ray induced developmental abnormalities in the mouse and their use in the analysis of embryological patterns: I. External and gross visceral changes. *J. Exper. Zool.* **144**:545, 1950.

Ryle, J. A.: Natural history of duodenal ulcer (Hunterian Lecture). *Lancet* **1**:327, 1932.

Sackler, R. R., Sackler, A. M., and Van Ophuijsen, J. H. W.: A three-year follow-up study of non-convulsive histamine biochemotherapy, electroconvulsive posthistamine therapy, and electric convulsive therapy controls. *Psychiatric Quart.* **27**:199, 1953.

Sakel, M.: A new treatment of schizophrenia. *Am. J. Psychiat.* **93**:829, 1937.

Sakel, M.: On the significance of the epileptic convulsion as a therapeutic factor in the pharmacological shock therapy of schizophrenia. *J. Nerv. & Ment. Dis.* **87**:140, 1938.

Sakel, M.: Therapy of schizophrenia by means of insulin hypoglycemia and hypoglycemic shock. *Wien. med. Wschnschr.* **84, 85**:1211 *et seq.*, 1934.

Sarason, S. B.: Individual psychotherapy with mentally defective individuals. *Am. J. Ment. Deficiency* **56**:803, 1952.

Sarason, S. B.: "Psychological Problems in Mental Deficiency." Harper & Brothers, New York, 1949.

Saroyan, W.: "Bicycle Rider in Beverly Hills." Charles Scribner's Sons, New York, 1952.

Saroyan, W.: "Rock Wagram." Doubleday & Company, Inc., New York, 1952.

Sarwer-Foner, G. J., and Ogle, W.: The use of reserpine in an open psychiatric setting. *Canad. M.A.J.* **73**:187, 1955.

Schacht, M., and Kempster, S.: Useful techniques in the treatment of patients with schizophrenia or borderline states. *Psychiatry* **16**:35, 1953.

Schaffner, B. (editor): "Conference on Group Processes. Transactions of the First Conference." Josiah Macy, Jr. Foundation, New York, 1955.

Schamberg, J. F., and Rule, A. M.: Studies of the therapeutic effect of fever in experimental rabbit syphilis. *Arch. Dermat. & Syph.* **14**:243, 1926.

Schottstaedt, W. W., Grace, W. J., and Wolff, H. G.: Life situation, behavior patterns and renal excretions of fluid and electrolytes. *J.A.M.A.* **157**:1485, 1955.

Schwing, G.: "A Way to the Soul of the Mentally Ill." Translated by R. Ekstein and B. H. Hall. International Universities Press, Inc., New York, 1954.

Sechehaye, M. A.: "Symbolic Realization." International Universities Press, Inc., New York, 1951.

Selye, H.: Critical period for inhibition of inflammation by a primarily neurogenic stress situation. *Psychosom. Med.* **17**:124, 1955.

Sem-Jacobsen, C. W., Petersen, M. C., Lazarte, J. A., Dodge, H. W., and Holman, C. B.: Intracerebral electrographic recordings from psychotic patients during hallucinations and agitation. *Am. J. Psychiat.* 112:278, 1955.

Senn, M. (editor): Symposium on the Healthy Genesis of Psychiatric Conditions in Early Childhood. In "Psychoanalytic Study of the Child." International Universities Press, Inc., New York, 1952.

Sharpe, W.: "The Diagnosis and Treatment of Brain Injuries." J. B. Lippincott Company, Philadelphia, 1920.

Sherrington, Sir C.: "The Brain and Its Mechanism." The Macmillan Company, New York, 1937.

Silverman, D.: Clinical and E.E.G. studies on criminal psychopaths. *Arch. Neurol. & Psychiat.* 50:18, 1943.

Silverman, D.: E.E.G. and treatment of criminal psychopaths. *J. Crim. Psychopath.* 5:439, 1944.

Simmons, L. W., and Wolff, H. G.: "Social Science in Medicine." Russell Sage Foundation, New York, 1954.

Simon, B., Holzberg, J., and Unger, J.: Study of judgment in the psychopathic personality. *Psychiatric Quart.* 25:132, 1951.

Simpson, W. M.: Artificial fever therapy of syphilis. *J.A.M.A.* 105:2132, 1935.

Simpson, W. M.: Artificial fever therapy of syphilis and gonococcic infections. *Brit. J. Ven. Dis.* 12:133, 1936.

Simpson, W. M.: Influence on chloride metabolism. *J.A.M.A.* 100:67, 1933.

Simpson, W. M., and Kendell, H. W.: Experimental treatment of early syphilis with artificial fever combined with chemotherapy. *Am. J. Syph.* 21:526, 1937.

Singer, H. D.: Mental and nervous disorders associated with pellagra. *Arch. Int. Med.* 15:121, 1915.

Sjögren, T.: Genetic-statistical and psychiatric investigations of a West Swedish population. *Acta psychiat. et neurol.* Suppl. 52, 1948.

Skeels, H. M., and Dye, H. B.: A study of the effects of differential stimulation on mentally retarded children. *Am. J. Ment. Deficiency* 44:114, 1938.

Slavson, S. R.: "Introduction to Group Therapy." International Universities Press, Inc., New York, 1952.

Smith, P. L.: Alcoholics Anonymous. *Psychiatric Quart.* 15:554, 1941.

Smith, H. W., and Cobb, S.: Relations of emotions to injury and disease. *Ann. Int. Med.* 19:873, 1943.

Smith, H. W., and Solomon, H. C.: Traumatic neuroses in court. *Ann. Int. Med.* 21:367, 1944.

Solomon, H. C.: The treatment of neurosyphilis. *J.A.M.A.* 81:1742, 1923.

Sontag, L. W.: A research institute on child growth and development reports progress. *Child* 16:54, 1951.

Southard, E. E.: Anatomical findings in senile dementia. *Trans. Am. Medico-Psychol. A.* 16:511, 1909.

Spicer, C. C., Stewart, D. N., and de R. Winser, D. M.: Perforated peptic ulcer during the period of heavy air raids. *Lancet* 1:14, 1944.

Spiedel, C. C.: Changes in nerve fibers during intoxication and recovery. *Scient. Month.* 44:178, 1937.

Spielmeyer, W.: The problem of the anatomy of schizophrenia. *A. Res. Nerv. & Ment. Dis., Proc.* 10:105, 1929.

Spies, T. D., Grant, J. M., Stone, R. E., and McLester, J. B.: Pellagra: Summary of one year's experience with nicotinic acid. *South. M. J.* 31:1231, 1938.

Spitz, R. A.: "Hospitalism: An Inquiry into the Personality." Josiah Macy, Jr. Foundation, New York, 1950.

Spitz, R. A.: The Psychogenic Diseases in Infancy: An Attempt at Their Etiologic Classification. In "Psychoanalytic Study of the Child." International Universities Press, Inc., New York, 1951.

Spitz, R. A.: The role of etiological factors in emotional development in infancy. *Child Development* 20:146, 1949.

Spitz, R. A., and Wolf, J. M.: An inquiry into the genesis of psychotic conditions in early childhood: II. Anaclitic depression. *Psychoanalyt. Stud. Child.* 2:313, 1946.

Sprague, G.: Psychopathology of constitutional psychopathic inferiority. *Bull. New York Acad. Med.* 17:911, 1941.

Stanton, A. H., and Schwartz, M.: "The Mental Hospital." Basic Books, Inc., New York, 1954.

Stein, C.: Studies in endocrine therapy in epilepsy. *Am. J. Psychiat.* 13:740, 1933.

Stevenson, J. E., Metcalfe, E. V., and Hobbs, G. E.: Eosinophile response in schizophrenic patients; influence of the diurnal cycle and the type of schizophrenia. *Arch. Neurol. & Psychiat.* 70:802, 1953.

Stevenson, L. D., McGowan, L., and Allen, A. M.: Changes in the brain in alcoholism. *Arch. Neurol. & Psychiat.* 45:56, 1941.

Stewart, W. A.: Electroencephalographic changes associated with different forms of experimentally produced increased intracranial pressure. *Bull. Johns Hopkins Hosp.* 69:240, 1941.

Stokes, J. H., Gammon, G. D., and Falk, M. S.: A Fifth Annual Report on Penicillin Alone in Neurosyphilis. In "Recent Advances in the Study of Venereal Diseases." National Institute of Health, U.S. Public Health Service, Washington, D.C., 1949.

Strecker, E. A.: The non-specificity of mental disease. *Ment. Hyg.* **7**:277, 1923.

Strecker, E. A.: Physical findings in the psychoneuroses. *Arch. Neurol. & Psychiat.* **6**:197, 1921.

Strecker, E. A.: The practice of psychiatry. *Arch. Neurol. & Psychiat.* **31**:403, 1934.

Strecker, E. A.: Psychopathology. *Arch. Neurol. & Psychiat.* **30**:1318, 1933.

Strecker, E. A.: Some thoughts concerning the psychology and therapy of alcoholism. *J. Nerv. & Ment. Dis.* **86**:191, 1937.

Strecker, E. A.: Why abnormal mental disorders develop. *Ann. Clin. Med.* **22**:63, 1923.

Strecker, E. A., and Appel, K.: "Discovering Ourselves." The Macmillan Company, New York, 1932.

Strecker, E. A., and Chambers, F. T.: "Alcohol: One Man's Meat." The Macmillan Company, New York, 1938.

Strecker, E. A., Ebaugh, F. G., and Ewalt, J. R.: "Practical Clinical Psychiatry," ed. 7. Blakiston Division, McGraw-Hill Book Company, Inc., New York, 1951.

Strecker, E. A., and Meyers, M. K.: "Clinical Neurology." Blakiston Division, McGraw-Hill Book Company, Inc., New York, 1927.

Strecker, E. A., and Willey, G. F.: "Prognosis in Schizophrenia." *A. Res. Nerv. & Ment. Dis., Proc.* **5**:403, 1925.

Sullivan, A. J.: Ulcerative colitis of psychogenic origin. *Yale J. Biol. & Med.* **4**:779, 1932.

Taylor, H. M., and Cross, A. R.: Treatment of acute alcoholism with insulin: report of a case. *J. Pediat.* **16**:341, 1940.

Thimann, J.: Conditioned reflex as a Rx for abnormal drinking. *New England J. Med.* **288**:333, 1943.

Thom, D. A.: "The Everyday Problems of Everyday Children." Appleton-Century-Crofts, Inc., New York, 1934.

Thomas, J. M., Semrad, E. V., and Schwab, R. M.: Studies of the blood proteins in delirium tremens. *Am. J. M. Sc.* **195**:820, 1938.

Thompson, W. R.: Early Environment—Its Importance for Later Behavior. In "Psychopathology of Childhood." Edited by P. H. Hoch and J. Zubin. Grune & Stratton, Inc., New York, 1955.

Thorne, F. C.: Counseling and psychotherapy with mental defectives. *Am. J. Ment. Deficiency* **52**:203, 1948.

Tietza, T.: Study of the mothers of schizophrenic patients. *Psychiatry* **12**:55, 1949.

Tillotson, K. J.: The practice of the "total push" method in the treatment of chronic schizophrenia. *Am. J. Psychiat.* **95**:1205, 1939.

Timberlake, W. H., Belmont, E., and Ogonik, J.: Personal communication.

Trulson, M., Fleming, R., and Stare, F.: Expert Committee on Mental Health, Subcommittee on Alcoholism, Technical Report Series. World Health Organization, Palais des Nations, Geneva, Switzerland, 1954.

Tucker, W. I., Fleming, R., and Raeder, O.: Electroconvulsive treatment in a general hospital. *New England J. Med.* **253**:451, 1955.

Underwood, G. H.: Emotional and psychic factors in the production of gastrointestinal diseases. *Texas J. Med.* **27**:798, 1932.

U.S. Department of Health, Education and Welfare: "Evaluation in Mental Health," Public Health Service, Washington, D.C., 1955.

Van Bogaert, L.: Post-infectious encephalomyelitis and multiple sclerosis. *J. Neuropath. & Exper. Neurol.* **9**:219, 1950.

Vander Veer, A. H., and Reese, H. H.: The treatment of schizophrenia with insulin shock. *Am. J. Psychiat.* **95**:271, 1938.

Vaughan, W. T., Jr.: Mental health for school children. *Children* **2**:203, 1955.

Vaughan, W. T., Jr.: "Survey of Community Psychiatric Resources in Massachusetts." Massachusetts Department of Mental Health, Boston, 1952.

Voegtlin, W. C.: Treatment of alcoholism by establishing a conditioned reflex. *Am. J. M. Sc.* **199**:802, 1940.

Waelder, R.: The structure of paranoid ideas: a critical survey of various theories. *Internat. J. Psycho-Analysis* **32**:167, 1951.

Wagner-Jauregg, J.: Die Behandlung der progressiven Paralyse und Tabes. *Wien. med. Wchnschr.* **71**:1105, 1921.

Wagner-Jauregg, J.: Fieberhandlung bei Psychosen. *Wien. med. Wchnschr.* **76**:79, 1926.

Wagner-Jauregg, J.: *Ars. Medici* **4**:42, 1926.

Wagner-Jauregg, J.: The treatment of general paresis by inoculation of malaria. *J. Nerv. & Ment. Dis.* **55**:369, 1922.

Wagner-Jauregg, J.: Ueber die Einwirkung der Malaria auf die progressive Paralyse. *Psychiat. Neurol. Wchnschr.* **20**:132, 1918.

Wagner-Jauregg, J.: Ueber die Behandlung der progressiven Paralyse mit Bacterientoxinen. *Wien. med. Wchnschr.* **25**:61, 1912.

Wagner-Jauregg, J.: Ueber die Behandlung der progressiven Paralyse. *Wien. med. Wchnschr.* **59**:2124, 1909.

Wagner-Jauregg, J., and Schacher, L.: Wie sind die bisharigen Erfolge der Malaria-behandlung der Paralyse? *Wien. med. Wchnschr.* **74**:646, 1924.

Wagner-Jauregg, J.: Ueber die Einwirkung fieberhafter Erkrankungen auf Psychosen. *Jahrb. Psychiat.* 7:94, 1887.

Wahl, C. W.: Some antecedent factors in the family history of 392 schizophrenics. *Am. J. Psychiat.* 110:688, 1954.

Weil, A., Liebert, E., and Heilbrunn, G.: Histopathologic changes in the brain in experimental hyperinsulinism. *Arch. Neurol. & Psychiat.* 39:467, 1938.

Weininger, O.: Physiological damage under emotional stress as a function of early experience. *Science* 119:285, 1954.

Weiss, E.: Psychosomatic aspects of hypertension. *J.A.M.A.* 120:1081, 1942.

Weiss, E., and English, S.: "Psychosomatic Medicine." W. B. Saunders Company, Philadelphia, 1949.

West, F. H., Bond, E. D., Shurley, J. T., and Meyers, C. D.: Insulin coma therapy in schizophrenia; a fourteen-year follow-up study. *Am. J. Psychiat.* 111:583, 1955.

White, W. A.: "Outlines of Psychiatry," ed. 10. Nervous & Mental Disease Publishing Company, New York, 1924.

White, W. A.: The unconscious. *Psychoanalyt. Rev.* 2:58, 1915.

Whitehead, D.: Improvement and recovery rates in dementia praecox without insulin therapy. *Psychiatric Quart.* 12:409, 1938.

Whitehorn, J. C.: Understanding psychotherapy. *Am. J. Psychiat.* 112:3, 1955.

Whiting, J. W. M., and Child, I. L.: "Child Training and Personality." Yale University Press, New Haven, Conn., 1953.

Wiener, N.: Problems of organization. *Bull. Menninger Clin.* 17:130, 1953.

Wiener, N.: "Cybernetics." John Wiley & Sons, Inc., New York, 1948.

Wiest, G.: Psychotherapy with the mentally retarded. *Am. J. Ment. Deficiency* 59:640, 1955.

Williams, D. J.: The electroencephalogram in acute head injuries. *Arch. Neurol. & Psychiat.* 4:107, 1941.

Williams, D. J.: The electroencephalogram in chronic post-traumatic states. *Arch. Neurol. & Psychiat.* 4:131, 1941.

Williams, R. J.: "Nutrition and Alcoholism." University of Oklahoma Press, Norman, Okla., 1951.

Williams, R. R., and Spies, T. D.: "Vitamin B₁ and Its Use in Medicine." The Macmillan Company, New York, 1938.

Wilse-Robinson, G.: The treatment of delirium tremens with insulin in subshock doses. *Am. J. Psychiat.* 97:136, 1940.

Wilson, D. C.: Pathology of senility. *Am. J. Psychiat.* 111:902, 1955.

Winkelstein, A., and Rothschild, L.: Psychosomatic background of peptic ulcer. *Am. J. Digest. Dis.* 10:99, 1943.

Witmer, H. L.: "Psychiatric Clinics for Children." Commonwealth Fund, Division of Publications, New York, 1940.

Wolf, S., and Wolff, H. G.: Genesis of peptic ulcer in man. *J.A.M.A.* 120:670, 1942.

Wolf, S., and Wolff, H. G.: "Human Gastric Function." Oxford University Press, New York, 1947.

Woolf, L. I., Griffith, R., and Moncrieff, A.: Treatment of phenylketonuria with a diet low in phenylalanine. *British M. J.* 1:57, 1955.

Woolley, D. W., and Shaw, E.: The biochemical and pharmacological suggestion about certain mental disorders. *Proc. Nat. Acad. Sc.*, 1954.

World Health Organization: "The Mentally Subnormal Child." Technical Report Series 75, Palais des Nations, Geneva, Switzerland, 1954.

World Health Organization: "Report of Expert Committee on Mental Health, Subcommittee on Alcoholism." Technical Report Series 48, Palais des Nations, Geneva, Switzerland, 1952.

Wortis, H., Wortis, S. B., and Marsh, F. I.: Chronic alcoholism. *Am. J. Psychiat.* 94:891, 1938.

Wortis, H., Wortis, S. B., and Marsh, F. I.: Vitamin C studies in alcoholism. *Am. J. Psychiat.* 94:891, 1938.

Wortis, J., Bowman, K. M., and Goldfarb, W.: Use of insulin in alcoholism. *M. Clin. North America* 24:671, 1940.

Wortis, J., and Lambert, R. H.: Irreversible or hyperglycemic insulin coma. *Am. J. Psychiat.* 96:335, 1939.

Wuth, O.: Treatment, etiology, and pathology. *J.A.M.A.* 88:2013, 1927.

Zabarenko, R. N., and Chambers, G. S.: Evaluation of glutamic acid in mental deficiency. *Am. J. Psychiat.* 108:881, 1952.

Zeligs, M. A.: War neuroses. *War Med.* 6:166, 1944.

Zimmerman, F. T., Burgemeister, B., and Putnam, T. J.: Effect of glutamic acid upon mental functioning in children and in adolescents. *Arch. Neurol. & Psychiat.* 56:489, 1946.

Index